Hither Shore

Interdisciplinary Journal
on Modern Fantasy Literature

Jahrbuch der
Deutschen Tolkien Gesellschaft e. V.

Violence, Conflict, and War in Tolkien

Gewalt, Konflikt und Krieg bei Tolkien

Interdisziplinäres Seminar der DTG
24.-26. April 2009, Hannover

Herausgegeben von:
Thomas Fornet-Ponse (Gesamtleitung),
Marcel Bülles, Thomas Honegger,
Rainer Nagel, Alexandra Velten,
Frank Weinreich

SCRIPTORIUM OXONIAE

Bibliografische Information der Deutschen Bibliothek

Die Deutsche Bibliothek verzeichnet diese Publikation in der Deutschen Nationalbibliografie; detaillierte bibliografische Daten sind im Internet über http://dnb.ddb.de abrufbar.

ISBN 978-3-9810612-4-6

Zweite Auflage: korrigierte Fassung vom 31.5.2010

Hither Shore, DTG-Jahrbuch 2009 veröffentlicht im Verlag »Scriptorium Oxoniae«

Deutsche Tolkien Gesellschaft e. V. (DTG)
E-Mail: info@tolkiengesellschaft.de

Scriptorium Oxoniae im Atelier für Textaufgaben e. K.
Brehmstraße 50 · D-40239 Düsseldorf
E-Mail: rayermann@scriptorium-oxoniae.de

Hither Shore, Gesamtleitung: Thomas Fornet-Ponse
Graurheindorfer Straße 64 · D-53111 Bonn
E-Mail: hither-shore@tolkiengesellschaft.de

Vorschläge für Beiträge in deutscher oder englischer Sprache (inklusive Exposé von ca. 100 Wörtern) werden erbeten an o.g. Adresse.

Alle Rechte verbleiben beim Autor des jeweiligen Einzelbeitrags. Es gilt als vereinbart, dass ein Beitrag innerhalb der nächsten 18 Monate nach Erscheinen dieser Hither-Shore-Ausgabe nicht anderweitig veröffentlicht werden darf.

Abwicklung: Susanne A. Rayermann, Düsseldorf
Vorlagenherstellung: Kathrin Bondzio, Solingen
Umschlagillustration: Anke Eißmann, Herborn
Druck und Vertrieb: Books on Demand, Norderstedt

Alle Rechte vorbehalten.

Inhalt

Preface 6

Vorwort 7

Tolkien Seminar 2009

Violence in *The Lord of the Rings* 10
Frank Weinreich (Bochum)

Perspectives on Just War in Tolkien's *Legendarium* 28
Annie Birks (Angers)

Gibt es Macht ohne Gewalt? 42
Thomas Fornet-Ponse (Bonn)

Gewalt und Gewaltdarstellung bei Tolkien
im Vergleich mit zeitgenössischen Gewalt- und
Aggressionstheorien 58
Friedhelm Schneidewind (Hemsbach)

Der Sängerkrieg:
Gesang und Gewalt in J.R.R. Tolkiens Mittelerde 70
Julian T.M. Eilmann (Aachen)

Von kühner Recken Streiten? Höfische Akteure und
Heroische Gewalt in Tolkiens *Farmer Giles of Ham* 86
Patrick Brückner (Potsdam)

Dagor dagorath & Ragnarök: Tolkien & the Apocalypse 102
Michaël Devaux (Livarot)

Clean Earth to Till: A Tolkienian Vision of War 118
Anna Slack (Cambridge)

The Legacy of Swords: Animate Weapons and the
Ambivalence of Heroic Violence 132
Judith Klinger (Potsdam)

Language and Violence:
The Orcs, the Ents, and Tom Bombadil 154
Martin G.E. Sternberg (Bonn)

The Problem of Closure:
War and Narrative in *The Lord of the Rings* 170
Margaret Hiley (Peterborough)

The Legends of the Trojan War in J.R.R. Tolkien 182
Guglielmo Spirito (Assisi)

›contraria contrariis curantur‹ – Krankheitsheilung
als Kampf in Tolkiens *The Lord of the Rings* 202
Petra Zimmermann (Braunschweig)

Zusammenfassungen der englischen Beiträge 218
Summaries of the German Essays 224

Rezensionen/Reviews

Adam Lam, Nataliya Oryshchuk (eds.): How We Became Middle-earth.
    A Collection of Essays on *The Lord of the Rings* 228
Harriet Margolis, Sean Cubitt, Barry King, Thierry Jutel (eds.):
    Studying the Event Film *The Lord of the Rings* 228
Stratford Caldecott, Thomas Honegger (eds.):
    Tolkien's *The Lord of the Rings*. Sources of Inspiration. 231
Jonathan B. Himes, Joe R. Christopher, Salwa Khoddam (eds.):
    Truths Breathed Through Silver. The Inklings' Moral and
    Mythopoeic Legacy. 233

Jeremy Mark Robinson: J.R.R. Tolkien. The Books, The Films,
   The Whole Cultural Phenomenon. Including a Scene-by-Scene
   Analysis of the 2001-2003 *Lord of the Rings* Films. 235
Krisztina Sebők: Roots of Middle-earth Seeds of Fantasy:
   Mythical and Literary Heritage in *The Lord of the Rings*,
   and J.R.R.Tolkien's Classic as Fantasy 236
Eduardo Segura: Mitopoeia y Mitología.
   Reflexiones Bajo la Luz Refractada. 238
Gregory Bassham, Eric Bronson: *Der Herr der Ringe* und die Philosophie.
   Klüger werden mit dem beliebtesten Buch der Welt. 239
Fabian Geier: J.R.R. Tolkien 242
Mark T. Hooker: The Hobbitonian Anthology of Articles about
   J.R.R. Tolkien and his *Legendarium*. 244
Douglas Charles Kane: Arda Reconstructed. The Creation
   of the Published *Silmarillion*. 246
Alex Lewis, Elizabeth Currie: The Epic Realm of Tolkien.
   Beren and Lúthien. 247
John S. Ryan: Tolkien's View: Windows into his World. 249
Thomas Scholz: Weit entfernte Wunder. Zur Konstruktion von
   Raum und Zeit in der englischen Fantasyliteratur am Beispiel
   von J.R.R. Tolkiens *The Hobbit*. 252
Pia Skogeman: Where the Shadows Lie: A Jungian Interpretation
   of Tolkien's *The Lord of the Rings*. 254
J.R.R. Tolkien: The Legend of Sigurd and Gudrún.
   Edited by Christopher Tolkien. 255
Tolkien Studies. An Annual Scholarly Review. Volume VI. 2009 257

Über die Autorinnen und Autoren 262

About our Authors 266

Siglen-Liste 270

Index 272

Preface

While the Tolkien Seminars of the past few years were dedicated to various individual areas of Tolkien's oeuvre – the *History of Middle-earth*, his "smaller works", and the *Hobbit* –, April 2009 saw the treatment of a shared and quite sensitive topic that could, and was supposed to, be found all throughout Tolkien's works: violence, conflict, and war. In looking at this topic, the emphasis was not to be so much on biographic aspects, but rather on questions such as: Have violence, conflict, and war informed Tolkien's works, from the *Hobbit* to the *Silmarillion* complex or his later texts, and if so, how? Can we make out pacifistic tendencies to compensate for the use of violence? Might there be deeper philosophical or theological reasons for the prominence of war and conflict?

We, as the German Tolkien Society, were especially pleased that we were able to win the support and participation of Prof. Dr. Rainer Emig, a renowned expert on war in literature. The success of our scientific work on Tolkien – and our ongoing commitment – has also been confirmed by the international recognition of the Seminar as well as this yearbook, as evidenced by the internationality of the papers. This type of international exchange can only benefit our research, due to the differences in scientific approach and cultural backgrounds.

The questions posed above could not be treated exhaustively in the course of the Seminar – especially because, as is usual, the papers and discussions opened up additional insights and questions, or encouraged more detailed research. The contributions collected here clearly show how manifold and interdisciplinary the positions held during the course of the Seminar were.

The scope of the contributions mirror the breadth of the works analysed, ranging from quantitative content analysis and (philosophical as well as theological) discussions on the Just War or the relation between power and violence to theories of aggression, language and songs as violence and literary as well as other sources, right down to the healing of illness as some kind of fight. While most of the attention naturally was focussed on *The Lord of the Rings* the *Silmarillion* complex or the "smaller works" also received some attention.

We would like to extend thanks to everyone involved in running the Seminar or creating yet another issue of this yearbook. First of all, thanks go to Prof. Dr. Rainer Emig and his staff at Leibnitz University, Hanover, for faultlessly organising the conference. Our gratitude also goes to Walking Tree Publishers for their gracious local cooperation and, of course, all contributors, my fellow editors, and finally our publisher Susanne A. Rayermann, as well as Kathrin Bondzio for typesetting.

Thomas Fornet-Ponse

Vorwort

Nachdem sich die Tolkien Seminare der letzten Jahre verschiedenen Bereichen des Werkes Tolkiens – der *History of Middle-earth*, den »Kleineren Werken« sowie dem *Hobbit* – gewidmet hatten, stand im April 2009 ein gemeinsames und durchaus brisantes Thema im Blickpunkt, das im gesamten Werk untersucht werden konnte und sollte: Gewalt, Konflikt und Krieg bei Tolkien.

Dabei sollte bewusst der Akzent weniger auf die biographischen Aspekte gelegt werden und stärker auf die Fragen, ob und wie Gewalt, Konflikt und Krieg Tolkiens Werke vom *Hobbit* bis zum *Silmarillion*-Komplex oder späteren Schriften bestimmen, ob es ausgleichende pazifistische Tendenzen zum Gebrauch von Gewalt gibt, ob es tiefer liegende philosophische und theologische Gründe für die Prominenz von Krieg und Konflikt gibt etc.

Besonders erfreulich für uns von der Deutschen Tolkien Gesellschaft war, dass wir mit Prof. Dr. Rainer Emig einen ausgewiesenen Experten für das Thema Krieg in der Literatur für die Zusammenarbeit gewinnen konnten. Eine weitere Bestätigung für den Erfolg unserer bisherigen wissenschaftlichen Arbeit – und insofern auch Verpflichtung – ist die sich in der Internationalität unserer Beitragenden niederschlagende überregionale Wahrnehmung des Seminars und des Jahrbuchs. Gerade aufgrund unterschiedlicher Wissenschaftstraditionen und kultureller Hintergründe kann ein solcher internationaler Austausch die Forschung nur voranbringen.

Die genannten Fragestellungen konnten im Seminar nicht in ihrer gesamten Breite erschöpfend behandelt werden – zumal wie üblich in den Vorträgen und Diskussionen noch zahlreiche weitere Einsichten und Problemstellungen aufgezeigt oder detaillierte Untersuchungen angeregt wurden. Die hier versammelten Beiträge zeigen deutlich, wie vielfältig und interdisziplinär die Perspektiven waren, die im Laufe des Seminars eingenommen wurden:

Die Bandbreite der Beiträge von einer quantitativen Inhaltsanalyse und (philosophisch-theologischen) Fragestellungen zum Gerechten Krieg oder dem Zusammenhang von Macht und Gewalt über Aggressionstheorien, Sprache oder Lieder als Gewalt und literarischen und anderen Quellen bis hin zur Krankheitsheilung als Kampf entspricht der Breite der untersuchten Werke –

denn auch wenn *The Lord of the Rings* verständlicherweise einen großen Raum einnahm, wurden auch der *Silmarillion*-Komplex oder die »Kleineren Werken« nicht vernachlässigt.

Schließlich sei noch den verschiedenen am Erfolg des Seminars und dem Zustandekommen einer weiteren Ausgabe des Jahrbuchs herzlich gedankt: Zunächst Prof. Dr. Rainer Emig und seinen Mitarbeitern und Mitarbeiterinnen an der Leibniz-Universität Hannover für die einwandfreie Organisation der Tagung; dem Verlag *Walking Tree Publishers* für die freundliche Unterstützung vor Ort; natürlich wie immer allen Beitragenden, meinen Mitherausgebern und der Mitherausgeberin im Board of Editors sowie schließlich der Verlegerin Susanne A. Rayermann sowie Kathrin Bondzio für die Vorlagenerstellung.

Thomas Fornet-Ponse

Violence in *The Lord of the Rings*
Frank Weinreich (Bochum)

Introduction[1]

antasy is a violent genre; there can be no doubt about this fact. There are some books, films and computer games which contain little or even no violence, but the majority of the stories told within fantasy tell tales of conflict, which is most often resolved through the use of violence. This is especially true for works of High Fantasy and Sword & Sorcery, which always have plots containing violence, and this most of the time on the scale of wars or even worldwide conflict which go hand in hand with a very huge number of wounded and killed people, be those men, dwarves, orcs, elves, dragons, demons or other more or less strange living (or undead) beings. And the audience of the genre feels entertained by the violence depicted, although violence for most of us is something which is avoided at almost all costs in real life. Nonetheless violence is entertaining, be it in fantasy, science ficton, or 'decent' murder mysteries as in Agatha Christie.

Many things are responsible for the entertaining qualities of violence, not the least of it human nature itself, which is, among other qualities, one of violent and aggressive capabilities. But the nature of storytelling itself can be pointed out as the most prominent reason for the attraction of violent contents. A story needs suspense and climactic developments, which are most easily provided through violent occurrences or the threat of violence. 'Tales' about gardening may be insightful and helpful, but they are not really a kind of storytelling. A story grips its audiences by depicting interesting people whose affairs have an adventurous touch and who gamble for high stakes.

Fantasy can most easily tell about the highest stakes imaginable. Fantasy tells stories that transcend the physical world, entering into the realms of magic and metaphysics. The threats in fantasy do not only address the physical, but often the souls and very essence of people. Stories reach extremes of success and failure which no other genre can provide, and these extremes could not be reached if violence were not involved in the stories told.

One could lament that humanity is entertained by violence, but it cannot be changed without changing human nature. Furthermore aggression and violence in storytelling can be put into useful contexts. The depiction of violence and war, as it is done for example in *All Quiet on the Western Front*, a story about

---

1 I wish to thank Dr. Margaret Hiley for carefully proofreading this article.

the Great War by Erich Maria Remarque, serves to tell the reader about the real horrors of war in the years 1914-1918 and thereby showing him or her the worth of peace. And *The Lord of the Rings* also has lots of moments where terror, oppression and the horrors of war are laid out before its reader, hopefully leaving them with at least a more thoughtful view on these topics.

Critics usually do not point out this thought-provoking potential of fantasy when commenting on the violent nature of the genre. Usually concerns are expressed that the depiction of violence may result in habituation. The audiences of books, films and computer games become used to resorting to violence as a means of solving problems, the argument goes, and the danger of that becomes greater the more graphic the depiction of violence is and the more the audiences are able to become involved in the stories told (books are the least dangerous, comics are more dangerous, films are worse and computer games with their interactivity are the worst). And even books can talk about violence in graphic and very vivid manner. Especially fantasy works of the last decade seem to do this more and more often and in ever more detail, be it Steven Erikson with the *Malazan* stories, very recently Mark Charan with his *Nights of Villjamur* or the new grandmaster of Fantasy, George R.R. Martin and his *Song of Ice and Fire*. In all these cases and many more books the tendency, as I see it, goes to ever more detailed depictions of violence and gore.

Having thought about this one might reasonably turn to the undisputed masterpiece of fantasy and read *The Lord of the Rings* with a special focus on violence. This is what this paper will proceed to do in the following. But others, of course, have given thought to the very same topic, for example Patrick Curry with *Defending Middle-earth* and Matthew Dickerson with *Following Gandalf*. And in Dickerson it is that a very astonishing observation can be found: "These are the things – friends, sunlight, grass – that are really important in the tale; this, and not war and battles is the stuff of life: the stuff that counts" (Dickerson 27).

In the subsequent chapters of his book *Following Gandalf* Dickerson goes on making similar statements. And Dickerson points out more than once that Tolkien is very restrictive in his descriptions of fighting, war, and violence (cf. for example 23, 33, 88). He gives examples of this, but does Dickerson's claim really hit the mark? That was a question I asked myself quite often while reading his book. *Following Gandalf* was published in 2004, one year after the release of the last of Peter Jackson's movies, and this interpretation of Middle-earth influenced my reading of Dickerson quite heavily, since the screenplays threatened to change my whole experience of *The Lord of the Rings*. On the one hand then there was Jackson's hack 'n slash (cf. Weinreich, *Herr*) which put me well back into my "Norman-and-Akers" experiences, on the other hand there was Dickerson's claim of a restrictive use of violence in the book. Curiosity arose: Who was right?

There is a way to lend a certain kind of objectivity[2] to the study of literary content: a quantitative analysis of content according to a transparent system of categories. From 2004 onwards I waited for such an analysis to be published, but somehow nobody seemed to be eager to do the dirty work. So when the DTG came up with *War, Violence and Conflict in Tolkien* as the topic of the 2009 seminar I felt somehow obliged to grab the book and start counting. So I counted the 2.5 million letters that make up *The Lord of the Rings* and am now able to present first findings on the amount and types of violence that can be found in the Ring trilogy. And in the course of this analysis some light will also be shed on the overall structure of *The Lord of the Rings*.

Theoretical Framework
Violence

The present content analysis of *The Lord of the Rings* focuses on the amount of violence in the novel itself. Violence, for the purposes of this study, is understood as in the definition of violence given by the World Health Organization (see next page). I wish to point out in advance that there is a difference between this study and the usual media violence research as it has been undertaken in the last fifty years. Media violence research (cf. Bonfadelli 20-23; Moser 175-180 and 184-192; Vollbrecht 146-175; Weinreich, *Medieneinflüsse*) usually focusses on cause and effect relations attributed to the consumption of media. More precisely it commonly can be understood as research that nearly exclusively deals with the consumption or use of movies, TV and computer games.

This is not the focus of my study. Media violence research has to undertake thoroughly designed empirical studies to try to give any valid statements about the effects of violence in the media. Multilevel design and a combination of questionnaires, observation and testing has to try to take into account the various dimensions that violence can have for the audience which is exhibited to open as well as hidden aspects of violence and its structural embeddedness (cf. Theunert). It follows that a content analysis in itself does not allow for any conclusions to be drawn about the effects of the content analysed. But that is not the point here. My points are first to describe the amount of violence

---

2 As will be pointed out in the following "objectivity" is of course not the right term, since even content analysis in the stern understanding of Bernard Berelson is an interpretative process that even with the due amount of methodical transparency can yield not more than a certain amount of intersubjective validity.

within a certain narrative in quantitative terms, second to point out the types of violence the reader encounters in the book and third to compare the violent with the non-violent parts of *The Lord of the Rings*.

Nonetheless it has to be explained what is meant by violence in *The Lord of the Rings*. In philosophy violence is mostly understood as an instrumentally[3] applied force (Arendt 47), whose use is always connected with certain ethical aspects like morality, justice, legislation and so on (Benjamin 29pp, see esp. 29[4]). Violence not only encompasses the use or suffering of physical force or power but the widest range of harm that can be done to somebody.

The sociologist and principal founder of the profession of peace and conflict studies, Johan Galtung, has developed the most influential theory of violence which understands violence as a harmful manifestation of power. Thus violence according to Galtung includes personal violence as physical or psychological violence against people (or other living beings) as well as structural violence which may manifest itself in uneven social relations stemming from the exertion of rulership, appointment of roles and also unfair distribution of goods and opportunities.

Violence in this sense can be understood as everything that is opposed to the definition of health according to the World Health Organization (WHO *Health*) as adopted in June 1946: "Health is a state of complete physical, mental and social well-being and not merely the absence of disease or infirmity."[5] In the sociological discussion of violence this usually excludes natural diseases, accidents and catastrophes. For the purposes of this study I also count as violence only acts or threats that are performed by sentient beings which are or could be harmful to other sentient beings.

While a broad definition of violence is very enlightening and useful in the criticism of social relations, politics, economics and so on, it goes too far for the purposes of the present study. Therefore I will leave out the scrutiny of structural

---

3   "Violence is the mid-wife of history; like the mid-wife she does not sire or give birth to history or revolution." (Arendt 15; my translation: "Die Gewalt ist die Geburtshelferin der Geschichte, und sie macht Geschichte oder Revolution so wenig wie die Hebamme das Kind zeugt oder gebiert.")
4   "Any cause becomes violence in the truest sense of this word as soon as it affects moral relations." (Benjamin 29; my translation: "[Z]ur Gewalt im prägnanten Sinne des Wortes wird eine wie immer wirksame Ursache erst dann, wenn sie in sittliche Verhältnisse eingreift.")
5   Preamble to the Constitution of the World Health Organization as adopted by the International Health Conference, New York, 19-22 June, 1946; signed on 22 July 1946 by the representatives of 61 States (*Official Records of the World Health Organization*, no. 2, p. 100) and entered into force on 7 April 1948.

violence and limit the categories of violence to the working definition of the World Health Organization. Violence as defined in the *World Report on Violence and Health* is: "the intentional use of physical force or power, threatened or actual, against oneself, another person, or against a group or community, that either results in or has a high likelihood of resulting in injury, death, psychological harm, maldevelopment, or deprivation" (WHO *Violence*).

Leaving aside the whole range of dimensions in which violence can appear, as is considered in Galtung's structural approach, *The Lord of the Rings* can be scrutinized by concentrating on occurrences of interpersonal violence. Violence in the narrative almost exclusively appears as interpersonal violence in communities of acquaintances (seldom) or strangers (mostly) and it consists of physical and psychological violence; we see very few examples of deprivation or neglect, and the narrative does not deal with sexual violence.

It has to be noted that the given definition of violence cannot be assumed to be equal to Tolkien's understanding of violence. The definition was developed while *The Lord of the Rings* was being written. But what I am interested in is how today's readers read and understand the book. This is, by the way, what usually is the focus of interest in media violence research.

System of Categories

The system of categories consisted of three basic categories with differentiated subcategories. The basic categories were content-based, that is classified as "Non-Violence", "Violence" and as a third main category, labeled "Inbetween", into which fell descriptions, moments, or scenes of tension but without mention of actual violence or the direct threat of violence. Examples of this category are longer parts of the walk through the Old Forest undertaken by Frodo, Sam, Merry and Pippin, or the description of Aragorn, Legolas and Gimli on the Paths of the Dead.

The main categories were then divided in more meaningful subcategories. The category "Non-Violence" was divided in two greater sub-categories, "Descriptions" and "Interaction". These sub-categories were then divided into more meaningful parts. The main category "Violence" was divided in actual violence on the one hand and seven categories dealing with violence from a distance.

See on the next page Figure 1 for a graphic representation of the system of categories.

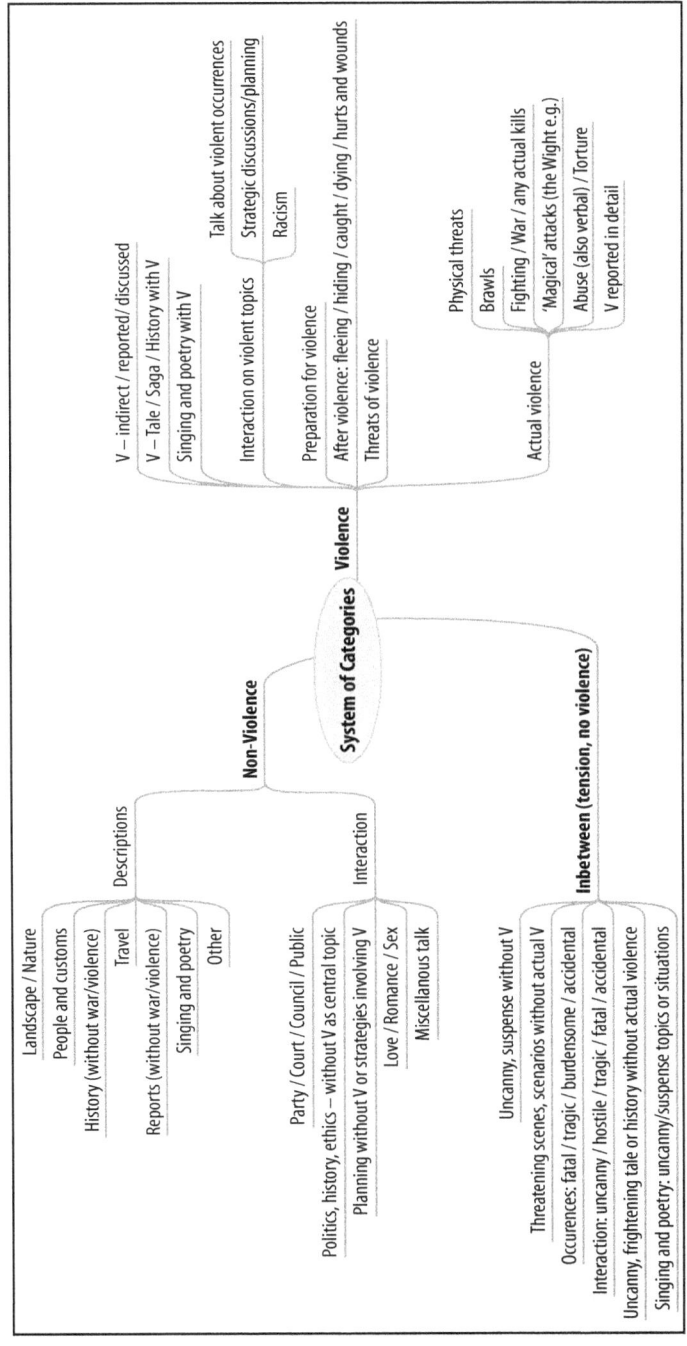

Methodology

The methodology is dealt with in a little more detail not only for reasons of due transparency, but also because I wish to encourage others to pursue the topic of content analysis in *The Lord of the Rings*. There are many, many aspects that wait for further studies, and perhaps some of you readers will carry this work further.

Analysis of Content

The analysis of content was developed as a research method that should yield objective, systematic and quantitative data of the communicated content. Content analysis should reduce subjective interpretations as far as possible (Früh 50ff). The bare contents of communication – in this case, 'contents of communication' refers to the topics that are told in *The Lord of the Rings* – are coded according to a transparent system of categories. The original claim of objectivity may not be valid, but nonetheless the method calls for a systematic and reproducible collection of data according to a transparent system of categories, by which the method "stands or falls" (Berelson 147).

The system of categories as the heart of the study has to be developed in orientation with a theoretical approach. In the present case, this approach has been the restricted theory of violence according to WHO as explained above. The categories were laid out as shown in Figure 1. They were mostly derived from the WHO definition of violence as "intentional use of force or power against persons or communities". Everything that does not fall under this category is declared as non-violent content. Violence in itself was differentiated and coded accordingly.

Besides the main topic of violence it was my goal to also identify the other contents that are found in *The Lord of the Rings*, though not in as detailed a manner as violence (at least for now).

The system of categories underwent peer discussion and was modified due to the peers' remarks. After performing this discursive validation of the system, intercoder-reliability was tested for. This was done to lend more stability to the system of categories. But since I was not able to delegate the coding process as a whole or to employ one or two other coders, the coding itself was performed by one person only, which may result in a lack of reliability when reviewed. Nonetheless intercoder-reliability was tested with two coders on two chapters from *The Fellowship of the Ring* and *The Return of the King* and was measured .77, which is a trustworthy result indicating a reliable system of categories.

Preparation of the Text

The paperback edition by HarperCollins (1993) formed the basis of the analysis. The edition was digitized, run through a character recognition program (Omnipage V 14.0) and transferred to a Word document, which then was read and corrected where the computer or software had made mistakes while processing the text.

The corpus examined did not encompass the whole text usually printed with *The Lord of the Rings*. The foreword, the chapter "Concerning Hobbits" and all Appendices were deleted. Runes and Elvish scriptures were omitted. The object of this study is just the text of the ongoing story without any additional information. The reason for this is that further information is given in content, style, and wording which differs from the story itself and therefore would be able to bias the analysis. That left me with a total amount of nearly 500.000 words or 2.5 million characters for the text of *The Lord of the Rings*.

A problem occurred concerning the counting of characters. Microsoft Word provides a statistic feature which counts characters, words, lines and paragraphs. Alas, this feature miscalculates and comes up with differing count every time a file is opened anew. The calculations regarding character count, which are the basis of the following analysis, differ on a level of 0.005 to 0.05 per cent and are evenly distributed throughout the whole corpus regardless of the amount of text counted. The miscalculations are therefore negligible since they are not able to produce statistically significant differences in the outcome of the quantitative content analysis.

The miscalculations are annoying, regardless of their statistical insignificance. So a trustworthy method of counting is called for and would be very much appreciated; by the way, Open Office also seems not to be able to yield this, as some trials with that program have shown.

Concerning replicability of the analysis and further quantitative research, almost all problems due to miscalculations can also be avoided using a fixed page set-up. Therefore the pages of the corpus of *The Lord of the Rings* were formatted with a width of 53 characters per line, no hyphenation, non-proportional typescript. Approximately 50 lines were set on each page, but from time to time one line more or less was unavoidable.

This set-up also compensates for the miscalculations of the statistic feature, because future reviewers or researchers will not have to rely on this feature and can perform comparative analyses by sticking to the standardized lines. Since every chapter begins anew with line 2 (leaving out the chapter headings) a possible slip in lines in one chapter is corrected with every new beginning of a chapter. This slip of line may occur due to OCR-problems in the recognition of blank spaces. Omnipage V. 14 was used for character recognition and I noticed that sometimes the space between quotation marks and characters was interpreted as blank space.

This results in negligible miscalculations but may lead at the end of lines in very few cases to an additional line consisting of one quotation mark only. Thus a line was added which another OCR-program would not have added, and so there may be one or two additional lines per chapter, which over the whole corpus would lead to increasing differences in line counts. Beginning every chapter afresh avoids this hypothetical problem.

The lines were given numbers, beginning anew with every chapter. Every blank line was deleted, no indentations were allowed. Since the citations depend on the line number per chapter, the omission of blank lines and indentations does not matter and cited texts can be found by their line, chapter and book alone.

Citations are given in volume, number of the chapter and number of line(s). "III, 1, 333-345" therefore means: *The Lord of the Rings* Book 3, being the first part of *The Two Towers*, Chapter 1, bearing the title "The Departure of Boromir", Lines 333-345.

Prepared in this way, I came out with three documents of *The Lord of the Rings*, *The Fellowship of the Ring / The Two Towers / The Return of the King*, with approximately 1.000.000, 825.000 and 720.000 characters, which amounts to a total of a little more than 2.5 million characters.

For a replication, revision or further examination of the text it is recommended to follow the preparational steps described. I cannot, of course, publish the digitized text. The Excel-sheets with my calculations are published under a Creative Commons License on my website. It therefore is possible to calculate further analyses or hit me on the head with my own numbers where I made a mistake. (www.polyoinos.de/download/download.html)

Results

The following results are just a few descriptive first impressions out of a much greater number of possible analyses. But even these first results yield interesting information and encourage further and deeper analysis, which everyone is invited to pursue.

Basic Data

	words***	characters***	violence	(actual violence)	non-violent (+ inbetween)
FotR *	179.720	978.299	11.5%	(4%)	88.5%
TT	154.399	826.264	21.5%	(10.5%)	78.5%
RotK **	136.201	718.200	30.5%	(11.5%)	69.5%
sum / arithmetic means	470.320	2.522.763	Ø: 20%	(Ø: 8.2%)	Ø: 80%

*without "Concerning Hobbits"
**without Appendices
***keeping in mind that Word counts slightly different every time a file is opened, counts differ in a range from 0.005 % to 0,05 % as described above

Table 1: basic data

Basic Data: content inbetween

The material coded as "Inbetween" is of mostly uncanny or tension building nature, where protagonists are approaching dangerous situations without an immediate threat of violence or actual violent occurrences. The main category "Inbetween" contributes 300.000 characters or 12% of the whole corpus. One could very well argue that this content should not be regarded as main category, but instead be counted as a subcategory of "Non-Violent". It then would amount to 18.5% of the non-violent portions of *The Lord of the Rings;* regardless of which category it is placed in, it constitutes 12.5% of the whole corpus. For the moment I will leave this undecided and will not go deeper into the findings of "Inbetween".

Basic Data: non-violent

However, non-violent content makes up 68% per cent of the narrative, i.e. 1.7 million characters of the whole corpus consist of the main category "Non-Violent". The main category "Non-Violent" (with "Inbetween" omitted) was divided into a first set of sub-categories, labelled "Descriptions" and "Interaction". These are nearly of the same extent, 845.000 to 843.000 characters, so descriptions and interactions each roughly make up a third of the whole of *The Lord of the Rings*.

The descriptive part of the narrative consists mainly of the depiction of travel (18.7% of the whole corpus) and the portrayal of people and customs. The descriptions of landscapes and architecture make up a little more than 10% of the descriptive part (which is about 3.5% of the whole corpus). Reports of events or historic occurrences and singing and poetry without violence amount to a lesser extent of approx. 6.8% for reports and 3.7% for poetry (which is about 2.3% and 1.2% of the whole narrative).

	characters	% of descriptions	% of the corpus
description of travel	469.874	55.6%	18.7%
description of people, customs	192.985	22.9%	7.7%
description of landscape, architecture	89.646	10.7%	3.5%
description: reports, non-violent	56.909	6.8%	2.3%
description: singing, poetry, non-v	30.875	3.7%	1.2%

Table 2: basic data – descriptions

The descriptive part of a tale or narrative in fantasy is responsible for the creation of depth in the imaginary world and its occurrences (cf. Weinreich, *Fantasy* 24pp.). If these descriptions are imaginative, they allow for a sense of wonder on the part of the reader and for the willing suspension of disbelief (Coleridge 169) that make up the fascination of the genre. Sheer numbers of course tell nothing about the quality of the descriptive part of *The Lord of the Rings*, but they show at least that Tolkien cared about giving depth and background to Middle-earth. As with all further analysis, a more useful appreciation of the quantitative analysis can only be provided if a comparison to other novels, movies and fantasy products is available. In this sense, the present content analysis can be not much more than a first step.

The other half of the non-violent part consists of the interaction between the people in Middle-earth, insofar as they are not concerned with topics of violence and war. The interaction can be divided roughly into miscellaneous talk and chit-chat, which covers more than 50% of all interaction. General councils add another third, while the distinctive planning of measures, approaches and strategies (as long as they are not strategies for fights or battles) make up only 6% of the interaction. Lastly interaction on certain topics like ethics, romance, politics can be found. These talks include romance, which with 18.000 characters covers less than 1% of the whole story. This could be an all time low for the genre.

	characters	% of descriptions	% of the corpus
interaction: talk	452.669	53.7%	18.1%
interaction: council	302.746	35.9%	12.1%
interaction: planning, strategy (non-v)	50.800	6%	2%
interaction: other	24.163	2.9%	1%

Table 3: basic data - interaction

While on the one hand interaction in narratives has to drive the story, on the other hand it illustrates the characters and as it were gives flesh to their bones. Thus interaction plays a great part in the ability of the reader to relate to the protagonists or even to identify with the characters. This is especially true of those portions of the interaction which do *not* have the main task of keeping the story going. Planning and councils tell mostly about the development of the plot, while miscellaneous talk may also do this to a certain extent. But foremost, these parts portray the characters which are talking or interacting. It is thus presumably a strength of *The Lord of the Rings* that nearly 20% of the whole story serves the purpose of building a relation between protagonists and readers.

Basic Data: violent content

The violent content was divided first into the actual description of violent occurrences which are depicted mostly as ongoing war and fighting, but also including actual threats, vivid reports, abuse and harmful magical influences. Secondly, violence-related material was coded as distant depiction of violence.

The validity of this distinction can be questioned. But with regard to the question of how the reader experiences *The Lord of the Rings*, it makes perfect sense to distinguish thus. There is a differing quality even in the experience of fictitious violence. Take for example a dry report of an ambush on Osgiliath, which tells only of the loss of soldiers and the bridge over the Anduin, and compare it to the vivid description of the fight on the walls of Helm's Deep. Certainly the experience differs. Thus one can argue that what affects the reader as violence is only actual fighting, threat and abuse. If one chose to argue such, it is not important incidentally how the violence depicted affects the reader – whether he suffers compassionately or whether he is inflamed and aggressive.

The difference in the extent of violence in *The Lord of the Rings* if coded thus is however great. The entirety of violent material, as I chose to code it, amounts to 20% of the corpus, actual and vivid fighting and violence amounts to 'only' 8.2%.

The descriptions of actual violence were divided into fighting, magical attacks (or defense), vividly reported violence, actual physical threats, abuse, and brawls. Two thirds of the amount of actual violent material are descriptions of fighting. If one adds the detailed reports of violence, which are reports of fighting and war, the descriptions of fighting amount to more than 80% of the violence. Neither brawls, nor threats nor magical attacks (the latter could also be added to the fighting) reach much more than a share of 5%. Interestingly, the descriptions of abuse, which do not seem likely to glorify violence and war, amount to 10% of the actual violence.

	characters	% of act. viol.	% of the corpus
fighting	131.744	63.4%	5.3%
magical attacks (or defense)	13.940	6.7%	0.5%
vivid reports of violence	31.155	15%	1.2%
physical threats	6.361	3%	0.3%
abuse	20.137	9.7%	0.8%
brawl	5.291	2.5%	0.2%

Table 4: basic data – actual violence

There is more diversity to the violence over all than can be observed on the part of actual violence. Besides actual violence, which amounts to 41% in the violence department of *The Lord of the Rings*, there are nine other sub-categories.

Firstly there is reported, but not vividly depicted violence. This can be divided into historic reports, like for instance the tale of the fall of Númenor, and into reports of contemporary violence on the other hand, as is the case when Éomer tells about the death of Théodred. This distinction is important since historic reports lend more depth to the fictitious world Middle-earth and have thus not only an explanatory and story-driving moment. Then there is interaction on violent topics to be found, and the preparation for violence as in the waiting for a battle. Another point is "threats", which I distinguish from threatening scenes which fall under actual violence. Threats are situations in which violence may burst out under certain circumstances, while a threatening situation is in itself violent. A threat of possible violence occurring is inherent for example when Pippin bids Beregond to stop Denethor's self-destruction. A threatening situation is given for Bill Ferny and the ruffians when the Hobbits scare them off by nearly using physical violence. Two other points are interactions with racist expressions, and singing and poetry including violent topics, as in the marching song of the Ents.

A very important last aspect of violence are situations which occur after actual violence has happened. These are situations in which people may be wounded, may be dying, may flee or may be caught and imprisoned. The importance in this lies in the possibility that these situations may illustrate suffering and other anti-violent aspects, which show the 'dark side' of violence, where violence is not entertaining anymore but shows its true face of hurt and grief. Therefore with scenes after violence, it was distinguished between situations which emphasize suffering and those that do not.

	characters	% of viol. over all	% of the corpus
actual violence	208.628	41%	8.2%
violence, reported, historic	12.049	2.4%	0.5%
violence, reported, contemporary	44.937	8.8%	1.8%
interaction on violence	25.624	5%	1%
preparation for violence	79.592	15.5%	3.1%
interaction, racism	2.247	0.4%	0.08%
threats	16.081	3.2%	0.7%
singing, poetry with violent topics	4.861	0.9%	0.2%
after violence, suffering	69.611	13.6%	2.8%
after violence, non-suffering	36.680	7.8%	1.5%

Table 5: basic data – violence overall

Interesting findings in the observation of violence overall in my opinion are the following ones. Firstly, there are comparatively few historical reports focussing on violence, despite the violent history of Middle-earth which was more or less fully developed at the time Tolkien wrote *The Lord of the Rings*. But *The Lord of the Rings* gives the reader the impression of a rich historic background – obviously therefore violence and war are not that important for the background of the story.[6]

Also quite amazing is the little interaction, i.e. talk, on violence: 25.000 characters. Compare that to the 840.000 characters of interaction overall. To a lesser extent the same is true for singing and poetry: 5.000 to 33.000 characters despite the common tradition in saga and legend to use poetry to tell of mighty deeds done well.

The last point I want to emphasize is the point of suffering when it comes to violence or its aftermath. Situations after fights are in majority scenes of hurt, grief and suffering as is shown in table 4. I also took another look at the section "actual violence" and sorted out the parts "fighting" and "magical attack". I came out with 150.000 characters or 6% of the whole corpus. These pieces were distinguished into fights where the heroic moment stands in the foreground and fights where suffering is emphasized.

	characters	% of descriptions	% of the corpus
fighting and magical attack, heroic	94.367	62.4%	3.8%
fighting and magical attack, suffering	56.957	37.6%	2.2%

Table 6: complementary data – fighting distinguished

To this result one also should add the nearly 1% of torture and abuse depicted in *The Lord of the Rings* which also is very unlikely to glorify violence. This first distinction of violence shows that Tolkien was well aware of the bad consequences of violence and that he was not in the least inclined to spare his reader these experiences.

---

6   This is only true for *The Lord of the Rings*; *The Silmarillion* and *The History of Middle-earth*, of course, depict the history of Arda as a history of battle and violence. But that is interestingly not emphasized in *The Lord of the Rings*, where the reader does not get the same expression of the world's history than in the rest of the *Legendarium*.

Conclusion

I want to close this first overview of an analysis of content of *The Lord of the Rings* at this point without going into the interpretation of the data presented. This, I hope will be the topic of discussion in the future. Three closing remarks may be allowed, though.

As to the question posed at the beginning of this study, the question of whose interpretation of *The Lord of the Rings* hits the mark, I think that Jackson's screenplay is not more than an entertaining action movie, adapting motifs from *The Lord of the Rings,* while Matthew Dickerson's *Following Gandalf* is a highly intelligent observation of what the most important narrative about Middle-earth really is about.

Secondly, even the impression of the sheer numbers of violent and non-violent portions of *The Lord of the Rings* show that violence, in the first place, is not the ruling topic in the narrative though *The Lord of the Rings* is *the* book on the "War of the Ring" (cf. Weinreich, *Ethos* 120).

And thirdly, where violence is made explicit, it is dealt with in a differentiated way. There is of course heroism and northern spirit. But there are also suffering, wounds, and grievance, and perhaps this will provide the longer lasting impressions. Tom Shippey, it seems, is right when he claims that Tolkien's narrative is "a war-book, also a post-war book, framed by and responding to the crisis of western civilisation" and that the author belongs in one group of writers with William Golding, George Orwell, Kurt Vonnegut and others of that kind (Shippey 329).

The Lord of the Rings is not the same as Erich Maria Remarque's *All Quiet on the Western Front* but it has much more in common with that book than with Ernst Jünger's *Storm of Steel* and it definitely has very little in common with the hack 'n slash of many other fantasy writers like J.F. Lange Jr. (John Norman), H.K. Bulmer (Alan Burt Akers), and Chris Evans or others. And that may very well be another piece of the mosaic that explains the success of this great tale.

Bibliography

Arendt, Hannah. *Macht und Gewalt*. München: Piper, 1993

Benjamin, Walter. »Zur Kritik der Gewalt«. *Zur Kritik der Gewalt und andere Aufsätze*. Frankfurt/M.: Suhrkamp, 1965, 29-65

Berelson, Bernard. *Content Analysis in Communication Research*. Facsimile of 1952 Edititon. New York: Hafner, 1971

Bonfadelli, Heinz. *Medienwirkungsforschung I. Grundlagen und theoretische Perspektiven*. Konstanz: UVK Medien, 1999

Coleridge, Samuel Taylor: *Biographia Literaria or Biographical sketches of my Literary Life and Opinions*. London, New York: Dent & Sons, 1975

Curry, Patrick: *Defending Middle-Earth*. Tolkien: Myth and Modernity. New York: St. Martin's Press, 1997

---. "Tolkien and His Critics: A Critique". *Root and Branch – Approaches Towards Understand-ing Tolkien*. Ed. Thomas Honegger. Zurich/Berne: Walking Tree Publishers, 2003, 81-148

Dickerson, Matthew. *Following Gandalf*. Epic Battles and Moral Victory in "The Lord of the Rings". Grand Rapids: Brazos, 2004

Galtung, Johan. *Strukturelle Gewalt. Beiträge zur Friedens- und Konflikt-forschung*. Rowohlt, Reinbek bei Hamburg, 1982

Moser, Heinz. *Einführung in die Medienpädagogik. Aufwachsen im Medienzeitalter*. 3. Auflage, Opladen: Leske & Budrich, 2000

Shippey, Tom. *The Road to Middle-earth*. How J.R.R. Tolkien created a New Mythology. Boston, New York: Houghton Mifflin, 2003

Theunert, Helga: »Gewalt«. *Grundbegriffe Medienpädagogik*. Ed. Jürgen Hüther. München: KoPäd 1997, 126-134

Vollbrecht, Ralf. *Einführung in die Medienpädagogik*. Weinheim und Basel: Beltz, 2001

Weinreich, Frank: »Medieneinflüsse«. *Medien und Informationstechnologien in Erziehung und Bildung*. Eds. Bardo Herzig, Renate Schulz-Zander, Gerhard Tulodziecki. [CD-ROM] Hagen: UVM, 2002

---. »Ethos in Arda. Charakteristika der Ethik in Mittelerde«. *Eine Grammatik der Ethik. Die Aktualität der moralischen Dimension in J.R.R. Tolkiens literarischem Werk*. Thomas Honegger, Andrew J. Johnston, Friedhelm Schneidewind, Frank Weinreich. Saarbrücken, Verlag der Villa Fledermaus, 2005, 111-134

---. *Fantasy. Einführung*. Essen: Oldib, 2007

---. »Der Herr der Ringe. J.R.R. Tolkien (1892-1973) lebte für die Fantasy.« *Die Fantastischen 6*. Ed. Ch. Kerner. Weinheim: Beltz, 2010 (in print)

World Health Organization. *WHO Definition of Health*. 1946. Online: www.who.int/about/definition/en/print.html (01-04-2009)

---. Ed. *World Report on Violence and Health*. 2009. Online: www.who.int.violenceprevention/approach/definition/en/index.html (01-04-2009)

Perspectives on Just War in Tolkien's *Legendarium*

Annie Birks (Angers)

Introduction

> All hopes for the future must take into account what will be done by (people) who do not want peace and justice.   (Wood 155)

This quotation from Millar Burrows might lead one to think that if everybody wanted peace and justice, the world would be a better place, and that those who are not that way inclined should be dealt with radically to preserve the future. Such an interpretation, however, can leave much to be desired, for the concepts of peace and justice are far from easy to delineate and the legacy left by what might appear as noble dealings is often far from healthy.

Tolkien once warned of being careful not to conquer Sauron with his own Ring for although success might come, the penalty is "to breed new Saurons and slowly turn Men and Elves into Orcs" (L 78). In other words you cannot use the fact that others are not doing the right thing to justify your personal intention of initiating war.

The problem is how to define good, just, noble etc. in a universally accepted sense. As long as there is discussion about what is right and what is wrong, there will always be discord. It seems that an acceptance or an encouragement of relativism is a breeding ground for conflict. And yet most great theologians and leaders admit that there is some underlying truth and only superficial differences. Aragorn's reply to Éomer in Rohan sheds light on Tolkien's views of relativism:

> "It is hard to be sure of anything among so many marvels. The world is all grown strange. Elf and Dwarf in company walk in our daily fields; and folk speak with the Lady of the Wood and yet live; and the Sword comes back to war that was broken in the long ages ere the fathers of our fathers rode into the Mark! How shall a man judge what to do in such times?"
> "As he ever has judged," said Aragorn. "Good and ill have not changed since yesteryear; nor are they one thing among Elves and Dwarves and another among Men. It is man's part to discern them, as much in the Golden Wood as in his own house". (LotR II 44)

Aragorn invites Éomer to discern the "Law of Nature" or "decent behaviour" which lies deeply in all human beings, as C.S. Lewis skillfully demonstrates in *Mere Christianity* and *The Abolition of Man*. Anyone comparing the "moral teaching of, say, the ancient Egyptians, Babylonians, Hindus, Chinese, Greeks and Romans", will be surprised to notice "how very like they are to each other and to our own" (Lewis 6).

Because war implies death-giving and, in Tolkien's words, is such an "utter stupid waste, not only material but moral and spiritual", "so staggering to those who have to endure it" (L 75), entering into it has to be highly justified. The genesis of Middle-earth as related in the *Ainulindalë* shows from the outset that in Tolkien's *Legendarium*, war is not an option. Conflict is inherent to the creation as soon as the seeds of harmony and discord are sown by the Ainur during their handling of the themes propounded by Ilúvatar. Therefore in Middle-earth, there will be war, the question becomes: how will it be waged?

Owing to the centrality of warfare in Tolkien's *Legendarium*, this paper will consider the motivations of the races and people engaged in war, whether the conflicts be waged with seemingly justifiable intentions or not, whether they be defensive, preventive or aggressive. In the light of scholarly viewpoints on the subject (such as that of Saint Augustine) and judging by the short and long-term outcomes of hostilities in the history of Middle-earth, an attempt will be made to identify perspectives on the concept of "just war" in Tolkien's secondary world.

I. The Just War Theory: Preliminary Considerations

1. *Jus ad Bellum* and *Jus in Bello*

Over the centuries, many scholars and thinkers have addressed the ethical question of warfare and have gradually developed a theory with a view to offering guidance to nations when faced with the imminence of war (cf. Fotion VII). Although the collective name "Just War Theory" encompasses disparate traditions, it boils down to several principles which will be used as guidelines in our reflections (cf. Regan 14).

Basically the theory revolves around two main questions: first, when is waging war justifiable and secondly, what is justifiable while waging war? The first question refers to the Latin phrase *Jus ad Bellum*, i.e. "Justice to war" and the second to *Jus in Bello*, i.e. "Justice in war". Although the two questions appear *a priori* linked, they require independent assessments: a just war may be fought unjustly, in keeping with the Latin maxim *Inter arma silent enim leges* ("in times of war, the law falls silent"), whereas an unjust war may be waged fairly, in strict adherence to the rules (cf. Waltzer 3, 21).

The philosopher and theologian Augustine of Hippo (354-430) is usually regarded as the originator of the doctrine although pre-Christian thinkers had already theorized on the necessity of military self-defence, such as Aristotle (384-322 BC) and Cicero (106-43 BC) (cf. Regan 14). Augustine's ideas provided an embryonic answer to the question on how to reconcile, on the one hand, the Christian law of love prohibiting the use of lethal force and, on the other hand, the necessity for a community to defend itself or to come to the aid of neighbours by inflicting harm on malefactors (cf. Regout 15, Regan 17).

Thomas Aquinas, the most influential theologian of the Middle Ages (1225-1274) endorsed the Augustinian theory and expanded it further. He gave the Just War Theory its scholarly status through his greatest work *Summa Theologica* (*The Summation of Theology*). However it was only in the 16th century that the doctrine became more firmly established thanks to Spanish theologians, such as Francisco de Vitoria (1492-1546). In 1625, the Dutch Christian jurist Hugo Grotius (1583-1685) integrated their ideas in his *De Jure Belli ac Pacis* (*On the Law of War and Peace*) (cf. Regout 15). This treatise contributed in a more modern secularized form to the development of the doctrine which was to serve as a benchmark to Nations trying to decide about the ethics of war and be integrated in international Law (cf. Simpson 63).

It is important to point out that not all theorists placed just war considerations within a theological framework even though it seems generally accepted that the reasoning process stems from and was first elaborated by theologians.

2. Augustine of Hippo's underlying Ideas on Just War

Before examining the principles in detail, let us first consider some of Augustine's underlying ideas on just war reasoning and their echoes in the unfolding of the history of Middle-earth. The Augustinian doctrine was essentially based on the principle that a just war is a means to obtain peace.

> Peace should be the object of your desire; war should be waged only as a necessity and waged only that God may by it deliver men from the necessity and preserve them in peace... Therefore, even in waging war, cherish the spirit of a peacemaker, that, by conquering those whom you attack, you may lead them back to the advantages of peace.[1] (Simpson 42)

---

[1] This quotation comes from Augustine, Letter 189 (A.D. 418) to Count Boniface.

Although the wish formulated at the end of the statement is difficult to imagine when fighting the Orcs of Mordor, these words cannot but bring to mind Faramir's view of war:

> I would not take this thing [the Ring], if it lay by the highway. Not were Minas Tirith falling in ruin and I alone could save her, so, using the weapon of the Dark Lord for her good and my glory. No, I do not wish for such triumphs, Frodo son of Drogo...
> I would see the White Tree in flower again in the courts of the kings, and the Silvers Crown return, and Minas Tirith in peace; Minas Anor again as of old, full of light, high and fair, beautiful as a queen among other queens: not a mistress of many slaves, nay, not even a kind mistress of willing slaves. War must be, while we defend our lives against a destroyer who would devour all; but I do not love the bright sword for its sharpness, nor the arrow for its swiftness, nor the warrior for his glory. I love only that which they defend: the city of the Men of Númenor.   (LotR II 348 pp)

This is far from the glorification of war for war's sake. Unlike his brother Boromir, Faramir was aware of the danger of the Ring and his engagement in war is in keeping with the Augustinian criterion.

Augustine went even further in his perception of peace. He did not just refer to a situation opposed to war; what he meant was a state of *tranquillitas ordinis* ("tranquillity in order"), "tranquillity in justice", "the harmony of order" (Regout 40). In his mind order came "when equal and unequal things are all in their place". Prosperity of the country, tranquillity and order in the community were also Thomas Aquinas' prime justification for a just war. Respect of right and order when "everything is indeed in its place" was one of Aquinas' characteristic principles. To him, justice demands that right be restored whenever the objective order of things is disturbed (cf. Regout 93).

3. Harmony of Order: a Glance at the *Ainulindalë*

At the outset of Tolkien's myth of creation, the Augustinian justification of waging war as a means of attaining peace, harmony and order is presented in a reversed form. Ilúvatar's propounded project for his creation in the form of musical themes begins with ordered tranquillity and invites each one, with their own free will, to play in harmony and unison, to adorn the music according to their own thoughts, devices and skills.

Owing to Melkor's handling of the themes, harmony and therefore order are totally disrupted. Melkor gives in to "an inordinate desire", which Augustine expressed as being the root of evil (cf. Davidson 102). That is "the desire for something that violates the rightful order of things", a sort of perversion of all legitimate desires. Melkor decides to compose his own music disregarding the divine score. Restoring harmony can therefore be viewed as a justifiable goal of war in Middle-earth.

Furthermore, the *Ainulindalë* shows that music is a time-related process: it starts, flows, stops and the pattern goes on with new harmonies and new discordant notes. But it appears that there is always a time when Ilúvatar considers that the struggle with discordance has continued long enough and has to be interrupted. Such is the case when he instructs the Valar "to take up again the mastery of Arda at whatsoever cost" (S 58) before the Battle of the Powers and later when he destroys Númenor.

However this state of respite only lasts a while for there will always be more discordant notes arising because the Melkorian ingredients are incorporated in the fibres of Middle-earth. At the very beginning of days, the Valar experience the principle of impermanence: whatever they build in Eä is destroyed by Melkor over and over again, until one day, in a sense, the Music halts with the Battle of the Powers and the chaining of Melkor.

It is interesting to note that their first experience of war unfolds in three stages. During the first war, which is waged before Arda is full-shaped, Melkor is defeated thanks to the intervention of Tulkas (sent by Ilúvatar) and forsakes Arda to go brooding in the outer darkness. The second war comes after he destroys the lamps Illuin and Ormal as the Valar are resting on the Isle of Almaren. Again he is defeated and escapes to his fortress Utumno. The third war is fought by the host of Valinor upon Ilúvatar's counsel to free the Quendi from the shadow of Melkor. The first victory of the Valar is swift; Melkor and his minions flee to Utumno. After a long siege and many battles Tulkas wrestles with him and takes him captive to Valinor.

The same pattern of ongoing conflict and war interspaced with major victories against evil and periods of relative peace runs throughout the history of Middle-earth. War in Middle-earth can therefore be seen as a means to achieve a new state of order or ordinate tranquillity insofar as Melkor's discord has permanently altered the original theme.

4. A Just War does not necessarily imply Short-Term Victory for the Just

ugustine was well aware that just war did not necessarily involve short-term victory on the part of the wronged belligerents, as is said in the Gospels: "He [Your Father who is in heaven] makes his sun rise on the evil and on the good, and sends rain on the just and the unjust." (Matthew 5, 45). But being a consequence of the original sin, calamities such as war can be used by God to punish the sinners, and provide opportunities for both the good and the sinners to amend (cf. Regout 41).

His vision of just war therefore encompasses the necessity of punishing and amending the wrongdoers for their own good. Such a vision is rooted in biblical narratives where Israel's defeats are sometimes due to the fact that wars are waged "presumptuously", i.e. "against Yahweh's will" or as part of His judgment (cf. Wood 18). War appears therefore as a means of expiation and redemption.

There are many examples in the *Legendarium* that just wars do not always lead to the defeat of the wrongdoers in the short term. It takes all the wars of Beleriand and thousands of casualties to reach a state of tranquillity with the expulsion of Morgoth. It is as though Ilúvatar, like the God of the Bible, uses these opportunities as a learning curve for the different races. As echoed in the later *Quenta Silmarillion* (II):

> Eru is Lord of All, and will use as instruments of his final purposes, which are good, whatsoever any of his creatures, great or small, do or devise, in his despite or in his service. But we must hold that it is his will that those of the Eldar that serve him should not be cast down by griefs or evils that they encounter in Arda Marred; but should ascend to a strength and wisdom that they would not otherwise have achieved: that the children of Eru grow to be daughters and sons. (MR 245)

II. The Principles of the Just War Theory
Exclusion of the Defensive War

Before listing the principles of Just War Theory and applying them to the history of Middle-earth, it is expedient to exclude the case of a defensive war. Indeed the issue is so obvious that Just War Theorists do not take it into account. Individuals and nations have the right and duty to defend themselves against any unjust attack within the limits of necessary protection. The same goes for the defence and protection of allies or friends.

One does not need to labour the point in the history of Middle-earth concerning the wars initiated by Morgoth and Sauron which obviously triggered opportunities for just-war responses on the part of the wronged parties.

If no attack has been launched but if an individual's or a nation's right has been violated in one way or another, an offensive war might then be justifiable. It can in fact be considered in some cases as a defensive war. Therefore offensive wars can be regarded as morally justifiable. However, owing to the terrible calamities engendered by war in general, theorists base their principles on the following presumption: offensive war is unjust, illegitimate and a crime unless it corresponds to certain specific criteria. Hence the following agreed upon principles:

The six Principles

i. Just Cause

A cause will be just only if it involves preventing or rectifying "wrongful or unjust action by another nation against itself or a third" (Regan 48). It must be in response to the perpetration of an actual and verifiable injury (cf. Simpson 27 pp.). For instance, it cannot be triggered off by pride, acquisitive appetite, the search for power or pure revenge.

In that respect, Feänor's reaction to his father's death and the theft of the Silmarils by Morgoth might appear at first sight as a just cause. Nevertheless his motivations do not seem to be legitimate according to the just-war principles insofar as he gives in to his inordinate desire of revenge and greed. The Doom of Mandos is hardly surprising by just-war standards. This illegitimate cause will lead to Feänor's death and all the terrible wars of Beleriand.

In a way, Feänor resembles his fellow-elves insofar as he wants things to remain stationary; he wants to recover the Silmarils in spite of the Valar's forbiddance. Yet, in the *Ainulindalë* the music shows that life flows and changes. As Tolkien wrote:

> The Elves' weakness is in these terms naturally to regret the past, and to become unwilling to face change: as if a man were to hate a very long book still going on, and wished to settle down in a favourite chapter. (L 236)

Tolkien viewed this trait as 'a sort of second type of fall'. The Elves are prepared to enter into war to keep things as they were. They build kingdoms in Middle-earth which resemble Valinor and yet perhaps their fate is to leave Middle-earth and move to the Blessed Realms, and not to reconstruct Valinor in Middle-earth. Although there might be nothing essentially wrong with lingering "in the mortal historical Middle-earth because they had become fond of it", what is discordant is their desire "to arrest change" (L 197, 236). The line is thin between preventing change and healing the wounds. The danger for the Elves is to be closer to "embalmers" than to "healers". This leads them to create the three Rings to protect themselves against change and thus give them a power over Middle-earth that they did not originally possess. Nevertheless in spite of Sauron's hope to "bring under his sway all those that desired secret power beyond the measure of their kind" (S 347), they do not fall under his control for their intention is not to dominate other wills. At the end of the Third Age, Sauron is destroyed; the Elves and the Rings go to Valinor. All change is ultimately for the good because it has its source in Ilúvatar. It is foretold in the original music.

If resisting change for the Elves is an inordinate desire, the refusal of mortality (or quest for immortality) for the men of Númenor who attempt to invade Valinor by force is another. As a direct consequence of this terrible act of sacrilege, the island is destroyed by Ilúvatar himself in the Change of the World. Another case of inordinate desire is the vengeance of the Dwarves at the Battle of the Thousand Caves. After slaying King Thingol in order to keep the Nauglamir, they are pursued to death by the Elves and "robbed" of the necklace. Their onslaught on Menegroth after the end of the protective girdle of Melian leads them to plunder and ransack the Halls of Thingol. Despite an initial victory, most of them are killed by Beren, Dior and the Laiquendi (green elves) at the Battle of Sarn Athrad.

Such is also the case of Thorin's greed behind his decision to fight his former allies after the death of the dragon. His desire to recover the Arkenstone is too great. Thorin is killed not in the battle he has contemplated waging and which, in fact, does not occur, but in the Battle of the Five Armies.

As part of the first principle, a preemptive strike might constitute a just cause if there is a high degree of certitude that threats are imminent. The threatened nation does not have to wait to be under attack to initiate hostilities (cf. Regan 51). It is a case of self-defense. The White Council's attack on Dol Guldur to drive out Sauron is a good example.

Finally, the wrongful or unjust action must be actual and verifiable, and of substantial importance (cf. Simpson 28). Trifles can in no way justify a military response. The refusal by the Teleri to provide the rebelling Noldor with ships did not justify the kinslaying at Alqualondë. In a more general way all the characters that become martially-minded to possess objects such as the Silmarils, the Nauglamir and the Arkenstone can be ranged in this category. Shippey explains the latter trait as being typical of our modern world, a form of underlying applicability : "Love of things, especially artificial things, could be seen as the besetting sin of modern civilization, and in a way a new one, not quite Avarice and not quite Pride, but somehow attached to both" (Shippey 214).

ii. Legitimate Authority

Just war principles exclude any idea of vengeance on the part of private individuals or citizens (cf. Simpson 28). Only legitimate authorities, such as a king, a prince or a government, who have been given the power of decision-making can decide whether to enter into a war of not. It is their duty to weigh the legitimacy of the cause with extreme prudence and practical wisdom and avoid acting rashly (cf. Regan 20). If they have a *prima facie* just cause to resort to war to defend their countries against potential armed attacks or to redress a cause, it might prove a fatal mistake to fail to do so.

This second condition implies that all forms of rebellion and civil war are excluded. However this principle presupposes that the ruler or head of state is *a priori* right and just and that he is not considered a possible enemy. If this were not to be the case, the leader of the rebellion becomes the legitimate authority. The latter is a question of division within one nation leading to two nations under one banner.

There is evidence in the history of Middle-earth that Tolkien was aware of this difficult and awkward situation, one that revolves around obedience to a central authority and how far it can be maintained before a form of civil disobedience or indeed civil war becomes the most just course of action. In his well-known essay on *Civil Disobedience*, the American writer and philosopher Henry David Thoreau (1817-1862) advocated that it is a man's duty to disobey the law of the land and to obey the much higher law of his own conscience when on those rare occasions there is a conflict between the two.

Thus on the one hand, Elendil, Éomer and Faramir do not rebel outwardly (insofar as they do not seek to organize a revolt) but they do disobey their respective leadership – Ar-Pharazôn, Theoden and Denethor – in martial affairs, as does Gandalf with regards to Saruman. And on the other hand the War of the Silmarils is entirely based on an unjust rebellion if we consider that the Valar are the legitimate authorities. Nevertheless, for most of the rebellious Noldor who followed Feänor, the legitimate authority was their leader.

Thoreau's description of the mass of men serving the state with, in most cases, "no free exercise whatever of the judgment or of the moral sense" brings to mind the blind servile attitude of Sauron's followers: these serve "not as men mainly, but as machines, with their bodies" putting themselves "on a level with wood and earth and stones", or as a "mere shadow and reminiscence of humanity" (Thoreau 345).

iii. Last Resort

However the properly instituted authorities are expected to strive to avert war by all reasonable means for it is the most harmful option. By starting the process, the authorities will be responsible for all the potentially terrible consequences (cf. Walzer 23). It falls to them to negotiate and if need be to ask for reparations. The wronged party has to remain vigilant and make sure that the negotiations are not a means for the threatening party to gain time and build up military forces and stockpile weapons (cf. Regan 67). In case of reparations, prudence dictates fairness if resentment and future conflict are to be avoided. If everything has been attempted and the guilty nation still refuses to give in, resorting to war might be the only solution.

The principle of last resort implies therefore the possibility of negotiation. One fateful example is that of Sauron being taken prisoner to Númenor by Ar-Pharazôn who was anything but vigilant because he was hardly motivated by the best intentions. Now whilst it may have been a "just" thing for Ar-Pharazôn not to make open war on Sauron, it becomes clear that, as with Morgoth, it is impossible to negotiate with this enemy in Middle-earth and that war will become unavoidable.

iv. Proportionality

Not all the wrongs – whatever the degree of severity involved – can justify engaging in war. Owing to the terrible calamities caused by warfare, it might be sometimes more appropriate to tolerate the lesser of two evils (cf. Regout 21). If fighting a justified war leads the wronged nation to employ disproportionate means against the guilty nation, then war is unjust.[2] Reason dictates a value judgment to determine whether the number of casualties and the high cost involved on the enemies' side can be justified (cf. Regan 63). Just war theorists generally agree that the damage caused to the guilty nation must not overweigh the original harm inflicted. Assessing such data is no easy task owing to the imponderables of war and life in general but it is part and parcel of the Just War Theory. If this condition is not met, war should not be undertaken.

This principle does not seem to be applicable to the main events in the history of Middle-earth given the excessively evil nature of the enemy. The closest we can get is the tolerance of Elves, Men and Dwarves towards Orcs wandering freely in Middle-earth during periods of relative peace.

v. Likelihood of Success

This principle is linked to the previous one insofar as estimates have to be made but this time in terms of benefits and loss on the part of the wronged party. It is burdened with the same uncertainty factors as it involves predicting the future without the possibility of weighing all the consequences.

---

2   Nevertheless some argue that the recourse to disproportionate means does not go against justice but against charity (cf. Regout 2).

Such a principle relies mainly on the legitimate authorities' faculty of reason and lucidity. However one might be hard pressed to pin down exactly what is meant by success. At the outbreak of war, total victory seems to be the prime purpose but when all resources are exhausted and the original aim considered as unachievable, one might be content with a less favourable result (cf. Simpson 16).

This is another area where the principle of just war does not seem to fit in well with Tolkien's Middle-earth. For, on a number of occasions we have only a glimpse of "hope without guarantee". In the War of the Ring for example, the chances of success are so slim that characters like Saruman decide to join the enemy or like Denethor decide not to fight and commit suicide. Yet Tolkien the sub-creator shows that, as long as the underlying cause is just, even if there is little chance of success, not attempting what constitutes in effect the only hope for peace, would amount to a form of suicide. In this case, ceasing to wage war would bring less tangible hope for the peoples of the West than would continuing the war with the little hope they had.

It must be stressed here that in Middle-earth warfare is often against an easily identifiable and undisputable source of evil such as Melkor or Sauron, and that without the destruction of the enemy there is little hope of peace. The applicability of Just War Theory to Middle-earth, it seems, is therefore underscored more by Middle-earth's ability to give us insights into how Tolkien considered that a war against evil should be fought, than by whether war in Middle-earth itself was just or unjust. The discord sown in the *Ainulindalë* again seems to make war a foregone conclusion.

We need to be careful not to make too close an analogy between our own primary world and Middle-earth, remembering Tolkien's dislike of analogy and preference for applicability. If Tolkien had meant Middle-earth to resemble our own in all its details he could be criticized for glorifying war. Careful study of Middle-earth shows us however, that the identification of evil, a major difficulty in our world, is often simplified in Middle-earth, but that the response to evil and war in Middle-earth is just as thorny a problem as in our own.

vi. The right Intention : *Jus ad Bellum* and *Jus in Bello*

Once all the basic guidelines on the relevance of initiating war are adhered to by the legitimate decision-makers, there arises another principle which, unlike the others, is not procedural in nature but which is directly related to the mental disposition of those who have made the decision and those who are going to perform the action (cf. Regan 84).

Indeed justifying a good reason to take offensive military action does not guarantee that the war will be waged with the right intention. For example the idea of exercising power or reaping benefits must not be part of the motives, even if this is considered as collateral from the very outset (cf. Regan 85). Conduct in combat must remain in keeping with the norms of justice whether it be related to the treatment of prisoners, or the discrimination of targets (actions threatening the lives of ordinary civilians must be avoided).

Furthermore the principle of proportionality is again at stake; for example resorting to excessive force against a stronghold ready to surrender or the decision to sacrifice an unjustifiable number of soldiers on both sides to satisfy one's own glory (Simpson 21). Intentionality which also relates to the *Jus in Bello* is the key moral concept and non compliance with it impairs a just cause (cf. Regan 98).

Examples of this on the scale of a race are difficult to find in Arda, but at the level of rulers or individuals they are more common. Objects of power such as the Palantirí or the Ring play an important role in exposing the mental disposition of those waging war. Saruman well illustrates non compliance with this principle. His fight stems from a good cause: defeating obvious evil. It is legitimate at the beginning. But gradually his motivations are tainted since they turn towards the Ring, domination and power. Denethor also wages a just war against Sauron but this also degenerates as he desires to keep his position as steward and also to acquire the Ring. Aragorn's and Gandalf's compliance with this principle is exemplary insofar as they will not seek any power, benefit nor glory for themselves.

In the two classic works[3] of military knowledge both entitled *The Art of War*, one by the Chinese military general Sun Tzu (544-496 BC) and the other by the Italian philosopher, writer and politician Niccolo Machiavelli (1469-1527), the non compliance with the *Jus in Bello* principle is rather noteworthy in some of the strategies put forward. These instances remind the Tolkien reader of Melkor or Sauron's recurring methods. For example, in Sun Tzu's treatise, the military authorities are encouraged to sow division among the enemies. All possible means are justified to reach this aim and notably the use of spies spreading false rumours and misleading information (cf. Sun Tzu 102). Consequently in the enemies' camp, suspicions will replace trust, and the slightest doubts will be regarded as the most convincing evidence to have any suspect executed. Generous rewards should be granted to all those who have joined your banners and many civilians from the enemies' camp will eventually become entirely devoted to your service ... Obviously if your plot happens to be unveiled, all

---

3   Although *The Art of War* by Sun Tzu is the oldest military treatise in the world, it is still referenced in modern military and business contexts. It is classical reading on warfare along with *The Art of War* and *The Prince by Machiavelli* and *Vom Kriege (On War)* by the Prussian soldier, military historian and theorist, Carl Philipp Gottlieb von Clausewitz (1780-1831). The latter's philosophical reflections on war "influenced many 20th-century strategists and historians". See *Encyclopedia Britannica*: http://www.britannica.com/

those involved would have to be unremittingly eradicated. (Cf. Sun Tzu 105) In Machiavelli's *Art of War*, the same advice is strongly recommended:

> Among all his other actions, a captain ought with every art to contrive to divide the forces of his enemy, either by making him suspect his own men in whom he confides, or by giving him a cause that has him separate his own troops and, through this, become weaker. (Machiavelli 134)

The mode of punishment of culprits praised by Machiavelli is a far cry from the attitude of pity and charity shown by Gandalf and Frodo towards Gollum:

> The wicked man was allowed to flee and all the soldiers to kill him. So that at once each threw stones or darts, or hit him with other arms, in such a manner that he went along barely alive, and very rarely did he escape. And such as did escape, were not allowed to return home, except with so many disadvantages and ignominies that it was much better to die. (Machiavelli 128)

This Roman practice also adopted by the Swiss is, according to the Italian military tactician "well considered and optimally done" (Machiavelli 128).

Conclusion

The *Ainulindalë* provides an explanation as to why there is discord, suffering and war in Middle-earth. Tolkien as someone who had seen two world wars in our primary world and who yet believed in a benevolent God does not necessarily try to explain why such a momentous experience both of good and evil exists in our own primary world. Rather he explores, through applicability, how people, like himself, caught up in such events can or should face up to them without using the enemy's ring by following what are essentially just-war principles. To quote again, more fully this time, the letter to his son Christopher in April 1944, Tolkien wrote:

> The utter stupid waste of war, not only material but moral and spiritual, is so staggering to those who have to endure it. And always was (despite the poets), and always will be (despite the propagandists) – not of course that it has been, is, and will be necessary to face it in an evil world. (L 75)

However compliance with the generally accepted just-war principles does not suffice to circumscribe Tolkien's yardsticks as to whether a war is just or not. As a Christian, Tolkien also incorporated in Middle-earth what some theologians call "synergism" (Wood 35), that is the fusion of divine and human activity. Hence not only the Heavenly host intervene explicitly in several circumstances, or even the creator himself as with the destruction of Númenor, but also in the form of miraculous turns of events, what Tolkien called eucatastrophes, brought about for example by charismatic individuals.

This is when you can feel, but not always detect explicitly in the narrative, that war is waged in a synergistic, and hence in a just manner. When such miraculous elements enter and play a dominant part, the divine blessing vouches for the legitimacy of the war in Middle-earth.

Bibliography

Carpenter, Humphrey, Ed. *The Letters of J.R.R. Tolkien*. London: George Allen & Unwin, 1981

Davidson, Scott A. "Tolkien and the Nature of Evil". *The Lord of the Rings and Philosophy*. Ed. G. Bassham and E. Bronson. Chicago: Open Court, 2004, 99-109

Fotion, Nicholas. *War and Ethics: A New Just War Theory*. London: Continuum, 2007

Lewis, C.S. *Mere Christianity* [1952]. San Francisco: HarperCollins, 2001

Machiavel, Nicolas. *Oeuvres Complètes de Machiavel*. Paris: Gallimard, 1952

Machiavelli, Niccolò. *Art of War*. Translated by Christopher Lynch. Chicago: University of Chicago Press, 2003

Regan, Richard J. *Just War Principles and Cases*. Washington D.C.: The Catholic University of America Press, 1996

Regout, Robert. *La doctrine de la guerre juste de Saint Augustin à nos jours*. Paris: Éditions A. Pedone, 1934

Shippey, Tom. *The Road to Middle-Earth* [1982]. London: HarperCollins, 1992

Simpson, Gary M. *War, Peace, and God: Rethinking the Just-War Tradition*. Minneapolis: Augsburg Fortress, 2007

Thoreau, Henri David. *Walden and Civil Disobedience*. New York: Washington Square Press, 1971

Tolkien, J.R.R., *The Two Towers* [1954]. London: HarperCollins, 1993

---. *The Silmarillion*, (1977), Christopher Tolkien (ed.), London: Allen & Unwin, 1979

---. *Morgoth's Ring. The History of Middle-earth X* [1993], Ed. Christopher Tolkien. London: HarperCollins, 2002

Tzu, Sun. *The Art of War*. Translated by Father Amiot. Barcelone: Mille et une nuits, 2008

Von Clausewitz, Carl. *De la guerre*. Translated by Denise Naville. Paris: Les Éditions de minuit, 1955

Walzer, Michael. *Just and Unjust Wars*. New York: Basic Books, 1977

Wood, John A. *Perspectives on War in the Bible*. Macon: Mercer University Press, 1998

Encyclopedia Britannica online: http://www.britannica.com/

Gibt es Macht ohne Gewalt?
Thomas Fornet-Ponse (Bonn)

Die Frage nach dem Zusammenhang von staatlicher Macht (im Sinne von Herrschaft) und Gewaltausübung, besonders mit Blick auf das Verhältnis zwischen Staat bzw. Gemeinwesen und Individuum gehört zu den zentralen Fragen politischer Philosophie. Dabei können verschiedene Fragenkomplexe genannt werden: Wie legitimiert der Staat seine Macht über Individuen, die auch die Einschränkung von Menschenrechten beinhalten kann? Muss ein Staat über das Gewaltmonopol verfügen? Wie ist bei Konfliktfällen zwischen staatlichen und individuellen Interessen vorzugehen? Zusätzlich zugespitzt werden diese Fragen, wenn wir einen Sonderfall des Verhältnisses zweier Staaten oder Gemeinwesen, den Kriegsfall, bedenken. Denn ein solcher hat schwerwiegende Konsequenzen für die Bevölkerung der beiden Staaten, sei es wegen der direkten Folgen der Kriegshandlungen wie Einschränkungen des Handels, der Bewegungsfreiheit, das höhere Gefährdungsniveau, Mobilmachung etc. oder wegen indirekter Folgen wie Rationierung, Evakuierung etc. Zudem treten latente oder akute Konfliktfälle zwischen staatlichen und individuellen Interessen besonders in Kriegszeiten zutage.

Damit erklärt sich auch, wieso es sich lohnen könnte, Tolkiens Werk auf diese Fragestellung hin zu untersuchen, auch wenn diese keineswegs im Vordergrund zu stehen scheint. Denn zweifelsohne spielen einerseits die Themenkomplexe Macht, Konflikt und Krieg eine eminente Rolle in seinem Werk, anderseits wird der Blick immer wieder auf Einzelpersonen und deren Funktion in der Geschichte gelenkt. Dementsprechend stehen nicht die Auseinandersetzung mit Sauron oder Melkor und die damit verbundene – und an anderer Stelle behandelte – Frage des gerechten Krieges im Vordergrund, sondern die bei diesen Konflikten deutlich werdenden Konsequenzen für das Verhältnis Gemeinwesen – Individuum.

1. Machtbegründung in Verfassungen mit und ohne Schwert: das Auenland, Gondor und Rohan

Hier können verschiedene Gemeinwesen in Betracht gezogen werden. Den Unterschied der politischen Herrschaftssysteme Gondors und des Auenlandes (über die am meisten bekannt ist) hat Frank Weinreich bereits untersucht, so dass ich mich auf seine Ergebnisse stützen kann. Er sieht im Auenland und in Minas Tirith »Beispiele für Staatsverfassungen (besser: Staatsverfasstheiten ...), die mit und ohne Schwert regieren« (90). Gondor wäre demnach ein Beispiel für einen faktisch gegebenen und evtl. von der Verfasstheit her als notwendig angesehenen Zusammenhang von Macht und Gewalt bzw. von der Notwendigkeit der Gewalt zur Legitimierung der Herrschaft, wohingegen das Auenland ohne dies auskommt.

Während in Gondor problemlos die personalen Träger der staatlichen Macht (zugespitzt auf König bzw. Truchsess) ausgemacht werden können, ist dies im Auenland nicht der Fall: »The Shire at this time had hardly any ›government‹« (LotR 9). Weinreich betont den anarchischen und wenig einheitlichen Charakter dieses politischen Gebildes und vergleicht es mit dem Ward-System zu Beginn der Vereinigten Staaten. Allerdings unterstreicht er den idyllisch überhöhten Charakter, wodurch der Bedarf an staatlicher Macht sehr begrenzt sei. Die konkrete Macht liegt nicht bei einer Institution wie dem Bürgermeister, der primär repräsentative Funktion besitzt, sondern primär bei den Familien- oder Sippenoberhäuptern. Wenn auch keine Zentralregierung vorliegt, können – wie besonders die Geschichte nach dem Ringkrieg zeigt – aristokratische Strukturen ausgemacht werden (z.B. ›Master of Buckland‹, Thain oder ›Warden of Westmarch‹), innerhalb derer von einem Gewaltmonopol ausgegangen werden kann.[4] Der Thain (nach dem Ende des Nordreichs gewählt, um die Autorität des Königs zu übernehmen) ist zur Zeit des Ringkrieges vor allem Oberhaupt der Tuks, da er zwar Vogt der Volksversammlungen und Hauptmann der Heerschau ist, diese allerdings nur in Notfällen einberufen werden, womit das Amt keine regelmäßige Funktion hat.[5] Der König in Fornost ist allerdings keineswegs vergessen: »For they attributed to the king of old all their essential laws; and usually they kept the laws of free will, because they were The Rules (as they said), both ancient and just« (LotR 9). Das einzige faktisch ›politische‹ Amt im Auenland war das des Bürgermeisters von Michelbinge, der alle sieben Jahre gewählt wird und weitgehend repräsentative Aufgaben innehat, dem aber Postmeister und First Sheriff des Auenlandes unterstehen. Mit den Sheriffs gibt es zwar eine Art Polizei, aber diese sind für den Innendienst nur zwölf Personen und fungieren eher als Feldhüter, bis sie unter Saruman zahlreicher und anders eingesetzt werden. Wie das Scouring of the Shire zeigt, gibt es kein Gewaltmonopol des Gemeinwesens, sondern sind die Familien und Sippen selber in der Lage (und gefordert), kriegerisch tätig zu werden. Damit kann von einer staatlichen Macht im Auenland kaum geredet werden; als Saruman wirksam wird, entsteht eine Zentralgewalt genau durch Gewaltanwendung, nachdem Lotho

---

[4] Martin Sternberg hat sich in einem Vortrag beim Tolkien Thing 2009 ausführlich dem Thema »Adel im Auenland« gewidmet.
[5] Nach dem Ringkrieg ernennt König Elessar 1434 den Thain, den Bürgermeister und den Meister von Bockland zu Beratern des Nordreiches (vgl. LotR 1071).

vorher eine große Menge Grundbesitz erworben hat, der dann von Saruman übernommen wird (vgl. LotR 989). Diese Macht wird so lange aufrechterhalten, wie sein Gewaltmonopol besteht – d.h. so lange, bis die Hobbits durch Frodo, Sam, Merry und Pippin zum gemeinsamen gewaltsamen Widerstand gegen die Menschen Sarumans gebracht werden. Diese Widerstandsfähigkeit hängt eng mit der dezentralen Struktur des Auenlandes und der weitgehenden Autonomie (und Autarkie) seiner Sippen zusammen und schränkt die Möglichkeit des Machterwerbs und der Machtausübung für Einzelpersonen sowie ihren Zugriff auf Mittel der Gewaltausübung enorm ein.[6]

Ganz anders verhält es sich mit Gondor bzw. dem wiedervereinigten Westreich, das Frank Weinreich ähnlich wie Númenor als juristisch und praktisch uneingeschränkt absolutistische Monarchie charakterisiert (vgl. auch van de Bergh 94). Beschränkt man dies auf die Kernelemente eines aus eigener Machtvollkommenheit handelnden Herrschers, der ohne politische Mitwirkung ständiger Institutionen regiert, und beansprucht keine zu großen Ähnlichkeiten zum Absolutismus eines Ludwig XIV., trifft dies auf die Könige Númenors wie des Westreiches zu. Die relative Eigenständigkeit von Fürsten Gondors wie Imrahil oder Faramir spricht indes eher dafür, ihr Verhältnis zum König als ein Lehensverhältnis anzusehen; schließlich gelang es französischen und englischen Herrschern (im Gegensatz zu deutschen), »sich in Vollendung dieser Vorstellung zum Oberlehnsherrn im ganzen Reich zu machen« (Diestelkamp 1808).

Unabhängig von einer genauen Bestimmung dieses Herrschaftsverhältnisses, die wegen der Fiktionalität des Tolkien'schen Werkes (und des Idealtypus Aragorn) ohnehin nur analog zu realweltlichen Herrschaftsverhältnissen möglich ist, wird der Machtanspruch nicht durch eine Wahl eines Gremiums legitimiert, sondern durch die Ableitung der Abstammung von Elendil und damit »von oben« (was wiederum ein Argument für den ›absolutistischen‹ Charakter ist). »Elendils Herrschaft wiederum gründet auf seiner Abstammung von Elros, der nach Auskunft der *Akallabêth* von den Valar selbst als Herrscher über Númenor eingesetzt worden war« (Weinreich 97). Die Familienzugehörigkeit ist dabei ein Ausschlusskriterium, weil sich auch bei dem eingetretenen Abbruch der Thronfolge die Aristokratie (inkl. der Truchsessen) nicht in der Lage sah, per Wahl einen neuen König zu küren; erinnert sei auch an den kin-strife sowie Denethors Antwort auf Boromirs Frage, wann ein Truchsess König werden könnte (vgl. LotR 1022, 655). Nach dem Tode Ondohers und seiner Söhne 1944 lehnt der Rat von Gondor den Anspruch Arveduis (als direkter Nachfahre Isildurs und Ehemann der Tochter Ondohers) ab und erkennt den Anspruch Eärnils an, da er zum königlichen Haus gehört.

---

6   Ob es den Hobbits tatsächlich aus Mangel an Erfahrung im Umgang mit Straf- und Gewalttätern unmöglich ist, entschlossen auf Aggression von außen zu reagieren, wie van de Bergh annimmt (vgl. 89), bezweifele ich. Als Gegenbeispiel können die Tuks genannt werden, die Widerstand geleistet haben.

Es handelt sich mithin bei Gondor bzw. dem wiedervereinigten Reich um ein Königtum von Gottes (bzw. der Valar) Gnaden, dessen Gründungsmythos als geschichtliches Ereignis vor langer Zeit präsentiert wird. Die Anerkennung des Anspruchs Aragorns auf den Thron durch das Volk auf die Anfrage Faramirs hat keine machtkonstitutive sondern zeremonielle Funktion (vgl. 945f); als König hat er sich bereits durch seine Taten im Krieg und seine Heilungen erwiesen, die zu seiner Anerkennung bzw. seinem Erkennen durch das Volk führen. Zudem verbindet er als Krieger und Magier/Weiser zwei der drei Funktionen der indoeuropäischen Mythologie und hat – was zu seiner mythologischen Aufladung beiträgt – eine wichtige Bedeutung für den dritten Bereich, die Agrikultur, da mit der Rückkehr des Königs auch die Fruchtbarkeit des Bodens verbunden ist: »Indeed the waste in time will be waste no longer, and there will be people and fields where once there was wilderness« (LotR 971; vgl. Alibert).

Aragorns absoluter Machtanspruch und seine Ausübung derselben wird deutlich nach der Zerstörung des Rings, weil er auch oberster Richter ist (vgl. 947f). Besonders instruktiv ist der Fall Beregonds, der in den Weihestätten Blut vergossen und seinen Posten verlassen hat, was gewöhnlich mit dem Tod bestraft wurde. Von der Todesstrafe sieht Aragorn ab wegen Beregonds Tapferkeit in der Schlacht und wegen seines Motivs, nämlich Faramir zu schützen. Die Versetzung zur und Ernennung zum Hauptmann der Wache Faramirs in Ithilien kann kaum als Strafe angesehen werden. Aragorn steht somit eindeutig über dem Gesetz, auch wenn er sich selbst an von ihm erlassene Gesetze, z.B. bezüglich der Autonomie des Auenlandes, hält (vgl. 1019). Weinreich sieht an diesem Beispiel Gnade und Gerechtigkeit des Königs deutlich werden, wobei Aragorn »unzweifelhaft der gute König par excellence« ist (98). Ferner erhebt Aragorn auch über die Ostlinge, Haradrim und die Sklaven Mordors keinen Machtanspruch, da er sie freilässt bzw. ihnen Länder gibt; auch über die Wasa und das Auenland will er nicht herrschen (vgl. 954, 1019). Er ist damit ein Beispiel für einen Monarchen, der seiner eigenen Macht Grenzen auferlegt – gerade darin besteht seine Weisheit und Größe.

Als Kontrastfigur dient Isildur, der sich nicht in der Lage sah, den Ring zu vernichten, womit der Niedergang des Doppelreiches einsetzte. Beide, gemeinsam mit Eärnur, nach dessen Auszug zum Kampf mit dem Hexenkönig der Thron Gondors verwaist war, zeigen deutlich, welch gravierende Folgen die Taten einzelner Monarchen in einem solchen absolutistischen System haben können (vgl. auch die anderen Könige 1020ff). Ohne selbst König zu sein, beansprucht Denethor wie die Truchsessen vor ihm diese Machtfülle, was bei seinem Versuch, sich selbst und Faramir verbrennen zu lassen, deutlich wird, worauf ihm Gandalf entgegenhält: »But others may contest your will, when it is turned to madness and evil« (LotR 834, vgl. Pippin zu Beregond 809). Er stellt damit dessen Machtanspruch in Frage, sieht die Vernunft als Kontrollinstanz und zögert nicht, diese selbst auszuüben; zudem erstrecke sich die Autorität Denethors auch nicht darauf, die Stunde seines Todes zu bestimmen, womit

Gandalf letztlich wohl naturrechtlich argumentiert. Eine solche Kontrollinstanz ist indes nicht institutionalisiert, weshalb diese Einzelpersonen solch gravierende Folgen bewirken können. Der enge Zusammenhang von politischer Qualität in Númenor und Gondor/Arnor und den moralischen Qualitäten seiner Herrscher kann nach Weinreich »als Warnung vor den Risiken der absoluten Monarchien« (100) interpretiert werden, da es viel seltener gute als weniger gute Könige gebe.[7]

Ohne dies ausführlich beschreiben zu können, sei kurz auf Rohan verwiesen, das ebenfalls als (absolutistische?) Erbmonarchie gestaltet ist, wobei sich die Legi-timation der herrschenden Familie über deren Abkunft von Eorl herleitet. Dies allerdings beruht auf der Anerkennung des Herrschaftsanspruchs der Familie durch das Volk. Dieser wird indes im Unterschied zu Gondor nicht über eine besondere und exklusive Qualität der Familie begründet, sondern über das Vertrauen des Volkes in die Familie. Deutlich wird dies bei der Bestimmung Éowyns als Herrschende in Abwesenheit Théodens und Éomers:

>›Behold! I go forth, and it seems like to be my last riding‹, said Théoden. ›I have no child. Théodred my son is slain. I name Éomer my sister-son to be my heir. If neither of us returns, then choose a new lord as you will. But to some one I must now entrust my people that I leave behind, to rule them in my place. Which of you will stay?‹
> No man spoke.
> ›Is there none whom you would name? In whom do my people trust?‹
> ›In the House of Eorl‹, answered Háma.
> ›But Éomer I cannot spare, nor would he stay‹, said the king; ›and he is the last of that House.‹
> ›I said not Éomer‹, answered Háma. ›And he is not the last. There is Éowyn, daughter of Éomund, his sister. She is fearless and high-hearted. All love her. Let her be as lord to the Eorlingas, while we are gone.‹
> ›It shall be so‹, said Théoden. ›Let the heralds announce to the folk that the Lady Éowyn will lead them!‹   (LotR 511f)

---

7   Weinreich sieht ferner die Verfassheit des Auenlandes als prinzipiell realisierbares pragmatisch-ideales Zusammenleben an, wohingegen das Gondor Elessars eine Utopie sei, weil es solche übermenschlich guten Herrscherfiguren nicht gebe. Damit will er natürlich nicht behaupten, es gebe keine absolutistischen Monarchien, sondern nur, dass der Idealfall, in dem ein solches System keine problematischen Folgen hätte, utopisch ist. Ähnlich sieht van de Bergh unter Berufung auf Petzold diese Herrschaftsform als nicht wünschenswert an (vgl. 94).

Das Haus Eorls hat zwar Vorrang, aber das ausschlaggebende Argument sind das Vertrauen und die Liebe des Volkes zu diesem Haus bzw. Éowyn im Speziellen. Bei einem Aussterben der Familie wählt es schlicht einen neuen Führer. Nachdem Théoden zu Merry sagte, Éomer müsse nach ihm König werden, ließ er ihm kurz vor seinem Tod das Banner geben und ernannte ihn zum König. Möglicherweise handelt es sich dabei nur um ein Zeremoniell, eventuell aber ist die Erbnachfolge zumindest in der nicht direkten Linie nicht zwingend vorgeschrieben bzw. hat der König Ernennungsrecht.

Bei allen drei Beispielen zeigt sich eine enge Verbindung zwischen zentralisierter Macht und dem Gewaltmonopol der Zentralgewalt – denn auch wenn das Auenland eine Verfassung ohne Schwert ist, entsteht eine solche durch die Gewaltanwendung der Menschen Lothos bzw. Sarumans. Weil sie aber nicht institutionalisiert ist und kein Gewaltmonopol besteht, kann die Säuberung des Auenlandes, d.h. die Rückkehr zur dezentralisierten Verfasstheit verhältnismäßig zügig und problemlos vollzogen werden.[8] In Gondor und Rohan hingegen besteht ein Gewaltmonopol der Zentralgewalt, wie sich u.a. an den Funktionen des Herrschers als oberstem Heerführer und als oberstem Richter zeigt. Ein bedeutender Unterschied besteht in der Begründung der Autorität der Zentralgewalt, da diese in Gondor letztlich auf die Einsetzung Elros' durch die Valar zum König über Númenor zurückgeführt wird und somit ihre Begründung von außerhalb des Staatswesens erhält. In Rohan hingegen ist es der Konsens der Bevölkerung.

2. Verhältnis Staat – Individuum

Über das Verhältnis der Zentralgewalt Gondors und Rohans zur Zivilbevölkerung ist nur sehr wenig bekannt. Gleichwohl können den wenigen Aussagen wichtige Hinweise entnommen werden. Die in beiden Ländern durchgeführten Evakuierungen im Kriegsfall, von denen mindestens die in Gondor per Befehl erfolgte (vgl. LotR 747), dürfen wegen der im Krieg auftretenden Ausnahmesituation allerdings nicht als Regelfall betrachtet werden. Sie zeigen aber zumindest die Verantwortung des Herrschers für Leib und Leben der Zivilbevölkerung. Gravierender sind die Edikte des Königs Elessar bezüglich des Drúadan-Waldes und des Auenlandes, da diese nicht nur die Bewegungsfreiheit ihrer Bürger, sondern grundsätzlich aller außer der Bewohner dieser Regionen einschränken:

---

8 Der Vollständigkeit halber sei angemerkt, dass dem Auenland mit einer Zentralregierung mit dem Recht auf verbindliche, letztinstanzliche Weisungen und deren Durchsetzung, gestützt auf ein Justizsystem, eine Verwaltung sowie Polizei und Militär und dem Anspruch auf ein Gewaltmonopol ein wichtiges Definitionsmerkmal von Staatlichkeit fehlt, wobei auch nicht alle realen Staaten sämtlichen Kriterien genügen. (Vgl. dazu Horn 7f)

> ›Behold, the King Elessar is come! The Forest of Drúadan he gives to Ghân-buri-ghân and to his folk, to be their own for ever; and hereafter let no man enter it without their leave!‹ (LotR 954)
> 1427 ... King Elessar issues an edict that Men are not to enter the Shire, and he makes it a Free Land under the protection of the Northern Sceptre. (1071)

Die beanspruchte Autorität erstreckt sich auch auf Fremde, wie sich bei dem Treffen Faramirs mit Frodo und Sam zeigt. Zum einen wird grundsätzlich mit dem Tode bestraft, wer ungebeten nach Henneth Annûn kommt (vgl. 670), was allerdings Kriegsrecht sein mag. Wichtiger ist die Entscheidung Faramirs, Frodo (und wen er unter seinen Schutz nimmt) für Jahr und Tag freies Wegerecht mit Ausnahme Hennet Annûns in ganz Gondor einzuräumen, sofern dies vor Ablauf der Frist nicht in Minas Tirith verlängert wird (vgl. 675). Nicht bekannt ist, ob die Untertanen frei waren, das Land zu wechseln oder ob dies unter Strafe stand.

Ein ähnliches Wegerecht für Fremde gilt in Rohan, wie Éomer erklärt: »It is against our law to let strangers wander at will in our land, until the king himself shall give them leave, and more strict is the command in these days of peril« (428). Gleichwohl setzt er sich über dieses Gesetz hinweg und bittet lediglich Aragorn darum, nach Erfüllung seiner Aufgabe nach Meduseld zu kommen und von Théoden die nachträgliche Autorisierung der Entscheidung Éomers zu erwirken.

Der Unterschied zwischen Rohan und Gondor im Verhältnis zwischen Herrscher und Bedienstetem kann an Pippins Eid vor Denethor verdeutlicht werden, mit dem er Treue und bedingungslosen Gehorsam explizit nicht nur dem Reich, sondern auch der Person des Truchsessen gelobt:

> Here do I swear fealty and service to Gondor, and to the Lord and Steward of the realm, to speak and to be silent, to do and to let be, to come and to go, in need or plenty, in peace or war, in living or dying, from this hour henceforth, until my lord release me, or death take me, or the world end. (740)

Dieser Eid wird von Denethor mit dem Versprechen der Vergeltung entsprechend der (guten oder schlechten) Taten angenommen. Bei Merry hingegen nimmt Théoden das Angebot seines Schwertes formlos an, legt ihm die Hände auf, segnet ihn und bestätigt Merrys Aussage, wie ein Vater zu ihm zu sein (vgl. 760). Chance drückt den Unterschied etwas zugespitzt aus: »The tyrant commands his followers by edict, rule, and law; the true leader commands through respect and love, like a benign father to a son« (100).

Daran zeigt sich, wie stark der Umgang der Herrscher mit ihren Untergebenen in solchen Verfassungen von der jeweiligen Persönlichkeit beeinflusst wird. Dementsprechend unterschiedlich ist der Umgang Théodens mit seinen Reitern und besonders mit Merry und der Denethors mit seinen Dienern und den Wachen Gondors und dabei auch mit Pippin – von ihrer unterschiedlichen Einstellung zu Gandalfs Rat zu schweigen. »Théoden is a kindly old man. Denethor is of another sort, proud and subtle, a man of far greater lineage and power, though he is not called a king« (LotR 737). Beide beanspruchen nicht nur höchste Autorität und Macht, sondern verfügen auch darüber (gleichwohl die Denethors zum Schluss von Gandalf angegriffen wird). Während Théoden aber nicht nur kurz vor seinem Tod Merrys Zuwiderhandeln gegen seinen Befehl vergibt, weil er die ehrenwerte Motivation erkennt (vgl. 824), sondern auch Gríma ziehen lässt und ihm ein Pferd nicht vorenthält (vgl. 509), schickt Denethor (zugegebenermaßen nach dem Tode Boromirs) nicht nur Faramir in den quasi sicheren Tod, sondern zögert auch nicht, Beregond anzugreifen, als dieser die Verbrennung verhindern will (vgl. 834).

In Aragorn verbinden sich idealtypisch die positiven Eigenschaften beider, wie sich nicht nur bei seinen Urteilen, sondern auch an seinem Umgang mit den Fahnenflüchtigen auf dem Weg zum Schwarzen Tor zeigt: »Aragorn looked at them, and there was pity in his eyes rather than wrath« (868).

3. Die Istari: persönliche Macht und Gewaltausübung

Darüber hinaus ist ein kurzer Blick auf die Istari erhellend: Von den Valar absichtlich als Berater und Ermutiger gesandt, die keine Machtpositionen einnehmen sollen, entfernt sich Saruman schon dadurch davon, dass er sich in Orthanc niederlässt, Isengard zu seiner Machtbasis ausbaut und letztlich auch auf politische Macht aus ist und dabei vor einem Eroberungsfeldzug gegen Rohan nicht zurückschreckt. Er begnügt sich nicht mit der ihm qua seiner Weisheit und Bildung zukommenden epistemischen Autorität, sondern strebt danach, diese auch unmittelbar wirksam werden zu lassen – und begründet sein Streben nach institutioneller Autorität mit seiner epistemischen Überlegenheit. Denn während Sauron auf totale Herrschaft aus ist, wird die andere Motivationslage Sarumans im Versuch, Gandalf zu überreden, deutlich: »The time of Elves is over, but our time is at hand: the world of Men, which we must rule. But we must have power, power to order all things as we will, for that good which only the Wise can see« (LotR 252). Als höchsten und letzten Zweck nennt er Wissen, Herrschaft und Ordnung als dasjenige, wozu sie nach Mittelerde gekommen sind; es sei nicht nötig, die Ziele zu verändern, sondern nur die Mittel. Er ist mithin der Versuchung der Weisen verfallen, mit politischer Macht das Gute, das sie erkennen und wollen, durchzusetzen, ohne auf diejenigen Rücksicht zu nehmen, für die sie das Gute durchsetzen wollen, bzw. ohne diese auf ihrem Weg dahin zu führen. Er zögert auch nicht, Gandalf festzusetzen. Als Gegenbeispiele können Gandalf und Galadriel der Versuchung zumindest dann widerstehen, als Frodo ihnen den Ring anbietet (vgl. 60, 356). Auf Sarumans qua Gewaltanwendung errichteter Herrschaft im Auenland habe ich bereits hingewiesen.

Gandalf übt zwar durchaus großen Einfluss aus, bleibt aber seiner Rolle als Berater treu – zumindest bis zu seinem Kampf mit dem Balrog. Nach seiner Rückkehr greift er wesentlich aktiver in die Geschehnisse ein und verfügt entweder über mehr (persönliche) Macht als vorher oder zögert weniger, sie einzusetzen. Dabei ist sein erklärtes Ziel die Überwindung Saurons und nicht, selbst zu herrschen. Den Umständen seines Einsatzes gegen Sauron geschuldet, wendet er immer wieder Gewalt an bzw. zeigt sich seine Macht gerade darin, dass er Gewalt anwendet, vor allem in Kriegshandlungen und gegen die Nazgûl, aber auch gegen Denethor, als dieser Beregond töten will – allerdings nur entwaffnend (vgl. 802, 834). In den entscheidenden Tagen übernimmt er bei Denethors Tod das Kommando bzw. beauftragt zunächst Imrahil, das Kommando zu übernehmen. Nach der Schlacht auf dem Pelennor einigen sich Imrahil, Aragorn und Éomer auf Anraten Aragorns darauf, ihm den Befehl in den kommenden Tagen und in der Auseinandersetzung mit dem Feind zu übergeben (vgl. 844). Dies kann aber angesichts der Aufgabe und zeitlichen Begrenzung als Fortsetzung seiner Beratungstätigkeit angesehen werden. Während Saruman also sein Streben nach institutioneller Autorität mit seiner epistemischen Autorität begründet, bewegt Gandalfs epistemische Autorität andere Protagonisten dazu, ihn befristet mit institutioneller Autorität auszustatten.

Auch bei Gandalf und Saruman wird mithin der enge Zusammenhang zwischen politischer Macht bzw. dem Streben nach Macht und Gewalt deutlich. Denn während Saruman nicht vor Gewaltanwendung zurückschreckt, um seine Ziele zu erreichen, setzt Gandalf Gewalt lediglich in Kampfhandlungen oder zur Entwaffnung ein, nicht aber, um andere Personen von der Richtigkeit seiner Ansicht zu überzeugen bzw. seine Ansicht durchzusetzen.

4. Ontologisch begründete Machtpositionen: Eru, die Ainur und die Kinder Ilúvatars

m *Silmarillion*-Komplex begegnen wir einer ganz anderen Konstellation der Fragestellung von Macht und Gewalt: Hier können zwar auch Staatswesen untersucht werden, aber mit Eru und den Valar tritt eine Dimension der Macht auf, die auf einem ontologischen Unterschied zwischen ihnen und den Kindern

Ilúvatars basiert. Die Valar werden von Eru als Hüter der Welt eingesetzt, der ihre Macht gegenüber Elben und Menschen allerdings begrenzt, bei deren Erschaffung auch keiner der Ainur mitgewirkt hat. »For which reason the Valar are to these kindreds rather their elders and their chieftains than their masters; and if ever in their dealings with Elves and Men the Ainur have endeavoured to force them when they would not be guided, seldom has this turned to good, howsoever good the intent« (Sil 41). Die Ainur sind qua ihrer persönlichen Macht in der Lage, Elben und Menschen zu etwas zu zwingen – und gerade Melkor und Sauron haben dies oft genug umgesetzt –, dies wird aber deutlich kritisiert. Sie nehmen durchaus Macht- bzw. Verantwortungspositionen ein, aber Älteste und Häuptlinge sind keine absolutistischen Herrscher. Vielmehr üben sie primär eine Dienstfunktion für sie aus, indem sie sie unterrichten, die Welt für ihre Ankunft vorbereiten und eine grundsätzliche Fürsorgefunktion ausüben (vgl. ausführlicher Fornet-Ponse, *Präsenz* 38f).[9]

Während bei Melkor durchgängig betont wird, es gehe ihm um Herrschaft, Gewalt und Tyrannei, wird Manwë als höchster und heiligster der Valar bezeichnet, er »has no thought for his own honour, and is not jealous of his power, but rules all to peace« (Sil 40). Dementsprechend werden die Elben nicht gezwungen, nach Aman zu kommen. Aber Melkor sät Uneinigkeit in Valinor, indem er die Eldar davon zu überzeugen sucht, sie würden von den Valar gefangen gehalten aus Furcht, sie könnten zu mächtig werden, um noch beherrscht werden zu können; daher sollen sie auch durch die einfacher beherrschbaren Menschen in Mittelerde ersetzt werden (vgl. 68). Dies ist zwar nicht der Fall, weil sie die Rückkehr der Noldor nach Mittelerde auch nach dem Kampf mit den Teleri nicht behindern und auch Fëanor nach der Zerstörung der Bäume nicht dazu zwingen wollen, die Silmaril herauszugeben. Es zeigt aber deutlich, wie leicht der Eindruck politischer Unterdrückung mithilfe von Stolz, Eifersucht oder Machtstreben erweckt werden kann; noch deutlicher wird dies bei Fëanors Rede und seinem und seiner Söhne Eid, wo auch von Galadriel und Fingon gesagt wird, sie wünschten, aus eigenem Willen zu herrschen.

Zudem üben die Valar nicht nur über Melkor nach ihrem Sieg im Krieg der Mächte Gerichtsbarkeit aus, sondern auch über Fëanor, nachdem er Fingolfin bedroht hat; er wird für zwölf Jahre aus Tirion verbannt. Danach soll der Vorfall für erledigt gelten, sofern niemand Einwände erhebt, was Fingolfin nicht tut (vgl. 70f).[10] Darüber hinaus befielt Manwë Fëanor als einzigem, zum Fest

---

9   Der Frage, inwiefern sie als Mitwirkende bei der Ainulindalë Macht über Elben und Menschen ausüben, bin ich andernorts nachgegangen, weshalb dies hier nicht weiter ausgeführt werden muss, zumal es dabei weniger um politische Macht und Gewalt als vielmehr um die Frage nach Freiheit und Determination geht. Vgl. Fornet-Ponse, *Freedom* und ders., *Freiheit*.
10 Dickerson erläutert ausführlicher die in dieser Entscheidung deutlich werdenden objektiven Wertmaßstäbe (vgl. 119ff).

zu kommen, bei dem Melkor und Ungoliant die Bäume zerstören. Unklar ist, ob die vom Boten Manwës geäußerte Exilierung Fëanors sich einem Urteil der Valar verdankt oder – wie es der Wortlaut eher nahe legt – eine zwangsläufige Konsequenz seines Eides ist: »But thou Fëanor Finwë's son, by thine oath art exiled. The lies of Melkor thou shalt unlearn in bitterness« (85). Denn er sei niemals in der Lage, einen der Valar zu überwinden, auch wenn er dreimal so mächtig wäre wie er ist. Insofern habe er vergebens geschworen. Etwas klarer sieht es nach dem Sippenmord an den Teleri bei der Prophezeiung des Nordens bzw. dem Fluch der Valar aus, die für alle gelte, die nicht umkehren und Urteil und Vergebung der Valar erbitten. Sie werden von Valinor ausgeschlossen, der Eid werde sie treiben und betrügen, außerhalb Amans würden sie im Schatten des Todes wohnen und der Welt müde werden.

Allerdings werden diese Folgen nicht von den Valar bewirkt, sondern sind die Konsequenzen der falschen Entscheidungen der Noldor und drücken somit die Gesetzmäßigkeiten Mittelerdes aus, wonach böse Handlungen letztlich selbstzerstörerische Folgen haben. Denn Manwë und besonders Ulmo kümmern sich auch im Exil noch um die Noldor, außerdem gewähren sie die Bitte Eärendils um Vergebung für die Noldor und Unterstützung im Kampf gegen Morgoth (vgl. 110, 125f, 185f, 239f, 247). Während sie aber über das Schicksal der Menschen keine Macht haben bzw. ihnen nicht erlaubt ist, dieses zu ändern, waren sie bei Lúthien und den Nachfahren Eärendils in der Lage, sie vor die Wahl zu stellen, sterblich zu werden (vgl. 187, 249, LotR 1010f).[11]

Diese Linie zeigt sich auch in der *Akallabêth*. Das Verbot für die Númenórer, zu weit Richtung Valinor zu segeln, soll sie nach Manwës Plan vor der Versuchung bewahren, Valinor aufzusuchen und die ihrem Glück gesetzten Grenzen zu überschreiten. In Unkenntnis des Sinns des Bannes der Valar entsteht im Verlauf der Zeit Widerstand und das auch aus dem Wunsch nach Unsterblichkeit geförderte Begehren, nach Valinor zu gelangen. Der Aussage des Boten Manwës, nicht das Land mache seine Bevölkerung unsterblich und sie würden dort nur schneller vergehen, zudem sei der Tod keine Strafe, sondern für Menschen der Lauf der Welt wie für Elben ihre Bindung an diese, schenken sie wenig bis keinen Glauben, obwohl sie sich noch längere Zeit aus Furcht vor den Valar an den Bann halten (vgl. 264f).[12] Im Zuge der Entfremdung der Könige von Númenor von den Valar verweigern diese ihnen Rat und Schutz, womit auch die Besuche aus Eressëa enden; sogar die Reue und Umkehr Tar-Palantirs kann den Zorn der Valar über die Anmaßung seiner Väter nicht besänftigen, zumal die Mehrheit der Bevölkerung ihm nicht folgte. Selbst als der Bann durch das

---

11 Den Sonderfall Miriel hat Michaël Devaux innerhalb seiner Ausführungen über Reinkarnation der Elben behandelt (vgl. 15-21).
12 In den Myths Transformed bietet Tolkien ausführliche Überlegungen an, wieso Sterbliche einen Aufenthalt in Valinor nicht vertragen könnten (vgl. MR 427ff).

Heer Ar-Pharazôns tatsächlich gebrochen wird, ziehen die Valar nicht in den Krieg oder üben Zwang aus, der über Gewitter etc. hinausgeht. Sie sehen sich nicht befugt, selbst mit dieser Situation umzugehen, und überlassen dies Eru, der daraufhin die Gestalt der Welt verändert und das Heer der Númenórer dabei vom Gebirge begraben lässt. Bewahrt werden – ausdrücklich »by grace of the Valar« (279) – lediglich Elendil, seine Söhne und ihr Volk.

Die Valar verfügen mithin über eine sehr große persönliche Macht, die sie allerdings gegenüber Menschen und Elben in der Regel nicht dazu verwenden (dürfen), über diese Herrschaft auszuüben. Vielmehr üben sie Gewalt nur in Kriegsfällen aus und fungieren als Richter in ihrem Reich nur bei eklatanten Verletzungen wie denjenigen der Noldor. Melkor hingegen strebt nach politischer Macht, erwirbt und erhält diese per Gewaltanwendung und muss wie Sauron in einem Krieg überwunden werden.

5. Kolonialisierung in Mittelerde: von Lehrern zu Tyrannen

Die Kolonialisierung Mittelerdes durch die Númenórer im Zweiten Zeitalter ist für unsere Fragestellung nicht nur wegen des inhärenten Zusammenhangs von Macht und Gewalt relevant, sondern zudem interessant, weil mit *Tal-Elmar* eine begonnene Geschichte vorliegt, in der Tolkien die Perspektive der Menschen in Mittelerde einnimmt. Im Umgang mit diesen zeigen sich deutlich der allmähliche Niedergang Númenors und der wachsende Einfluss Saurons.

Wegen des Bannes der Valar sind die Númenórer Richtung Osten gesegelt und hatten Mitleid mit den Menschen in Mittelerde, die schwach und furchtsam geworden waren und zudem über wenige Kulturtechniken verfügten. Zunächst treten die Númenórer großzügig und als Tutoren auf: »Corn and wine they brought, and they instructed Men in the sowing of seed and the grinding of grain, in the hewing of wood and the shaping of stone, and in the ordering of their life, such as it might be in the lands of swift death and little bliss« (Sil 263). Auf diese Weise erwerben sie sich Achtung und Respekt der Menschen, die sie teilweise sogar als Götter ansehen.

In späterer Zeit, unter Tar-Ciryatan und Tar-Atanamir, verändert sich ihre Einstellung zu den Menschen Mittelerdes: Nun geht es ihnen vor allem darum, Wohlstand anzuhäufen, weshalb sie Tribut verlangen. Dies verstärkt sich in den nachfolgenden Generationen, in denen auch ihre Niederlassungen in Mittelerde stark ausgebaut werden. Während die Númenórer in früherer Zeit nur kurze Zeit dort lebten und bald wieder nach Hause zurückkehrten, lassen sich nun viele dort nieder, »but they appeared now rather as lords and masters and gatherers of tribute than as helpers and teachers« (266f). Diese Entwicklung setzt sich weiter fort, wobei auch Kriege geführt werden, um den Herrschaftsbereich auszudehnen. Der nächste und letzte Schritt von den ursprünglichen Geschenkbringern über die Regierenden zu Kriegsbringern und Sklavenhaltern findet unter dem Einfluss Saurons statt: Die Menschen von Mittelerde werden gejagt, ihrer Güter beraubt, versklavt und viele von ihnen auf den Altären geopfert. Die Númenórer werden nun gefürchtet, »and the memory of the kindly kings of ancient days faded from the world and was darkened by many a tale of dread« (274). Ar-Pharazôn wird auf diese Weise mit Sauron als seinem Berater und eigentlich Herrschendem der größte Tyrann seit Morgoth.

Die Geschichte *Tal-Elmar* ist in diesem Verlauf zwar nicht exakt zu datieren, da Tolkien sich noch nicht entschieden hatte, ob sie noch vor der Überführung Saurons nach Númenor oder nachher spielt. Tal-Elmar unterscheidet sich durch Hautfarbe und Physiognomie von den übrigen Einheimischen in seinem Dorf, was wohl daran liegt, dass seine Großmutter Elmar den Erzählungen nach selbst zu einem anderen Volk aus dem Osten gehörte und von seinem Großvater Buldar nach dem Sieg in einer Schlacht gegen sie zur Frau genommen wurde. Als Elmar Buldar vorhält, sein Volk sei einfach und lieblos, entgegnet er ihr, ihr Volk sei grausam, gesetzlos und die Freunde von Dämonen. »Thieves are they. For our lands are ours from of old, which they would wrest from us with their bitter blades. White skins and bright eyes are no warrant for such deeds« (PM 425). Sie hält dagegen, auch sein Volk hätte das Land erobert. Im Unterschied zu den Kriegen gegen Melkor oder Sauron können diese Eroberungskriege nicht gerechtfertigt werden; es handelt sich nicht um Verteidigungskriege.[13]

Ohne dies genau bestimmen zu können, scheinen die ersten Feldzüge der Númenórer eher mit dem Eroberungsfeldzug Sarumans vergleichbar, dem es um die Herrschaft des Weisen geht, als mit den versklavenden Eroberungskriegen Melkors oder Saurons. Wie der Vater Tal-Elmars ihm erklärt, haben sie drei Völker als Feinde: die wilden Menschen der Berge und der Wälder, das Volk seiner Mutter aus dem Osten und die Hohen Menschen der See. Sein Bericht kann als Vermischung der ersten und der späteren Phase des Umgangs der Númenórer mit den Menschen Mittelerdes verstanden werden, könnte aber auch den Unterschied zwischen den Getreuen, die allerdings eher Umgang mit den Elben in den Anfurten pflegten, und den Männern des Königs ausdrücken:

> They came in boats, but not such as some of our folk use that dwell nigh the great rivers or the lakes, for ferrying or fishing. Greater than great houses are the ships of the Go-hilleg ... Thus they will come to the shore, where there is shelter, or as nigh as

---

13 M.E. zutreffend sieht Janet Croft in folgender Aussage Faramirs eine gute Zusammenfassung der Einstellung Tolkiens zum Krieg: »War must be, while we defend our lives against a destroyer who would devour all; but I do not love the bright sword for its sharpness, nor the arrow for its swiftness, nor the warrior for his glory. I love only that which they defend: the city of the Men of Númenor« (LotR 656, vgl. Croft 147).

> they may; and then they will send forth smaller boats laden with goods, and strange things both beautiful and useful such as our folk covet. These they will sell to us for small price, or give as gifts, feigning friendship, and pity for our need; and they will dwell a while, and spy out the land and the numbers of the folk, and then go. And if they do not return, men should be thankful. For if they come again it is in other guise. In greater numbers they come then: two ships or more together, stuffed with men and not goods, and ever one of the accursed ships hath black wings. For that is the Ship of the Dark, and in it they bear away evil booty, captives packed like beasts, the fairest women and children, or young men unblemished, and that is their end. Some say that they are eaten for meat; and others that they are slain with torment on the black stones in the worship of the Dark. Both maybe are true. (PM 427)

Im weiteren Verlauf der Geschichte landen einige Schiffe und Tal-Elmar begegnet den Númenórern. Zu dieser Begegnung hat Tolkien verschiedene Alternativen überlegt, aber nicht sehr weit ausgeführt. Ein durchgängiges Motiv ist aber die Besetzung des Landes und die Vertreibung der von ihnen so genannten dunklen Völker (bzw. gegebenenfalls die Bedrohung des Königs Sauron) durch die Númenórer (vgl. 436f).

Deutlich wird in beiden Perspektiven der Aufbau einer Herrschaftsstruktur durch Feldzüge und Unterwerfung der Bevölkerung, wobei die frühe Phase, in der die Númenórer nicht als Herrscher, sondern als Lehrer kamen, als Kontrastfolie dient. In ihr erfüllen die Númenórer den Menschen Mittelerdes gegenüber eine analoge Funktion wie die Valar gegenüber den Kindern Ilúvatars; sie werden aber allmählich und unter dem Einfluss Saurons – wie viele andere in Tolkiens Werk – durch ihre Überlegenheit dazu verführt, diese nicht zum Wohl der Anderen, sondern zu ihrem eigenen Vorteil einzusetzen, was letztlich zur Versklavung der anderen Menschen führt.

Conclusio

Auch wenn nicht sämtliche staatlichen Gebilde in Tolkiens Werk berücksichtigt werden konnten, hat sich ein klares Bild ergeben: Tolkien hat kein (utopisches) Staatswesen beschrieben, in dem es eine zentralisierte Macht gibt, die ohne Gewaltmonopol bzw. ohne den Anspruch auf gewaltsame Durchsetzung ihrer Entscheidungen auskommt. Das Auenland ist zwar ein Beispiel für ein Staatswesen ohne Gewaltmonopol, verfügt aber auch nicht über eine zentralisierte Organisationsstruktur. Bei Númenor und Gondor handelt es sich um

Monarchien, die sich auf eine externe Einsetzung des ersten Königs zurückführen und dem König die Machtfülle und damit das Gewaltmonopol zugestehen. Unklar bleibt, ob dies eher absolutistische Züge trägt oder eher im Rahmen eines Lehenswesens zu verstehen ist. In Rohan liegt auch eine Monarchie vor, die allerdings eher vom Konsens der Bevölkerung getragen ist, aber dem König auch das Gewaltmonopol überlässt. Eine institutionalisierte Kontrollinstanz gibt es nicht. Der Machtanspruch erstreckt sich nicht nur auf die Untergebenen und Untertanen, sondern auch auf die im Lande Reisenden.

Ein sehr wichtiges Element zieht sich durch alle untersuchten Aspekte: die Versuchung, die eigene Macht über andere Personen auszuüben und sie zu beherrschen, anstatt ihnen zu helfen. Während die Valar fast ausnahmslos der Versuchung nicht erliegen und besonders Aragorn als leuchtendes Vorbild dargestellt wird, gibt es mit Melkor, Sauron, Saruman, Denethor, den Númenórern etc. zahlreiche Gegenbeispiele. Ein weiser Umgang mit Macht besteht darin, sie zum Wohle der anderen einzusetzen, also beratend und helfend tätig zu sein, sowie sie nicht über bestimmte Grenzen hinaus anzuwenden oder ausweiten zu wollen. In dieser Versuchung liegt die Wurzel kriegerischer Auseinandersetzungen, da dieser Drang des Mehrhabenwollens, der Pleonexia, die schon Thykides in seiner Pathologie des Krieges als eine Ursache hervorhebt (vgl. III, 82), zu Eroberungskriegen führt und auf der anderen Seite nach Tolkien ein Verteidigungskrieg gerechtfertigt und hinsichtlich der metaphysischen Dimension seines Werkes sogar notwendig ist.

Bibliographie

Alibert, Laurent. »L'influence indo-européenne en Arda et ses limites«. *Tolkien, trente ans après (1973-2003)*. Hg. Vincent Ferré. Paris: Christian Bourgois, 2004, 117-136

Chance, Jane. *The Lord of the Rings. The Mythology of Power*. Kentucky: University Press of Kentucky, 2001

Croft, Janet Brennan. *War and the works of J.R.R. Tolkien*. Westport and Oxford: Praeger, 2004

Devaux, Michaël. "'The Shadow of Death' in Tolkien". *2001: A Tolkien Odyssey. Proceedings of Unquendor's Fourth Lustrum Conference, Brielle, The Netherlands, 9 June 2001*. Hg. Ron Pirson. Leiden: De Tolkienwinkel, 2002, 1-46

Dickerson, Matthew. *Following Gandalf. Epic Battles and Moral Victory in* The Lord of the Rings. Grand Rapids: Brazos, 2003

Diestelkamp, Bernhard. »Lehen, -swesen; Lehnrecht. I. Allgemein; Frankenreich und Deutsches Reich«. *Lexikon des Mittelalters*. Bd. 5. Darmstadt: Wissenschaftliche Buchgesellschaft, 2009, 1807-1810

Fornet-Ponse, Thomas. "'In the webs of fate' – Freiheit und Determination in der *Ainulindalë* und der Narn". *Inklings-Jahrbuch* 23 (2005): 153-179
---. "Freedom and Providence as antimodern elements?" *Tolkien and Modernity 1.* Hg. Thomas Honegger, Frank Weinreich. Zürich/Bern: Walking Tree Publishers, 2006, 177-206
---. »Die steigende Präsenz von Philosophie und Theologie«. *Hither Shore* 3 (2006): 37-50
Horn, Christoph. *Einführung in die Politische Philosophie.* Darmstadt: Wissenschaftliche Buchgesellschaft, 2003
Thukydides. *Der Peloponnesische Krieg.* Stuttgart: Reclam, 2000
Tolkien, John Ronald Reuel. *The Lord of the Rings.* London: HarperCollins, 1995
---. *The Silmarillion.* Edited by Christopher Tolkien. London: HarperCollins, 1999
---. "Tal-Elmar". *The Peoples of Middle-earth. HoMe XII.* Hg. Christopher Tolkien. London: HarperCollins 1997, 422-438
van de Bergh, Alexander. *Mittelerde und das 21. Jahrhundert. Zivilisationskritik und alternative Gesellschaftsentwürfe in J.R.R. Tolkiens The Lord of the Rings.* Trier: WVT, 2005
Weinreich, Frank. »Von Verfassungen mit und ohne Schwert – Impressionen idealer Herrschaftsformen in Mittelerde als Ausdruck des politischen Verständnisses von J.R.R. Tolkien«. *Hither Shore* 2 (2005): 89-104

Gewalt und Gewaltdarstellung bei Tolkien im Vergleich mit zeitgenössischen Gewalt- und Aggressionstheorien

Friedhelm Schneidewind (Hemsbach)

Einleitung

Immer wieder wird diskutiert, ob und wie weit Tolkien in seiner Darstellung von Krieg und Gewalt durch seine persönlichen Erfahrungen, etwa im Krieg, beeinflusst wurde oder durch politische und soziale Ereignisse während jener Zeit, in der er *Der Herr der Ringe* schrieb: In Deutschland gab es eine nationalsozialistische Schreckensherrschaft, während einiger Jahre herrschte Krieg. Für mich als Biologen und Anthropologen stellte sich jedoch schon beim ersten Lesen 1976 die Frage, welches Menschenbild (wenn ich den Begriff Mensch hier einmal ganz weit fasse) Tolkien in seiner Beschreibung von Mittelerde als Grundlage diente.

Die Lektüre des *Silmarillion* drei Jahre später bot mir nicht nur die Möglichkeit, dieser Frage vertieft nachzugehen, sondern auch ein besonderes Erlebnis: Zu diesem Zeitpunkt hielt ich ein Referat in einem Anthropologieseminar zum Thema »Die Aggressivität des Menschen – Trieb oder reaktives Verhalten?« und reflektierte natürlich auch in diesem Zusammenhang das, was ich über Mittelerde las. Es war mir eine besondere Freude, 30 Jahre später auf dem Tolkien Seminar 2009 einen Vortrag zu halten, in dem ich das Thema von damals aufgreifen und einer breiteren Öffentlichkeit darlegen konnte.

Warum sollte es interessant sein, ob Tolkien die zu seiner Zeit verbreiteten Theorien zu Aggression und Aggressivität kannte, was er davon hielt? Weil die Entscheidung für eine der beiden Hauptrichtungen, die es in dieser Diskussion gibt, mit entscheidend ist für das Welt- und Menschenbild und Grundlage für die Handlungsmuster der beschriebenen Personen.

Auch heute machen sich viele Menschen nicht ausdrücklich Gedanken darüber, welche Vorstellung von der Aggressivität der Menschen sie haben. Ihre Entscheidungen im Umgang mit anderen, bei der Wahl von Sanktionen oder auch von Politikrichtungen werden jedoch von dieser Vorstellung geprägt, ob nun bewusst oder nicht.

Interessant ist in diesem Zusammenhang, dass die beiden Hauptvorstellungen über die Aggression des Menschen schon zur Zeit von Tolkiens Jugend bekannt waren und diskutiert wurden; während seiner aktiven Schaffensphase waren sie fast schon so ausgearbeitet wie heute und dürften gebildeten Menschen zumindest in den Grundzügen bekannt gewesen sein.

Im ersten Teil dieses Artikels definiere und erläutere ich die Begrifflichkeiten, im zweiten Abschnitt stelle ich kurz die wichtigsten Theorien und Modelle vor und im dritten Teil zeige ich, dass Tolkiens Werk eindeutig eine bestimmte der beiden Hauptrichtungen widerspiegelt.

Aggression und Aggressivität

Aggressivität und Aggression sind gar nicht so leicht zu definieren, da schon in der Definition oft ein Erklärungsansatz verborgen liegt. Nicht einmal der Unterschied ist immer ganz klar. Schauen wir uns zunächst die »quasi-offizielle« Definitionen im Duden an:

Ag|gres|si|vi|tät, die; -, -en:
1. <o. Pl.> a) (Psych.) mehr od. weniger unbewusste, sich nicht immer offen zeigende **aggressive Haltung** eines Menschen: seine A. beim Sport ausleben;
b) **offen aggressive Haltung, aggressives Verhalten; Angriffslust**.
2. **einzelne aggressive Handlung**

Ag|gres|si|on, die; -, -en [lat. aggressio = Angriff, zu: aggressum, 2. Part. von: aggredi = angreifen]:

1. (Völkerr.) rechtswidriger militärischer Angriff auf ein fremdes Staatsgebiet; feindliche, militärische -en gegen Nachbarstaaten.

2. (Psych.) a) **durch Affekte ausgelöstes, auf Angriff ausgerichtetes Verhalten des Menschen, das auf einen Machtzuwachs des Angreifers bzw. eine Machtverminderung des Angegriffenen zielt**;

b) **feindselige, ablehnende Einstellung, Haltung**: jmd. ist voller -en ...[1]

Das ist nicht sonderlich klar! Verbreitet ist heute folgende Definition: Aggression ist »jegliche Verhaltensform, die das Ziel hat, andere Lebewesen zu schädigen oder zu verletzen, welche motiviert sind, dem zu entgehen, oder Dinge zu beschädigen bzw. zu zerstören, insoweit dies nicht ihre gesellschaftlich zugewiesene Aufgabe ist« (Roberts 17).

Ein Mensch, der ein Auto verschrottet, ist damit nicht aggressiv, wenn er dies als gesellschaftliche Aufgabe, etwa als Angestellter in der Schrottpresse, erledigt, sehr wohl aber, wenn er dies im Rahmen einer Demonstration mit irgendeinem Auto am Straßenrand tut.

---

[1] DUDEN Universalwörterbuch, CD-Rom, Mannheim: Duden-Verlag 2003. Herv. F.S.

Schon darüber aber, nämlich inwieweit die gesellschaftliche Relevanz eine Rolle spielen soll, wird gestritten, noch mehr darüber, ob das Motiv einer Handlung gegenüber Menschen oder Tieren eine Rolle spielen soll. Ist Verteidigung, also beispielsweise Notwehr, Aggression? Die Meinungen gehen auseinander. Ist das Töten eines Tieres in jedem Falle eine Aggression? Manche Tierschützer würden zustimmen, Menschen hingegen, die Fleisch essen, werden wohl kaum geneigt sein, das Schlachten als Aggression zu betrachten. Über dieses Thema zu diskutieren ist kaum möglich, ohne moralische und/oder soziale Aspekte einzubeziehen.

Heutzutage wird gerne unterschieden zwischen instrumenteller und emotionaler Aggression (Roberts 17) sowie negativer und positiver Aggression. Ein paar Aspekte seien hier, ohne Anspruch auf Vollständigkeit, aufgezählt: Als negative Ausdrucksformen oder Aspekte von Aggression werden häufig genannt:

- offene Aggression gegenüber Lebewesen (physisch): körperliches Bedrohen, Schlagen, Verletzen, Töten …

- offene Aggression gegenüber Sachen (physisch): Beschädigung, Zerstörung, Verunreinigung, Vernachlässigung …

- offene verbale oder nonverbale Aggression: Beleidigen, Spott; Gestik, Mimik, Sprachstil, Umgangsformen …

- indirekte Aggression: Entzug von Zuwendung, scheinbar sachliche Geringschätzung, Kränkung, Schikane, üble Nachrede, Mobbing (kann in direkte Aggression umschlagen) …

- emotionale Aggression: Stress, Ärger, Wut, Groll, Hass, Neid (evtl. auch Autoaggression) …

- verdeckte Aggression: Phantasien …

- »motivierte« Aggression: Vergeltung, Rache …

Heute wird Aggression aber oft auch positiv bewertet, besonders im Geschäftsleben, etwa in folgenden Zusammenhängen oder Ausdrucksformen:

- Wetteifern, spielerische Aggression

- selbstbewusstes Auftreten, Durchsetzungsfähigkeit, »In-Angriff-Nehmen«, »Kampfwillen«, »Killerinstinkt«

- »aggressives Vorgehen« in Werbung, Öffentlichkeitsarbeit/PR, Verkauf …

- Schutz, Abwehr/Verteidigung, Notwehr/Nothilfe, Angriff »zur Verteidigung«/Präventivschlag

- Rangordnungs-»Kämpfe«

Friedhelm Schneidewind

- im Tierreich: Wettbewerb um Rang, Ressourcen, Fortpflanzungsmöglichkeiten, Nahrungserwerb, Räuber-Beute-Beziehung; von manchen werden diese Ausdrucksformen auch Menschen zugeordnet, etwa Aggression gegenüber Tieren

In den letzten gut 100 Jahren gab es viele Theorien und Erklärungsversuche zur Aggression. Sie lassen sich im Wesentlichen in zwei grundlegende Auffassungen unterteilen:

- Aggressivität/Aggression basiert auf Trieb(en), ist affekt-induziertes Verhalten. In der Regel ist dieser Ansatz verbunden mit der Vorstellung eines inneren Bedürfnisses nach Aggression und führt zu verschiedenen Vorstellungen, wie dessen Ausleben verhindert werden kann.

- Aggressivität/Aggression ist ein reaktives Verhalten, auf innere wie äußere Anlässe und/oder Reize. In diesem Zusammenhang werden häufig Verhaltensmodelle entwickelt und/oder Vorstellungen, wie aggressives Verhalten (auch) durch die Beeinflussung der Umwelt vermieden oder vermindert werden kann.

Es ist hier weder der Platz noch die richtige Gelegenheit, weitergehend auf die verschiedenen Modelle und Theorien einzugehen. Hierzu sei auf die umfangreiche Literatur verwiesen.[2] Ich will aber einen kurzen Überblick geben über die wichtigsten Ansätze, die in einer breiteren Öffentlichkeit diskutiert wurden und wahrscheinlich zumindest in ihren populärwissenschaftlichen Ausprägungen auch Tolkien als gebildetem Mann bekannt gewesen sein dürften.

- Sigmund Freud (1856-1939) trat 1905 und später erweitert 1915 mit der These an die Öffentlichkeit, Aggression basiere auf dem *Aggressionstrieb*. Diesen sah Freud zunächst als Komponente der »Ich-Triebe« an, ab 1920 aber als eigenen (primären) Trieb, als Hauptvertreter des Todes- oder Destruktionstriebes (Zerstörungstrieb, »Thanatos«). Diesen stellte er der Libido, der sexuellen Triebkraft, dem Liebestrieb »Eros« als zweiten Hauptantrieb menschlichen Verhaltens und Antagonisten gegenüber. Als Abwehrmechanismus dient laut Freud vor allem die *Sublimierung* oder *Sublimation* (von lat. *sublimare*, erhöhen): die Umwandlung, die Umleitung der Energie auf andere sozial anerkannte oder zumindest tolerierte Formen der Aktivität, auf unschädliche »Ventilsitten« wie Sport. Oder aber Gewaltbereitschaft und Zerstörungslust werden »neutralisiert«, indem sie mit erotischer Triebkraft verbunden werden. Kulturelle Leistungen führte Freud vor allem auf Sublimierungen des Sexualtriebs zurück, die sich etwa in intellektueller Arbeit oder künstlerischer Betätigung äußerten, die

---

2   Insbesondere auf Bärsch, Hacker, Heinemann, Heitmeyer, Michaelis, Nolting und Selg.

Sublimation der Aggression, etwa von Wut, zeige sich eher in sinnvollen körperlichen Aktivitäten wie Holzhacken oder Putzen oder eben Sport. Es komme so zur Reduzierung des angestauten Drucks, zur Katharsis. Aggression stehe als Energiepotential zur Veränderung zur Verfügung.

- Konrad Lorenz (1903-1989) veröffentlichte 1937 die Theorie der Doppelten Quantifizierung und das psychohydraulische Instinktmodell. Eine innere spontan ansteigende Handlungsbereitschaft, eine endogene Energie, staut sich immer mehr auf (siehe Grafik[3]). Durch einen Schlüsselreiz (häufig ein AAM, ein »angeborener Auslösemechanismus) wird ein »Abfluss« dieser Energie ermöglicht, die »Reizschwelle« überwunden, die Lorenz sich als zu überwindende zentrale Hemmung vorstellte (in der Grafik Ventil und Feder, der Schlüsselreiz wirkt als Gewicht): Es wird aggressives Verhalten ausgelöst, also Energie abgelassen. Wenn sich diese zu sehr anstaut, muss allerdings ebenfalls ein Ablauf stattfinden, da durch den Druck, den diese Energie ausübt, sonst irgendwann »der Kessel platzt«. Durch sein 1963 veröffentlichtes populärwissenschaftliches Buch *Das sogenannte Böse* fand die These vom Aggressionstrieb oder gar -instinkt in der nicht-wissenschaftlichen Öffentlichkeit breite Aufmerksamkeit. Wie Freud plädierte auch Lorenz für ein »Umleiten« der Aggression hin zu gesellschaftlich akzeptiertem Handeln.

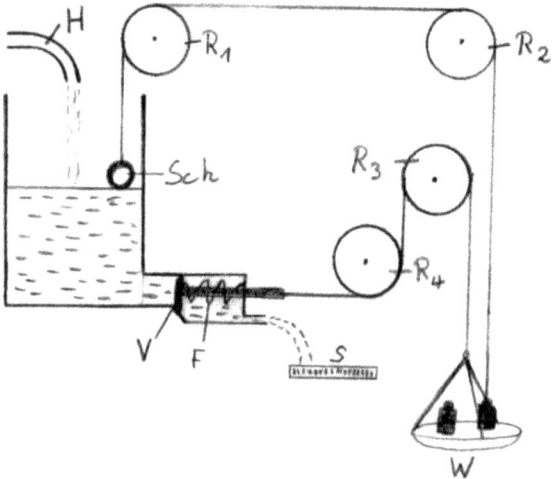

---

3   Diese Grafik gehört zu meinem in der Einleitung erwähnten Vortrag von 1979. H = Hahn, aus dem die endogene Energie strömt, V = Ventil, F = Feder, S = Skala zur Messung der Aggressivität, R = Rollen, W = Waagschale mit Gewichten, Sch = Schwimmer.

Noch heute wird in Teilen der Verhaltensforschung und biologischen Anthropologie wie auch der Psychoanalyse ein eigenständiger Aggressionstrieb angenommen, nicht selten als wesentlicher primärer Aggressionstrieb. Zu den modernen Vertretern gehör(t)en u.a. der deutsch-amerikanische Psychoanalytiker, Philosoph und Sozialpsychologe Erich Fromm (1900-1980)[4], der österreichische Lorenzschüler und Begründer der Humanethologie Irenäus Eibl-Eibesfeldt (geb. 1928) und der amerikanisch-österreichische Psychiater, Psychoanalytiker und Aggressionsforscher Friedrich Hacker (1914-1989)[5].

In der modernen Biologie und Anthropologie wird die These vom Aggressionstrieb als endogener, stets sprudelnder Energiequell kaum noch vertreten. Der »Todestrieb« im Sinne von Freud ist aus evolutionsbiologischer und -theoretischer Sicht nicht haltbar, da kein natürlicher Selektionsmechanismus denkbar ist, der ihn hervorbringen könnte.[6]

Dass die Vorstellung vom Aggressionstrieb aus sozialpsychologischer Sicht unzureichend ist, führte schon früh zu alternativen Modellen. John S. Dollard (1900-1981) und Neal E. Miller (1909-2002) stellten 1939 das Frustrations-Aggressions-Modell vor, wonach Aggression immer eine Folge von Frustration ist: Auf Frustration kann (nicht muss!) Aggression folgen, auf Wunschversagung kann Verstimmung oder Angriff folgen. Aggressionen sind danach immer Frustrationsfolgen, abhängig vom Grad der Neigung zu Frustrationsreaktionen, vom Grad der Behinderung einer Reaktion, von der Zahl der frustrierenden Reaktionen und von der Zahl gelöschter nicht-aggressiver Reaktionen. Dieses einfache Modell wird heute nur noch selten vertreten[7], war aber zu Tolkiens

---

4 Fromm führt Destruktivität (»bösartige Aggression«) zwar auch auf die gesellschaftlichen Umstände zurück, insbesondere den Kapitalismus, vor allem aber auf Charakterstrukturen. Neben Sadismus und Nekrophilie beschreibt er auch die »spontane Destruktivität«.

5 Aus der psychoanalytischen Tradition Freuds kommend, verband Hacker die Thesen von Lorenz zur angeborenen, triebhaften Natur der Aggression (»biologische Programmierung«) mit behavioristischen Thesen: »Aggression ist eine Grundverhaltensform, die durch Schmerz, Angst, Wut, Provokation, Bedrohung der Stellung in der Rangordnung, Überfüllung und andere innere und äußere Reize ausgelöst, verstärkt oder vermindert und durch Lernerfahrung entscheidend beeinflusst werden kann« (Hacker 158). Und er empfiehlt das »Bewusstwerden der eigenen Aggression«, denn damit begännen »jene Prozesse, die (zwar nicht automatisch, aber doch möglicherweise durch genaue und intime Kenntnis der Aggressionswandlungen und Aggressionsverwandlungen) Gewalteskalation unterbrechen« (Hacker 418).

6 Die Evolution funktioniert über die Vermehrung, nur darüber lässt sich der »Erfolg« eines Individuums bzw. seiner Gene feststellen, nur so können letztere weitergegeben werden. Dass sich ein Mechanismus entwickelt, der Individuen dem Tode näherbringt, ist nur denkbar, wenn entweder dadurch die Vermehrungschancen verbessert werden (etwa wenn sich die Kinder von einem Elternteil ernähren), oder es um das Sterben nach der fortpflanzungsfähigen Zeit geht, also im Alter. Beides passt nicht zum »Todestrieb«. (Übrigens gibt es auch keinen »Selbsterhaltungstrieb«, jedenfalls nicht im Sinne eines biologischen Triebs oder Instinktes).

7 Kritisiert wird u.a., dass in diesem Modell die Zuschreibung von Kausalität eine Rolle spiele: Frustration führe nur dann, und selbst dann nicht immer, zu Aggression, wenn

Zeit bekannt und wurde viel diskutiert und kann als Grundlage aller folgenden Reaktionsmodelle der Aggression dienen.

Andere Modelle in der Folge betonten stärker das Bekräftigungslernen, beispielsweise das frühe S-O-R-Modell[8] von Edward Lee Thorndike[9] (1874-1949), einer der »Väter« des Behaviorismus, und das Modell der operanden Konditionierung von Burrhus Frederic Skinner (1904-1990): Die Anwendung von aggressiven Verhaltensmustern bringt Erfolg, diese »Erfolgsbelohnung« lässt in Zukunft erneut aggressiv handeln. Das Verhalten wird spontan »emittiert« und anschließend durch seine Konsequenzen geformt (»selection by consequences«). Heute werden auch zahlreiche andere Hypothesen vertreten, die sich keineswegs alle widersprechen, sondern zum großen Teil ergänzen.[10]

Während das Triebmodell außerhalb der Psychoanalyse nur noch wenig Anerkennung findet, gilt die Reaktionshypothese als gut begründet. Die Kontroverse allerdings, ob Aggression eher als Frustrations- und/oder Angstfolge zu begreifen oder doch eher lerntheoretisch zu erklären ist, gilt als noch nicht entschieden.

Der deutsche Philologe und Psychologe Wolfgang Michaelis (geb. 1939) stellte 1974 ein ausgeklügeltes und nach meiner Auffassung schlüssiges systemtheoretisches Modell der Aggression vor. Danach entscheidet sich der Organismus jeweils für ein ihm angemessen erscheinendes Verhalten zur Erhaltung und/oder (Wieder-)Herstellung seiner Homöostase (oder Homoiostase: hier verstanden als subjektives Wohlbefinden, auch bei Wesen, die kein Bewusstsein haben). Dies kann die Flucht sein oder eben auch Aggression: Handlung(en) auf Kosten

---

ihr Ursprung einer anderen Person oder einer Sache zugeschrieben werde(n könne). Diese Kritik allerdings unterschlägt wiederum Auto-Aggressionen oder Übersprungshandlungen.

8 S = (Umgebungs-)Reiz (*stimulus*), R = Reaktion (*reaction*), O = Konsequenz, Verstärker (*outcome*)

9 In seiner Lerntheorie stellte er 1898 u.a. das Gesetz der (Aus-)Wirkung vor (*law of effect*) über Lernen als Prozess aus Versuch und Irrtum und Lerneffekte durch Bildung von Assoziationen zwischen Reizen/Stimuli und befriedigenden Konsequenzen (Belohnung). Mit John B. Watson einer der Begründer des Behaviorismus und Vorläufer von Frederic Skinner.

10 Für erwähnenswert halte ich insbesondere das Angst-Aggressions-Modell des Tübinger Philosophen und Psychoanalytikers Rolf Denker (1923-1999), das kognitiv-neoassoziationistische Modell von Leonard Berkowitz (1962), einer der schärfsten Kritiker der Katharsis-Hypothese, das Lernen am Modell oder Beobachtungslernen (bekanntester Vertreter dieser Theorie ist der kanadische Psychologe Albert Bandura, geb. 1925), die daraus weiterentwickelte Skripttheorie von L. Rowell Huesmann (1988) und die rational-funktionalistisch ausgerichtete sozial-interaktionististische Theorie von Tedeschi und Felson (1994), nach den drei Motiven für Aggression – Kontrolle/Soziale Macht, (Wiederherstellung von) Gerechtigkeit, Soziale Identität/Positive Selbstdarstellung – auch das 3-Motiv-Modell genannt. Siehe zu den letzten drei Modellen die Foliensammlung von Hallfahrth.

und/oder gegen den Widerstand eines anderen Organismus oder im weiteren Sinne auch einer Sache.
So sehr sich in den letzten 60 Jahren auch die Vorstellungen und Modelle im einzelnen verändert haben: Die grundlegenden Richtungen, die beiden wesentlichen Alternativen, nämlich Aggression als trieb- oder reaktionsbegründetes Verhalten zu verstehen, waren zu der Zeit, als Tolkien *Der Herr der Ringe* schrieb, schon ausgebildet und wurden diskutiert. Es bleibt zu untersuchen, ob Tolkiens Werk Hinweise darauf liefert, welcher Vorstellung von Aggression und Aggressivität Tolkien anhing.

Aggressionsvorstellungen bei Tolkien

Es gibt keine klare und eindeutige Aussage von Tolkien zu Aggressionsmodellen oder -theorien. Beim einzigen Mal, da der Begriff Aggression auftaucht, geht es um Frodo und sein Verhältnis zu den Ringgeistern. Dieses kann man laut Tolkien

> … mit der Situation eines kleinen tapferen Mannes mit einer fürchterlichen Waffe gegenüber acht grimmigen Kriegern vergleichen, die von großer Stärke und Beweglichkeit und mit vergifteten Klingen bewaffnet sind. Die Schwäche des Mannes war, daß er seine Waffe noch nicht zu gebrauchen wußte **und von Temperament und Erziehung her der Gewalt abgeneigt war.**
> (Nr. 246 vom September 1963, B 433, Herv. FS)

Dies zeigt, dass Tolkien zumindest in diesem Fall davon ausging, dass Aggressivität sowohl durch Veranlagung wie durch Erziehung gesteuert wird. Dies entspricht einem eher reaktiven Modell.
Ein einziges Mal beschreibt Tolkien in seinem veröffentlichten Werk ein Wesen als »angriffslustig« (»aggressive«). Dieses Wesen aber ist erstens eine Sache, nämlich das Schwert Caudimordax (Tailbiter/Schwanzbeißer/Schweifschläger), und zweitens so angriffslustig auch nur gegenüber einer bestimmten Spezies, nämlich Drachen, weshalb sich der Drache Chrysophylax zu Recht fragt:

> Und wie, um alles in der Welt, verhält man sich zu einem tollkühnen Bauern und einem so ruhmreichen und angriffslustigen Schwert? (BGH 73)

Anderen Wesen gegenüber ist das Schwert harmlos, also haben wir selbst hier eine Reaktion und kein triebhaftes Verhalten.

Doch schauen wir uns das Hauptwerk an. Wenn wir es wirklich mit einem Aggressionstrieb zu tun hätten, wie von Freud oder Lorenz angenommen, müssten die Personen entweder andauernd aggressiv sein oder aber sublimieren. Wie oben erwähnt, ist Frodo beispielsweise »von Temperament und Erziehung her der Gewalt abgeneigt« (B 433). Sowohl er als auch Sam kämpfen nur, wenn es um das nackte Überleben geht und/oder als (auch emotionale) Reaktion, wie in Moria: »Plötzlich und zu seiner eigenen Überraschung fühlte Frodo einen heißen Zorn in seinem Herzen aufflammen. ›Das Auenland!‹, rief er, sprang neben Boromir, bückte sich und hieb mit Stich auf den abscheulichen Fuß« (HdR 365). Auch Sam kämpft gegen Gollum und dann gegen Kankra in deren Höhle (HdR 799 ff), weil er muss. Erst später »sah er rot vor Wut« (HdR 799). Und die Wut ist es, die es ihm ermöglicht, Kankra zu besiegen:

> Dann griff er an. Kein wütenderer Ansturm war je in der wilden Welt der Tiere gesehen worden, wo selbst ein verzweifeltes kleines Geschöpf, mit winzigen Zähnen bewaffnet, einen Turm aus Horn und Fell anspringen wird, der über seinem gefallenen Gefährten aufragt. (HdR 801)

Das ist die literarische Umsetzung verschiedener Reaktionsmodelle, hier findet sich Michaelis' systemtheoretischer Ansatz nahezu pur.

Ein Paradebeispiel für einen Kämpfer aus Reaktion und nicht aus Trieb ist Faramir: ein tapferer Krieger, der aber nur kämpft, wenn und weil er muss, nicht aus Freude am Kampf oder zur Triebbefriedigung, und der auch nicht gerne tötet: »Aber ich erschlage Mensch oder Tier nicht ohne Not, und auch nicht gern, wenn es nötig ist« (HdR 732). Später erläutert er Sam und Frodo:

> Krieg muss sein, solange wir unser Leben verteidigen gegen einen Zerstörer, der sonst uns alle verschlingen würde; aber das blanke Schwert liebe ich nicht um seiner Schärfe willen, den Pfeil nicht um seiner Schnelligkeit willen, den Krieger nicht um seines Ruhmes willen. Ich liebe nur das, was sie verteidigen ... (HdR 740)

Selbst den Gegnern wird der blinde Aggressionstrieb abgesprochen: Im Buch drückt Sam dies so aus:

> ... Er fragte sich, wie der Mann wohl hieß und wo er herkam und ob er wirklich ein böses Herz gehabt hatte, oder welche Lügen oder Drohungen ihn zu dem langen Marsch von seiner Heimat veranlasst hatten; und ob er nicht in Wirklichkeit lieber in Frieden dort geblieben wäre ... (HdR 728)

In der Verfilmung hat Peter Jackson diesen klugen Satz leider gestrichen. Er taucht nur in der Extended Version auf und wird dort Faramir in den Mund gelegt.
Schließlich haben viele der Angreifer, auch wenn sie von Sauron missbraucht werden, durchaus nachvollziehbare eigene Gründe für ihren Angriff auf Rohan und Gondor, wurden sie doch teilweise wie etwa die Dunländer von den Rohirrim früher von ihrem Land verdrängt!

Es gäbe noch viele Stellen, die man zitieren könnte, um zu belegen: Gewalt stellt in *Der Herr der Ringe* keine oder nur eine unbefriedigende oder unzureichende Lösung dar. Auch das spricht sehr für ein Reaktions-Verständnis von Aggression bei Tolkien, denn nur dann lässt sie sich vermeiden.[11]

In *Der Hobbit* sieht es ähnlich aus. Die Hobbits agieren nur »aggressiv«, wenn es nötig ist. Sogar der »Bösewicht« des Buches, der Drache Smaug, verzichtet auf unnötige Gewalt. Er lässt die Seestadt in der Regel in Ruhe und frönt nicht irgendwelchen Aggressions- oder Zerstörungstrieben. Er ist es zufrieden, solange er in Ruhe auf seinem Schatz liegen und ab und zu jagen kann. Erst als er sich angegriffen wähnt und bestohlen, wird er aggressiv und greift die Seestadt an.

Die »Monster« in *Bauer Giles von Ham* sind nicht aggressiv aus purer Angriffslust oder ohne Grund. Der Riese kommt in die Heimat des Bauern, weil er sich bei einem »Spaziergang« verirrt (BGH 15), und der Drache Chrysophylax, weil er auf fette Beute hofft in einem Land ohne Gefahren, wie es der Riese ankündigt: »… massig zu futtern …« – und das ohne gefährliche Menschen oder gar Ritter (BGH 37). Chrysophylax scheut wenn möglich den Kampf, er kämpft nur als Reaktion, zur Verteidigung seines Reviers oder seines Schatzes:

> Ohne Warnung oder Förmlichkeit kam er zum Kampf hervorgestürzt. Er überfiel sie mit Getose und Gebrüll. In weiter Entfernung von seinem Heim hatte er sich nicht allzu kühn gezeigt, trotz uralter kaiserlicher Abstammung. Doch jetzt packte ihn ein heiliger Zorn; denn er kämpfte nun vor seiner eigenen Tür, und sein ganzer Schatz war zu verteidigen. Er kam um einen Bergrücken wie eine Tonne voller Donnerkeile mit dem Getöse eines Sturmwinds und einem Strahl roter Blitze. (BGH 101)

Und nachdem er besiegt und gefangen wurde, wird er zahm:

---

11 Dies wird durch die Ergebnisse der Untersuchung von Frank Weinreich bestätigt, siehe seinen Artikel in diesem Band.

> Chrysophylax blieb lange in Ham, sehr zum Vorteil von Giles; denn ein Mann, der einen zahmen Drachen besitzt, ist natürlich geachtet... So geschah es nach einigen Jahren, als Giles sich rundum gesichert fühlte, daß er den armen Wurm nach Hause ziehen ließ. Sie schieden unter vielen Beteuerungen gegenseitiger Wertschätzung und einem Nichtangriffspakt. Im Grunde seines schlechten Herzens fühlte der Drache für Giles eine so freundliche Zuneigung, wie sie ein Drache überhaupt für jemanden fühlen kann. (BGH 129. 137)

Wir haben es hier klar mit reaktivem Verhalten zu tun, nicht triebgesteuertem, wie auch beim Zauberer Artaxerxes, der den Hund Rover in einen Spielzeughund verwandelt, nachdem er von ihm angegriffen und verletzt wurde (*Roverandom* 11f), oder bei den Koboldkriegen in *Die Briefe vom Weihnachtsmann* (1933).

Schlussbemerkung

Wohin wir in Tolkiens Werk auch schauen: Stets finden wir eine moderne Auffassung von Aggression und Aggressivität als Reaktion auf persönliche und/oder gesellschaftliche, familiäre oder soziale Situationen oder Bedrohungen, und nur selten Wesen, die »einfach so« aggressiv sind.

In *Der Herr der Ringe* und allgemein in Tolkiens Werk haben wir »... ein geradezu modernes und sehr humanes Verständnis von Ethik ...« (Weinreich 9) und eben auch ein modernes Verständnis von Aggression und Aggressivität.

Bibliographie

Bärsch, Sibylle und Tim. *Theorien zur Gewalt.* Schwerte: Amt für Jugendarbeit der EKvW, 2007
Bandura, Albert. *Lernen am Modell.* Stuttgart: Klett-Cotta, 1976
---. *Aggression. Eine sozial-lerntheoretische Analyse.* Stuttgart: Klett-Cotta, 1979
Denker, Rolf. *Aufklärung über Aggression: Kant, Darwin, Freud, Lorenz.* Stuttgart/Berlin/Köln/Mainz: Kohlhammer, 1966
---. *Angst und Aggression.* Stuttgart/Berlin/Köln/Mainz: Kohlhammer, 1974
Dollard, John, and Neil E. Miller. *Frustration and Aggression.* London: Paul Trench Trubner, 1944

Fromm, Erich. *Anatomie der menschlichen Destruktivität*. Reinbek bei Hamburg: Rowohlt, 1977

Hacker, Friedrich. *Aggression. Die Brutalisierung der modernen Welt*. Wien: Molden, 1971

Hallfarth, Carolin: *Theorien der Aggression Teil III*. Folien zu einem Seminar. Bielefeld, 2007: http://www.uni-bielefeld.de/ikg/zick/Theorien%20der%20Aggression%20Teil%20III.ppt (15.08.2009)

Heinemann, Evelyn. *Aggression – Verstehen und bewältigen*. Berlin et.al.: Springer, 1996

Heitmeyer, Wilhelm (Hg.). *Gewalt. Beschreibungen, Analysen, Prävention*. Bonn: Bundeszentrale für politische Bildung, 2006

Heitmeyer, Wilhelm, und Hans-Georg Soeffner (Hg.). *Gewalt. Entwicklungen, Strukturen, Analyseprobleme*. Frankfurt/Main: Suhrkamp, 2004

Lorenz, Konrad: *Das sogenannte Böse*. Wien: Borotha-Schoeler, 1963

Michaelis, Wolfgang. *Verhalten ohne Aggression? Versuch zur Integration der Theorien*. Köln: Kiepenheuer und Witsch, 1976

---. *Perspektiven der Theorienbildung über die Aggression*. Kiel: Universität (Habil.-Schrift), 1977

Nolting, Hans-Peter. *Lernfall Aggression. Wie sie entsteht – wie sie zu vermindern ist. Eine Einführung*. Reinbek bei Hamburg: Rowohlt, 1978 [2005]

Otten, Sabine, und Amélie Mummendey. »Sozialpsychologische Theorien aggressiven Verhaltens«. *Theorien der Sozialpsychologie* (Band 2). Dieter Frey und Martin Irle (Hg.). Bern, Göttingen, Toronto, Seattle: Hans Huber, 2002

Robertz, Dorothee und Frank: *Konflikt-Training mit Kindern und Jugendlichen*. Hamburg: Robertz, 2001

Selg, Herbert, Ulrich Mees und Detlef Berg: *Psychologie der Aggressivität*. Göttingen: Hogrefe, 1997

Tolkien, John Ronald Reuel. *Der Hobbit oder Hin und zurück*. Mit Illustrationen von Alan Lee. Stuttgart: Klett-Cotta, 2009

---. *Der Herr der Ringe* (übersetzt von Margarete Carroux, neu durchgesehen von Lisa Kuppler). Stuttgart: Klett-Cotta, 2009

---. *Farmer Giles of Ham – Bauer Giles von Ham*. Zweisprachige Ausgabe. München: Deutscher Taschenbuch Verlag, 1999

---. *Das Silmarillion*. Hg. Christopher Tolkien, Assistenz Guy Gavriel Kay. Stuttgart: Klett-Cotta, 1978

---. *Die Briefe vom Weihnachtsmann*. Stuttgart: Klett-Cotta, 1977

---. *Roverandom*. Hg. Christina Scull und Wayne G. Hammond. Stuttgart: Klett-Cotta, 1999

---. *Briefe*. Hg. Humphrey Carpenter unter Mitwirkung von Christopher Tolkien. Stuttgart: Klett-Cotta, 2002

Weinreich, Frank. »Ethos in Arda. Charakteristika der Ethik in Mittelerde«. *Eine Grammatik der Ethik. Die Aktualität der moralischen Dimension in J.R.R. Tolkiens literarischem Werk*. Thomas Honegger, Andrew James Johnston, Friedhelm Schneidewind, Frank Weinreich. Saarbrücken: Verlag der Villa Fledermaus, 2005

Der Sängerkrieg: Gesang und Gewalt in J.R.R. Tolkiens Mittelerde

Julian Tim Morton Eilmann (Aachen)

Ein Sängerkrieg in Tolkiens Mittelerde? Was haben wir uns darunter vorzustellen? Irritiert es nicht, im Rahmen einer Tagung, die sich mit Konfliktaustragung, Gewalt und Krieg im Werk Tolkiens beschäftigt, Gesang und Poesie zum Thema zu machen?

Die berechtigte Frage muss also lauten: Was haben Lieder und Gesang mit Gewalt und Krieg zu tun? Wie wir feststellen werden, eine ganze Menge. Denn wie im Folgenden deutlich wird, findet Konfliktaustragung in Tolkiens Werk nicht nur mithilfe von Waffengewalt statt. Manche Auseinandersetzung wird mit Worten ausgetragen.

Beim Stichwort »Wortstreit« denkt man im Kontext von Tolkiens Schriften natürlich zuerst an die rhetorisch geschliffenen Rededuelle, wie sie beispielsweise zwischen Gandalf und Denethor oder Saurons Mund ausgetragen werden. Ein anderes Rededuell, der Wortstreit zwischen Húrin und Morgoth, ist innerhalb von Tolkiens Mythologie sogar legendär. Ein Kampf der Worte wäre eine Aufgabe für eine rhetorische Analyse, um die es hier ausdrücklich nicht gehen soll.

Im Fokus dieser Untersuchung soll vielmehr folgender Befund stehen: Neben der rhetorischen Auseinandersetzung findet der Streit der Worte innerhalb von Tolkiens Werk auch auf eine ganz besondere Art und Weise statt, denn gestritten wird nicht nur mit Worten allein, sondern mit poetischer Sprache, genauer gesagt mit lyrischem Gesang. Auf diese Weise hält das Moment der Poesie Eingang in das Feld der Konfliktaustragung.

> Thus befall the contest of Sauron and Felagund which is renowned. For Felagund strove with Sauron in songs of power, and the power of the king was very great; but Sauron had the mastery, as is told in the Lay of Leithian. (S 200)

Mit diesen eindrucksvollen Worten beschreibt Tolkien den Beginn eines Kampfes in seiner Erzählung *Of Beren and Lúthien*, die im Zentrum des *Silmarillion* steht. Der hier geschilderte Kampf wird jedoch nicht mit Schwert und Schild ausgetragen, sondern mit Gesang.

Auch im *Herrn der Ringe* wird der Leser mehrfach Zeuge eines Kampfes, bei dem die Antagonisten sich gegenseitig durch Lieder der Macht bezwingen wollen. Besonders deutlich wird dies in der Auseinandersetzung zwischen Tom Bombadil und dem Grabunhold. Der Grabunhold gewinnt Macht über die Hobbits, die die Hügelgräberhöhen durchstreifen, indem er ein Lied anstimmt, das in einen Zauberspruch bzw. eine Beschwörung übergeht. Die Furcht, die der Grabunhold verbreitet, und die Kontrolle, die er damit über seine Feinde gewinnt, scheint tatsächlich in hohem Maße in der Macht seines Zaubergesangs zu bestehen, der Frodo buchstäblich zu Eis erstarren lässt.

Tolkien beschreibt den Vorgang dieser Überwältigung durch Gesang mit großer Anschaulichkeit und vermittelt uns auf diese Weise ein beeindruckendes Bild der destruktiven Wirkung eines solchen Liedes der Macht:

> Suddenly a song began: a cold murmur, rising and falling. The voice seemed far away and immeasurably dreary, sometimes high in the air and thin, sometimes like a low moan from the ground. Out of the formless stream of sad but horrible sounds, strings of words would now and again shape themselves: grim, hard, cold words, heartless and miserable... Frodo as chilled to the marrow. After a while the song became clearer, and with dread in his heart he perceived that it had changed into an incantation. (LotR 137)

Tom Bombadil bricht schließlich die Macht des Unholds ebenfalls mithilfe eines »song of power« (vgl. ebd. 139). So heißt es charakteristischerweise über seine Lieder: »His songs are stronger songs« (ebd.). Erstaunlicherweise ist es Toms Gesang, die Macht der Poesie, die die Kräfte des Bösen bezwingt. In einer anderen Szene, in der »songs of power« eine entscheidende Rolle spielen, bricht Tom Bombadil die Macht eines anderen Widersachers, des Weidenmanns. Über den Weidenmann heißt es: »he's a mighty singer« (ebd. 124).

Vielen Lesern des *Herrn der Ringe* mag diese Formulierung bei der ersten Lektüre merkwürdig vorkommen, was u.a. dadurch unterstützt wird, dass Frodo und die anderen Hobbits die Irritation des Lesers teilen und mit Tom Bombadils Formulierung ebenfalls wenig anfangen können (vgl. ebd.). In den Augen Tom Bombadils jedoch wird der Weidenmann durch die Bezeichnung »mighty singer« (ebd.) offensichtlich mehr als eindeutig charakterisiert. Dem Leser hingegen wird erst durch den Kontext des Kampfes zwischen Tom und dem Weidenmann ersichtlich, dass die Formulierung, der Weidenmann sei ein mächtiger Sänger, nicht darauf abzielt, dem Baumgeist ein besonders ausgeprägtes künstlerisches Sangestalent zu attestieren.

Im Gegenteil, der Begriff Sänger ist in diesem Kontext ein Synonym für den Magier und Zauberer (vgl. Eilmann 121). Bemerkenswert ist, wie Tom Bombadil den Weidenmann bezwingt:

›What?‹ shouted Tom Bombadil, leaping up in the air. ›Old Man Willow? Naught worse than that, eh? That can soon be mended. I know the tune for him. Old grey Willow-man! I'll freeze his marrow cold, if he don't behave himself. I'll sing his roots off. I'll sing a wind up and blow leaf and branch away.‹ ... Tom put his mouth to the crack [of the tree] and began singing into it in a low voice. (LotR 117)

Wir finden in dieser Textpassage zahlreiche Hinweise auf die Anwendung eines »song of power«. So behauptet Tom, er kenne die richtige Melodie, um dem Weidenmann erfolgreich entgegenzutreten. Ähnlich dem Terminus »a mighty singer« (ebd. 124) müsste jedoch auch diese Formulierung unverständlich bleiben, wäre man sich nicht der Kontextbedeutung bewusst, wonach eine Verbindung von Gesang und Machtausübung besteht. »[To] know the tune« (ebd. 117) bedeutet hier offenbar: den passenden »song of power« zu kennen.

Am Ausgangspunkt meiner Untersuchung steht somit die Feststellung, dass auch Lieder und Gesang in Tolkiens Mittelerde-Mythologie ein Mittel zur Konfliktbewältigung darstellen. Tolkien hat, wie wir sehen, für Lieder, die einen solchen Zweck erfüllen, einen bestimmten Begriff geprägt: Er spricht von »songs of power«. Dieser Begriff verweist auf die zentrale Problemantik, um die es im Folgenden gehen soll: das Verhältnis von Kunst und Macht bzw. Gewalt.

Die Problematik des Terminus' lässt sich bereits an seinen sprachlichen Bestandteilen ablesen. Als ein Begriff der Widersprüche setzt er sich aus den Wörtern »song« und »power« zusammen. Untersucht man Tolkiens theoretische Schriften hinsichtlich der unterschiedlichen Konnotationen dieser beiden Begriffe, dann wird man feststellen, dass »song« mit den positiv besetzten Begriffen Kunst, Bezauberung, Poesie und Ästhetik in Verbindung gebracht wird, während »power« mit dem semantischen Begriffsfeld Macht, Beherrschung, Verhexung und Gier negativ assoziiert ist: »›power‹ is an ominous and sinister word in all these tales« (L 152).

Der Begriff »songs of power« macht demnach auf ein ästhetisches und ethisches Problem aufmerksam, denn es stellt sich die Frage, inwiefern Kunst und die Ausübung von bzw. das Streben nach Macht miteinander vereinbar sind. Darf ein Sänger bzw. Künstler seine poetische Begabung dazu nutzen, Ziele zu erreichen, die jenen moralisch zweifelhaften Bereich berühren, den Tolkien mit »power« in Verbindung bringt? Es wird sich zeigen, dass die Verantwortung des Künstlers bei der Anwendung seines kreativen Potentials in der Tat eines der zentralen Themen in Tolkiens Werk darstellt. Für Tolkien kristallisiert sich die Problematik des rechtmäßigen Liedgebrauchs (»song of power«) im grundlegenden Gegensatz von Kunst und Magie heraus.

Julian Eilmann

Die Versuchung des Künstlers: Zum Verhältnis von Magie und Gesang

Der Gegensatz von Kunst und Magie wird für Tolkien virulent, da diese Gegenüberstellung den Kern seiner Poetologie berührt. Bekanntlich steht im Zentrum seines Kunstschaffens der Begriff der »sub-creation« (FS 47). Der Urwunsch des Menschen besteht nach Tolkien im so genannten Zweitschöpfertum, einer Form des künstlerischen Schaffens, die in Analogie zum göttlichen Schöpfertum steht. So gelangt Tolkien zu der Schlussfolgerung, dass der Menschen bereits durch seine Fähigkeit zur spielerischen Sprachschöpfung zum Zweitschöpfer werde:

> But how powerful, how stimulating to the very faculty that produced it, was the invention of the adjective: no spell or incantation in Faërie is more potent... When we can take green from grass, blue from heaven, and red from blood, we have already an enchanter's power...; and the desire to wield that power in the world external to the minds awakes. It does not follow that we shall use that power well on any plane... But in such ›fantasy‹, as it is called, new form is made; Faërie begins; Man becomes a sub-creator. (ebd. 22)

Auf diese Weise wird der kreative Adjektivgebrauch mit der »enchanter's power« gleichgesetzt, jener Form der poetischen Bezauberung, die für Tolkiens Kunstverständnis zentral ist. Tolkiens Versuch, diese Kraft der (elbischen) Bezauberung näher zu definieren, führt ihn zum Vergleich von Kunst und Magie, wobei Tolkien den Begriff »Magie«, der für ihn als Autor phantastischer Literatur sicherlich verlockend gewesen sein muss, ablehnt:

> We need a word for this elvish craft, but all the words that have been applied to it have been blurred and confused with other things. Magic is ready to hand, and I have used it above..., but I should not have done so: Magic should be reserved for the operations of the Magician. (ebd. 53)

In beiden hier zitierten Passagen spricht Tolkien die ethische Dimension des zweitschöpferischen Handelns an. Die Problematik resultiert dabei aus dem Wunsch des Künstlers bzw. des Menschen als Gattungswesen, den eigenen Geistesschöpfungen wirkliches Leben einzuhauchen: »the desire to wield that power in the world external to the minds« (ebd. 22). Dieser aus ästhetischer Sicht gerechtfertigte Wunsch kann jedoch zur Pervertierung des Individuums führen, denn der Künstler ist der Verführung durch die Macht ausgesetzt: durch das ihm gegebene kreative Potential (s.u.).

Wenn dieser Wunsch nach (grenzenloser) kreativer Realisation auf eine zentrale Problematik des Tolkien'schen Werks verweist, wie wird dann in Tolkiens poetologischen Schriften und Briefpassagen zwischen Kunst und Magie differenziert? Tolkien unterscheidet Kunst und Magie, indem er die Magie dem Bereich Technik zuordnet. So heißt es bei ihm: »[Magic] is not an art but a technique; its desire is *power* in this world, domination of things and wills« (ebd. 53). Technik ist hier im abwertenden Sinne gebraucht: als ein Werkzeug, das der direkten Anwendbarkeit und ethisch fragwürdigen Zielen dient. Das kreative Potential des Menschen wird im magischen Gerbrauch pervertiert und durch die Ausrichtung auf praktische Ziel- und Wunscherfüllung profanen Zwecken untergeordnet.

Eine solche Definition der Magie als einer pragmatischen »technique«, die auf Machterwerb und rücksichtslose und gewalttätige Veränderung der Dingwelt ausgerichtet ist, stimmt mit einem in der Kulturwissenschaft verbreiteten Magieverständnis überein. So kommt Karl Beth in seiner Diskussion des Verhältnisses von Magie und Religion ähnlich wie Tolkien zu der Einschätzung, dass die Zauberei in erster Linie eigennützig auf das Subjekt des Magiewirkenden ausgerichtet ist. In diesem Sinne formuliert er: »Die Magie ist egozentrisch« (Beth 45). Unterstützend zu Tolkiens These einer ausgeprägten Nähe der magischen Künste zur Technik[1] betont der Volkskundler Leander Petzoldt: »Was Magie in erster Linie bestimmt, ist ihr instrumenteller Charakter« (Petzoldt viii); und Robert Stockhammer stellt fest: »Magie wäre Technik, insofern sie als Mittel zu einem damit erreichbaren Zweck gilt« (Stockhammer 5).

Wenn sich Magie nach Tolkien durch ihre egozentrische Funktionalisierung als Technik zu erkennen gibt, was kennzeichnet dann im Gegensatz dazu die Kunst? Tolkien charakterisiert die Kunst in deutlicher Abgrenzung zur Zauberei, wenn er in *On Fairy-Stories* formuliert:

> Art of the same sort [as magic], if more skilled and effortless, the elves can also use...; but the more potent and specially elvish craft I will, for lack of a less debatable word, call Enchantment. Enchantment produces a Secondary World into which both designer and spectator can enter, to the satisfaction of their senses while they are inside; but in its purity it is artistic in desire and purpose. (FS 53)

---

1 Tolkien beschreibt das auf Magie und Technik fußende Machstreben der Despoten Mittelerdes so: »The Machine is our more obvious modern form though more closely related to Magic than is usually recognized.« und »The Enemy in successive forms is always ›naturally‹ concerned with sheer Domination, and so the Lord of magic and machines.« (L 146)

Wie wir sehen, legt Tolkien großen Wert darauf zu betonen, dass Kunst bzw. das elbische »enchantment« in Abgrenzung zur Magie nicht auf irdischen Machterwerb abzielt, sondern allein künstlerische Ziele verfolgt: »in its purity it is artistic in desire and purpose.« Auch an anderer Stelle in seinen theoretischen Schriften thematisiert Tolkien die genuin ästhetische Ausrichtung der elbischen Verzauberung, u.a. bei seiner Definition des Quenya-Begriffs *Olos*:

> Olo – s: vision, ›phantasy‹: Common Elvish name for ›construction of the mind‹ not actually (pre)existing in Ea apart from the construction, but by the Eldar capable of being by Art (Karmë) made visible and sensible. Olos is usually applied to fair constructions **having solely an artistic object** (i.e. not having the object of deception, or of acquiring power). (UT 396, Herv. J.E.)

Durch die Abgrenzung des künstlerischen Zweitschöpfertums von der egozentrischen Magie betont Tolkien die ästhetische Orientierung der Kunst (»having solely an artistic object«). Darüber hinaus erhält der Künstler einen genuin ethischen Auftrag. So heißt es über die Magie der Maiar und Eldar:

> Their magia the Elves and Gandalf use (sparingly): a magia producing real results (like fire in a wet faggot) **for specific beneficient purposes**. Their goetic effects are entirely artistic and not intended to deceive. (L 200, Herv. J.E.)[2]

Entscheidend in dieser Briefpassage ist die von mir hervorgehobene Formulierung: Elbische Verzauberung (»enchantment«) bzw. Kunst darf im Kontext der Mittelerde-Mythologie nur eindeutig wohltätigen Zielen dienen. In dieser Forderung einer moralisch einwandfreien Zielausrichtung besteht das signifikante Unterscheidungsmerkmal zu den »vulgar devices of the laborious, scientific magician« (FS 10).

Vergegenwärtigt man sich nach den bisherigen Erörterungen noch einmal den von Tolkien konstruierten Gegensatz zwischen Kunst und Magie, dann wird man feststellen, dass der Bereich der Magie mit durchweg negativ konnotierten Begriffen in Verbindung gebracht wird: »delusion«, »bewitchment«, »domination« und in besonderem Maße »power« (ebd. 53f). Das destruktive Potential des korrumpierten Magiers manifestiert sich auch in anderen Formulierungen Tolkiens, die einen absoluten und zerstörerischen Herrschaftsanspruch gegenüber der lebendigen Welt und ihren Geschöpfen zum Ausdruck bringen (»terrify and subjugate«; L 200, »bulldozing the real world or coercing other wills«, »tyrannos

---

2   Zur Verwendung der Begriffe *goeteia* und *magia* in Tolkiens Werk vgl. die kontroverse Diskussion bei Hageböck 47ff und Kegler/Fornet-Ponse/Kegler 220-23.

re-forming of Creation«; L 146). Als maßgebliches Charakteristikum wird dem Magier demnach die oben angesprochene egozentrische Weltsicht und verbunden damit eine nahezu unendliche Gier nach autokratischer Macht zugesprochen (»the desire for Power«, L 145; »greed for self-centred power«, FS 53).

Demgegenüber steht Tolkiens Kunst-Definition, der, wie bereits deutlich wurde, die in hohem Maße positiv besetzten Termini »sub-creation« und »enchantment« zuzuordnen sind. Darüber hinaus kennzeichnet die Kunst eine sowohl ästhetische als auch wohltätige Zielausrichtung (»artistic in desire an purpose«, FS 53; »specific beneficient purposes«, L 200) mit dem Wunsch, gemeinsam mit dem Gegenüber schöpferisch tätig zu werden (»That creative desire... seeks shared enrichment, partners in making and delight, not slaves«, FS 54).

Wenn dies die grundlegenden Unterschiede zwischen Magie und Kunst sind, und wenn »domination«, »power« und »bewitchment« wesentliche Merkmale magischen Handelns darstellen, handelt dann Felagund in seinem Sangeskampf mit Sauron nicht ebenfalls als Magier? Die für den Zauberer so charakteristische Gier nach egozentrischer Macht (»greed for self-centered power«, FS 53) wird man Felagund sicherlich nicht unterstellen. Dennoch stimmt auch er seine Lieder der Macht zum Zwecke der »domination« an, auch ihm geht es um die Beherrschung und Bezwingung seines Feindes. Schließlich tragen auch Felagunds »songs of power« (S 200) bereits im Titel das Element der Macht. Darüber hinaus weist auch die metaphernreiche und poetische Beschreibung der magischen Auseinandersetzung zwischen Felagund und Sauron im *Silmarillion* darauf hin, dass hier ein Kampf auf Leben und Tod ausgetragen wird:

> He [Sauron] chanted a song of wizardry, / Of piercing, opening, of treachery, /Revealing, uncovering, betraying. / Then sudden Felagund there swaying, / Resisting, battling against power, / Of secrets kept, strength like a tower, /And thus unbroken, freedom, escape; / Of changing and of shifting shape, / Of snares eluded, broken traps, / The prison opening, the chain that snaps. // Backwards and foreward swayed their song.   (S 200f)

Im Gegensatz zu Tolkiens Definition der Elbenkunst als »entirely artistic« steht im Zentrum des Wettstreits von Sauron und Felagund eben nicht das charakteristische »desire for a living, realised sub-creative art« (FS 53), ein Streben, das sich nach Tolkien grundlegend von der Zauberei unterscheidet. Ganz im Gegenteil, hier können wir einen Elben bei der Ausübung von Magie beobachten. Auch Tom Bombadil gibt sich, wie oben bereits deutlich wurde, durch die Bezwingung von Weidenmann und Grabunhold mithilfe von Zauberliedern als Magier zu erkennen. Die Frage, die sich aus diesen Befunden ergeben muss: Steht die Kunst der poetischen Bezauberung tatsächlich am anderen Ende einer gedanklichen Linie von Magie und Kunst?[3] Tolkien selbst bietet eine mögliche Lösung dieser Problematik an. Nicht der Magie- bzw. Kunstgebrauch an sich ist gut oder schlecht, allein die Intention ist entscheidend:

> Neither [*magia* and *goeteia* as two forms of magic] is, in this tale, good or bad (per se), but only by motive or purpose or use. Both sides use both, but with different motives. The supremely bad motive is... domination of other »free« wills.   (L 199f)

Der künstlerisch-magische Liedgebrauch steht demnach im Zeichen eines latenten Widerspruchs: Einerseits heißt es, Magie und Kunst unterscheiden sich grundlegend in ihrer Zielrichtung, andererseits entscheiden allein die guten oder schlechten Absichten über die ethische Beurteilung des Künstlers/Magiers bei der Anwendung der »elvish craft« (FS 53). In Bezug auf die Anwendung der Elbenkunst als Magie bedeutet dies jedoch: Der Künstler hat eine ethische Verantwortung; seine Intentionen entscheiden über die Güte oder Verwerflichkeit seiner Handlungen.

Diese moralische Gratwanderung des Künstlers hat Tolkien in seiner Poetologie mehrfach problematisiert. Von entscheidender Bedeutung ist dabei seine eindringliche Warnung in *On Fairy-Stories*:

> Fantasy can, of course, be carried to excess. It can be ill done. It can be put to evil uses. It may even delude the minds out of which it came.   (ebd. 55)

Diese Warnung vor der Pervertierung des Künstlers durch seine eigene Schöpfungskraft hat zur Folge, dass die Forderung »we shall use that power well« (ebd. 22) eine Maxime darstellt, die das Handeln des Künstlers maßgeblich bestimmen muss, will er nicht zu einem jener gefallenen Künstler werden, die ihre gottgegebene Gabe missbrauchen.

Lúthien Tinúviel: Sirenengesang in Mittelerde

Bevor wir uns abschließend näher mit dem Ethos und der Gefährdung des Künstlers im Kontext von Tolkiens Schöpfungsmythos beschäftigen, soll nun die Figur Lúthien Tinúviels ins Zentrum der Diskussion rücken. Denn an ihr können einige der bisher gewonnenen Ergebnisse verdeutlicht und weitere

---

3   »Faërie itself may perhaps most nearly be translated by Magic – but it is magic of a peculiar mood and power, at the furthest pole from the vulgar devices of the laborious, scientific, magician.« (FS 10)

Einsichten zur Bedeutung der »songs of power« in Tolkiens Werk gewonnen werden.

In welchem Zusammenhang stehen die Sirenen der griechischen Mythologie mit Lúthien Tinúviel? Diese Frage mag irritieren, denn auf den ersten Blick scheinen Lúthien und die Sirenen nichts miteinander gemeinsam zu haben. Lúthien ist weder ein Mischwesen aus Vogel und Frau noch hat sie Ähnlichkeiten mit Meerjungfrauen, wie Sirenen in der literarischen Überlieferung häufig dargestellt werden. Die Analogie zwischen Lúthien und den Sirenen besteht in der Tat nicht in Äußerlichkeiten, sondern lediglich in einem einzigen, wenn auch entscheidenden Aspekt: Sirenen zeichnen sich durch den Liebreiz und die Macht ihres Gesangs aus. Dieser Gesang wird einem der bekanntesten Helden der Antike, Odysseus, in einer Episode der Sage fast zum Verhängnis. Wie die bisherigen Ausführungen gezeigt haben, kann das Zauberlied in Mittelerde eine ähnliche Bedeutung haben.

Im Falle Lúthiens hat der Vergleich mit den Sirenen in zweifacher Hinsicht Relevanz: Lúthien teilt mit den antiken Fabelwesen sowohl die physische Schönheit als auch ihr Talent für Zaubergesang. So heißt es im *Silmarillion* über Lúthiens Erscheinung und Fähigkeiten: »The fame of the beauty of Lúthien and the wonder of her song had long gone forth from Doriath« (S 205).

Auf Basis der bisherigen Ergebnisse liegt die Schlussfolgerung nahe, dass die Formulierung »wonder of her song« hier nicht in erster Linie ästhetische Qualitäten meint, sondern auf ein magisches Potential hindeutet. Ähnlich den Sirenen besitzt Lúthien Macht durch ihre vollendete körperliche Schönheit (»fame of the beauty«) und das Wunder ihrer Lieder. Dass auch Lúthien über »songs of power« gebietet, wird an verschiedenen Stellen im *Silmarillion* deutlich.

Ähnlich wie der griechische Sagenheld Orpheus in die Unterwelt hinabsteigt, um Eurydike durch die Macht seines Gesangs zu befreien, kann Lúthien den in Saurons Kerkern gefangenen Beren nur durch die Zuhilfenahme zweier machtvoller Zaubergesänge retten:[4]

---

4   Auf die Parallele zwischen Lúthien und Orpheus hat bereits Tolkien selbst hingewiesen: So sei die Geschichte der zwei Liebenden »a kind of Orpheus-legend in reverse, but one of Pity not of Inexorability« (L 193). Dass Lúthien in Tolkiens Kosmos als ein weiblicher Orpheus erscheint, wird nicht nur in der durch Zaubergesänge vollbrachten Rettung Berens deutlich. Insbesondere das Ende der Erzählung betont den Orpheus-Bezug. So gelingt es der Elbin, ihren verstorbenen Liebhaber zurück ins Leben zu rufen, indem sie vor Mandos ein Lied anstimmt, das innerhalb von Tolkiens Kosmos geradezu legendär ist: »The song of Lúthien before Mandos was the song most fair that ever in words was woven, and the song most sorrowful that ever the world shall hear... For Lúthien wove two themes of words, of the sorrow of the Eldar and the grief of Men, of the Two Kindreds that were made by Ilúvatar to dwell in Arda, the Kingdom of Earth amid the innumerable stars. And... Mandos was moved to pity, who never before was, nor has been since« (S 220).

> In that hour Lúthien came, and standing upon the bridge that
> led to Sauron's isle she sang a song, that no walls of stone could
> hinder. Beren heard and he thought that he dreamed; for the stars
> shone above him, and in the trees the nightingales were singing.
> And in answer he sang a song of challenge... But Lúthien heard his
> answering and she sang a song of greater power. (ebd. 204)

Die magische Wirkung (»a song that no walls could hinder«) wird hier eindeutig mit poetischer Sprache erzielt. Offenbar sind nicht die Worte allein für die magische Wirkung verantwortlich, sondern ebenso die Art des lyrischen Vortrags. Zauberei erscheint hier als eine Form der poetischen Sprachmagie (vgl. Eilmann 120f). An anderer Stelle der Erzählung wird erkennbar, dass im Falle Lúthiens tatsächlich ähnlich den Sirenen leibliche Schönheit und magischer Gesang für den Erfolg eines Unternehmens ausschlaggebend sind. So kommt es in Morgoths Thronsaal zur Konfrontation zwischen den beiden Liebenden mit dem dunklen Herrscher von Angband. Jedoch ist es nicht Beren, der den Feind überwindet und die Wiedergewinnung des Silmarils ermöglicht. Es ist Lúthien, der es gelingt, Morgoth zu bezwingen:

> She was not daunted by his eyes; and... she eluded his sight, and
> out of the shadows began a song of such surpassing loveliness, and
> of such blinding power, that he listened perforce; and a blindness
> came upon him... All his court were cast down in slumber, and
> all the fires faded and were quenched (S 212f)

Lúthiens Lied ist beides: Meisterhaftes Kunstwerk (»a song of such surpassing loveliness«) und Zauberspruch (»and of such blinding power«). Darüber hinaus stellt Lúthiens »song of power« ein entscheidendes Plotelement dar, denn ohne ihren magischen Zaubergesang hätte der Silmaril nicht zurückgewonnen werden können.

Wichtig ist es, an dieser Stelle auf einen weiteren Aspekt dieser Szene näher einzugehen: Nachdem das Lied verklungen ist, befindet sich der ganze Hofstaat in schlafenden Zustand. Offensichtlich besteht die Macht dieses speziellen Liedes darin, die Zuhörer mit Blindheit zu schlagen (»blinding power«) und sie in Schlaf zu versetzen. Wir können demnach festhalten: Lúthiens Zaubergesang ist ein Schlafzauber.

Auch an anderer Stelle in seinem Werk beschreibt Tolkien einschläfernden Zaubergesang: Zum Beispiel ist der Weidenmann Anwender eines Schlafzaubers. Er wird, wie bereits erwähnt, als Zauberkundiger (»a mighty singer«, LotR 124) eingeführt, der die Hobbits mit magischen Mitteln am Verlassen des Alten Waldes hindern möchte. Tolkien legt bei seiner Schilderung des Geschehens sehr großen Wert darauf, deutlich zu machen, dass hier tatsächlich ein Lied die magische Wirkung herbeiführt:

> They looked up at the grey and yellow leaves, moving softly against the light, and singing... it seemed that they could almost hear words, cool words, saying something about water and sleep. They gave themselves up to the spell and fell fast asleep at the foot of the great grey willow. (LotR 114)

Dass Blätterrauschen wie ein Flüstern klingen kann, ist in keiner Weise verwunderlich. Die Textbelege weisen jedoch eindeutig darauf hin, dass das Singen, das die Hobbits vernehmen, tatsächlich als ein magischer Gesang aufzufassen ist. So spricht auch Sam selbst von einem Schlafzauber, unter den sie gefallen sind: »I don't like this great big tree. I don't trust it. Hark at it singing about sleep now« (ebd. 115).
Eindeutig wird hier ein Lied für die Ausübung von Macht funktionalisiert. Dieses Zauberlied hat jedoch keinerlei Kunstcharakter, sondern ist bloße »technique« (FS 53) im Sinne Tolkiens. Es zielt auf »power in this world, domination of things and wills« (ebd.).

Um das Phänomen des gesungenen Schlafzaubers besser zu verstehen, sind die Forschungen von Gisela Just hilfreich, die sich eingehend mit magischer Musik und Gesang im Märchen beschäftigt hat. So weist Just darauf hin, dass in einer phantastischen Erzählung wie dem Märchen der Schlaf, in den man durch Gesang versetzt wird, kein gewöhnlicher Schlaf ist. Ein solcher Schlaf ist ein magischer Schlaf, und ein solches Lied ist ein Zauberlied (vgl. Just 80). Zur Funktion des gesungenen Schlafzaubers kommt Gisela Just zu folgendem Ergebnis: »Der Zauberschlaf währt nicht hundert Jahre (wie bei Dornröschen), nur gerade so lange, bis der Schlafende das, was er tun wollte, nicht mehr tun kann« (ebd.).

Auch in Tolkiens Werk werden gesungene Schlafzauber in dieser Form verwendet. Sowohl Lúthien Tinúviel als auch der Weidenmann nutzen ihr kreativmagisches Potential in dieser Form. Während jedoch Lúthiens Gesang noch einen deutlichen Kunstcharakter besitzt (s.o.), handelt es sich beim Schlafgesang des Weidenmannes um Magie im negativen Sinne.
Die jeweils unterschiedlichen ethischen Motive der Sänger lassen somit vor dem Hintergrund von Tolkiens Diskussion des Verhältnisses von Kunst und Magie eine Wertung der magischen Handlung zu. Die gewonnenen Ergebnisse führen uns zu einem Aspekt, der abschließend eine weitere Perspektive zulässt.

Julian Eilmann

Der pervertierte Künstler

Wie wir feststellen konnten, kreist die Frage nach dem Verhältnis von Gesang und Gewalt entschieden um das Problem der ethischen Verantwortung des Künstlers. Da Tolkien das Konzept des Zweitschöpfertums ins Zentrum seiner Poetologie rückt, muss er das Wesen der Kunst genauer untersuchen. Zwar definiert Tolkien Magie hinsichtlich ihrer Ziele gewissermaßen als das Gegenteil der Kunst, dennoch macht sein literarisches Werk deutlich, dass Zauberei und Kunst auf dieselben schöpferischen Wurzeln zurückgehen. Aus diesem Grund kann Magie durchaus als pervertierte Kunst und der Magier als der korrumpierte Künstler begriffen werden. Wie ist das zu verstehen?

Wie deutlich wurde, sind in Tolkiens Mythologie Kunst und Magie beide Ausdruck des kreativen Schöpfungspotentials des Menschen. Beiden kreativen Ausdrucksformen liegt somit derselbe Schöpfungswille zugrunde. Diese ausgeprägte Schaffenskraft ist es jedoch gerade, die den Künstlern bzw. Magiern zum Verhängnis wird. Diejenigen, die in der »elvish craft« (FS 53) besonders begabt sind, sind auch in hohem Maße der Gefahr ausgesetzt, ihr Potential zu missbrauchen. Melkor, Sauron und Feanor sind die prominentesten Beispiele dieser Künstlerfiguren, die ihre Schöpfungskraft überschätzen bzw. für ethisch fragwürdige Zwecke verwenden.

So resultiert die Rebellion Melkors gegen den Schöpfergott Illúvatar gerade aus Melkors Willen, selbst erstschöpferisch tätig zu werden, und nicht lediglich im Rahmen der ihm gegebenen Möglichkeiten zweitschöpferisch zu wirken. Wir erfahren über Melkor im *Silmarillion*:

> But as the theme [of Illúvatar] progressed, it came into the heart of Melkor to interweave matters of his own imagining that were not in accord with the theme of Illúvatar; for he sought therein to increase the power and glory of the part assigned to himself. To Melkor among the Ainur had been given the greatest gifts of power and knowledge, ... He had often gone alone into the void places seeking the Imperishable Flame; for desire grew hot within him to bring into Being things of his own. (S 4)

Melkor wird hier als große Künstlerfigur präsentiert, die über immense kreative Fähigkeiten verfügt, eigene Gedanken in die Tat umsetzen will und nach der unmittelbaren Schöpfungskraft verlangt. Weil Melkor als ein Wesen mit den »greatest gifts of power and knowledge« in Tolkiens Kosmologie beschrieben wird, liegt es nahe, Melkor als die größte Künstlerfigur in Tolkiens Werk zu verstehen. Der Fall Melkors, seine Wandlung von einem der Ainur zum schwarzen Feind der Welt, ist demnach ein Verrat des Künstlers an der Kunst bzw. an der Schöpfungskraft. Mehr noch: Da die Kunst bei Tolkien eindeutig als gottgegebene Gabe bezeichnet wird, stellt die Pervertierung des Künstlers gleichzeitig einen Verrat am Schöpfergott selbst dar.

Versteht man Melkor in dieser Weise als fehlgeleiteten Künstler, dann können seine späteren verwerflichen Taten (z.B. die Missgestaltung der Welt oder die Erschaffung der Orks, wenn man sie ihm denn zusprechen möchte) als versuchte erstschöpferische Handlungen verstanden werden. Diese Versuche, die Ausdruck seines wesensmäßigen Unvermögens sind, aus sich selbst heraus zu schaffen, sind jedoch letztlich zum Scheitern verurteilt. Melkors Despotismus, seine Negation bzw. Zerstörung aller anderen zweitschöpferischen Leistungen (z.B. die Vernichtung der zwei Bäume Valinors), spiegelt seine luziferische Rolle als Schwarzer Feind (vgl. S 23 u. 67) und ist somit als Ausdruck eines fehlgeleiteten Künstlertums deutbar. Aus diesem Grunde ist es auch nicht weiter verwunderlich, dass der gescheiterte Zweitschöpfer Morgoth als Meister der verderbten Zauberkunst alle negativen Aspekte verkörpert, die Tolkien der Magie zuordnet (s.o.).

Tolkien selbst hat den Fall des schöpferischen Subjekts, dem die notwendige Demut vor Schöpfer und Schöpfung fehlt, mit großer Eindringlichkeit in einem seiner Briefe geschildert:

> [My mythology] is mainly concerned with Fall, Mortality, and the Machine. With Fall inevitably, and that motive occurs in several modes. With Mortality, especially as it affects art and the creative (or as I should say, the sub-creative) desire which seems to have no biological function and to be apart from the satisfactions of plain ordinary biological life, with which, in our world, it is indeed usually at strife. This desire is at once wedded to a passionate love for the real primary world, and hence filled with the sense of mortality, and yet unsatisfied by it. It has various opportunities of ›Fall‹. It may become possessive, clinging to the things made as ›its own‹, the sub-creator wishes to be the Lord and God of his private creation. He will rebel against the laws of the Creator – especially against mortality. Both of these (along or together) will lead to the desire for Power, for making the will more quickly effective, – and so to the Machine (or Magic). (L 145)

Dass die Korrumpierung des von einer existentiellen schöpferischen Sehnsucht (»creative... desire«) getriebenen Individuums mit einer Hinwendung zu Magie und Technik einhergeht, macht unmissverständlich klar, welchen Stellenwert dieses Thema in Tolkiens Gesamtwerk einnimmt.

Auf weitere Beispiele aus dem Mittelerde-Kosmos soll an dieser Stelle nicht mehr eingegangen werden. Interessant ist jedoch, dass selbst eine Figur wie Saruman als ein korrumpierter Künstler verstanden werden kann, denn auch er ist ein Wesen, das über »Olos« (UT 396), die Elbenkunst, gebietet. Bei Sarumans magischen Künsten dominiert jedoch das Element der Technik (vgl. Hageböck 64f). Da auch in seinem Falle die notwendige Demut fehlt und er das schöpferische Potential in destruktiven Akten missbraucht, wird auch der ehemals Weiße Zauberer zu einem gefallenen Zweitschöpfer und fortan zu einem »Lord of magic and machines« (L 146).

Zusammenfassung und Ausblick

Gefallene Künstlerfiguren wie Melkor oder Saruman haben uns noch einmal das spannungsvolle Verhältnis von Kunst und Magie verdeutlicht. Konfliktaustragung findet in Tolkiens Werk nicht nur mit Waffengewalt statt, auch Lieder und Gesang können hierbei zum Einsatz kommen. Tolkien hat für Lieder, die auf diese Weise verwendet werden, den Begriff »songs of power« geprägt. Solche Zauberlieder verweisen innerhalb von Tolkiens Mythologie auf das schöpferische Potential der Kunst, jenes Moment der poetischen Bezauberung, das im Falle der »songs of power« jedoch auch das Element der negativ konnotierten »domination« enthält. Tolkiens Lieder der Macht verweisen demnach auf den problematischen Gegensatz von Kunst und Magie, der zentral für Tolkiens Ethik der Kunst ist.

Die ethische Problematik, die sich durch die »songs of power« ergibt, zeigt sich in den Konflikten, die mit ihnen ausgetragen werden. Die Auseinandersetzung zwischen Sauron und Felagund ist hierfür beispielhaft, denn sie bringt den Sänger, wie deutlich geworden ist, in eine ethisch schwierige Situation. Vor dem Hintergrund von Tolkiens Erörterung des Verhältnisses von Kunst und Magie entscheiden in einer solchen Konfliktsituation die Motive des Sängers darüber, ob eine solche Verwendung von Gesang als Machtmittel moralisch verwerflich ist oder nicht.

Des Weiteren wurde deutlich, dass »songs of power« u.a. in Form von Schlafzaubern zur Anwendung kommen. Auch hierbei entscheiden die Intentionen der Zauberanwender über die moralische Wertung.

Insgesamt bleibt festzuhalten, dass die Frage nach dem angemessenen Gebrauch von »songs of power« in Konfliktsituationen auf das Herz von Tolkiens Poetologie zurückverweist, nämlich auf die Bedeutung des schöpferischen Potentials für den Menschen als Gattungswesen. Da Tolkien nicht müde wird, die Bedeutung dieser kreativen Kraft des Menschen zu betonen, eine Kraft, die er sogar als ein regelrechtes Menschenrecht bezeichnet[5], wird deutlich, dass es Tolkien in seinem dichterischen Werk vehement um eine Verteidigung der poetischen Phantasie geht, ja um eine regelrechte Apologie der Kunst. Aber diese Frage weiter zu verfolgen, muss einer späteren Studie vorbehalten bleiben.

Bibliographie

Beth, Karl. »Das Verhältnis von Magie und Religion«. *Magie und Religion. Beiträge zu einer Theorie der Magie*. Hg. Leander Petzoldt. Darmstadt: WBG, 1978, 27-46

Eilmann, Julian. »Das Lied bin ich. Lieder, Poesie und Musik in J.R.R. Tolkiens Mittelerde-Mythologie«. *Hither Shore 2* (2005): 105-135

Fornet-Ponse, Thomas, Karl u. Adelheid Kegler: »Was bedeutet die Untersuchung von Magie für Tolkiens Werk? Eine Entgegnung auf Michael K. Hageböck«. *Inklings-Jahrbuch 22* (2004): 212-242

Hageböck, Michael K. »Kunst und Technik: Anmerkungen zu Tolkiens Magie Begriff«. *Inklings-Jahrbuch 21* (2003): 37-85

Just, Gisela. *Magische Musik im Märchen. Untersuchungen zur Funktion magischen Singens und Spielens in Volkserzählungen*. Frankfurt: Verlag Peter Lang, 1991

Petzoldt, Leander. *Magie und Religion. Beiträge zu einer Theorie der Magie*. Darmstadt: WBG, 1978

Stockhammer, Robert. *Zaubertexte. Die Wiederkehr der Magie und die Literatur 1880–1945*. Berlin: Akademie Verlag, 2000

Tolkien, J.R.R. *The Lord of the Rings*. London: HarperCollins, 1995

---. *The Letters of J.R.R. Tolkien*. Hg. Humphrey Carpenter. London: HarperCollins, 1981

---. »On Fairy-Stories«. *Tree and Leaf*. London: Unwin, 1964, 1-81

---. *The Silmarillion*. Hg. Christopher Tolkien. London: HarperCollins, 1999

---. *Unfinished Tales of Númenor and Middle-earth*. Hg. Christopher Tolkien. London: Allen&Unwin, 1980

---

5 »Fantasy remains a human right: we make in our measure and in our derivative mode, because we are made: and not only made, but made in the image and likeness of a Maker.« (FS 56)

Von kühner Recken Streiten?
Höfische Akteure und Heroische Gewalt in Tolkiens *Farmer Giles of Ham*

Patrick Brückner (Potsdam)

> Mit dem guoten swerte, / daz hiez Balmunc
> durch die starken vorhte / vil manec recke junc,
> die si zem swerte héten / und an den küenen man,
> daz lánt zúo den bürgen / si im tâten undertân.
> (*Nibelungenlied* St. 95)

Ritter?

enn man[1] über Krieg und Gewalt bei Tolkien sprechen will, dann ist sicherlich *Farmer Giles of Ham* nicht der Text, an den in diesem Zusammenhang zuerst gedacht wird, sondern wohl eher *The Lord of the Rings*. Spricht man über *Farmer Giles of Ham,* so stehen meistens die komischen Tendenzen im Zentrum der Interpretation (so die Forschung sich mit diesem Text überhaupt beschäftigt). In diesem Befund werden die durchaus vorhandenen Szenen subsummiert, in denen Gewalt eine Rolle spielt.[2] Dies scheint auf den ersten Blick auch legitim, mutet die Gewalt in diesem Text doch nicht mehr an als ein Beitrag zur Komik des Textes. Es gibt lediglich ein individualisiertes Opfer zu beklagen: den bedauernswerten Pfarrer von Oakley (vgl. FGH 48). Dessen Tod jedoch – er wird vom Drachen gefressen – geht durch die Information »the parson of Oakley had been stringy« (FGH 68) in der Komik des Textes auf. Ebenso scheinen der Held Giles of Ham, die Ritter, der König und selbst der Drache allesamt lediglich als parodistische Figuren entworfen.

Doch Tom Shippey hat recht, wenn er sagt, »the story makes a point, and a rather aggressive« (Shippey 290); doch zielt diese Aggressivität auf mehr als nur die Verspottung des »›correct and sober taste‹ of [Tolkiens] literary contemporaries« (Shippey 291).

---

[1] Der Text verwendet die Formulierung man und die männliche Schreibform (z.B. Leser). Aus Gründen der Lesbarkeit und Kürze wird auf die Schreibweisen frau, »...-Innen« oder Verdoppelungen wie »Leser und Leserinnen« verzichtet. Es wird freundlich gebeten, hieran keinen Anstoß zu nehmen.

[2] Jane Chance Nitzsche sei als ein Beispiel genannt, die ausführt: »*Farmer Giles of Ham* represents Tolkien's only medieval parody« (Chance 85).

Farmer Giles of Ham ist geeignet zu zeigen, nach welchem Prinzip Tolkien Entstehung von Geschichte – im Falle *Farmer Giles of Ham* »the origin of some difficult place-names« (FGH 6) – konzipiert.³

Dass Gewalt dabei (auch in *Farmer Giles of Ham*) eine wesentliche Rolle spielt, wird deutlich, wenn man eine der vielleicht zentralen Fragen im Text ernst nimmt, nämlich die Frage, was ein Ritter sei.

Die Frage, was einen Ritter ausmacht, wird im Text immer wieder gestellt (vgl. z.B. FGH 46, 70). Sie wird auch immer wieder unterschiedlich beantwortet: ein Schwert, eine Rüstung, ein Ritterschlag, »a red letter [from the King]« (vgl. FGH 46, 70, 94) kann einen Ritter machen. Oder ist »courage ... all that is needed« (FGH 46)?

Bevor geklärt werden kann, was in *Farmer Giles of Ham* einen Ritter ausmacht, scheint es hilfreich, diese Frage durch einen mittelalterlichen Dichter beantworten zu lassen. Hartmann von Aue lässt seinen Helden Iwein im gleichnamigen Text auf die Frage, was wohl ›aventiure‹ sei, antworten:

> nû sich wie ich gewâfent bin:
> ich heize ein riter und hân den sin
> daz ich suochende rîte
> einen man der mit mir strîte,
> der gewâfent sî als ich.
> daz prîset in, und sleht er mich:
> gesige aber ich im an,
> sô hât man mich vür einen man,
> und wirde werde danne ich sî.
>
> (*Iwein* V. 529-536)⁴

Es scheint offensichtlich, dass Gewalt und Gewaltfähigkeit ursächlich vorausgesetzt werden müssen, wenn man von einem mittelalterlichen Ritter spricht.

Gewaltfähigkeit ist ein konstituierendes Element für die Identität des höfischen Ritters, weil durch sie ›êre‹ generiert wird. Die beste ›aventiure‹ verweist auf den besten (weil gewaltfähigsten) Ritter, wobei als die vorrangige Gefahr eben nicht der Verlust des Lebens, sondern der Verlust von ›êre‹ anzunehmen

---

3   Ein Indiz für den konzeptuellen Charakter des *Farmer Giles of Ham* mag der Fakt sein, das Tolkien diese Geschichte »in lieu of a paper ›on‹ fairy stories« (L 39) vor der Lovelace Society vortrug.

4   Sieh her welche Rüstung ich trage (wie ich bewaffnet bin). Man nennt mich Ritter, und ich habe die Absicht auszureiten auf die Suche nach einem Mann, der mit mir kämpfe und der Waffen trägt wie ich. Schlägt er mich, so bringt ihm das Ruhm ein, siege aber ich über ihn, so sieht man einen echten Mann in mir und ich habe mehr Ehre als bisher.

ist. Dies ist jedoch existenziell, betrifft und zerstört dieser Verlust doch die Identität des Ritters.[5]

Nun wird ›ère‹, also der Einsatz, um den im ritterlichen Kampf des höfischen Modells gefochten wird, im Regelfall in und durch gegenseitige Anerkennung der Kämpfenden generiert. Es geht eben nicht um die physische Vernichtung des Gegners, sondern um dessen (freiwillige) Unterwerfung unter den besseren Ritter, der im vorausgehenden Kampf ermittelt wird. Dies bedingt also jeweils zwei Ritter, die an diesem Spiel um den Einsatz ›ère‹ teilnehmen. Kämpfen heißt für einen Ritter in diesem Fall immer auch ein Erkennen und Anerkennen des Anderen als Ritter. So wird die Identität Ritter für beide Kämpfenden in einer wechselseitigen Reziprozität generiert. Der Ort für diese ritterliche Gewalt ist die ›aventiure‹ und stellt einen höfischen Akt dar, der einem Normenkatalog (Herausforderung, Nennen des Namens etc.) unterworfen ist. Folglich agiert der Ritter nie als vereinzeltes Individuum (auch wenn er allein auf ›aventiure‹-Fahrt ist), sondern ist immer in eine höfische Ordnung eingebunden und setzt sich immer zu dieser in Beziehung. Im Falle Iweins ist dies der Artushof[6] (vgl. Haferland, *Interaktion* 73 ff).

In Tolkiens *Farmer Giles of Ham* wird die Frage nach Ritterschaft zuallererst in Bezug auf den Titelhelden der Geschichte gestellt. Die Dorfbewohner diskutieren sie vor dem Auszug gegen den Drachen. Auch der Drache selbst bezeichnet Giles als Ritter und der König benutzt diese Bezeichnung in Zusammenhang mit ihm. Die Grundlage, auf der diese Bezeichnung an Giles herangetragen wird, ist seine bewiesene Gewaltfähigkeit, die ihn in die Lage versetzt »to deal with giants, dragons, and other enemies of the King's peace« (FGH 90).

Giles selbst jedoch behauptet von sich mehrmals: »I am no knight« (FGH 46, 70). Ob er damit Recht hat, wird noch zu fragen sein, doch erscheint es sinnvoll, zunächst die Frage zu stellen, was denn einen Ritter in Tolkiens *Farmer Giles of Ham* ausmacht und wie sich dieses Konzept mit dem mittelalterlichen in Verbindung bringen lässt. Denn tatsächlich gibt es dort Rittertum: in der Gestalt der Ritter des Königs, des Königshofes, und letztlich in der Präsenz des Königs selbst.

---

5   Der Ritter Iwein etwa verliert »vil gar vreude und den sin« (Frohsinn und Verstand, *Iwein* V. 3215) und »verlôs sîn selbes hulde« (Er begann sich selbst zu hassen, *Iwein* V. 3221), nachdem seine ›êre‹ öffentlich gemindert wurde. Die direkte Folge dieser Minderung ist ein kompletter Verlust seiner ritterlichen Identität: »er brach sîne site und sîne zuht / und zarte abe sîn gewant, / daz er wart blôz sam ein hant. / sus lief er über gevilde / nacket nâch der wilde. / ... der lief nû harte balde / ein tôre in dem walde.« (Er vergaß seine Gesittung und Erziehung und riss sich das Gewand vom Leibe, dass er splitternackt war. So lief er über das Feld nackt der Wildnis zu. ... der lief nun als Wahnsinniger im Wald umher, *Iwein* V. 3234-3261)

6   Der Begriff ›aventiure‹ ist untrennbar mit dem mittelalterlichen Ritterbegriff verbunden. Iwein wird nicht gefragt, was ein Ritter, sondern was ›aventiure‹ sei, und erklärt doch in seiner Antwort, was ein Ritter ist (vgl. *Iwein* V. 527).

Spricht man über die Ritter am Hofe des Königs des Middle Kingdom, so fällt zunächst auf, dass diese sich in einem Dienstverhältnis befinden. Der Ritter, der ausgewählt wird, um sich auf die Suche nach einem Drachenschwanz für das Weihnachtsessen zu begeben, wird »for the duty of hunting« (FGH 32) ausgewählt und als der König nach dem ersten Drachenkampf in Ham einreitet, werden mit den Worten »liege« und »suzerain« (FGH 82) Termini verwendet, die deutlich auf feudales Recht verweisen. Ritter und König bilden einen feudalen Verbund in dem Herrschaft offensichtlich auf (Lehns-)Recht basiert. Der Anspruch, den der König bei diesem Anlass auf den Drachenhort – er sagt, der gesamte Schatz des Drachen sei seinen Vorfahren gestohlen worden – erhebt, zeigt dies ebenso wie die Selbstproklamation eben zum obersten Lehnsherr des Berglandes (FGH 82). Die Vasallität, die für die Ritter des Hofes angenommen werden kann (der König kann sie zum Zug gegen den Drachen auffordern und sie müssen folgen; vgl. FGH 90), hat zur Folge, dass die persönliche Bewährung des Ritters in Tolkiens Text offenbar immer auch als Machtdemonstration des politischen Verbandes zu verstehen ist.

Der einzelne Ritter erwirbt jedoch im Text persönliche êre im Turnier, das als quasi spielerische Variante der ›aventiure‹ betrachtet werden kann. Gleichzeitig muss dieses Turnier im Text als Grund der Ritter für die Unmöglichkeit gegen den Drachen zu ziehen herhalten (vgl. FGH 44). Der Drache ist für die mittelländischen Ritter offensichtlich leichter hinzunehmen als die Aussicht, durch einen Kampf gegen ihn das Turnier zu verpassen und so die eigene Chance auf den Erwerb von ›êre‹ zu gefährden (vgl. FGH 44). Das Turnier, in dem ›êre‹ nach dem im Iwein auffindbaren Muster der gemeinsam-gegnerischen Reziprozität im Kampf generiert wird, muss also in *Farmer Giles of Ham* als die bessere ›aventiure‹ im Vergleich zum Drachenkampf verstanden werden und besitzt deshalb zwangsläufig für die höfischen Ritter den Vorrang.

Diese Logik ist eigentlich zwingend, denn die ›aventiure‹ dient nicht allein dem individuellen Ehrerwerb, sondern sie konstituiert höfische Ordnung. In dieser Logik ist auch die symbolische Jagd nach dem Drachenschwanz zu verstehen, die alljährlich den schon erwähnten Jagd-Dienst mit sich bringt. Der Hof und das höfische Fest sind hier als »gewaltfreier und gleichwohl von êre erfüllter« (Czerwinski 454) Raum zu denken, der aber nur durch herausragende Gewaltfähigkeit konstituierbar ist. Deshalb ist einerseits die Aussendung des Ritters durchaus sinnvoll, weil durch sie eben jene Gewaltfähigkeit des Einzelnen und damit des gesamten Hofes demonstriert wird. Der Ausritt ist ganz und gar ethischer Natur. Der Drache taugt deshalb als ›aventiure‹, aber nur insoweit, als ein Sieg über ihn, der die höfische Ordnung stört, zu einer Anerkennung durch ein oder mehrere reziproke Individuen (also andere Adelige) und dadurch letztlich durch die höfische Öffentlichkeit führt und das höfische Ideal herstellt. Das weihnachtliche Essen des Drachenschwanzkuchens bedient sich dieses Musters.

Auf der anderen Seite entsteht hier eine Art von Komik, über die noch zu reden sein wird und durch die Sinnentlehrung der gesamten Prozedur bedingt ist. Denn obwohl es ja offensichtlich Drachen gibt, bleibt der Ausritt des zum Jagd-Dienst ausersehenen Ritters nur symbolisch. Der am Ende kredenzte Drachenschwanz ist aus Kuchen (vgl. FGH 32). Die Funktion, die allerdings von Dorfbewohnern erwartet wird, nämlich die des Beschützers des Landes (FGH 44), erfüllen die Ritter in *Farmer Giles of Ham* nicht.

Dies darf allerdings keinesfalls mit fehlender Gewaltfähigkeit verwechselt werden, wie eben das Turnier als spielerische, aber auch die Schlacht an der Brücke von Ham (FGH 122) als militärische Form der Gewaltausübung zeigen.

Helden!

Welche Rolle übernimmt nun der titelgebende Held Giles in dieser Geschichte? Mehr noch als die Ritter erscheint er als ein Träger der Komik im Text. Eine Parodie auf die ohnehin schon komischen Ritter des Königshofes. Doch greift dieser Befund zu kurz.[7] Natürlich ist die Vertreibung des Riesen,

---

7 Auf die Komik, die diesem Text zweifellos innewohnt, kann hier nicht im gebührenden Maße eingegangen, doch soll kurz versucht werden, ihren Sinn zu erhellen. Sicherlich sind es gerade die komischen Elemente, die den Text als »entirely lighthearted« (Shippey 289) erscheinen lassen. Doch was ist der Sinn dieser Komik. Shippeys Interpretation von der Verspottung des korrekten, nüchternen Geschmacks seiner literarischen Zeitgenossen (Shippey 291) erscheint hier als vielleicht nicht weitreichend genug. Es soll kurz versucht werden, einen anderen Ansatz aufzuzeigen. Dieser ergibt sich, wenn man sich dem *Beowulf* zuwendet, ein Text, der, wenn man *Farmer Giles of Ham* genauer betrachtet, in diesem deutliche Spuren hinterlassen hat (vgl. Brückner 272 ff). Alois Wolf weist auf den Fakt hin, dass »die Hauptgestalt dieses großangelegten Epos in den verschiedenen Formen der Überlieferung keine Spuren hinterlassen hat. Er gehört also mit Sicherheit nicht zur germanischen Heldensagenprominenz... Das heißt aber andererseits, dass dieser Beowulf sagenhistorisch nicht besonders belastet war« (Wolf 87). Aus dieser Feststellung entwickelt Wolf die Überlegung, dass es im *Beowulf* nicht nur um die »Sicherung der Autorität des Berichteten [geht], sondern darum, die Andersartigkeit dieses Geschehens in der heldischen Vorzeit zu verdeutlichen« (Wolf 107). Die Modellhaftigkeit, mit der Heldensage als Aspekt einer umfassenden Vergangenheitskunde im *Beowulf* inszeniert wird, legt es nahe, einen sagenhistorisch unbelasteten Heroen als Akteur zu wählen (vgl. Wolf 87). Um Vergangenheitskunde geht es auch im *Farmer Giles of Ham*, daran lässt die Vorrede keinen Zweifel. Es handelt sich, so der Text, um ein »origin [that] has been preserved: a legend, perhaps, rather than an account; for it is evidently a late compilation« (FGH 6). Wenn man Wolfs These nun auf Giles anwendet, könnte hier ein Grund für die komischen Elemente im Text liegen. Ähnlich wie beim *Beowulf*-Dichter scheint das Problem eines ›etablierten‹ Helden darin zu liegen, dass dieser die Auswahl an möglichen Perspektiven einschränkt, »es sei denn, man hätte das ganze Sagengefüge aus dem [dieser Held] stammte, über den Haufen geworfen« (Wolf 87). Die Komik, die der Figur Giles anhängt, könnte als ein Mittel verstanden werden, ihn aus der Perspektive des ›etablierten‹ Helden herauszunehmen. Dies würde zum Beispiel die höchst anachronistische ›blunderbuss‹ erklären, die Giles, anders als das Schwert Tailbiter, nicht in den Verdacht geraten lässt, er könnte einem bekannten epischen Helden nachempfunden sein.

die mittels der ›blunderbuss‹ auf höchst unritterliche Weise geschieht (vgl. FGH 20 ff), komisch; und auch die von den Dorfbewohnern für den Drachenkampf angefertigte Rüstung – sie improvisieren Kettenhemd und Helm (vgl. FGH 60 f) – parodiert in einer schlechten Imitation die Ausstattung eines Ritters. Die Parodie wäre einleuchtend, wäre da nicht das Schwert Tailbiter, ein Geschenk des Königs an Giles nach der Vertreibung des Riesen (vgl. FGH 32). Dieses Schwert, einst im Besitz des legendären Drachentöters Bellomarius (vgl. FGH 54), ist ein Zeichen für die Brisanz, die der Figur Giles bereits am Anfang des Textes anhaftet.

Dass Giles Recht hat, wenn er immer wieder sagt, er sei kein Ritter, zeigt sich schon sehr früh im Text; doch dies liegt nicht daran, dass er eine bloß komische Figur ist, sondern an einem anderen Prinzip, nach dem die Figur funktioniert. Ein erster Beleg für dieses andere Prinzip ist die Methode, mit der für Giles ›êre‹ generiert wird. Nach dem Sieg über den Riesen »the news had spread to all the villages within twenty miles. He [Giles] had become the Hero of the Countryside« (FGH 30). Auffällig ist, in welchen Zusammenhang Giles selbst diesen Fakt setzt: Er beginnt »old heroic songs« (FGH 30) zu singen. Was also fehlt, ist die Reziprozität, die für den Ehrerwerb des Ritters nötig ist. Zwar kommt auch Anerkennung vonseiten des Hofes (durch Schwert und den erwähnten »red letter«, FGH 30), doch scheint dies für Giles keine vorrangige Bedeutung zu besitzen, wie der Disput der Dorfbewohner zeigt, bei dem Giles sagt: »There's more to knighthood than a sword... Anyway I've my own business to attend to« (FGH 46).

Dass Giles wahrlich kein (höfischer) Ritter ist, wird bei dessen erster Begegnung mit dem Drachen Chrysophylax deutlich. Chrysophylax beklagt, nachdem er in Giles einen Ritter erkannt zu haben glaubt, die fehlenden ritterlichen Gepflogenheiten. Es sei »the custom of knights to issue a challenge in such cases [der Begegnung mit einem potentiellen Gegner] after a proper exchange of titles and credentials« (FGH 70).

Dies ist, wie schon erwähnt, eine der Stellen im Text, in der Giles sagt: »I am no knight. I am Farmer Ægidius of Ham; and I can't abide trespassers. I've shot giants with my blunderbuss before now... And I issued no challenge neither« (FGH 70 f). Giles' offensichtlich unritterliches Verhalten resultiert hier (anders als die improvisierte Rüstung) nicht aus einem Defizit, das ihn komisch erscheinen ließe, sondern zeigt deutlich das andere (nicht höfisch-ritterliche) Prinzip, nach dem die Figur funktioniert.

Denn betrachtet man die kurz darauf folgende Szene, wird die Differenz zu den Rittern im Text deutlich: »[Giles] stepped towards Chrysophylax, waving his arms as if he was scaring crows. That was quite enough for Tailbiter. It circled flashing in the air; then down it came, smiting the dragon on the joint of the right wing, a ringing blow that shocked him exceedingly« (FGH 72).

Giles Angriff folgt keinem höfischen Muster, sondern geschieht im Zorn. Dies mag unritterlich erscheinen. Doch in der Antwort der Dorfbewohner auf die Frage, was einen Ritter ausmacht (»courage is all that is needed«, FGH 46), findet sich ein weiteres Indiz für die Art von Heldentum, die Giles verkörpert.

Zwar scheint es mit Giles' Mut nicht zu weit her zu sein, dreimal muss er von den Dorfbewohnern aufgefordert und bedrängt werden, ehe er gegen den Drachen zieht (vgl. FGH 46, 48, 54), doch dann »it came over him all of a sudden that he would take Tailbiter and go dragon hunting« (FGH 56).

Das Schwert Tailbiter scheint bei diesem ganzen Vorgang eine nicht unwesentliche Rolle zu spielen. Als Geschenk des Königs für den Sieg über den Riesen in den Besitz von Giles gelangt, wird es von den Dorfbewohnern erst als Signifikant einer möglichen Ritterwürde des Bauern gedeutet (vgl. FGH 46). Doch ist das Schwert weit mehr als nur dies: »This sword... will no stay sheathed, if a dragon is within five miles, and without doubt in a brave man's hands no dragon can resist it« (FGH 54). Dieses Schwert befand sich einst im Besitz des legendären, in Liedern besungenen Drachentöters Bellomarius; und der Augenblick, in dem es Giles ›überkommt‹, gegen den Drachen zu ziehen, überschneidet sich mit einer Erinnerung an die Geschichten über eben jenen Helden (vgl. FGH 46). Die Identität des Helden wird nun durch seine Taten gegen das Ungeheuer definiert und eben nicht durch ritterliche Waffengänge (wie sie am Hofe des Königs üblich sind).

Bellomarius ist ein Held und Drachentöter. Was aber unterscheidet einen Helden und einen Ritter in dieser Logik? Wieder kann eine mittelalterliche Quelle einen Anhaltspunkt geben. Im *Deutschen Heldenbuch* (im Druck von 1590) wird beschrieben, was ein Held ist und wie die Helden auf die Erde kamen: Gott schuf die Zwerge, damit sie Metall und Stein bearbeiten, und die Riesen, um die Zwerge vor den wilden Tieren und den Drachen zu beschützen. Doch die Riesen waren zu wild.

> Dar nach über liczel iar da wurden die rysen den zwergen gar vil zů leid thůn. Vnd wurden die risen gar böß vnd vngetrü. Darnach beschůff got die starcken held das was da czů-mal ein mittel volck vnder der treier hant volck. Vnd ist zů wissen das die helden gar vil iar getrüw vnd byderbe warent. Vnd darumb soltent sie den zwergen zů hilff kumen wyder die vngetrüwen risen, vnd wider die wilden tier vnd würm. Das lant was in den zeiten gancz vngebunden, Darumb macht got starcke held vnd gab in die natur das ir můt vnd sinn můstent stan auff manheit nach eren vnd auff streit vnd krieg. (*Heldenbuch* V. 14-23)[8]

Das immer zornige und kampfbereite Schwert ist also weniger die Waffe eines höfischen Ritters als vielmehr die eines archaischen Helden. Als magische und legendäre Waffe repräsentiert das Schwert Tailbiter die mythische und heroische

---

8 liczel = wenig, byderbe = tüchtig.

Qualität seines Trägers. Doch damit sie ihre Wirkung entfalten kann, sind eben auch ›a brave man's hands‹ nötig. Das Prinzip der magischen Waffe im mittelalterlichen Epos, die schon für sich mythische Qualität repräsentiert, vertritt in ihrer Bedeutung den Helden. Dazu verrät die Kenntnis über die Waffe etwas vom Status der Person, die sie führt (vgl. Friedrich 289).

Dass Giles im Besitz einer solchen magischen Waffe ist, kann nun keineswegs als Zufall betrachtet werden. Der Text begründet es mit einer Tat, die ganz der Definition des *Heldenbuches* folgt: dem Kampf gegen einen Riesen (vgl. FGH 20 ff). Nach der Logik des *Heldenbuches*, das Held und Riesen (und auch den später im Text erscheinenden Drachen) als eine einander bedingende Einheit beschreibt, muss davon ausgegangen werden, dass Giles durch seinen Kampf mit dem Riesen eben ein solcher ›heroe‹ ist. Auch wenn dieser Kampf auf den ersten Blick komisch erscheint, so beschreibt doch der Text einen offensichtlich reizbaren Akteur, ähnlich den Helden im *Heldenbuch*: »Farmer Giles had a short way with trespassers that few could outface« (FGH 20). Der Schuss auf den Riesen wird »without thinking« (FGH 20) abgegeben, der Gewaltakt gegen den Riesen geschieht also ebenso affektgeladen wie das Herausschnellen des Schwertes in Anwesenheit eines Drachen.

Giles ist also, bereits bevor er in den Besitz von Tailbiter gelangt, kein höfischer Ritter, wohl aber eine Figur, die eben jene ›brave man's hands‹ besitzt, die mit Tailbiter in der Lage sind, einen Drachenkampf zu bestehen. Denn folgt man dem Text, dann bedarf es offensichtlich keines Ritters, um den Drachen zu besiegen, sondern vielmehr eines archaischen Helden. Mit Blick auf das *Heldenbuch* wird auch deutlich, dass mit dem Erscheinen des Helden der Eintritt vom Vorhistorischen (der Schöpfungsgeschichte) in die Geschichte (das Heroic Age) markiert wird, der durch Gewaltakte gekennzeichnet ist. Es ist anzunehmen, dass dieser Übertritt in *Farmer Giles of Ham* durch den Kampf mit dem Riesen geschieht.

Warum jedoch wird nun im Text die Frage gestellt, was einen Ritter ausmacht? Zunächst einmal wohl darum, weil beide sozusagen dasselbe Feld bespielen, denn »Aventiure und Mythos teilen sich nicht nur die Semantik des Erzählten und den Raum des Magischen, sondern auch dessen Unverfügbarkeit. Das, was ereignishaft auf den Ritter in der Aventiure zukommt, partizipiert am Mythischen, wird aber in eine Prüfung überführt, konkretisiert und dadurch aller erst beherrschbar. Eine Aventiure kann bewältigt« (Friedrich 279) und in einen sozialen Rahmen überführt werden.

Deshalb kann ein höfischer Ritter natürlich einen Drachen erschlagen; Iwein selbst, dessen Definition für ›aventiure‹ wir schon gehört haben, erschlägt einen Drachen und eilt einem Löwen zu Hilfe, der mit diesem in einen Kampf geraten ist (vgl. *Iwein* V. 3833-3864). Im *Yvain*, der französichen Vorlage des Hartmann'schen Textes, wird das

> Eingreifen [des Ritters zugunsten des Löwen] durch Mitleid für
> »la beste fantil et franche« (*Yvain* V. 3375), das edle und stolze
> Tier, begründet. Im *Yvain* ist also der Kampf mit dem Drachen
> kein willkürlicher Gewaltakt, nicht nur Demonstration von Stärke,
> sondern zeigt Qualitäten..., die einem ritterlichen Verhaltenskodex
> entsprechen, ...seine ethischen Qualitäten, denen ein Normenkodex
> zugrunde liegt, durch den seine Tat integrative Wirkung hat in dem
> Sinne, dass sie ihn als einen derjenigen ausweist, die sich [einem]
> gemeinschaftlichen Ideal unterstellen. (Unzeitig-Herzog 45 f)

Dieses Muster findet sich auch in *Farmer Giles of Ham*, allerdings nur noch rudimentär. Zwar haben die Suche nach dem Drachen zu Weihnachten und der Drachenschwanzkuchen integrierende Funktion, doch ein echter Drache wie Chrysophylax in *Farmer Giles of Ham* offensichtlich nicht (mehr). Die Ritter des Königs ziehen, wie gesagt, das Turnier dem Kampf gegen das Ungeheuer vor. Beleg dafür ist ihre Unfähigkeit, während des vom König befohlenen zweiten Zuges gegen den Drachen auch nur Drachenspuren zu erkennen, was hingegen Giles kein Problem bereitet (vgl. FGH 96). Auch der folgenden Konfrontation mit dem Drachen Chrysophylax, der jetzt nicht mehr auf ritterlichem Verhalten besteht, sondern »with a great wrath« (FGH 100) angreift, können die Ritter nicht standhalten. Giles jedoch und das heroische Schwert besiegen den Drachen abermals und erringen nun den Drachenhort – oder doch wenigstens große Teile davon (vgl. FGH 100 ff).

Sinngebung durch Gewalt

Mit dem zweiten Sieg über den Drachen ist die Geschichte von Farmer Giles jedoch noch nicht zu Ende, denn dieser Kampf bringt eine Erfahrung von Gewalt an die Oberfläche des Textes, die keinen integrativen Sinn für den Königshof aufweist, sondern vielmehr für diesen fremdartig und bedrohlich erscheint.

Giles' Sieg über den Drachen ist wie jeder Akt der Überwindung des Fremden im Heldenepos ein gewalttätiger (vgl. Haug, *Grausamkeit* 78), der gänzlich verschieden ist vom Akt des ›êre‹ austauschenden Kampfes als ein Abmessen des höchsten Adels in Gewalt (vgl. Czerwinski 438). Für Giles selbst muss angenommen werden, dass, wie beim Helden der mittelalterlichen Heldensagen oder Epen, die Gewalttätigkeit des besiegten monströsen Gegners in den Sieger übergeht. Giles erhält das Schwert nach dem Sieg über den Riesen, und der Sieg über den Drachen bringt ihm den Besitz des Schatzes. Das muss aber gleichzeitig bedeuten, dass Giles aus Sicht des Hofes durch den Sieg über den Drachen zum Außenseiter, zum potentiellen Gegner und zur Bedrohung wird, anders als Yvain, der höfische Ritter, für den der Drachenkampf gerade einen

Akt der Integration in die höfische Welt darstellt (vgl. Unzeitig-Herzog 46). Schon allein der Sieg über den Drachen, der gerade nicht durch und für den höfischen Personenverband errungen wird, sondern allein von dem archaischen Helden (Giles zieht gegen den Drachen, wie Siegfried es im *Nibelungenlied* für die Fahrt nach Island empfiehlt, nämlich allein, »in recken wîse«; *Nibelungenlied* St. 341/1), lässt die Opposition zwischen höfischer Gesellschaft und archaischem Helden oder auch Personenverband und persönlicher Stärke deutlich werden.

Die Figur Giles vertritt im Text ein anderes Muster als die Ritter des Hofes und der König selbst und bestreitet deshalb zu Recht, ein Ritter zu sein. Spätestens nach Inbesitznahme des Drachenhorts entspricht er dem Typus des archaischen Helden. Bis hierhin ist zwar der Drache, als einbrechendes Fremdes, befriedet, die Geschichte allerdings ist damit noch nicht beendet.

Das Fremde ist dem Gewohnten gegenüber das Radikal-Andere, eine Bedrohung und Herausforderung zugleich. »Es geht... darum, die fremde Welt in ihren Repräsentanten zu besiegen und unschädlich zu machen« (Haug, *Schwierigkeit* 315). Bis zum zweiten Sieg über Chrysophylax folgt Giles im Großen und Ganzen diesem Muster. Walter Haug weist jedoch mit Blick auf den archaischen Helden darauf hin: »mit dem Sieg allein ist es noch nicht getan. Denn immer wieder ist das eigentlich prekäre Problem die Rückkehr des Helden in seine Gemeinschaft« (Haug, *Schwierigkeit* 316). Der Grund dafür liegt darin, dass der Sieg über das Ungeheuer mehr als nur die brachiale Erledigung des Fremden darstellt, vielmehr bewirkt die Erfahrung des Monsters eine Art Anverwandlung. «Das heroische Bild dafür ist, daß der Held, der dem Ungeheuer entgegentritt, selbst ungeheuerlich wird» (Haug, *Schwierigkeit* 316).

In *Farmer Giles of Ham* wird dieses Prinzip offensichtlich auf die Spitze getrieben. Der Drache überlebt den Kampf (und bleibt »respectable«, vgl. FGH 110). Giles jedoch nimmt nicht nur einen Großteil des Hortes in Besitz (vgl. FGH 106 ff), sondern geht nun ein Bündnis mit dem Drachen ein, das direkt gegen den Königshof, also die höfische Ordnung gerichtet ist (vgl. FGH 110). Die »Dämonisierung [die] der Sieger als Abbild des besiegten Dämons [trägt]« (Haug, *Grausamkeit* 80), nimmt hier also eine tatsächliche Form in Gestalt des Drachen an.

In *Farmer Giles of Ham* liegt also eine Option der Begegnung mit dem Fremden nicht nur im Gewaltakt, sondern auch in der Möglichkeit, sich dem Anderen durch dessen Preisgabe der Machtmittel (im Fall des Drachen also des Schatzes) anzuverwandeln. Der Drache schwört Giles Gefolgschaft. Mehr noch: Er bietet an, »[to] carry all this treasure back to your honour's [Giles] own house and not to the King's. And I will help you to keep it, what is more« (FGH 110). Spätestens hier ist der Konflikt zwischen dem monströs gewordenen Giles[9] und dem Königshof offensichtlich.

---

9   Der gewaltauslösende Moment geht hier vom Drachen aus. Dies verdeutlicht, wie sehr Giles sich dem Drachen anverwandelt hat.

Doch zunächst scheint Giles' Rückkehr in seine Gemeinschaft nicht sonderlich problematisch. Im Gegenteil: Er wird von den Dorfbewohnern bejubelt (vgl. FGH 114). Der Konflikt besteht lediglich zwischen Giles und der höfischen Ordnung, repräsentiert durch den König, der nun, um seine (selbst)proklamierten Rechtsansprüche gebracht, zum Kriegszug rüstet. Wieder ist hier die Logik der Machtdemonstration des politischen Verbandes zu finden, die schon den zweiten Zug gegen den Drachen prägt, und wieder werden Ritter und Soldaten versammelt (vgl. FGH 120). Aus Sicht des Königs kann dieser letzte Kriegszug des Textes nur als berechtigt erscheinen: Giles stellt die, wie schon erwähnt, genealogisch und auf Tradition fußenden Ansprüche des Königs infrage. Giles allerdings ist im Besitz des Schatzes, den er, wie es einem archaischen Helden entspricht, erworben hat. Die Tatsache, dass Giles es unterlässt, wie befohlen an den Königshof zurückzukehren, kann als Variation des Schemas von der Schwierigkeit der Wiedereingliederung des Drachentöters in seine Gemeinschaft verstanden werden. Während der König darauf setzt, dass dies, wie zwischen Giles und dem Drachen, durch Preisgabe des Machtmittels geschieht, verweigert sich Giles diesem Integrationsmittel, so wie er sich schon einer Antwort auf die Anrede ›liege‹ enthalten hat.

Die Schwierigkeit der Rückkehr in die Gemeinschaft scheint hier also eher eine Schwierigkeit der Integration in die höfische Gesellschaft zu sein. Letztlich scheint es für das höfische Zeremoniell unmöglich, die heroische Ordnung dauerhaft zu integrieren.[10] Demzufolge kann angenommen werden, dass im Text mit höfischem Rittertum und heroischer Ordnung auch zwei Konzepte von Herrschaft aufeinanderprallen: das des Vasallenkönigs und jenes, das Herrschaft herleitet aus persönlicher Stärke (die, wie der Text zeigt, zumindest im Middle Kingdom allein dazu befähigt, den Frieden zu sichern).

Die Konfrontation zwischen Giles und dem Königshof läuft also letztlich auf die Frage hinaus, wer herrschen soll. Der Text selbst favorisiert von vornherein das heroische Modell: Bellomarius, der frühere Besitzer des heroischen Schwertes, war einerseits zwar Ritter, ist aber gleichzeitig als archaischer Held, eben als Drachentöter zu denken. Dass der Text nun diesen Helden über die Genealogie in Verbindung mit dem aktuellen König bringt, zeigt, dass Herrschaft in *Farmer Giles of Ham* einmal an das Modell des Helden (also an das heroische Prinzip) gebunden war (vgl. FGH 54). Der König war, als er noch Bellomarius hieß, der stärkste Held. Diese Verbindung zwischen heroischem Prinzip und Königswürde allerdings ist im beschriebenen Vasallen-Königtum, wie es bis zum Erscheinen des Drachen Chrysophylax im Text zu finden ist, verloren gegangen. Das Heldenschwert liegt unbenutzt und unerkannt in der Waffenkammer des Königs und gilt als unmodern (vgl. FGH 32), bis es in die Hände von Giles gerät.

---

10 Zu diesem Problem vgl. Haferland, *Mündlichkeit* 77 f.

Der Erwerb des Schwertes gepaart mit dem Erscheinen des Drachen bewirkt bei Giles eine Modifikation seiner Identität hin zum Drachentöter. Der Drachenkampf ist deshalb nötig,[11] weil er das Muster prägt, in dem die überwundene Gewalt auf den Heroen übergeht (vgl. Haug, *Grausamkeit* 81). Damit geht aber zwangsläufig einher, dass der von außen kommende Held eine soziale Krise für den Hof auslöst, die – wenn sie unbewältigt bleibt – dessen Existenz bedroht. Die Reaktion auf diese Krise kann nur Gewalt sein: Es sei an Siegfried aus dem *Nibelungenlied* erinnert, der letztlich deswegen erschlagen wird, weil er als Drachenkämpfer unerträglich erscheint (vgl. Haug, *Schwierigkeit* 16). Gewalt ist es auch in *Farmer Giles of Ham*, die das Problem des unerträglichen, die Herrschaft bedrohenden Drachenkämpfers lösen soll, nachdem die Integration durch Austausch und höfisches Zeremoniell von Giles verweigert wurde (vgl. FGH 118). Wieder wird also vom König ein Ritterheer aufgeboten, und wieder endet die Schlacht an der Brücke von Ham mit einer Zerschlagung desselben durch den Drachen (vgl. FGH 124 ff).

Die endlose Dynamik des Heroen, im Text deutlich durch die Verbindung des vorhistorischen Helden Bellomarius mit Giles, die durch das Schwert Tailbiter initiiert wird, erweist sich dem sozial integrierten Ritter und Königtum überlegen. Das Prinzip der Machtdemonstration des politischen Verbandes (also der höfischen Ritterschaft) zeigt sich in *Farmer Giles of Ham* dem der persönlichen Bewährung im Kampf als unterlegen.[12] Zu guter Letzt begreift dies auch der König. Als er nach der Flucht seiner Ritter zurückkehrt, fürchtet er »any man or dragon on the face of the earth« (FGH 126) nicht mehr. Giles versagt dem König den Zweikampf mit den Worten »go home and get cool« (FGH 128). Einer Abkühlung bedarf aber nur der in Zorn geratene Held.[13]

Dass der Zweikampf trotzdem nicht stattfindet, liegt an der herausgehobenen Stellung, die der Drachenkampf für Tolkien einnimmt. Wenn für ihn der Sieg Beowulfs über Grendel ein Sieg »over the lesser and more nearly human« (BMC 32) im Vergleich zum »older and more elemental« (BMC 32) Drachen ist, so kann ein Zweikampf, wenn auch in heldischem Zorn ausgefochten, nicht an einen Drachenkampf heranreichen, zumal der Verdacht nahe liegt, es könne sich doch um einen Zweikampf höfisch-ritterlicher Akteure handeln, der, wie gezeigt, gegenseitige Reziprozität erzeugen würde.

Da der Text aber eine im Text als älter suggerierte Leitvorstellung von politischer Herrschaft präferiert, muss dieser Verdacht ausgeschlossen werden.

---

11 Auf die Funktion des Drachen in *Farmer Giles of Ham* kann hier nur oberflächlich eingegangen werden. Mehr dazu vgl. Brückner 242.
12 Vgl. dazu Müller 172ff.
13 Ein Beispiel dafür findet sich in der irischen Heldensage von CuChulainn, der nach seinem Kampf gegen die drei Söhne des dämonischen Wesens Nechta in drei Fässer Wasser gesteckt werden muss, ehe er ohne Gefahr für den Hof wieder in diesen integriert werden kann (vgl. Haug, *Grausamkeit* 80).

Der Untergang der höfischen Ordnung im Middle Kingdom ist nicht durch eine Verhöfischung des Konflikts aufzuhalten.

Nicht die Integration des monströs gewordenen Helden in die höfische Gesellschaft löst den Konflikt, sondern der heroische Legitimationstypus (vgl. Müller 176) setzt sich durch. Die Antwort auf den Einbruch des Fremden (des Drachen) ist in *Farmer Giles of Ham* letztlich nicht Gewalt, sondern Öffnung und Anverwandlung (vgl. Haug, *Grausamkeit* 86). In dieser Logik erscheinen in *Farmer Giles of Ham* am Ende nicht Drache und Drachenkämpfer als das eigentlich Fremde, sondern der Königshof, der sich in seinem höfischen Zeremoniell dem archaischen Helden als unterlegen erweist.

Folgt man dem, dann enthält *Farmer Giles of Ham* einen Weltentwurf, in dem immer wieder neu die Geschichte des überlegenen Heroen in einer unterlegenen Umgebung erzählt wird (vgl. Müller 175). Der Bellomarius war Drachentöter, und Giles' Taten sind letztlich die gleichen Taten wie die des legendären Helden. In der Wiederholung des immer gleichen Geschehens wird Geschichte episch und mittels einer heroischen Siegerdialektik immer wieder neu und doch gleich produziert. Dass sich das Fremde in Gestalt eines Drachen materialisiert, macht dies überdeutlich.[14]

Der Einbruch von Geschichte ist in *Farmer Giles of Ham* gekoppelt an einen Einbruch des Fremden, der immer mit Gewalt einhergeht.[15] Damit folgt der Text im Prinzip der Logik der mittelalterlichen Heldensage, zu der Walter Haug erklärt:

> Sich auf das einlassen, was fremd und gefährdend entgegensteht, das bedeutet..., dass man davon affiziert wird. Wenn man der Gewalt mit Gewalt begegnet, wird man als Sieger von dem überwältigt, was man bezwungen hat. Wenn man versucht, auf das Fremde einzugehen..., dann löst dies eine Reaktion aus, die doch wieder die Gewalt... heraufbeschwört. (Haug, *Grausamkeit* 86)

Hierin liegt die eigentliche Aggressivität des Textes. Heroische Gewalt, so scheint es, ist für Tolkien eine Triebfeder zur Produktion von epischer Geschichte. In *Farmer Giles of Ham* allerdings beschränkt sich Geschichte letztlich auf die erwähnte Herkunft einiger Ortsnamen wie beispielsweise »Worminghall, the spot where Giles and Chrysophylax first made acquaintance« (FGH 134).

---

14 Zum Zusammenhang von Drachen und epischer Geschichtsauffassung bei Tolkien vgl. Brückner 217 ff.
15 Für Haug ist der Eintritt in das Heroic Age gebunden an den Eintritt in die Geschichte. Der ›heroe‹ ist von der Gewalterfahrung geprägt, die dieser Eintritt in sich birgt (vgl. Haug, *Grausamkeit* 78).

Die Heiterkeit, die der Geschichte zugeschrieben wird, und die Annahme Shippeys »Tolkien felt no urge to take any of it [*Farmer Giles of Ham*] seriously« (Shippey 289), resultieren wohl aus dem Fakt, dass Geschichte hier also vordergründig als Wort- bzw. Sprachgeschichte inszeniert wird. Damit erscheint die Brisanz des Textes wohl eher mäßig. Wenn man jedoch Haug folgt, der über die Heldensage ausführt, dass »eine Dialektik [in dieses Muster] eingeschrieben ist, das ... nur narrativ ausgefaltet werden kann« (Haug, *Grausamkeit* 86), dann weist die Geschichte in *Farmer Giles of Ham* modellhaften Charakter für Tolkiens episches Geschichtsverständnis in seinen literarischen Werken auf, in dem der Einbruch der Geschichte durch Gewalt, die immer wieder Gewalt produziert, der Regelfall ist.

Bibliographie

Brückner, Patrick. »Der Dichter hält es seltsamerweise für lohnend, Drachen zum Thema zu machen ... Der Drache als poetologisches Konzept von Realität bei J.R.R. Tolkien«. *Good Dragons are Rare – An Inquiry into Literary Dragons East and West*. Ed. Thomas Honegger and Fanfan Chen. Frankfurt u.a.: Peter Lang, 2009, 217-271

Chance Nitzsche, Jane. *Tolkien's Art. A Mythology for England*. London: Macmillan Press, 1979

Chrestien de Troyes. *Yvain*. Hg. und Übers. Ilse Nolting-Hauff. München: Wilhelm Fink Verlag, 1983

Czerwinski, Peter. *Der Glanz der Abstraktion. Frühe Formen von Reflexivität im Mittelalter*. Frankfurt und New York: Campus Verlag, 1989

Das Deutsche Heldenbuch. Ed. Adelbert von Keller. Nach dem mutmasslich ältesten Drucke. Stuttgart: Bibliothek des Litterarischen Vereins, 1867

Das Nibelungenlied. Ed. und Übers. Helmut De Boor. Zweisprachig Mittelhochdeutsch/Neuhochdeutsch. Leipzig: Dieterich'sche Verlagsbuchhandlung, 1959

Eming, Jutta. *Funktionswandel des Wunderbaren. Studien zum ›Bel Inconnu‹, zum ›Wigalois‹ und zum ›Wigoleis von Rade‹*. Trier: WVT, 1999

Friedrich, Udo. »Transformationen mythischer Gehalte im *Eckenlied*«. *Präsenz des Mythos. Konfigurationen einer Denkform in Mittelalter und Früher Neuzeit*. Ed. Udo Friedrich und Bruno Quast. Berlin und New York: De Gruyter, 2004, 275-297

Hartmann von Aue. *Iwein*. Ed. Karl Lachmann u.a. Übers. Thomas Cramer. Berlin und New York: De Gruyter, 1981

Haferland, Harald. *Höfische Interaktion. Interpretationen zur höfischen Epik und Didaktik um 1200*. München: Wilhelm Fink Verlag, 1998

---. *Mündlichkeit, Gedächtnis und Medialität. Heldendichtung im deutschen Mittelalter*. Göttingen: Vandenhoeck & Ruprecht, 2004

Haug, Walter. »Die Grausamkeit der Heldensage. Neue gattungstheoretische Überlegungen zur heroischen Dichtung«. *Brechungen auf dem Weg zur Individualität. Kleine Schriften zur Literatur des Mittelalters*. Ed. Walter Haug. Tübingen: Max Niemeyer Verlag, 1997, 72-90

---. »Von der Schwierigkeit heimzukehren. Die *Walthersage* in ihrem motivgeschichtlichen und literaturanthropologischen Kontext«. *Die Wahrheit der Fiktion. Studien zur weltlichen und geistlichen Literatur des Mittelalters und der frühen Neuzeit.* Ed. Walter Haug. Tübingen: Max Niemeyer Verlag, 2003, 315-29

Müller, Jan-Dirk. *Spielregeln für den Untergang. Die Welt des Nibelungenliedes.* Tübingen: Max Niemeyer Verlag, 1998

Shippey, Tom. *J.R.R. Tolkien. Author of the Century.* Paperback Ed. London: Harper Collins, 2001

Tolkien, John Ronald Reuel. "Beowulf: The Monster and the Critics". *The Monster and the Critics and Other Essays.* Ed. Christopher Tolkien. London: Harper Collins, 2006, 5-48

---. *Farmer Giles of Ham/Bauer Giles of Ham.* Zweisprachig Englisch/Deutsch. München: DTV, 1999

---. *The Letters of J.R.R. Tolkien.* Paperback Edition. Ed. Humphrey Carpenter with assistance of Christopher Tolkien. Boston & New York: Houghton Mifflin, 1981

Unzeitig-Herzog, Monika. »Vom Sieg über den Drachen: alte und neue Helden«. *Chevaliers errants, demoiselles et l'Autre: höfische und nachhöfische Literatur im europäischen Mittelalter. Festschrift für Xenja von Ertzdorff zum 65. Geburtstag.* Ed. Trude Ehlert. Göppingen: Kümmerle, 1998, 41-61

Wolf, Alois. *Heldensage und Epos.* Tübingen: Gunter Narr Verlag, 1995

Dagor dagorath and Ragnarök: Tolkien and the Apocalypse

Michaël Devaux (Livarot)

DAGOR DAGORATH is an Israeli 'Symphonic *Black/Death Metal*' music band. Let us put this straight: that is not the music I am to tell you about ... Let us go back to the music of creation in Tolkien. *The Silmarillion* leads off indeed with the *Ainulindalë* as the Bible does with *Genesis*, but does not end with an *Apocalypse* (see Kocher 5f). This is a rather paradoxical absence for three reasons at least.

First, one could expect the creator of a world to unfold its story from beginning to end. Yet we know that if Middle-earth teems with details, Tolkien was careful not to say that he had described the whole of it (L 188). A world, by definition, is inexhaustible save by an infinite mind, which the sub-creator is not. Then, bringing the world to its end is one of the toughest challenges to meet. Yet, it is met in the tradition Tolkien belongs to, and even by some of his friends, which makes its absence in his work all the more paradoxical. Why did he not meet this challenge as well? Because even though their styles are different, the first novel of Charles Williams, *War in Heaven* (1930), takes root in the *Book of Revelation*[1] ; and C.S. Lewis describes the end of Narnia in *The Last Battle* (1956). Louis Bouyer, his French friend, a theologian of *l'Oratoire*[2], wrote a *Prélude à l'Apocalypse* (1982). And another minister turned Catholic, Mgr Robert Hugh Benson, had published *The Lord of the World* in 1906. One could then expect Tolkien to deal with the end of the world in the *Legendarium*. If nothing is said about it in *The Simarillion* it is because of the intervention of Christopher Tolkien and Guy Gavriel Kay (see Kane 236f). This is how Tolkien actually presented 'The Simarillion' to Milton Waldman in 1951:

> [1] This legendarium ends with a vision of the end of the world, its breaking and remaking, and the recovery of the Silmarilli and the 'light before the Sun'—after a final battle which owes, I suppose, more to the Norse vision of Ragnarök than to anything else, though it is not much like it. (L 149)[3]

---

1 *The Book of Revelation* XII, 7-12. See the articles of Schrader and Leigh (who also tackles the issue in the Lewis of *The Cosmic Trilogy*).
2 Bouyer, who was a minister before converting to Catholicism, was a friend of Tolkien's and the first to publish an article about him in France in 1958. See Devaux, *Tolkien*.
3 As far as we know, Tolkien always writes Ragnarök thus. We shall follow him, unlike Tom Shippey, for instance, who spells it with an *o caudata*. – The quotations preceded

Michaël Devaux

Two questions stem from this text. It is first about pinpointing in *The History of Middle-earth* what Christopher pushed aside when he published *The Silmarillion*; and about trying to understand why he rejected that theme. Let us identify straight away the texts in question. The 'Great End' is a recurring theme in *The Book of Lost Tales* ([**4-6**] see in particular LT 1 219). The sections 19 of the *Sketch of the Mythology* (SM, 40-41, [**7**]) and most of all of the *Qenta Noldorinwa* (SM, 165 [**8**]), and the conclusion of the *Quenta Silmarillion* (LR 333, § 31-32; XI, 247 [**9-10**]) are the most decisive texts. These texts do not make up a sizeable corpus and they are always short.

Then, the *letter to Waldman* tells us that Tolkien has a quite peculiar literary debt, for it is said to bear little likeness ("it is not much like it") to its professed model... And yet it is claimed to be the best: "more... than to anything else"? Who are the other pretenders? Ovid's *Metamorphoses* (which we shall not speak of) and the *Apocalypse of John* are the references which spring to mind. How can Tolkien say that *Dagor dagorath* owes more to *Ragnarök* than to the *Apocalypse*? Which similarities are there? Does the situation evolve between the first drafts of *The Book of Lost Tales* and the philosophical and theological ideas he put down in writing after he had retired?

It's this evolution we shall try and unfold to begin with. We shall then see how an apocalyptic text can be a problem in terms of interpretation in/for Tolkien's writings.

I. *Dagor dagorath*: from Ragnarök to Armageddon[4]

The link between *Dagor dagorath* and *Ragnarök* may be more visual than phonetic in the first place. These Sindarin and Old Norse words look akin ('a', 'g' and 'r' can be found in both). It is as obvious, if not more, with the Armageddon of the *Apocalypse* (with the additional similar 'o' and 'd' letters). But what about the meaning and the scenes or scenarios of the end of the world?

To carry this study through, we shall need to be able to make a distinction between the different versions of the texts of *The Silmarillion*. We have, in a previous study (focused on the *Ainulindalë*), suggested the following categories. By *original* is meant those features which belong to the myth from its inception. This distinction may be refined by considering different degrees of originality. *Original, sensu stricto*, is used to designate only what is present from the

---

by a number make up the texts which are essential to follow the evolution of Tolkien; they can be found (again) in the appendices.
4 For this section, see Whittingham, chap. vi.

first version on. Anything which is introduced at a later stage and remains to the end (i.e. from version *n* on) will be called *subsequent*. *Unique* designates features which are found only in one version or a group of versions; and finally *fundamental* is used for anything which conveys an overall concept. Equipped with those distinctions, we can now compare *Dagor dagorath* and *Ragnarök*.

A. Ragnarök

1. Meaning

Let us keep in mind the Sindarin meaning of *Dagor dagorath*: 'Battle of Battles'. What is the meaning of Ragnarök? The traditional translation, after Wagner, is 'Twilight of the Gods'. This translation is based on the *ragna rökr* reading, but the most common one is *ragna rök* which means '(consummation of the) destiny of the Powers'. Let us bear in mind that in the *Prose Edda*, Ragnarök is described in chapter 51 of *The Gylfaginning* (*The Tricking of Gylfi*) and in the 'Wise-Woman's Prophecy' in *Völuspá*.

2. Summary of the *Eddas*

A brief (maybe too much) reminder: Ragnarök starts with a three-year winter during which great battles take place, then follow three sunless winters. A wolf swallows the Sun and another the Moon. The stars also vanish out of the sky, the earth quakes. The sea crashes onto the earth. Four characters stand for the evil powers: the wolf *Fenrir*, *Jörmungand* (the *Miðgarðr* serpent), their father *Loki* and *Surtr*. During the battle on the plain of *Vígríðr*, they respectively fight *Óðinn*, *Þórr*, *Heimdallr* and *Freyr*. *Þórr* defeats the snake, but falls down from his venom. *Fenrir* kills *Óðinn*, but *Víðarr* crushes the wolf. *Loki* and *Heimdallr* kill each other. *Surtr* slays *Freyr*, casts fire down onto the earth and consumes all the worlds. But the earth reappears out of the water and some return unhurt, *Víðarr*, the sons of *Þórr*, and a human couple (*Líf* and *Leif-þrasir*) in particular. So *Ragnarök* is a description of a battle of the gods, on a plain, with a front line of eight fighting gods. Everybody dies; and the phenomenon is cyclical: it is an eternal return.

3. Ragnarök in Tolkien?

a. A prophecy. – The form of what is called the 'Second Prophecy of Mandos' in Tolkien cannot fail to echo the prophecy of the *völva* Thorbjörg in *Völuspá*. The prophetic form is original even though its name changed in the course of time[5].

---

5 Tolkien uses the following phrases: Prophecy of the North, (Second) Prophecy of Mandos, Doom of Mandos; cf. Prophecy of Gilfanon (LT 2 283). Tolkien himself used the

b. The moon and the sun. – In terms of content now, *The Book of Lost Tales* has it that the Sun and the Moon quarrel because of Melko, they pass the Gates and are destroyed[6]. In the *Prose Edda*, the wolves swallow both sun and moon. It is also said that 'the stars will vanish out of the sky'. Similarly, Tolkien devised Melko as the origin of eclipses and meteor showers (LT 2 281). The theme of the destruction of the moon and the sun is original, but the cause of this destruction undergoes changes. Originally, in *The Book of Lost Tales*, they destroy each other, Melko being indirectly responsible by stirring up the quarrel between them. Their destruction directly at the hands of Melkor is subsequent to the *Qenta Noldorinwa* and can be found in the *Quenta Silmarillion*.

c. The combatants. – The Second Prophecy of Mandos predicts a battle on the plain of Valinor[7]. Some of the combatants are identified. Dragons (LT 2 116) and monsters (LT 2 170) are known to be on Morgoth's side. Afterwards comes Eärendil, then Tulkas, with Túrin on his left and Fionwë on his right. The equivalences between the *Edda* and the *Legendarium* characters (apart from the problem, which we shall return to later, that they give rise to regarding the allegorical status of myths in Tolkien) are but partial. One can certainly identify Óðinn with Manwë, and Þórr with Tulkas. Tolkien himself did it in a note of *The Book of Lost Tales*[8].

i) The presence of **Tulkas** at the Great End is original since it appears in *The Book of Lost Tales*. More exactly it is subsequent to *The History of Eriol*. Tulkas is indeed mentioned in what is conveniently referred to as 'the Second Prophecy of Mandos': "Gilfanon also prophesies concerning the Great End, and of the Wrack of Things, and of Fionwë, Tulkas, and Melko and the last fight on the Plains of Valinor" (LT 2 283). So be it for Tulkas, but what about **Manwë**?

ii) He will undoubtedly be there, but very few are the texts in which he is mentioned. What is more, they are not in the 'internal' corpus, but can be found in reflexive notes, which stand outside the legends themselves. Thus a 1972 note on Gandalf has it that "Manwë will not descend from the Mountain until the Dagor Dagorath, and the coming of the End, when Melkor returns" (UT 511). And the *Notes on motive in the Silmarillion* say that: "The 'Elder King' is obviously not going to be finally defeated or destroyed, at least not before some

---

subheading *The Second Prophecy of Mandos* for the end of the *Quenta Silmarillion*, see WJ 247.

6 [4] "For 'tis said that ere the Great End come Melko shall in some wise contrive a quarrel between Moon and Sun, and Ilinsor shall seek to follow Urwendi through the Gates, and when they are gone the Gates of both East and West will be destroyed, and Urwendi and Ilinsor shall be lost. So shall it be that Fionwë Úrion, son of Manwë, of love for Urwendi shall in the end be Melko's bane, and shall destroy the world to destroy his foe, and so shall all things then be rolled away" (LT 1 219).

7 This is an original element, in accordance with the categories mentioned *infra*.

8 "... Óðinn, Þórr... and they identified them with Manweg, Tulkas..." (LT 2 290)

ultimate 'Ragnarök'..." (MR 399). So Manwë may be killed. Whether he is or not, it does seem that he takes part in the Battle of Battles.

iii) The case of **Fionwë** is quite close to Manwë's since he is his son[9] or herald. It should be pointed out that, originally, in the very first text (LT 1 219), he is the only one to be mentioned in the final battle against Melkor. He is the one who destroys the earth and puts an end to the world as collateral damage ... Túrin is afterwards brought in (LT 2 116). Then Fionwë and Túrin will be on Tulkas' right and left sides respectively (SM 165, LR 333). Fionwë may be thought to resemble Surtr since he is the destroyer of the earth. But that is an inconclusive resemblance ... How much then should Túrin and *Heimdallr* resemble each other to make the overall comparison conclusive?

iv) The case of **Túrin** is a complex one[10]. Contrary to Manwë, he appears in many a text, but what is said about him changes a great deal. He and Nienóri are first mentioned after they die 'as shining Valar among the blessed Ones' (LT 2 116): Christopher Tolkien, in his comments, spoke of the 'deification' (LT 2 137; SM 73) of Túrin. The 'spirit of Túrin' (*Sketch*, SM 40) is then mentioned "and him it names among the [sons of] Gods" (SM 165 [and n. 9 p. 166]), before being only granted "a place... among the sons of the Valar": he then comes back from the 'Halls of Mandos' (LR 333). The re-humanisation of Túrin is complete when Tolkien writes that he is "returning from the Doom of Men" (WJ 247). Túrin's deification is thus an original and fundamental theme, which is only present in *The Book of Lost Tales*. The more time passes, the less Túrin is presented as a Vala. Conversely, the more his humanity comes out and spreads till Tolkien makes him the avenger of all men. Indeed, he first only avenges "the children of Húrin" (SM 40), that is to say his family, before "all Men" are added to it (SM 165; LR 333). Whatever these evolutions[11], from the start, he is the one who kills Morgoth with his sword (Mormakil, LT 2 116). In no way does he resemble *Heimdallr*, the guardian of *Bifröst*. But it is Eärendil who operates as a guardian.

v) **Eärendil** is not present at the end of the world described in *The Book of Lost Tales*. His presence is subsequent to *Sketch* where it is said that Eärendil 'descends' as he sees the battle. It is only from the *Qenta Noldorinwa* that Eärendil descends upon Melkor when the Sun and the Moon are destroyed. The last battle begins *afterwards*. This is a fundamental change, for, in one

---

9 See texts 2 and 4; in SM 149 he is the son of Tulkas.
10 Garbowski has underlined one instance (279): how to admit, in a Christian work, that Túrin has an important role in the apocalypse, even though he committed suicide?
11 In *The Legend of Sigurd and Gudrún*, Christopher Tolkien comments on the parallel (LSG 184f) between the version of Ragnarök written by his father in which Sigurd has an original place quite similar to the one Túrin will eventually have (LSG 63, 247). Tolkien claims this novelty (LSG 53f). Could it be possible that the evolution (re-humanisation) of Túrin depended on the ideas of Tolkien about Sigurd?

case, he comes down after the battle has started whereas, in the other, he is at the origin of it. But it is therefore not quite clear what his role is: does he really fight or does he only give his Silmaril at the end, being decisive before and after but not during the battle? It is certain that he instigates the battle by driving Melkor from the airs, but nothing more is said. The *Qenta Noldorinwa* explains that "Eärendel shall descend and surrender that flame which he hath had in keeping" (LR 333).

To summarise the link between *Dagor dagorath* and Ragnarök, let us say that in *The Book of Lost Tales*, the battle only takes place between gods: Melkor, Fionwë, and Túrin (deified). It is a twilight of the gods indeed. Yet, the more time passes, the less it is about the gods! It seems Eärendil intervenes, he pursues Melkor and topples him. Túrin no longer is a god. The part played by men becomes more important. A marginal note even indicates that Beren shall be there (WJ 247)! The initial paradox is consequently twofold: the more time passes and the less Tolkien's end of the world resembles Ragnarök, yet he held onto this model until the end of his life. To account fully for this quite persistent paradox, let us do the other part of the study by comparing *Dagor dagorath* to Armageddon.

B. Armageddon

he battle of Armageddon mentioned in the *Apocalypse of John* (XVI, 16) refers to a place: 'the Mountain of Megiddo' (90 km north of Jerusalem). *Dagor dagorath* means 'the Battle of Battles' and *Ragnarök*, 'destiny of the Powers', and both occurred on a plain. But this difference should not conceal the fact that one is dealing with another 'prophecy'[12]. Trying to follow the 'episodes' of the Apocalypse in order to find them in *Dagor dagorath* is even less fruitful than with *Ragnarök* since the common elements between the two are very sparse. So, instead of starting from the text of St John to see what can be found in Tolkien, we shall work the other way round. Five elements can be pointed out.

1. Morgoth destroys the Sun and the Moon. In the *Apocalypse*, this destruction is progressive and takes place in three stages before they are declared to be useless[13].

---

12 *The Apocalypse of John* I, 3; XIX, 10; XXII, 7, 18-19.
13 See *The Apocalypse of John* VI, 12, VIII, 12, IX, 2; and XXI, 23 for the uselessness. In *The Book of Lost Tales*, Melko causes the meteor shower ("Melko stalks high above the air seeking ever to do a hurt to the Sun and Moon and stars (eclipses, meteors)", LT 2 281): in *The Apocalypse of John*, this phenomenon is also present (VI, 3, VIII, 12, IX, 1 and XII, 4).

2. Eärendil[14] then descends upon Morgoth as a white flame to cast him out into the earth. This version of the tale, subsequent to the *Qenta Noldorinwa*, possibly takes up two apocalyptic *loci*. One can indeed read that a fire comes down out of heaven to devour the nations who obey the devil on the one hand[15], and on the other hand that the devil is "cast out into the earth" by St Michael[16]. Let us incidentally point out that the designation of Morgoth as the devil is an established fact in Tolkien (MR 412; L 191, 195).
3. Morgoth is then killed by Túrin's sword, as those who had been deceived by the Antichrist are killed by the 'sword' of the Word of God[17].
4. After recovering the Silmarilli, the Mountains of Valinor are levelled as the mountains are moved out of their places during Armageddon[18].
5. The elves shall then awaken and their dead shall rise in the same way as Hades gives up the dead and there shall be no more death[19].

Out of these five possible common points, one and three are original (or at least date from *The Book of Lost Tales*); and two, four and five are subsequent to the *Qenta Noldorinwa*. If one adds the battle of Michael/Manwë against, possibly, the Devil/Morgoth (XII, 7-9, XX, 2), which we saw was mentioned rather late by Tolkien, then the Christianisation of *Dagor dagorath* seems obvious. Indeed, contrary to what happens with *Ragnarök*, the more time passes, the more there are common points with the *Apocalypse*[20]. But these are sparse elements. We started from Tolkien's text to see if they could be found in the *Apocalypse*. The scenario being so different, that is how it had to be done. Moreover, those common points are sometimes loosely connected! The scenario of *Dagor dagorath* consequently seems to remain closer to *Ragnarök*, but the conception of the

---

14 Eärendil is "the morning star" (SM 154, 196), which is also mentioned in *The Apocalypse of John* II, 28, XXII, 16.
15 "... and fire came down out of heaven, and devoured them. And the devil that deceived them was cast into the lake of fire and brimstone..." (*The Apocalypse of John* XX, 9-10).
16 "... Michael and his angels *going forth* to war with the dragon... And the great dragon was cast down, the old serpent, he that is called the Devil and Satan, the deceiver of the whole world; he was cast down to the earth, and his angels were cast down with him." (*The Apocalypse of John* XII, 7,9).
17 "... his name is called the Word of God... out of his mouth proceedeth a sharp sword, that with it he should smite the nations... [They] were killed with the sword of him that sat upon the horse..." (*The Apocalypse of John* XIX, 13, 15, 21, cf. II, 16).
18 "And every island fled away, and the mountains were not found" (*The Apocalypse of John* XVI, 20, cf. VI, 14).
19 "... death and Hades gave up the dead which were in them... death shall be no more" (*The Apocalypse of John* XX, 13 and XXI, 4). For a broader study of the theme of resurrection in Tolkien, we shall direct the reader to our analyses in 'Tolkien, l'effigie des elfes'. We shall not deal with the related issue of Judgement Day either (Lewis took up Judgement Day in *The Last Battle*).
20 It could also be maintained rather easily that Ragnarök itself already borrows elements from *The Apocalypse of John*. For instance, a beast comes out of the abyss (XI, 7).

world changes for Tolkien to move closer to the biblical vision. *Ragnarök* is in particular an eternal return whereas there is only one Arda Healed in Tolkien, such as the New Jerusalem (III, 12, XXI, 1-2). We therefore argue that *originally* and '*structurally*', *Dagor dagorath* has more in common with *Ragnarök*, that is to say a battle of the gods, but that *fundamentally*, the more time passes, the more the apocalyptic part modifies the representation of Arda by always incorporating more Christian elements, so much so that *Ragnarök* now stands so far away that the debt to the original model hardly bears any likeness to it any more; as the common points become more numerous on the Catholic side. Such could be the explanation of the literary debt without any likeness. Our categories which make a distinction between the original and the fundamental may help clarify this paradox. A last point of interpretation remains: why did Tolkien not completely re-write the apocalyptic version of *Dagor dagorath*? Why is he content with sprinkling those elements this way if they are that fundamental? Why does he remain so attached to the *Ragnarök* model throughout his life[21]? We are here dealing with the question of the status of the eschatological interpretation in Tolkien.

II. The Eschatological Interpretation

his question gives rise to, at least, two series of problems. We shall first briefly look at the three ways of reading the *Apocalypse of John* and then at the four meanings of Scripture in general.

A. Tolkien and the Prophetic Reading

he first reading is eschatological or **futuristic,** according to which the *Apocalypse* deals with the end times of the world, that is to say the future[22]. The second one is preteristic or **historical**: past events are here dealt with. The *Apocalypse* would describe the struggle of the Church against the Jews and the pagans before Constantine allowed Christianity. The **prophetic** reading is eventually a sort of synthesis of the two mentioned above: the *Apocalypse* would recap the whole history of the Church, past and present. Seven ages of the Church can then be identified (they correspond to the seven horsemen).

---

21 See texts [1] and [3] in the appendices and the 1972 'very rough notes' on Gandalf: 'under Men's dominion Middle-earth shall seek until Dagor Dagorath and the Doom cometh' (UT 512). Even quite late then, Tolkien remains attached to the idea of an end of Arda which bears a likeness to *Ragnarök*.
22 About the three sorts of reading, see Armogathe 130, 204-205.

Can we try and see where Tolkien fits into these different readings? Several elements speak in favour of a prophetic reading. First, the end of the world is indeed announced as a future event in the *Notes on motive in the Silmarillion*: "The 'Elder King' is obviously not going to be finally defeated or destroyed, at least not before some ultimate 'Ragnarök' – which even for us is still in the future..." (MR 399). Second, Tolkien does contemplate seven ages in the letter to Rhona Beare[23]. But third and most of all, *landmarks of the* Apocalypse *can be found scattered in the history of Middle-earth.*

a) The most obvious of these landmarks is the chaining of Melkor. In the *Apocalypse*, the devil is bound for a thousand years before being set free[24]. It is no different with Melkor, bound in chains for 300 years (between 1100 and 1400 of the First Age) and then released.

b) Another key element which could be summoned to substantiate the claim that the *Apocalypse* is scattered in the history of Middle-earth is the ambivalence of the phrase 'the last battle'.

i) Tolkien actually uses it to refer to both the Last Battle at the end of the First Age and to speak about the last battle at the end of times. The last battle is literally split into two, as it were, only the use of capital letters to refer to the first (being the more important of the two) tells one from the other!

ii) *Dagor dagorath* is the last battle, the Battle of Battles. In that sense, it completes the great battles of Beleriand: *Dagor-nuin-Giliath* (the Battle under the Stars in Sindarin), *Dagor Aglareb* (the Glorious Battle in Sindarin), *Dagor Bragollach* (the Battle of Sudden Flame in Sindarin), and *Nirnaeth Arnoediad* (the (battle of) Unnumbered Tears in Sindarin). All these battles were fought against Melkor. The battles of the Second and Third Ages shall be against Sauron. Only *Dagor dagorath* shall be another battle against Melkor. Could it be any other way? Could the battle in the superlative be fought against the devil's lieutenant?

iii) The scattering of the end of the world in the history of Middle-earth is all the more obvious if one looks at the succession of the Ages. The end of the First Age is marked by the disappearance of the Silmarilli after Melkor was cast into the Void. From this point of view, with a mirror-like effect, the end of the First Age announces the end of the world: Morgoth returns to the world and, once he has been definitively defeated, the Silmarilli are reunited for the light of the Trees to shine again. The end of the First Age paves the way for the end of the world. It is the condition upon which its scenario is based. The link between the Last Battle and the last battle shows here again.

The end of the Second Age is brought about by the disappearance of the Ring, yet beforehand an apocalyptic and cosmic upheaval takes place with the Downfall of Númenór. So once again the end of this Age is linked with the end of the world.

---

23 'I imagine we are actually at the end of the Sixth Age, or in the Seventh' (L 283).
24 *The Apocalypse of John* XX, 2, 7.

Eventually, the end of the Third Age is apocalyptic. A great deal of commentators, and not the least well-read in theology, saw it there. It is for instance the case of Father Louis Bouyer, this friend of Tolkien's we mentioned at the start, who speaks of *The Lord of the Rings* in his own book entitled *Prélude à l'Apocalypse*!

> You are like all the French, you have not read Tolkien! You are the only ones not to have read it yet. But you have to! He does not tell stories, but our history. But of course..., the history recorded in his journal, because this is what it is, believe me, is not what happened yesterday but what will happen tomorrow.

In other words, recounting the end of the Third Age is a way of speaking of our future. The end of the world takes place in a mythical past so as to be a better teaching of the *eschaton*. Paul Airiau underlined the inspiration that was common to both Tolkien and Bouyer, which he described as an eschatologism[25]. This point of view is also shared by another theologian, Father Jean-Yves Lacoste, when he writes that:

> ... fairy does not only deal with time, *chronos*: it is fundamentally linked with the *aeon*, with the completion of time or of a time. The experience of the hobbit in the eponymous book considered as a prologue to *The Lord of the Rings*, could be described as a caricature of existence only taken in time. It hardly deals with history, all the more so with eschatology. But when it enters history, it also simultaneously enters a history that has an end. History and eschatology are present together in *The Hobbit*. Neither *its* history, nor its completion are our history and our eschatology. But there are clear enough manifestations of the interweaving of the historical and of the *eschaton*, or to put it another way of the integration of chronos into the *aeon*, so that the subcreated world actually accounts for the real world. (363)

---

25 "The two of them [sc. Tolkien and Bouyer] eventually share a common Catholic position: an eschatologism that insists on the fallen situation of the world dominated by Satan, but redeemed by Christ, who, in sacramental and liturgical life, already allows us to live on earth the end of times... This eschatological Catholicism owes a lot to the patristics of the IIIrd-Xth centuries (up to the start of scholasticism even)... the closeness of Tolkien with the theology of the eschatological 'third party' of the 1950s thus leads us to consider that he is part of a broader movement... The mythical thought and its symbols completely recovered by God are now more than ever available for a propedeutical catechisation of modern man, by anticipating in their fashion the eschatological expectation." (Airau, *catholicisme* 134, 135, 137, 138). The (optimistic) eschatologism of Father Bouyer as opposed to (pessimistic) apocalypticism is explained by Airiau, *L'Église* 84-92, 119-121.

The end of the Third Age described in *The Lord of the Rings* is then also likely to be read from an apocalyptic point of view. Aragorn has been identified by some to the Christ of the *Apocalypse*[26]. Middle-earth is going through a phase of decline, the Shadow of Sauron is spreading, there are numerous attacks of wild animals, similarly to what happens in the *Apocalypse*[27]. Several arguments consequently speak in favour of a prophetic reading (as we have defined it) of the *Apocalypse* in Tolkien scattered in the history of Middle-earth. If that even applies to *The Lord of the Rings*, the question of its allegorical reading has to be asked to finish with.

B. The Allegorical Meaning?

t is well known how, for *The Lord of the Rings*, Tolkien rejected the allegorical interpretation. This must be true for the *Legendarium* as a whole. But the question of allegory is decisive for the reading of the *Apocalypse of John* itself. Tolkien, as a medievalist, could not ignore the doctrine of the fourfold senses of Scripture[28]. They are usually presented as follows: "*Littera gesta docet, quid credas allegoria, moralis quid agas, quo speres anagogia*, the literal teaches the facts, the allegorical teaches what you should believe, the moral [tropological] what you should do, the anagogic what you should hope [aim for]". One has surely recognised here the mnemonic distich of the Dominican Augustine of Dacia (1282†) in the *Rotulus pugillaris* (chap. 1). His didactic verse summarises St Thomas Aquinas (*Summa Theologica*). There are two main senses: the historical sense and the spiritual sense (divided into three).

In Origen's *De Principiis*, *explanatio spiritualis* (*pneumatike diegesis*), the anagogic and the allegorical are closely associated[29]. The truth of what has to be believed inevitably fits in with what is of all eternity, because the *eschaton* prepares for eternity. As Tolkien says, "Allegory and Story converge, meeting somewhere in Truth. So that the only perfectly consistent allegory is a real life; and the only fully intelligible story is an allegory" (L 121). These words by Tolkien on allegory are not very well-known. One actually remembers that Tolkien contrasts applicability, which leaves the reader free to choose, with allegory in which the author dominates the reader. Which precise aspect of allegory to grasp then to understand Tolkien's obvious refusal to re-write *Dagor dagorath* after *Apocalypse*?

---

26 It is Wytenbroek's case, the greater part of his article (p. 8b-12a) focuses on the Christlike analysis of Aragorn. The first reviews of *The Lord of the Rings* did identify his apocalyptic dimension, see Johnson 27 (B99) and 32 (B174).
27 Wytenbroek 7f, cf. Sookoo 20f.
28 See de Lubac 1 24-25.
29 See de Lubac 2 628.

Tolkien does not re-write the Apocalypse allegorically because he leaves the reader free to choose. Yet, he leaves all the elements to fit in with the story of salvation, for the God of Isaac, Abraham and Jacob to be the Lord 'of angels, and of men – and of elves' (FS 78, § 105). While it is up to the reader to decide what the meaning of the story is, the fundamentally Catholic elements are present. Tolkien actually goes as far as introducing what is absolutely necessary to the *Apocalypse*, that is to say the victory of good, namely: Jesus Christ. But that is not all. Let us make these fundamental points clear before concluding.

C. The Catholic-Orientated Elements

aint John leads off the *Apocalypse* mentioning the 'Revelation of Jesus Christ'. At the end of times, the Antichrist shall appear and Jesus Christ shall come back to destroy him. The final victory is Christ's. In Tolkien, if it is not known who the Antichrist by Satan's side will be (Sauron?), it is known that Eru will enter into Arda[30] and that he will re-enter into it[31]. Clyde S. Kilby as he spoke of those *Athrabeth* texts recognised "... Christ's incarnation..., and the final consummation at Christ's return" (62). Doing so, Tolkien was on the verge of crossing the line that he had set himself when he wrote that he would not dare write about the Incarnation (L 237).

Here is another fundamentally Catholic element, which is only subsequent to the version of the *Quenta Silmarillion* (§ 32, LR 333): "Thereafter shall Earth be broken and re-made". The whole theme of Arda Healed is a reminder of the Celestial Jerusalem.

Likewise, the Second Music[32] reminds one of the 'new song' (*Apocalypse* XIV, 3) or of the clamour of the crowd gathered in front of the throne of the Lamb (XIX, 1) or even of the *Sanctus* (which comes from the *Book of Isaiah* VI, 3) sung during what is now called the extraordinary form of the Roman Rite.

---

30 "[T]he One will himself enter into Arda" (MR 321).
31 Note 11 of the *Commentary* of the *Athrabeth*: "... in the *Ainulindalë*, in which reference is made to the "Flame Imperishable". This appears to mean the Creative activity of Eru (in some sense distinct from or within Him), by which things could be given a 'real' and independent (though derivative and created) existence. The Flame Imperishable is sent out from Eru, to dwell in the heart of the world, and the world then Is, on the same plane as the Ainur, and they can enter into it. But this is not, of course, the same as the re-entry of Eru to defeat Melkor." (MR 345)
32 Garbowski has given the specifics of the eschatology of the Second Music. According to him, Tolkien implemented two eschatologies from the start (Ragnarök's dark one and the Second Music's more joyful one, p. 273); and it would then have become more and more difficult for him to integrate an Armageddon once the *Legendarium* was conceived as a mythopoetic supplement to our history (p. 274).

Conclusion

First, the more time passes, the more the Catholic elements play a part in the history of Tolkien. Yet, the Norse reference remains essential, should it be at the expense of the paradox of a literary debt that bears little resemblance to it, while the Catholic similarities are building up... But the apocalypse, precisely, is diluted in the history of Middle-earth.

Because second, the problem of interpretation is decisive. Tolkien did not re-write *Dagor dagorath* as an allegory of the *Apocalypse*, but got very close to it. He paved the way by building up the similarities. But the correspondences are not perfect matches. We have seen the importance of distortions, how heterogeneous they are (a scene of Eärendil has two different sources). In short, what is essential is here, but redistributed according to the logic of the history of Middle-earth. Tolkien wrote a history which resembles reality; he turned his *Legendarium* into a parable after the meaning defined by his friend Father Murray[33]. From this viewpoint, the history of Tolkien is an acceptable allegory.

But third, the *Dagor dagorath* text is not an allegory *with* the *Apocalypse* text, because it would also have meant deciding on the allegorical reading *of* the *Apocalypse* and that would have amounted to depriving twice the reader of the freedom to choose.[34]

Appendix

[1] This legendarium ends with a vision of the end of the world, its breaking and remaking, and the recovery of the Silmarilli and the 'light before the Sun' – after a final battle which owes, I suppose, more to the Norse vision of Ragnarök than to anything else, though it is not much like it. (L 149)

[2] Manwë will not descend from the Mountain until the Dagor Dagorath, and the coming of the End, when Melkor returns To the overthrow of Morgoth he sent his herald Eönwë. (UT 511)

[3] The 'Elder King' is obviously not going to be finally defeated or destroyed, at least not before some ultimate 'Ragnarök' – which even for us is still in the future, so he can have no real 'adventures'. But, if you keep him *at home*, the issue of any particular event (since it cannot then result in a final 'checkmate') can remain in literary suspense. Even to the final war against Morgoth it is Fionwë son of Manwë who leads out the power of the Valar. When we move out Manwë it will be the last battle, and the end of the World (or of 'Arda Marred') as the Eldar would say. (MR 399)

---

33 For a bibliography of R. Murray, see 'Robert Murray: publications', *The Heythrop Journal*, 36, 1995, 4, p. 521-528.
34 It is our pleasurable duty to thank Bertrand Bellet, Paul Airiau and, most of all, our translator David Ledanois.

The Book of Lost Tales

[4] For 'tis said that ere the Great End come Melko shall in some wise contrive a quarrel between Moon and Sun, and Ilinsor shall seek to follow Urwendi through the Gates, and when they are gone the Gates of both East and West will be destroyed, and Urwendi and Ilinsor shall be lost. So shall it be that Fionwë Úrion, son of Manwë, of love for Urwendi shall in the end be Melko's bane, and shall destroy the world to destroy his foe, and so shall all things then be rolled away. (LT 1 219)

[5] Turambar indeed shall stand beside Fionwë in the Great Wrack, and Melko and his drakes shall curse the sword of Mormakil. (LT 2 116)

[6] Melko is thus now out of the world – but one day he will find a way back, and the last great uproars will begin before the Great End... Gilfanon also prophesies concerning the Great End, and of the Wrack of Things, and of Fionwë, Tulkas, and Melko and the last fight on the Plains of Valinor. (LT 2 282-283)

Sketch of the Mythology (1926)

[7] When the world is much older, and the Gods weary, Morgoth will come back through the Door, and the last battle of all will be fought. Fionwë will fight Morgoth on the plain of Valinor, and the spirit of Túrin shall be beside him; it shall be Túrin who with his black sword will slay Morgoth, and thus the children of Húrin shall be avenged. In those days the Silmarils shall be recovered from sea and earth and air, and Maidros shall break them and Belaurin with their fire rekindle the Two Trees, and the great light shall come forth again, and the Mountains of Valinor shall be levelled so that it goes out over the world, and Gods and Elves and Men shall grow young again, and all their dead awake... Eärendel's boat is drawn over Valinor to the Outer Seas, and Eärendel launches it into the outer darkness high above Sun and Moon. There he sails with the Silmaril upon his brow and Elwing at his side, the brightest of all stars, keeping watch upon Morgoth. So he shall sail until he sees the last battle gathering upon the plains of Valinor. Then he will descend. (SM 40)

Quenta Noldorinwa (c. 1930)

[8] Thus spake the prophecy of Mandos, which he declared in Valmar at the judgement of the Gods, and the rumour of it was whispered among all the Elves of the West: when the world is old and the Powers grow weary, then Morgoth shall come back through the Door out of the Timeless Night; and he shall destroy the Sun and the Moon, but Eärendel shall come upon him as a white flame and drive him from the airs. Then shall the last battle be gathered on the fields of Valinor. In that day Tulkas shall strive with Melko, and on his right shall stand Fionwë and on his left Túrin Turambar, son of Húrin, Conqueror of Fate; and it shall be the black sword of Túrin that deals unto Melko his death and final end; and so shall the children of Húrin and all Men be avenged. Thereafter shall the Silmarils be recovered out of sea and earth and air; for Eärendel shall descend and yield up that flame that he hath had in keeping. Then Fëanor shall bear the Three and yield them unto Yavanna Palúrien; and she will break them and with their fire rekindle the Two Trees, and a great light shall come forth; and the Mountains of Valinor shall be levelled, so that the light goes out all over the world. In that light the Gods will again grow young, and the Elves awake and all their dead arise, and the purpose of Ilúvatar be fulfilled concerning them. But of Men in that day the prophecy speaks not, save of Túrin only, and him it names among the Gods. (SM 165)

Quenta Silmarillion (mid-1930 and after)

[9] Thus spake Mandos in prophecy, when the Gods sat in judgement in Valinor, and the rumour of his words was whispered among all the Elves of the West. When the world is old and the Powers grow weary, then Morgoth, seeing that the guard sleepeth, shall come back through

the Door of Night out the Timeless Void; and he shall destroy the Sun and Moon. But Eärendel shall descend upon him as a white and searing flame and drive him from the airs. Then shall the Last Battle be gathered on the fields of Valinor. In that day Tulkas shall strive with Morgoth, and on his right shall stand Fionwë, and on his left Túrin Turambar, son of Húrin, coming from the halls of Mandos;[35] and the black sword of Túrin shall deal unto Morgoth his death and final end; and so shall the children of Húrin and all Men be avenged. Thereafter shall Earth be broken and re-made, and the Silmarils be recovered out of Air and Earth and Sea; for Eärendel shall descend and surrender the flame which he hath had in keeping. Then Fëanor shall take the Three Jewels and bear them to Yavanna Palúrien; and she will break them and with their fire rekindle the Two Trees, and a great light shall come forth. And the Mountains of Valinor shall be levelled, so that the Light shall go out over all the world. In[36] that light the Gods will grow young again, and the Elves awake and all their dead arise, and the purpose of Ilúvatar be fulfilled concerning them. But of Men in that day the prophecy of Mandos doth not speak, and no Man it names, save Túrin only, and to him a place is given among the sons of the Valar. (LR 333)

Bibliography

Airau, Paul. *L'Église et l'Apocalypse du XIXe siècle à nos jours*. Paris: Berg, 2000

---. »Catholicisme et actualisation du merveilleux médiéval. Le cas de J.R.R. Tolkien et Louis Bouyer«. *Fantasy, le merveilleux médiéval aujourd'hui*. Ed. A. Besson & M. White-Le Goff. Paris: Bragelonne, 2007, 131-142

Armogathe, Jean-Robert. *L'Antéchrist à l'âge classique. Exégèse et politique*. Paris: Mille et une nuits, 2005

Bouyer, Louis (C.O.) [under the pseud. of Lambert, Louis]. *Prélude à l'Apocalypse ou les derniers chevaliers du Graal*. Limoges: Criterion, 1982

Carpenter, Humphrey (Ed.). *The Letters of J.R.R. Tolkien*. London: HarperCollins, 1995

Devaux, Michaël. »Louis Bouyer & J.R.R. Tolkien: une amitié d'écrivains«. *Tolkien, les racines du légendaire*. Ed. M. Devaux. Genève: Ad Solem 2003, 85-146

---, »L'effigie des elfes«. *Tolkien, l'effigie des elfes*. Ed. M. Devaux. Paris: Ad Solem, 2010, 21-91

Flieger, Verlyn & Douglas A. Anderson (Eds.). *Tolkien On Fairy-stories*. Expanded Edition with Commentary and Notes. London: HarperCollins, 2008

Garbowksi, Christopher. "Tolkien's Eschatology of Hope: From Ragnarok to Joyous Subcreation". *Journal for the Study of the Pseudepigrapha Supplement Series* 43 (2002): 271-283

Johnson, Judith A. *J.R.R. Tolkien. Six Decades of Criticism*. London: Greenwood Press, 1986

Kane, Douglas Charles. *Arda Reconstructed. The Creation of the Published* Silmarillion. Bethlehem: Lehigh University Press, 2009

Kilby, C.S. *Tolkien &* The Silmarillion. Wheaton: Harold Staw, 1977

Kocher, Paul. *A Reader's Guide* The Silmarillion. London: Thames and Hudson, 1980

---

[10] **Quenta Silmarillion (1958-1960)**
35 > Túrin Turambar, son of Húrin, returning from the Doom of Men at the ending of the World. (In margin: and Beren Camlost).
36 > Large X in the margin. (WJ 247)

Lacoste, Jean-Yves. »Anges et hobbits : le sens des mondes possibles«. *Freiburger Zeitschrift für Philosophie* 36 (1989): 341-373

Leigh, David J. (S.J.). "The Problem of Violence Against the Other in Twentieth-Century Apocalyptic Fiction". *Christianity and Literature* 57 (2008): 253-268

Lubac, Henri de (S.J.). *Exégèse médiévale. Les Quatre sens de l'Écriture.* 4 vols. Paris: Aubier, 1959-1964

Murray, Robert (S.J.). "J.R.R. *Tolkien and the Art of the Parable*". *Tolkien: A Celebration.* Ed. J. Pearce. London: Fount, 1999, 40-52

Schrader, R.J. "*Sehnsucht* and the Varieties of Religious Experience in Charles William's *War in Heaven*". *Renascence. Essays on Values in Literature* 30 (1978): 99-110

Sookoo, Lara. "Animals in Tolkien's World". *Tolkien Encyclopedia. Scholarship and Critical Assessment.* Ed. M.C. Drout. New York: Routledge 2006, 19-21

Tolkien, John Ronald Reuel. *The Book of Lost Tales 1. History of Middle-earth I.* Ed. Christopher Tolkien. London: HarperCollins, 2000

---. *The Book of Lost Tales 2. History of Middle-earth II.* Ed. Christopher Tolkien. London: HarperCollins, 2000

---. *The Shaping of Middle-earth. History of Middle-earth IV.* Ed. Christopher Tolkien. London: HarperCollins, 2000

---. *The Lost Road and other writings. History of Middle-earth V.* Ed. Christopher Tolkien. London: HarperCollins, 2000

---. *Morgoth's Ring. History of Middle-earth X.* Ed. Christopher Tolkien. London: HarperCollins, 2000

---. *The War of the Jewels. History of Middle-earth XI.* Ed. Christopher Tolkien. London: HarperCollins, 1994

---. *Unfinished Tales of Númenor and Middle-earth.* Ed. Christopher Tolkien. London: HarperCollins, 2000

---. *The Legend of Sigurd and Gudrún.* Ed. Christopher Tolkien. London: HarperCollins, 2009.

Whittingham, Elizabeth A. *The Evolution of Tolkien's Mythology. A Study of the History of Middle-earth.* Jefferson – London: McFarland, 2007

Wytenbroek, J.R. "Apocalyptic Vision in *The Lord of the Rings*". *Mythlore* 54 (1988): 7-12

Clean Earth to Till: A Tolkienian Vision of War

Anna Slack (Cambridge)

Apologia

It is no secret that a subject as expansive as war is always a hard one to pin down. Tolstoy was able to write on the matter at considerable length, and many are the philosophers and war historians who have always done so. This paper is a preliminary investigation into how war is envisioned in what amounts to one sample of Tolkien's canon of works: accordingly, it cannot and does not pretend to offer a thorough and conclusive investigation into every facet of that vision. Rather, it is an exploration into some aspects of it that seem significant.

This exploration will focus on *The Lord of the Rings*, examining the causes, motives, waging and ends of war in the context of the literary and spiritual underpinnings of Tolkien's work. The first question we must ask is what, so far as literary tradition is concerned, are the *causus belli*?

Causus Belli

> Was this the face that launched a thousand ships
> And burnt the topless towers of Ilium?[1]

Many genres of literature intersect over the question of war, handling it differently depending upon the time and function of their writing. One thing is certain: in one form or another, conflict is expected. It drives story-telling.

Conflict arises on a sliding scale. It ranges from the microcosmic, focused entirely on inter-personal relations at the level of the individual, and goes through dozens of variations to reach, as is so often the case with the grander end of literature, the macrocosmic, where the focus is on the disputes between nations or worlds. In this latter case of macrocosmic conflict, war and violence by definition almost inevitably play a part in the proceedings. But how do we come to be embroiled in a macrocosmic conflict?

This question has troubled philosophers for many years. We can perhaps summarise a very complex process by saying that wars are entered into either

---

[1] Christopher Marlowe, *Doctor Faustus*, Scene xviii l.99-100

to avenge or defend against a perceived or actual wrong, or for gain. The two circumstances can have a considerable measure of overlap.

In the literary genre of fantasy, and especially that sub-genre called heroic fantasy, we will typically encounter a plot where the macrocosmic 'wrong' facing the heroes is that of unlawful dominion. The villain of the piece is either actively seeking or has already obtained a particular gain. Whether he is seizing an inheritance, object of power or entire realm, the heroes' task is either to stop the villain from achieving his ends or to overthrow him and restore the usurped order. It is the description of the heroes' efforts that make up the story that we read.

It's clear that on a basic level *The Lord of the Rings* uses this kind of plot; all the protagonists' efforts are towards keeping Sauron from seizing unlawful control of Middle-Earth. We can see similar traits in other works of modern fantasy: in Narnia, the Pevensies are called upon more than once to drive out usurpers, Prydain's Taran defends against Arawn's increasing power and Earthsea's archmage Ged confronts Cob as he seeks immortality at the cost of the archipelago. Widening our scope a little, Luke Skywalker and his space-faring kindred face exactly the same problems. What unites the heroes of these heroic genres is that they all face villains seeking to destroy or control something that is not theirs to seek. Evil tries to corrupt, pervert and destroy while good tries to redeem, restore and be just.

A villain with his sights set on unlawful dominion is prone to dealing out destruction and violence and doing whatever it takes to obtain his end. Consequentially the stakes in these kinds of stories are often unimaginably high. Failure is measured in suffering and death, and not only for the heroes. This ripple effect means that the heroes' actions take on global or even universal significance. When the final battle-lines are drawn we end up with a rendering of good on one side and evil on the other. Thanks to the macrocosmic nature of this conflict, these lines aren't usually metaphorical either – light and dark quite literally go to war.

War in Heaven

The war of good versus evil forms a very particular thread in western storytelling traditions. If we trace it back just a couple of hundred years we find it featuring heavily in Milton's *Paradise Lost*. The concept we encounter is that of war in heaven, good and evil clashing on the grandest scale imaginable. Of course, the meeting of such forces is not unique to the Christian tradition – but its crucially defining element with that tradition is that good is ultimately and unquestioningly victorious. This is a kind of prevailing wind that quietly breathes life into the genre of heroic fantasy: good triumphs. When it does, virtues other than strength and swords – like hope, charity, and courage – often seem to count the most, and the most unlikely and lowly pieces – farmboys, children, and peasants – are played against the powers of darkness in the endgame. The biblical parallels are clear: weakness becomes strength, the humble are raised up and the wicked are brought low.

Yet Christianity is not the only tradition wielding power over the fantasy genre. Under our umbrella of the war of good against evil we find a cornucopia of other traditions informing our narratives. They are predominantly pre-Christian and especially, in Tolkien's case, northern. With them come easily-recognisable heroic staples: feats of arms, desperate last stands, battles against impossible odds and deeds done for honour, glory, reputation, and song. Over time, these ideas bled into the later, more christianised notions of mediaeval romances, whose sword-wielding knights were, in their imitation of Christ, also called to moral and spiritual virtue that would have grave consequences in the temporal world.[2]

This is the melting pot from which heroic fantasy emerges. The tropes and stances of warfare, whether rooted in sagas and heroic epic or in later Christian ideas of moral and spiritual courage, is a vital ingredient and defining element of the genre.

So, we have the conflict of good and evil and the various virtues and vices of the pagan and Christian traditions. By any culture's definition, righteous or just action is laudable and heroic. Violence and war must be faced with physical skill and spiritual strength. Sometimes, as in the case of Spenser's knight Guyon throwing down the 'bowres of blisse' in *The Faerie Queene*, physical deeds are morally and spiritually motivated. The rule seems simple: fight the good fight, and all will be well.

But life in a work of modern heroic fantasy is more complicated than this. For writers of Tolkien's generation, and in many cases those writing after him even up to our own day, we also have to add to this mix the issues thrown up by a world disenchanted with morality, heroism and above all with war. Fantasy lives still in the literary shadow of the Great War, and many writers, especially in Tolkien's time, swallowed that era's aversion to war and its relentless questioning of whether bloodshed and sacrifice can ever be justified or achieve the good, whatever that might be. In other words, can war ever be good, whether it is thought of as a 'just war' or not?

Tolkien's works are birthed in these complex literary circumstances, just as Tolkien's writing is itself birthed in times of war and nurtured by 'the desire to express [his] feelings about good, evil, fair [and] foul' (L 78). Perhaps because

---

2 In terms of the relations between virtue and physical action, *Gawain and the Green Knight* is a highly articulated case in point.

of the press of disillusionment in his contemporaries and his own encounters with violence, Tolkien found himself driven to talk about good, evil, and war. The emerging fantasy genre, a product of the classics and sagas and Christian thought, was his chosen vehicle. Tolkien powerfully reconnected heroic fantasy to its literary and war-faring roots, creating a vision of war that stood against the *status quo* of his time. He does this by re-establishing war's morality in terms of its temporal and spiritual ends. Tolkien builds up a picture of a just war, but never denies the very human complexity of being in the line of battle.

Spectrums of Response

n *The Lord of the Rings*, Tolkien presents us with the vast canvas of a world at war where each culture and character responds differently to the threat posed by the dark lord. In fact, just as some critics have called Tolkien's most famous work a travelogue we might also call it an opinion poll, one whose results show attitudes to war that would be at home among cultures far earlier than ours, as well as our own. Everyone that we meet on the road to Mordor has a slightly different take on the war that will end the Third Age. There are those who help and those who hinder, those who are passionate and those who are indifferent, those who stridently face the situation with all their courage and those who will not look it in the eye.

Tolkien presents us with a spectrum of responses – some of them canonically heroic, some of them decidedly post-modern, and all of them very human. Most characters can be read as a confluence of the literary and historical tradition they represent and that tradition's stance on virtue and on war. Tolkien uses these points of confluence as a way of exploring and re-envisioning a just war.

An excellent example of this kind of exploratory confluence is in the Rohirrim and, more specifically, in Théoden. Rohan is a culture that seems at once Anglo-Saxon, Norse, and Classical: it has a sense of northern spirit in its literary links to the tale of *Beowulf* and in its emphasis on deeds and song. This same emphasis also links the Rohirrim to the heroes of ancient Greece, whose deeds sought glory, *kleos*, while in nomenclature Théoden's people are clearly linked to the Anglo-Saxons. Tolkien presents us with a people whose concerns seem to be centred on war:

> Where now the horse and the rider? Where is the horn that was blowing?
> Where is the helm and the hauberk, and the bright hair flowing?
> Where is the hand on the harpstring, and the red fire glowing?
> (LotR 497)

This elegiac verse by 'a forgotten poet' is clearly indebted to the Anglo-Saxon alliterative tradition. It shows us that song-making for the Rohirrim, as for many historical peoples, is commemorative, and demonstrates that a driving purpose for these songs is to remember war, and those lost in it. The song for the horse and the rider connects war ('the helm and the hauberk'), beauty ('the bright hair flowing'), song ('the hand on the harpstring') and the singing of songs by the fire ('the red fire glowing') together. By doing so, Tolkien suggests that song and war encompass every aspect of the Rohirrim's existence, from the cradle to the grave. Peter Jackson took up this idea in his film version: in the extended edition of *The Two Towers* we see Éowyn singing a funerary dirge for Théodred:

> Bealocwealm hafað fréone frecan forth onsended giedd sculon singan gléomenn sorgiende on Meduselde.
>
> [*An evil death has set forth the noble warrior / A song shall sing sorrowing minstrels in Meduseld...*][3]

The fact that the death was evil and the warrior noble compounds our sense that the warrior's participation in war was a just one. At the same time, the minstrel's lament guarantees that this noble warrior will be remembered.

When Théoden is contemplating the final defence of the Hornburg Tolkien again sketches for us, how outstanding deeds of martial heroism – and remembering them in song – is of crucial concern to the Rohirrim:

> When dawn comes, I will bid men sound Helm's horn, and I will ride forth. Will you ride with me then, son of Arathorn? Maybe we shall cleave a road, or make such an end as will be worth a song – if any be left to sing of us hereafter.   (LotR 527)

Théoden uses the vocabulary of epic: Aragorn is the epithetical 'son of Arathorn', the killing is presented in terms of cleaving – a vivid verb suggesting mass bloodshed – and the deed is to be worth a song. Théoden's connecting of song, memory and noble deeds done in war is a rendering of an ethos familiar to us from both Classical and Northern sources – a cursory glance through the pages of *Beowulf* or Homer's *Iliad* would furnish us with many examples for comparison. These ideas add up to show us that, for the Rohirrim, the battlefield is a place where virtue is proven by noble, violent deeds and songs are written to perpetuate that nobility.

---

3   Quote and translation from: www.warofthering.net/forum/vbulletin225/upload/show-thread.php?t=5852 (06-12-2009)

With epic language and gestures left, right, and centre, we seem to be dealing with a culture that exclusively values martial and physical prowess. However, Tolkien adds another layer of depth to the Rohirrim when King Théoden parts with Wormtongue:

> 'Give him a horse and let him go at once, wherever he chooses [,' said Gandalf]. [']By his choice you shall judge him.'
> 'Do you hear this, Wormtongue?' said Théoden. 'This is your choice: to ride with me to war, and let us see in battle whether you are true; or to go now, whither you will. But then, if we ever meet again, I shall not be merciful.' (LotR 509)

It is subtle, but in this short quotation we see moral notions of judgement, mercy, and forgiveness underscoring warring acts – and all are crucially tied to the element of choice. Théoden makes it clear that battle is a place where a man can prove true in his fealty, but he also implicitly agrees with Gandalf that Wormtongue's choice is the keenest measure of his truth. It is implied that achievement in battle is only worthy if it is 'true', and that truth can only be judged by a man's choices. The heroism of choice is a much more Christian idea – one that is crucial to Frodo's non-violent protagonism – and Tolkien here suggests that the moral and spiritual capacity to be true and choose rightly must be the precursor to any deed in battle. This concept of what we might call *jus in delectu* – not just in war but just in choice – is crucial to Tolkien's view of the relations between morality, deeds, and war.

The aligning of morality with martial skill is a step towards the world of mediaeval romance, and a firm step away from our first impressions of Théoden's hall as a place of song and glory, firmly in the tradition of Hrothgar's own. Despite the best efforts of Augustine, St. Thomas Aquinas, and the company of just war theory, uniting morality and war under one banner can seem contradictory, and doubly so to those enchanted by blind pacifism. Indeed, once Théoden arrives at Isengard, Saruman is quick to try to work the apparent incongruity of the epic stance and moral choice against our heroes:

> Am I to be called a murderer, because valiant men have fallen in battle? If you go to war, needlessly, for I did not desire it, then men will be slain. But if I am a murderer on that account, then all the House of Eorl is stained with murder; for they have fought many wars, and assailed many who defied them. (LotR 566)

Saruman uses heroic language ('valiant men', 'slain') to cast moral aspersions on Théoden, implying that war and morality are incompatible. Morality affects the semantics of war: if he wishes to be moral Théoden will have to reinterpret all the heroic deeds that the Rohirrim hold so dear as nothing more than murder. In other words, Saruman insists that morality must equate with inaction and pacifism. The Rohirrim are not pacifists and therefore cannot be moral. Saruman's intent is to divorce warfare from its moral and heroic roots.

This conversation with Saruman represents a different kind of conflict for Théoden – this is not a battle against 'flesh and blood' but against the convincing power and authority of Saruman's voice. It is an 'inner war' (L 82), and it is Théoden's growing moral courage that enables him to withstand the onslaught:

> 'We will have peace,' he said, *now in a clear voice*, 'we will have peace, when you and all your works have perished – and the works of your dark master to whom you would deliver us.'
> (LotR 566, emphasis mine)

Théoden's language here is uncompromising and may even seem extreme, yet it is unquestioningly the right answer. Théoden has become a channel for a steely glimmer of the heroism of moral choice, epitomised throughout *The Lord of the Rings* by Frodo. The biblical – and in every way apocalyptic – resonance of his words takes us back to the idea of a battle of light against dark, one that is conducted both in a temporal and spiritual plane.

It also gives us a bold picture of the ultimate goal of war – peace, as defined by the perishing of all the works of evil. That Théoden's voice here is 'clear' is a signal to the reader that he is doing rightly and that, in line with Pauline tradition,[4] Tolkien views moral and spiritual capacity as vital and as necessary in war as feats of arms. War is waged in the material and the spiritual worlds, but on both planes it must be waged with *clarity*.

We have seen the Rohirrim move from the ranks of the classical and northern traditions towards the mediaeval allegorical stance of the inner war, where morality and physical courage must have a symbiotic relationship. We have also seen how Tolkien uses this progression to highlight the compatibility of spirituality, morality, and arms – a mixture that would have seemed out of place to a generation still reeling from Paschendale and the Somme. Having taken, in Théoden's encounter with Saruman, a step towards the apocalyptic, Tolkien also ideologically here sets the scene for the Rohirrim at the battle of the Pelennor where, driven forward by a moral conviction in the justice of joining battle:

---

[4] Cf. Ephesians.

> They sang as they slew, for the joy of battle was on them and the sound of their singing that was fair and terrible came even to the city. (LotR 820)

The admixture of singing that is 'fair and terrible' with battle creates the flavour of an apocalyptic vision: the representation has something in common with passages in the book of Revelations. Tolkien presents a brief and stunning prefiguring of the war in heaven whose eschatological nature heightens our perception of the necessity of the moral strength needed to face evil. It also acknowledges the inherent contradiction at the heart of war – it is both fair and terrible.

Tolkien compounds his argument for the necessity of moral conviction by presenting Denethor as a foil to Théoden. While Théoden has clarity Denethor has become clouded by despair:

> 'Pride and despair!' he cried... 'thy hope is but ignorance. Go then and labour in healing! Go forth and fight! Vanity! ... The West has failed... I will have naught: neither life diminished, nor love halved, nor honour abated.' (LotR 835f)

Denethor's moral sin of despair withdraws him from battle and compels him into taking his own life – an act only previously performed by 'heathen kings, under the domination of the Dark Power' (ibid)[5]. Tolkien uses Denethor to underline the necessity of choosing hope and taking a stand in war, showing his belief that '... it has [been,] is and will be necessary to face [war] in an evil world' (L 75). In his letters Tolkien writes of the material, moral, and spiritual 'waste' of war – of which Denethor, in his lack of stewardship, moral discernment, and overarching despair, seems emblematic. This same despair pejoratively labels both fighting and healing as 'vanity' – and, paradoxically, Tolkien's use of Denethor here brings healing to the reader's attention as one of the ends of war.

Denethor is not alone in grappling with despair; another character hounded by it is Éowyn:

> [Merry] caught the glint of clear grey eyes; and then he shivered, for it came suddenly to him that it was the face of one without hope who goes seeking death. (LotR 785)

---

5   It is interesting to note that the word *heathen* is one of the few religiously charged words to remain in the text following Tolkien's careful removal of them. This heightens the notion that despair is a moral sin.

This use of clear is very different to when we saw it used to describe Théoden's moral clarity. Tolkien is not suggesting that Éowyn's desire to seek death is morally correct or glorious. Rather, by juxtaposing the apparent clearness of her eyes with their colour, 'grey', he suggests the clouding of her internal, moral clarity by despair. While going to battle may be an outward gesture of nobility and courage the signal to the reader (compounded by Merry's shivering) is that there is no moral virtue behind this gesture. Tolkien shows that despair can look very much like heroism from the outside, but that heroism without internal moral decisiveness is 'without hope'. I have little doubt that Tolkien had seen it like in fellow soldiers in the trenches.

You may be thinking that this use of the virtues of hope and the vices of despair as a way of defining a character's moral capacity is a clean-cut system inside a work of fantasy: hope = good = just in war, despair = bad = violent in war. But we all know that the real world is more complicated than this. Like Samwise on the road to Mordor, we are afflicted by hope and despair in turns, and have likely all felt how it affects our judgements. Tolkien has often been charged with 'escapism', and perhaps a superficial and simplistic view of Tolkien's dialogue of hope and despair has contributed to that charge. Although he is showing us a moral system Tolkien is not giving us a 'disneyfied' vision of hope and despair. On the contrary, he makes the very human recognition that at the toughest moments in our lives – at the end of all things or at the very brink – 'hope and despair are akin' (LotR 862):

> '... you would have us retreat to Minas Tirith... and there sit like children on sand-castles when the tide is flowing?' said Imrahil.
> 'That would be no new counsel,' said Gandalf. 'Have you not done this and little more in all the days of Denethor? But no! I said this would be prudent. I do not counsel prudence. I said victory could not be achieved by arms. I still hope for victory, but not by arms.' (LotR 860)

The dialogue between hope and despair as moral forces for driving temporal warfaring action is made very clear during the last debate. In fact, the Aristotelian sense of the word 'prudent' here alerts us, as readers, to the tricky mid-way between hope and despair that the heroes are attempting to fare. The decision to march out and make a last stand is canonically and classically heroic, while the determination to do so self-sacrificially for Frodo, thus leaving his heroism of choice and pity the hoped-for time to triumph, has definite moral connotations. The march is neither entirely altruistic nor entirely desperate. If we weigh it we find that Aragorn's decision defies canonisation – it is too altruistic to sit in the heroic camp and too desperate to sit in the moral one. In this regards it is the denouement to Tolkien's vision of war. War is not glorified. Tolkien recognises that the real, historic world, unlike the world of sub-creation, cannot simply be divided into canons of northern or moral heroism or into camps of light and dark, good and evil. As Tolkien put it in his letters: 'In real (exterior) life men are on both sides: which means a motley alliance of orcs, beasts, demons, plain naturally honest men, and angels' (L 82). While acknowledging this historical grey-scale in the morality of men, Tolkien's portrayal of his heroes suggests that the 'naturally honest men and angels' are those who inform their deeds with moral clarity – and that, if waged with moral clarity, war can be just and good.

The End of All Things and The Ends of War

At this point we must ask: What are the ends of war? The canvas of a battle of light against dark, and the associated underpinning of both spiritual and temporal war, could lead us to the conclusion that, for Tolkien, the end of war is in apocalypse – if our heroes are driven to act morally and righteously against evil villains then war must lead to the final showdown between good and evil.

While this is an understandable conclusion to draw it isn't a whole one. Although, dramatically speaking, the story ends with the destruction of the Ring and the crowning of Aragorn that is not where Tolkien chooses to end his narrative. To those who complain of the 'multiple endings' of *The Lord of the Rings* this can seem incomprehensible. Why doesn't Tolkien stop at what seems to be the natural end of his tale – where the fighting finishes?

This refusal to end the story with the end of the fighting points to a much deeper vision of war. For the first traces of our answer we must look back to the despair of Denethor. Tolkien unveils that despair as moral corruption and underscores that message by showing us how even in his despair, Denethor paradoxically thinks of healing. Although the Steward dismisses healing as an unthinking travail he is still aware that it is the compassed goal of those who desire to keep on fighting. And when Éowyn, another victim of despair, comes to understand her heart her new-found clarity shows her that she 'will be a shieldmaiden no longer, nor vie with the great Riders, nor take joy only in the songs of slaying. [She] will be a healer, and love all things that grow and are not barren' (LotR 943). There are, as Tolkien put it in his letters, those who are needed for 'things other than war'.

As *The Lord of the Rings* winds to its conclusion peace, as defined by healing, sowing and rebirth and the turning of swords into ploughshares, is shown as the end of war – but Tolkien does not hand us peace on a silver platter. It is a process, as the ever practical Samwise Gamgee observes, of 'clear[ing] up the mess' which takes 'a lot of time and work' (LotR 997). Unlike many writers of the genre, Tolkien invests time and effort into considering the after-effects of war – and he does not sugar-coat it. Sometimes, what seem to us as the best possible legacy of moral choices doesn't quite work out.

After the scouring of the Shire Frodo – who, in being 'wounded by knife, sting, tooth and a long burden' is both temporally and spiritually injured – 'drop[s] quietly out of all the doings of the Shire' (LotR 1002). The Shire has been saved, 'but not for [him]'. Tolkien acknowledges that an inevitable consequence of war is that not all 'victors [are] able to enjoy victory' (L 235). This is something he would not have been able to show had the story ended at Mount Doom. Haunted by darkness and the lingering horror that he did not give up his life to destroy the Ring,[6] Frodo withdraws from his active narrative role, encouraging Sam to take it in his place:

> The title page had many titles on it, crossed out one after another.
> 'Why, you have nearly finished it, Mr. Frodo!' Sam exclaimed...
> 'I have quite finished, Sam,' said Frodo. 'The last pages are for you.' (LotR 1004)

In his depiction of Frodo's consuming hurt, Tolkien shows us that those who are too deeply tainted by war long after the 'hidden paths' that lead to 'a far green country under a swift sunrise'. The spiritual heroism that sustained Frodo to the Crack of Doom has been exhausted. Frodo is juxtaposed with Sam, who takes an active role in healing the Shire and whom Frodo calls his 'heir'. By presenting Sam as an heir to 'everything [Frodo] had and might have had' (LotR 1006), Tolkien is also making Sam the heir to Frodo's moral heroism of choice. It is something Sam must use when deciding what to do with his gift from Galadriel:

> 'I'm not sure the Lady would like me to keep it all for my own garden, now so many folk have suffered,' said Sam.
> 'Use all the wits and knowledge you have of your own, Sam,' said Frodo, 'and then use the gift to help your work and better it...' ...
> So Sam planted saplings in all the places where specially beautiful or beloved trees had been destroyed... and at the end he found that he still had a little of the dust left; so he went to the Three-Farthing Stone, which is as near the centre of the Shire as no matter, and cast it in the air with his blessing. (LotR 1000)

---

6 In some ways, this could be seen as a christianised or 'martyrish' version of classical *kleos*.

Initially under Frodo's tutelage and then independently, Sam comes to embody how the moral heroism of choice so necessary in war is to be turned into a force of rejuvenation once violence is ended. Tolkien's description of the following summer seems to compound the spiritual virtue of Sam's choice: 'Not only was there wonderful sunshine and delicious rain, in due times and perfect measure, but there seemed something more: an air of richness and growth, and a gleam of a beauty beyond that of mortal summers that flicker and pass upon this Middle-Earth' (ibid). The heroism that led in times of war to the destruction of the Ring leads, in times of peace, to clean fields and glimpses of something beyond this mortal coil – and perhaps, in the long run, to a new heaven and a new earth.

The Fields That We Know

We have seen how Tolkien's vision is clearly conscious of the temporal and spiritual aspects of war, and the necessity of acting from a clear moral standpoint. This vision of war in the sub-created world enables the division of good from evil, hope from despair and morality from indifference, attributes that contribute to an apocalyptic feel but which serve to highlight the virtue and necessity of moral, spiritual and temporal good. Ultimately, *The Lord of the Rings* recognises war as something to be faced with courage and faith for, as Tolkien writes in his letters: 'evil labours with vast power and perpetual success – in vain: preparing always only the soil for unexpected good to sprout in' (L 76).

This is a vision that recognises the final haven of humanity from war in a place where there shall be 'no more weeping', and sees that our earth-bound lives are caught in a struggle against evil. Throughout his work and especially his letters, Tolkien acknowledges that in our temporal plane we will always be called upon to go to war, whether literally or metaphorically. Evil will happen, but each of us has a moral and spiritual obligation to stand against it where we find it, and to pursue peace:

> Other evils there are that may come... yet it is not our part to master all the tides of the world, but to do what is in us for the succour of those years wherein we are set, uprooting the evil in the fields that we know, so that those who live after us may have clean earth to till. What weather they shall have is not ours to rule. (LotR 861)

These fields, cleaned by clear-hearted moral heroism, are the ultimate end of war – and they are to be worked no less courageously in times of peace.

Bibliography:

The Holy Bible, New International Version.

Carpenter, Humphrey, Ed. *The Letters of J.R.R. Tolkien*. London: HarperCollins, 1995

Marlowe, Christopher. *Doctor Faustus*. London: Methuen Educational Ltd, 1987

Tolkien, John Ronald Reuel. *The Lord of the Rings*. London: HarperCollins, 1995

The Legacy of Swords: Animate Weapons and the Ambivalence of Heroic Violence

Judith Klinger (Potsdam)

I. The Sword's Double Nature: Heroic Violence

> 'Will you not take the sword?' said Gandalf. Slowly Théoden stretched forth his hand. As his fingers took the hilt, it seemed to the watchers that firmness and strength returned to his thin arm. (LotR 506)

If the watchers' impressions are taken seriously – that is, literally – a sword is much more than a mere tool of war. But does the blade possess an innate power which it lends to the hand that wields it? Or does touching the hilt renew the king's confidence through recollection alone? Whatever the answer may be, this initial moment of contact restores the old king's charisma as a leader of warriors and prefigures his final heroic battles and glory beyond death: "Out of doubt, out of dark, to the day's rising | he rode singing in the sun, sword unsheathing" (LotR 954), so the Rohirrim will eventually commemorate their fallen leader. The sword's radiance – associated with song and sunlight – remains inseparably linked to battle-death, bereavement and the darkness of the tomb: a fundamental ambivalence that surrounds the sword not only in Tolkien's texts.[1] "[T]he wages of heroism is death," Tolkien wrote about *Beowulf* (BMC 26).

The power of the sword, both literally and figuratively, depends entirely on this ambivalence: it joins and divides light and darkness – nothing more, nothing less. But what exactly does that mean – and, more importantly, what are the systems of meaning that circumscribe the sword as source, carrier and symbol of violence in Tolkien's texts? After all, the modern mind can grasp the sword only in the symbolic mode. As an emblem, a historical artefact or a ceremonial item, it is still a potent signifier of authority and justice, or perhaps of brutal aggression, and may represent traditional (if quaint) values

---

[1] Cf. *Beowulf* ll. 2247-54: Heald þu nu, hruse, nu hæleð ne moston, | eorla æhte! Hwæt, hyt ær on ðe | gode begeaton. Guðdeað fornam, | feorhbealo frecne, fyra gehwylcne | leoda minra, þara ðe þis lif ofgeaf, | gesawon seledream. Ic nah hwa sweord wege | oððe feormie fæted wæge, | dryncfæt deore; duguð ellor sceoc. *Now hold thou, earth, since heroes may not, | what earls have owned! Lo, erst from thee | brave men brought it! But battle-death seized | and cruel killing my clansmen all, | robbed them of life and a liegeman's joys. | None have I left to lift the sword, | or to cleanse the carven cup of price,| beaker bright. My brave are gone.*

such as heroic courage, strength and integrity. But the sword itself no longer renders these things present – as it clearly does for Théoden, whose vigour and charisma revive at the touch of the hilt. Considering the specific form of violence attached to the sword therefore involves grappling with pre-modern systems of meaning that shape experiences very unlike our own. The beauty of a sword is no more a matter of aesthetics than the danger to life and limb it embodies: it arises from historical cultures whose appreciation of violence differs dramatically from the widespread modern attitude of abhorrence (often in combination with aesthetic distance).

In Tolkien's Middle-earth texts, we encounter a dialogue between these historically discrepant – even conflicting – attitudes. It has become a critical commonplace to connect the descriptions of battle and post-war devastation in *The Lord of the Rings* to the author's biographical experiences in the trenches of World War I (cf. Shippey 155-57, Garth 310-312, Livingston). Tolkien himself carefully reduced the parallels to the landscape: "The Dead Marshes and the approaches to the Morannon owe something to Northern France after the battle of the Somme", he wrote in a letter (L 303). Certainly, the mingled, rotting corpses in the Marshes as well as the Hill of the Slain that marks the dreadful end of the Battle of Unnumbered Tears recall the modern experience of war with its mass graves: death strikes indiscriminately and, instead of praise and glory, leaves only decomposing bodies behind. However, less attention has so far been paid to Tolkien's figuration and reinterpretation of heroic violence (and heroic death), epitomized by the sword.[2]

The image, use and meaning of the sword in Tolkien's texts about Middle-earth owes much to medieval traditions, and the most prominent parallels are easily identified: Excalibur, King Arthur's sword, founds his claim to legitimate rulership rather in the same way that Andúril heralds Aragorn's claim to the throne of Gondor (cf. Flieger 132). As 'heroic signifiers',[3] the unique swords carried by Tolkien's protagonists are reminiscent of Durendal, the unbreakable 'holy' sword of Roland in the Old French *Chanson de Roland*, or Balmung, the sword of Siegfried the dragon-slayer in the Middle High German *Nibelungen-*

---

2   With the notable exception of the paper by K.S. Whetter and R. Andrew McDonald, who point out: "Tolkien makes it clear almost from the moment that the swords are introduced that they are no ordinary weapons... These swords, replete with names, runes, histories, and magical properties, make their presence felt at crucial moments in both *The Hobbit* and *The Lord of the Rings*; indeed, they are celebrated as living personalities in Middle-earth, just as the historical and literary weapons of the 'real Middle-earth' on which they were modelled were also celebrated by poets, bards, and writers of the middle ages." (6f)

3   "Throughout *The Lord of the Rings* especially, but also in *The Hobbit*, as in comparable tales from medieval Europe and the Classical world, arms and armour – often, but not always, swords – are important heroic signifiers. Indeed, often specific heroes are associated with specific weapons, weapons which add to that hero's heroic stature and reputation, and which may in fact prove to be unique to that individual." (Whetter/McDonald 22)

lied – or its Icelandic counterpart Gram, Sigurd's sword in the *Volsunga saga*. In Tolkien, as in medieval culture, illustrious swords appear as the insignia of rulers that either accompany them into their burial mounds or pass on as heirlooms from one generation to the next. A renowned sword may possess a 'lineage' of its own or a mythical origin, it is often decorated with emblems and inscriptions that invoke its supernatural potency or magical properties.[4] Sacred relics are embedded in the sword of Roland, whereas Sigurd is advised to carve 'victory runes' into hilt and blade (*Volsunga saga* ch. 21, p. 36). The blades the four hobbit travellers receive after their escape from the barrow closely recall medieval sword-lore: "leaf-bladed, damasked in gold and red, they are the work of Westernesse, wound about with spells for the bane of Mordor" (LotR 405). "The parallels are particularly evident in some places," Whetter and McDonald note, "such as Merry's Westernesse blade melting after striking the Nazgûl king, and the giant sword that Beowulf uses to slay Grendel's mother melting 'just like ice' (1608), leaving only the hilt" (Whetter/McDonald 24). But beyond such parallels, what defines the specific type of violence associated with these swords of medieval tradition, and how is it represented and modified by Tolkien?[5]

If the sword announces and magnifies the epic hero (cf. Whetter/McDonald 25; Flieger 131f), it points to the fact that heroic violence is a privilege and a distinction. Throughout the middle ages, the sword constitutes noble (male) identity, distinguishing the lord from the peasant or the cleric. But from epic literature, the individual hero stands out, set apart by the victories – and the defeats – he encounters at sword-point. His sword connects physical attributes, especially courage and endurance, to the singular deeds that sustain the hero's honour and reputation, define his identity, and, in some cases, secure the social order that is (re-)established through his courageous interventions. The warrior's blade may thus be transformed to the ruler's attribute of legitimate power and become a sign of peace and justice: In this sense, heroic violence integrates and consolidates cultural order. Yet heroic violence is as double-edged as the sword itself: Not only does it frequently culminate in death and defeat, it is by nature extreme and excessive. In order to achieve the singular, perilous feat, the hero must be stronger, bolder and hardier than the men of his community – and, ideally, his enemies.

---

4   Cf. *Beowulf* ll. 1687-1698. – For a closer examination of the parallels, see Whetter/McDonald 8-11.
5   Cf. Whetter/McDonald 24: "by and large what we have is influence rather than explicit borrowing: blades of Middle-earth glow magically of their own accord in the presence of enemies or in battle, whereas blades of early medieval Europe gleam and glint in the sunlight; swords of early medieval Europe were rarely inscribed on the blades themselves, whereas this seems a more common place for inscriptions in Middle-earth."

Judith Klinger

A recent debate among German medievalists centres on the question of whether the epic hero (as opposed to the hero of courtly romance[6]) is an exemplary or an exorbitant figure. Is he a role model, representing collectively recognized ethics and social standards? Or is there something uncanny to the outstanding hero, whose violence exceeds social measure and therefore defies ethical restraints?[7] If the former is the case, heroic violence "makes sense" in that it establishes meaningful order; in the latter opinion, heroic violence steps outside cultural order with its distinctions of 'good' and 'evil' and provides no meaning beyond itself. Walter Haug has argued strongly that the hero's stature is owed to encounters with profoundly alien enemies, beyond the bounds of the known. His ability to confront and defeat supernatural, monstrous creatures constitutes his identity – yet his close contact with the agents of Otherness renders him superhuman and monstrous in turn. He may therefore become a disintegrating force in his own right, as the example of Siegfried, the dragon-slayer shows: After his bath in the dragon's blood, Siegfried's skin becomes as impenetrable as the dragon's hide.[8] Imbued with ominous force, his incessantly heroic attitude challenges and endangers the social hierarchies of the Burgundian court and precipitates his death. Heroic exorbitance thus implies a profoundly destructive potential.

However, in many texts, heroic violence displays both facets and is played out on the brink between integrative and destructive effects. This fundamental ambivalence may be grasped in condensed form in the Middle High German *übermuot*, a term used to express both praise and criticism.[9] Tolkien discusses the Old English equivalent *ofermod* ('overboldness') in his essay about the Anglo-Saxon *Battle of Maldon* and identifies an element of excess in the 'northern heroic spirit':

> Yet this element of pride, in the form of the desire for honour and glory, in life and after death, tends to grow, to become a chief motive, driving a man beyond the bleak heroic necessity to excess – to chivalry. 'Excess' certainly, even if it be approved by

---

[6] The definition suggested by Whetter and McDonald – "epic-heroic literature is best defined by its focus on one or more potentially tragic heroes and the question (or questions) of the nature, consequences, and costs of heroism" (26) – may suffice here to mark the crucial difference.
[7] The former position is held by Heinzle, whereas von See and Haug have argued for the latter view.
[8] The parallelism of dragon-slayer and dragon is underlined in *Beowulf* l. 2844-2845: hæfde æghwæðer ende gefered lænan lifes (*each had brought about for the other the end of transitory life*).
[9] Cf. BMZ: "herzhafter muth, übermuth, stolz, hochfahrendes wesen, üppigkeit, vergnügungssucht"; Lexer: "stolz, übermütig".

> contemporary opinion, when it not only goes beyond need and
> duty, but interferes with it. (HB 144)

Excessive heroic violence, necessarily ambivalent, figures prominently in Tolkien's works, and the monstrous aspect of the hero is never more marked than it is in the story of Túrin who adopts the name *Mormegil*, Blacksword. By contrast, Aragorn with Andúril, the 'Flame of the West', clearly represents the socially integrative facet of heroic violence.

However, it would be altogether limiting to reduce the meaning of illustrious swords in Tolkien's texts to this tension between constructive and destructive violence. When Túrin's black sword answers his final plea for death in a 'cold voice' that 'rings' from the blade, the sword not only fulfils the hero's tragic fate, it also exhibits a will of its own. Swords of this kind are more than property or heroic signifiers: they participate in the events as animate agents with histories and identities of their own. According to Melian, there is 'malice' in the sword Túrin carries (S 243; CH 97), but other blades – especially the distinguished swords in *The Lord of the Rings* – are carriers and mediators of light. Some, like Frodo's Sting, possess the ability to recognize the Dark Lord's servants and will then emit 'a cold light' (LotR 302). Elrond says of Narsil that "its light [was] extinguished" (LotR 237, S 356), but before it was broken, the blade "shone with the light of the sun and of the moon" (S 354). These extraordinary swords also seem to absorb and preserve memories across vast expanses of time and play an active part in the fulfilment of their destinies.

It will therefore be necessary to examine the underlying connections between swords, fate and history and the sword's animating mystique. I will pursue these aspects by focussing on three prominent swords – Andúril, Anglachel, Sting – and the different approaches to heroic violence represented by Aragorn, Túrin and Frodo (or rather, Frodo and Sam).

II. The Sword That Was Broken: Charismatic Kingship and the Dialectic of Defeat

> It is a thing passing strange to me," says the Warden of the Houses of Healing, "that the healing hand should also wield the sword. It is not thus in Gondor now, though once it was so, if old tales be true. But for long years we healers have only sought to patch the rents made by the men of swords" (LotR 937).

Aragorn, however, achieves a union of apparent opposites that substantiates his claim to kingship: these tokens – the sword and the 'healing hand' – manifest his royalty as a personal quality that can be directly experienced.[10] Yet the

---

10 Cf. LotR 842: "For it is said in old lore: The hands of the king are the hands of a healer. And so the rightful king could ever be known."

renowned sword and the healing touch are also more closely linked than the Warden realizes. From the Merovingians onward, the ruler's 'healing touch' was crucial to the concept of sacred kingship in medieval England and France (cf. Bloch). That the disease (scrofula) healed by the king's miraculous touch was also known as *King's Evil* (or 'king's disease') led James Frazer to speculate about a belief "that it was caused as well as cured by contact with a king."[11]

Of course, there is no reason to suspect that Aragorn has caused the disease he cures. However, Frazer's notion suggests a double-edged charisma that stems from the king's connection to the divine or the supernatural sphere.[12] In *The Lord of the Rings*, Aragorn's dual role as warrior and healer[13] echoes this ambivalence and raises the question what exactly it is that qualifies him for the throne. His descent from Isildur alone does not suffice (although Aragorn is frequently addressed as 'Isildur's heir'), and Aragorn himself is careful not to upset the political balance in Gondor with a prematurely pronounced claim.[14] In fact, neither 'legality' nor "functional 'competence' based on rationally created rules"[15] sustain Aragorn's claim: instead, the 'healing touch' and the sword evince his charisma as a leader. According to Max Weber, a charismatic ruler is "set apart from ordinary men and treated as endowed with supernatural,

---

11 Frazer 269: "among our own remote ancestors scrofula may have obtained its name of the King's Evil from a belief... that it was caused as well as cured by contact with the divine majesty of kings." (Cf. Bloch III.134, Bloch/LeGoff 88) – The Icelandic *Kormak's Saga* connects injury and cure to *Skofnung*, a sword with magical properties: "the sword has a life-stone said to offer healing powers to those whom the blade has injured" (Complete Sagas I: 193-94; Whetter/McDonald 19).

12 It can be argued that Aragorn's ability to cure victims of the 'Black Breath' stems from the same spiritual power that allows him to confront Sauron in the Orthanc Stone – a feat that troubles his companions: "'You have looked in that accursed stone of wizardry!' exclaimed Gimli with fear and astonishment in his face. 'Did you say aught to – him? Even Gandalf feared that encounter.' 'You forget to whom you speak,' said Aragorn sternly, and his eyes glinted. 'Did I not openly proclaim my title before the doors of Edoras? What do you fear that I should say to him? ... Nay, my friends, I am the lawful master of the Stone, and I had both the right and the strength to use it, or so I judged. The right cannot be doubted. The strength was enough – barely'" (LotR 763). Once again, the hero's identity is achieved by his struggle with a monstrous enemy, but such a close encounter may infect him with a dangerous amount of Otherness.

13 Compare Frodo's succinct poetic description of Gandalf in similar terms: "A deadly sword, a healing hand" (LotR 350).

14 Cf. LotR 843: "'... But this City and realm has rested in the charge of the Stewards for many long years, and I fear that if I enter it unbidden, then doubt and debate may arise, which should not be while this war is fought. I will not enter in, nor make any claim, until it be seen whether we or Mordor shall prevail...' But Éomer said: 'Already you have raised the banner of the Kings and displayed the tokens of Elendil's House. Will you suffer these to be challenged?' 'No,' said Aragorn. 'But I deem the time unripe; and I have no mind for strife except with our Enemy and his servants.'"

15 Cf. Weber's description of power in the modern state: "Finally, there is domination by virtue of 'legality', by virtue of the belief in the validity of legal statute and functional 'competence' based on rationally created rules. In this case, obedience is expected in discharging statutory obligations. This is domination as exercised by the modern 'servant of the state' and by all those bearers of power who in this respect resemble him" (Weber, *Essays* 79).

superhuman, or at least... exceptional powers and qualities... which are not accessible to the ordinary person" (Weber, *Theory* 358; cf. Kraemer).

First and foremost, it is the compelling, auratic presence of his sword that manifests Aragorn's exceptional qualities. During his initial encounter with Éomer, he draws Andúril which "shone like a sudden flame as he swept it out", before he identifies himself by name and lineage.

> Gimli and Legolas looked at their companion in amazement, for they had not seen him in this mood before. He seemed to have grown in stature while Éomer had shrunk; and in his living face they caught a brief vision of the power and majesty of the kings of stone. For a moment it seemed to the eyes of Legolas that a white flame flickered on the brows of Aragorn like a shining crown.
> (LotR 423)[16]

Doubtless, this is a mythical moment of revelation: Andúril seems to trigger Aragorn's unfamiliar 'mood' and provides the very light by which he can be seen as king. But Narsil-Andúril has a dual identity and a history of its own: It is "the Sword that was Broken and is forged again" (LotR 423). The dialectic of continuity and rupture, loss and recovery, is central to the meaning of the royal sword.

In Narsil, the Broken Sword, resides a condensed account of heroic defeat in the battle against a superior, monstrous enemy.[17] Although the blade breaks as Elendil falls,[18] Isildur manages to strike a blow with the hilt-shard that cuts the One Ring off Sauron's hand.[19] Defeat and sacrifice enable a spectacular,

---

16 "Aragorn threw back his cloak. The elven-sheath glittered as he grasped it, and the bright blade of Andúril shone like a sudden flame as he swept it out. 'Elendil!' he cried. 'I am Aragorn son of Arathorn and am called Elessar, the Elfstone, Dúnadan, the heir of Isildur Elendil's son of Gondor. Here is the Sword that was Broken and is forged again! Will you aid me or thwart me? Choose swiftly!' ... Éomer stepped back and a look of awe was in his face. He cast down his proud eyes. 'These are indeed strange days,' he muttered. 'Dreams and legends spring to life out of the grass...'" (LotR 423).

17 In the *Volsunga saga*, Sigurd's father Sigmund dies in battle against Odin who shatters his sword. The fragments are bequeathed to Sigmund's unborn son. As a man, Sigurd kills the dragon Fáfnir with the reforged sword, named Gram. Here, the breaking and remaking of the sword are part of a cycle of defeat and victory. By contrast, *The Lord of the Rings* records no singular heroic feat that restores symmetry in equal fashion: although the sword is reforged, its heroic supremacy belongs to the past.

18 The breaking of a sword when its owner is killed or mortally wounded is a frequent event, from Frodo's barrow-sword (which breaks at the Ford of Bruinen) and Boromir's broken blade at Parth Galen to the nameless soldier whose death Sam contemplates in Ithilien: a clear indication that the life of the sword is entwined with that of its owner.

19 "Elendil fell, and Narsil broke beneath him; but Sauron himself was overthrown, and Isildur cut the Ring from his hand with the hilt-shard of his father's sword, and took it for his own" (Elrond; LotR 237).

unexpected victory: an event rendered ever present by the shards of Narsil. The weapon's brokenness thus signalizes the double edge of heroic violence with its promise of ultimate gain and its risk of irrecoverable loss.

In the course of history, the Broken Sword not only becomes the chief heirloom of Isildur's house,[20] it also functions as an ambivalent emblem that refers to both the unbroken line of descendants and the ruptured rule. It is nowhere explained why Narsil was not immediately reforged, but Elrond predicts that this will be done only when the One Ring is found again.[21] The choice to reforge Narsil therefore does not belong to Aragorn:[22] the right time is chosen for him by the larger forces of history and fate. By reverse, the history shaped by Narsil-Andúril is not one of linear temporality, of causes and effects: rather it connects significant moments of reversal with their dialectic implications.[23]

The dualism of Narsil-Andúril preserves a memory of defeat and disintegration as the other side of heroic self-assertion. During the battle of Helm's Deep, the reforged sword stirs hope even while the former loss is invoked: "A shout went up from wall and tower: 'Andúril! Andúril goes to war. The blade that was broken shines again!'" (LotR 521).[24] It is this specific legacy that shapes

---

20 "For here [i.e. in Rivendell] the heirs of Valandil have ever dwelt in long line unbroken from father unto son for many generations. Our days have darkened, and we have dwindled; but ever the Sword has passed to a new keeper" (Aragorn; LotR 242).
21 "Thus Narsil came in due time to the hand of Valandil, Isildur's heir, in Imladris; but the blade was broken and its light was extinguished, and it was not forged anew. And Master Elrond foretold that this would not be done until the Ruling Ring should be found again and Sauron should return; but the hope of Elves and Men was that these things might never come to pass" (S 356).
22 Here, the contrast with Roland's wilful attempt to break Durendal should be noted. Dying, Roland fears that the sword he once received from Charlemagne may fall into his enemies' hands and thus bring shame to France (*Chanson de Roland* CLXXII), but he also considers the sword an inalienable part of his own noble identity (and its temporal limitations): *Quant jo mei perd, de vos n'en ai mais cure* (CLXXI, v. 2305). The sword's refusal to be broken defies Roland's *ofermod* and isolated heroic choice. Aragorn's choice, on the other hand, bows to the needs of the collective and Elrond's insight into atemporal patterns of fate.
23 The parallel Whetter and McDonald draw with Arthur's Excalibur as the symbol for the beginning and end of an era rather simplifies these implications: "Excalibur also marks Arthur's reign, for just as it comes from the stone or lake at the beginning of his reign, so it is returned to the waters whence it came after the final battle in which Arthur is (fatally) wounded. Narsil-Andúril similarly defines the Third Age, for it is used by Isildur to hew the finger with the One Ring from Sauron, thus closing the Second Age, while the reforging of the blade heralds the destruction of the Ring, the dissolution of Sauron, and the return of Aragorn son of Arathorn as king, thus closing the Third Age" (Whetter/McDonald 23f).
24 The dream prophecy that brings Boromir to Rivendell – "seek for the Sword that was broken" – already implies that the broken blade, not the reforged sword, emblematizes Gondor's salvation. Although Boromir remains sceptical and characteristically places greater trust in heroic strength: "Mayhap the Sword-that-was-Broken may still stern the

Aragorn's approach to heroic violence and lends legitimacy to his claim. In the story of Andúril, martial feats are characteristically downplayed: Although Aragorn wields it in several battles, dramatic scenes highlighting the sword's deadly qualities are rare, and there is no indication of excess. While Narsil is the primary agent of heroic violence, Andúril features far more prominently as an instrument of integration: for instance when it initiates Aragorn's and Éomer's companionship as 'brothers in arms'.[25] The 'healing touch' therefore complements an approach to power and kingship based on intimate knowledge of rupture and defeat.

Finally, another shift that occurs when Narsil becomes Andúril must be noted. While Narsil once "shone with the light of the sun and of the moon" (S 354),[26] Andúril carries the heraldic signs of "the crescent Moon and the rayed Sun" (LotR 269):[27] it represents and reflects light but never seems to emit a radiance of its own.[28] If the radiance of a sword indicates the glory of heroic violence, this transition from actual presence to symbolic representation also suggests how Aragorn's kingship will mitigate violence and reduce its significance for the understanding of legitimate power.[29]

---

tide – if the hand that wields it has inherited not an heirloom only, but the sinews of the Kings of Men" (LotR 261).

25 Cf. LotR 429: "'Farewell, and may you find what you seek!' cried Éomer. 'Return with what speed you may, and let our swords hereafter shine together!'" LotR 521: "Together Éomer and Aragorn sprang through the door, their men close behind. The swords flashed from the sheath as one. 'Gúthwinë!' cried Éomer. 'Gúthwinë for the Mark!' 'Andúril!' cried Aragorn. 'Andúril for the Dúnedain!'" LotR 830: "And so at length Éomer and Aragorn met in the midst of the battle, and they leaned on their swords and looked on one another and were glad."

26 Tolkien explained the name's etymology with reference to these sources of light: "*Narsil* is a name composed of 2 basic stems without variation or adjuncts: √NAR 'fire' & √THIL 'white light'. It thus symbolised the chief heavenly lights, as enemies of darkness, Sun (*Anar*) and Moon (in Q) *Isil*" (L 425).

27 Together with the seven stars, these emblems refer to the realm of Gondor and its ancient royal cities of Minas Arnor ('Tower of the Setting Sun') and Minas Ithil ('Tower of the Rising Moon'). In his letter comment on the sword's names, Tolkien also specifies that "*Andúril* means Flame of the West (as a region) not of the Sunset" (L no. 347, 425).

28 "Very bright was that sword when it was made whole again; the light of the sun shone redly in it, and the light of the moon shone cold, and its edge was hard and keen" (LotR 269). Only in one instance – discussed below – does Andúril give off light, but the circumstances are extraordinary.

29 A similar approach is articulated by Faramir, whose leadership resembles that of Aragorn: "War must be, while we defend our lives against a destroyer who would devour all; but I do not love the bright sword for its sharpness, nor the arrow for its swiftness, nor the warrior for his glory. I love only that which they defend: the city of the Men of Númenor" (LotR 656).

III. The Black Sword: A Monstrous Hero in the Hands of Fate

In Narsil-Andúril, heroic exorbitance is tempered and refracted by the knowledge of defeat; in the Black Sword, Anglachel-Gurthang, the monstrous aspect of heroic aggression breaks through. Both Aragorn and Túrin are charismatic leaders; their lives and their choices are to a large extent shaped by external conditions – such as outstanding ancestry, a history of war and exile, and a legacy of loss. In both stories, possession of an exceptional sword is intimately entwined with the hero's fate. Yet Aragorn becomes a role model of successful leadership, whereas Túrin is a figure of excess. Although a ruler's heir himself, he assumes a leading role in various communities – often with ambivalent, if not disastrous results – but never regains his inherited dominion.

From the earliest version in *The Book of Lost Tales* (1919) to the recently published *Children of Húrin* (2007), the tale of Túrin Turambar underwent considerable revisions. However, several key elements were present from the beginning: the curse of Melko/Morgoth,[30] the tragic killing of Beleg, the Black Sword, the dragon's spell, Túrin's marriage to his unrecognized sister, and his eventual death by his own sword.[31] The tale of the heroic dragon-slayer is at the same time a story about an isolated man's struggle for his social place and identity that enmeshes him ever more deeply in the calamitous fate he tries to overcome.[32] Túrin's heroic stature and personal tragedy depend largely on his pride (*ofermod*) as well as his qualities as a leader and a warrior. And here, the element of excess – carefully hedged and balanced in the story of Aragorn – unfolds its full, destructive potential. The sword that comes into Túrin's hands complements and advances this dynamic.

---

30 From the earliest version of the story, Melko's curse falls on Húrin's family and children: "And this was the torture he [Melko] devised for the affliction of Urin the Steadfast, and setting him in a lofty place of the mountains he stood beside him and cursed him and his folk with dread curses of the Valar, putting a doom of woe and a death of sorrow upon them... 'Behold,' said Melko, 'the life of Turin thy son shall be accounted a matter for tears wherever Elves or Men are gathered for the telling of tales'" (LT2 71). Cf. CH 63: "'Behold! The shadow of my thought shall lie upon them wherever they go, and my hate shall pursue them to the ends of the world.'"
31 The latter part of the story echoes motifs from the conclusion of Kullervo's life in the *Kalevala*: Like Túrin, Kullervo has caused his sister's death and ends his life with his own sword.
32 That Túrin renames himself Turambar, 'Conqueror of Fate', is already present in the earliest version as well: "'Nay, from this hour shall none name me Turin if I live. Behold, I will name me a new name and it shall be Turambar!' Now this meaneth Conqueror of Fate, and the form of the name in the Gnome-speech is Turumart. Then uttering these words he made a second time at the drake, thinking indeed to force the drake to slay him and to conquer his fate by death, but the dragon laughed" (LT2 86).

The history and role of Anglachel-Gurthang (Gurtholfin, 'wand of death', in *The Book of Lost Tales*) changed considerably in the course of Tolkien's revisions. Both in the earliest prose and the subsequent verse *Children of Húrin*, Túrin received the sword from Orodreth for his fight against the dragon Glaurung (earlier: Glorund), which then gave him the name Mormegil (earlier: Mormakil).[33] Only when Tolkien began to conceptualize the *Silmarillion* did the Black Sword pass from Beleg to Túrin under the most tragic of circumstances.[34] The story of Anglachel's otherworldy origins appears to have been a late – though highly significant – addition:[35]

> Then Beleg chose Anglachel; and that was a sword of great fame, and it was so named because it was made of iron that fell from heaven as a blazing star; it would cleave all earth-dolven iron.
> (CH 96; cf. S 242)

The alien sword, forged from the ores of a meteorite, enters as an emblem and a focus of all that is Other, inducing a destructiveness that both incorporates

---

33 "Turin begged Orodreth for a sword, and he had not wielded a sword since the slaying of Beleg, but rather had he been contented with a mighty club. Now then Orodreth let fashion for him a great sword, and it was made by magic to be utterly black save at its edges, and those were shining bright and sharp as but Gnome-steel may be. Heavy it was, and was sheathed in black, and it hung from a sable belt, and Turin named it Gurtholfin the Wand of Death; and often that blade leapt in his hand of its own lust, and it is said that at times it spake dark words to him" (LT2 83).

34 In the verse Túrin, the sword already plays a more prominent role, as Beleg himself enchants the blade that will soon kill him with a 'whetting spell' before he frees Túrin: "Then sought his sword, and songs of magic | o'er its eager edge with Elfin voice | there Beleg murmured, while bluely glimmered | the lamp of Flinding neath the laced thorns. | There wondrous wove he words of sharpness, | and the names of knives and Gnomish blades | he uttered o'er it: ... | the sweeping sickle of the slashing tempest, | the lambent lightning's leaping falchion | even Celeg Aithorn that shall cleave the world. | Then whistling whirled he the whetted sword-blade | and three times three it threshed the gloom, | till flame was kindled flickering strangely | like licking firelight in the lamp's glimmer | blue and baleful at the blade's edges" (LB 45f, ll. 1203-1223). The implication is that 'doom' conspires with Beleg's spell, which turns against him (cf. l. 1240: "too dark his magic"). In the final revision of the tragic event, fate itself interferes: "but fate was that day more strong, for the blade of Eöl the Dark Elf slipped in his [Beleg's] hand, and pricked Túrin's foot" (CH 154). Once he realizes what he has done, Túrin wants to kill himself with the – yet unnamed – blade (LB 56, ll. 1359-60) and for a long time refuses to handle a sword ("but it pleased him little, | who trusted to targe and tempered sword, | whose hand was hungry for the hilts it missed | but dared never a blade since the doom of Beleg | to draw or handle" LB 76, ll. 2152-2156). That Túrin afterwards wields Beleg's own sword, which is reforged into a 'black blade with shining edges', first emerges in the earliest *Silmarillion* texts (1926-1930; SM 29: "He has Beleg's sword forged anew, into a black blade with shining edges, and he is from this given the name of 'Mormakil' or black-sword").

35 It first appears in the *Silmarillion*, to which reference is made in WJ 321. No other details about the date and evolution of this addition have so far been published.

and counters the individual will to violence. When Túrin first seizes the Black Sword, "crazed with anguish", indiscriminate aggression is unleashed "by the help of doom" (LB 46, l. 1252, 1254) and turned against his dearest friend.

While Tolkien apparently traced the sword's history from its destiny back to its origin, this reversal is in keeping with the temporal structure of the tale which, from the very beginning, is overshadowed by its fated conclusion. As Morgoth's curse indicates, the tale of Túrin is by no means the story of a modern individual governed by linear psychological progress. Thus the dragon-slayer already incorporates the monstrous aspect of heroic violence prior to his encounter with the dragon. Anglachel-Gurthang may therefore be viewed as Túrin's fated counterpart that mirrors his shifting identities[36] and contradictory roles: "treacherous to foes, faithless to friends, and a curse unto his kin", Glaurung calls him (CH 243).

Although the Black Sword's capacity of speech can be traced back to the earliest *Túrin* version,[37] it is remarkably incapable of understanding difference: "blood is blood", it tells Túrin, who "cherished Gurtholfin beyond all his possessions, for all things died, or man or beast, whom once its edges bit" (LT2 108).[38] Gurtholfin/Gurthang, the 'iron of death', thus manifests a collapse of differences, generating violence where it should be radically excluded:[39] murder of a 'brother in arms' and incest constitute violations of the essential boundaries that safeguard cultural order. Yet from his earliest years, Túrin enters every community as an outsider who, by means of exorbitant heroism, creates and eventually destroys his own place within each society. Anglachel-Gurthang

---

36 Túrin adopts and receives many names in the course of his life; beside Mormegil (Blacksword) and Turambar (Master of Fate), he also names himself "Agarwaen, the son of Úmarth (which is the Blood-stained, son of Ill-fate)" after the killing of Beleg (CH 159).

37 Cf. LT2 83 ("it is said that at times it spake dark words to him") and 112: "There stood Turambar spent at last, and there he drew his sword, and said: 'Hail, Gurtholfin, wand of death, for thou art all men's bane and all men's lives fain wouldst thou drink, knowing no lord or faith save the hand that wields thee if it be strong. Thee only have I now – slay me therefore and be swift, for life is a curse, and all my days are creeping foul, and all my deeds are vile, and all I love is dead.' And Gurtholfin said: 'That will I gladly do, for blood is blood, and perchance thine is not less sweet than many a one's that thou hast given me ere now'; and Turambar cast himself then upon the point of Gurtholfin, and the dark blade took his life."

38 "But what lord or loyalty do you know, Túrin finally asks Gurthang, save the hand that wields you? From no blood will you shrink" (CH 256). Similarly, Kullervo's unnamed sword in the *Kalevala* admits that it enjoys drinking blood, regardless of whether it is innocent or guilty: "Why should I not eat what I like | not eat guilty flesh | not drink blood that is to blame? | I'll eat even guiltless flesh | I'll drink even blameless blood." (*Kalevala* 36: 332-336).

39 Cf Girard 49: "Order, peace, and fecundity depend on cultural distinctions; it is not these distinctions but the loss of them that gives birth to fierce rivalries and sets members of the same family or social group at one another's throats."

embodies the Otherness of excessive violence as well as Túrin's liminal position as a born leader and an outcast.

That Gurthang remains the only sword with the gift of speech in Tolkien's works is inseparable from the degree of Otherness contained in the tale of Túrin. As an exorbitant hero, Túrin becomes a stranger to the world of Men and Elves until the only Other he can communicate with is the alien Black Sword.[40] Yet his presumption to overcome fate itself is taken through a surprising reversal. According to the second prophecy of Mandos, the 'Conqueror of Fate' will return for the cataclysmic battle at the end of time: "and it shall be the black sword of Túrin that deals unto Melko his death and final end; and so shall the children of Húrin and all Men be avenged" (SM 165). Túrin has become as strange to Men as his blade: he is now counted among the gods.[41]

IV. By Light of the Sword: A Hobbit's Journey through the Dark

Hobbits, on the other hand, are at first strangers to heroic violence.[42] The swords they carry belong to foreign cultures of past eras: the blades that Frodo, Sam, Merry and Pippin take from the barrow were forged in Númenor and played their part in the long-past war against Angmar during the early Third Age. The origins of Sting, the sword that passes from Bilbo to Frodo to Sam, are even more remote: it was made in Gondolin, the enclosed elven city of the First Age. Yet, as Whetter and McDonald observe, the actual history of Sting unfolds only in *The Hobbit* and *The Lord of the Rings*, whereas other

---

40 Túrin's companionship with Anglachel begins with shared mourning for Beleg: "its blade was black and dull and its edges blunt. Then Gwindor said: 'This is a strange blade, and unlike any that I have seen in Middle-earth. It mourns for Beleg even as you do...'" (CH 157). In Nargothrond, Arminas reproaches him for taking "counsel only with your own wisdom, or with your sword" (CH 175).

41 "But of Men in that day the prophecy speaks not, save of Túrin only, and him it names among the gods" (SM 165). – In *The Book of Lost Tales*, Turambar already appears beside Fionwë, but the demise of Morgoth only falls to him in the 'Sketch of the Mythology' from 1926. Tolkien retained this feature through all subsequent revisions of the 'Great End'.

42 Swords are foreign to Hobbit culture and rarely used: After his adventure, Bilbo hangs Sting above the mantelpiece until he leaves the Shire again. While there is no interdict against physical violence as such, social order is generally sustained without recourse to arms or sanctions enforced by violence. (Cf. LotR 6: "Though slow to quarrel, and for sport killing nothing that lived, they were doughty at bay, and at need could still handle arms. They shot well with the bow, for they were keen-eyed and sure at the mark.")

illustrious swords have pre-existing histories.[43] Though Sting is not without martial legacy – as its response to orcs illustrates – its meaning is to a large extent shaped by the hobbit hands that wield it. If it successively provides Bilbo, Frodo and Sam with a warrior's identity, the resulting heroism also reflects the hobbits' disposition and approach to violence.

Like Andúril, Sting is rarely seen in blood-thirsty action. While Frodo makes use of it in Moria and wounds a troll,[44] Sting's finest heroic hour does not arrive until Frodo and Sam find themselves cornered by Shelob – the most monstrous and alien enemy in the entirety *The Lord of the Rings*:

> Then Frodo's heart flamed within him, and without thinking what he did, whether it was folly or despair or courage, he took the Phial in his left hand, and with his right hand drew his sword. Sting flashed out, and the sharp elven-blade sparkled in the silver light, but at its edges a blue fire flicked. (LotR 705)

The redoubled radiance as well as the parallelism of Phial and blade point to a specific property that sets Sting apart from all other swords so far discussed. Its full heroic potential is finally realized in the hands of Sam who wields Sting in his desperate fight against Shelob:

> He sprang forward with a yell, and seized his master's sword in his left hand. Then he charged. No onslaught more fierce was ever seen in the savage world of beasts; where some desperate small creature armed with little teeth alone, will spring upon a tower of horn and hide that stands above its fallen mate... Sam... still stood upon his feet, and dropping his own sword, with both hands he held the elven-blade point upwards..., fending off that ghastly roof; and so Shelob, with the driving force of her own cruel will, with strength greater than any warrior's hand, thrust herself upon a bitter spike. (LotR 711)

---

43 Cf. Whetter/McDonald 15: "what we see in *The Hobbit* and *The Lord of the Rings* is actually the unfolding of the history of Sting – in contrast to Narsil-Andúril or Glamdring, which already have pre-existing histories. It is significant that Sting is not like these other blades in this respect, for that focuses our attention on its role in the hobbits' adventures and the way they become heroes in spite of themselves. But the acquisition of swords is one of the things that herald the hobbits' transformation."

44 Frodo's previous sword from the barrow never strikes a harmful blow. Frodo wields it in defence on Weathertop, albeit without causing an injury, and employs it to signal his resistance against the Nazgûl at the Ford of Bruinen, where the spiritual onslaught alone breaks the blade.

Only with the aid of an ancient sword that liberates excessive violence does the hobbit transform into a dragon-slayer.[45] Yet ultimately, Shelob's monstrous Otherness and *her own cruel will* generate an extreme of vicious aggression, whereas Sam is driven by love, grief and loyalty: motivations that point to the integrative rather than the destructive side of violence.[46] The noblest purpose Sting serves and subsequently helps achieve is Frodo's return from apparent death and his liberation from the Tower of Cirith Ungol.

In its entirety, the Cirith Ungol episode highlights Sting's most significant qualities: the sword becomes a source of light and guidance. With its mysterious blue radiance that announces the presence of enemies (not least: Gollum), Sting offers counsel and warning, up to the point where it illuminates Sam's path into the Tower: "He drew his sword again and beat on the stone with the hilt, but it only gave out a dull sound. The sword, however, blazed so brightly now that he could see dimly in its light" (LotR 724). Like the Phial, Galadriel's gift to Frodo, Sting has become "a light... in dark places when all other lights go out" (LotR 367). Secondly, Sting restores companionship instead of operating as an instrument of severance: In a revealing variation of the fatal encounter between Beleg and Túrin,[47] the tragedy of loss receives an almost eucatastrophic twist[48] in *The Lord of the Rings*. Instead of forging a connection of inescapable guilt and mourning, like Anglachel-Gurthang, Sting secures and renews the hobbits' bond, culminating in an unparalleled case of shared ownership. Ultimately, the question whether Frodo or Sam is Sting's final and rightful keeper remains undecided.[49]

---

45 Interestingly, Tolkien contemplated the idea that Bilbo might slay Smaug during an early stage in the creation of *The Hobbit* (cf. HH I 364). In the finished text, the narrator at first comments ironically on Gandalf's claim that Bilbo will yet prove to be *as fierce as a dragon in a pinch*, which he calls *poetical exaggeration* (H 27), yet the wizard's prediction holds true for Bilbo, whose most heroic fight pits him against the Spiders of Mirkwood, and more so for Sam in his battle against Shelob.

46 In this, one may also recognize a reflection of Tolkien's personal preferences: "It is the heroism of obedience and love not of pride or wilfulness that is the most heroic and the most moving" (HB 148).

47 Túrin's desperate grief and suicidal response in the verse *Children of Húrin* (LB 56) closely resemble Sam's responses at Ciritch Ungol (LotR 714f). An early draft also features a 'Lament' that Sam composes for Frodo (WR 185, 189), echoing Túrin's elegy for Beleg, *Laer Cú Beleg, the Song of the Great Bow* (CH 157).

48 For Tolkien's definition of 'eucatastrophe', the "joyous turn" as well as the "true form" and "highest function" of a fairy-story, see OFS 154.

49 To the modern recipient, this may amount to nothing more spectacular than an unclear property situation; in a heroic context, it constitutes a puzzling paradox. Just the One Ring can only be worn by one hand (LotR 253: "only one hand at a time can wield the One", Gandalf tells Saruman), so can a sword only ever belong to one warrior. Aragorn even threatens death to anyone who will touch Andúril when he sets his sword aside by the doors of Meduseld (LotR 500: "Death shall come to any man that draws Elendil's sword save Elendil's heir"). Sting is the only famous blade wielded by two living protagonists in the course of one war and which serves them both indiscriminately.

At the same time, the gift of heroic violence that a sword confers can never fully merge into the other virtues that it may possess. Characteristically, Sting comes to Sam through death and "black despair" (LotR 714),[50] and exposes him to a fearfully isolated experience of heroic battle.[51] But is such an 'outlandish' experience at all compatible with the traditions of the Shire?

Upon their return to their own society, all four hobbit travellers can look back on heroic achievements;[52] the swords they carry announce changed identities[53] and (re-)introduce[54] their community to heroic violence: a necessary adjustment, as it serves to liberate the Shire from foreign occupants. Yet while Merry and Pippin lead the Battle of Bywater, Frodo does not lift a weapon again, and Sam draws his sword one last time in defence when Saruman attacks Frodo (LotR 996). In the aftermath of these events, Merry and Pippin (with their Númenórean swords) exhibit an integrative, collectively accepted form of violence. Even in the supposedly peaceful Shire, "it warmed all hearts to see them go riding by with their mail-shirts so bright and their shields so splendid" (LotR 1002). The heroism of Frodo and Sam, on the other hand, remains hidden, its invisibility announced most clearly by their continued wearing of the 'magical' cloaks from Lórien.[55]

---

50 Sam's initial impulses – to commit suicide or avenge Frodo by killing Gollum – reflect a warrior's heroic attitude, but as Sam examines his options, his love for Frodo once again becomes the dominant motivation. For a closer examination of Sam's transformed understanding of death in this episode see Klinger 187-190.
51 Sam's intention to die fighting for the protection of Frodo's dead body amounts to an excess of loyalty and heroism that endangers the Quest: "They'll see the flame of the sword, as soon as I draw it, and they'll get me sooner or later. I wonder if any song will ever mention it: How Samwise fell in the High Pass and made a wall of bodies round his master" (LotR 718). Necessarily, such a last stand beside Frodo's body would be the end of the Quest.
52 Pippin in particular does not hesitate to demonstrate a heroic approach during the hobbits' first encounter with the changed situation in the Shire: "'I am a messenger of the King,' he said. 'You are speaking to the King's friend, and one of the most renowned in all the lands of the West. You are a ruffian and a fool. Down on your knees in the road and ask pardon, or I will set this troll's bane in you'" (LotR 982).
53 Cf. Whetter/McDonald 25: "Both in *The Hobbit* and *The Lord of the Rings* heroes are equipped with swords that, to a certain extent, define them. The swords also help to signify growth or change. Thus, it is about the time Bilbo kills the spiders and starts to acquire some sense of what he is capable of that he decides to name his sword 'Sting'... Sam's increasing importance and stature are similarly announced by Sting, for when Frodo and Sam are knighted in 'The Field of Cormallen,' Frodo reiterates his permanent handing over of Sting to Sam (VI.iv.233; VI.ii.204), just as Bilbo had earlier passed it to Frodo."
54 LotR Appendix A 1018 reveals that hobbit archers served the last king of Arnor in the war against Angmar.
55 Cf. LotR 1002: "The two young Travellers [Merry and Pippin] cut a great dash in the Shire with their songs and their tales and their finery, and their wonderful parties. 'Lordly' folk called them, meaning nothing but good; for it warmed all hearts to see them go riding by with their mail-shirts so bright and their shields so splendid, laughing and singing songs of far away; and if they were now large and magnificent, they were unchanged otherwise,

However, this disappearance of heroic violence must not be confused with rejection, let alone pacifism.[56] When Frodo announces in Mordor "I do not think it will be my part to strike any blow again" (LotR 905), he expresses not a willed, personal choice but insight into the patterns of the 'great tale' that he and Sam have 'fallen into' (cf. LotR 696) and in which Frodo plays a specific, pre-ordained part.[57] In the final confrontation with Saruman, he stays Sam's hand with reference to Saruman's former greatness and warns against the "evil mood" of such a killing (LotR 996): a statement that distinguishes different types of aggression and implies the contagious nature of excessive violence.

Even though violence as such is not rejected, the essence of Frodo's and Sam's heroism – epitomized by Phial and sword – becomes publicly invisible: these mementoes recall the sharp clash of light and darkness that marks the crisis of Cirith Ungol, where the Quest is literally poised on the edge of a knife. At this juncture, Sting displays the power to join and divide in equal measure: the very paradox of the sword that remains on the outside of hobbit culture and points to a lingering Otherness that surrounds Frodo and Sam.[58]

V. Beyond Violence: the Mystique of the Sword

The ambivalence of heroic violence, as Tolkien portrays it, is not determined by the individual's choices and disposition alone. The warrior and his blade form a close alliance, and it is the sword in particular that connects heroic feats with the struggles and conflicts that pervade the history of Middle-earth.[59] But what are the specific properties that enable certain swords to mediate between individual will, history and fate?

---

unless they were indeed more fairspoken and more jovial and full of merriment than ever before. Frodo and Sam, however, went back to ordinary attire, except that when there was need they both wore long grey cloaks, finely woven and clasped at the throat with beautiful brooches..."

56 As Michael Livingston suggests: "That Frodo is characterized by shock, sadness, and an unwillingness to partake in violence is, once again, evidence of shell-shock. His pacifism could stand alongside similar impulses among veterans from any number of wars, though Tolkien would, of course, know it from the Somme" (Livingston 86).

57 Frodo applies the same choice of words when he answers Sam's question "Don't the great tales never end?' 'No, they never end as tales,' said Frodo. 'But the people in them come, and go when their part's ended. Our part will end later – or sooner.'" (LotR 697)

58 In an entirely different context – during the celebration on the Field of Cormallen – the paradox re-emerges as subjective experience: "their joy was like swords, and they passed in thought out to regions where pain and delight flow together" (LotR 933).

59 In the fight against the Lord of the Nazgûl Dernhelm/Éowyn is transformed into a sword and embodies its paradox: "Still she did not blench: maiden of the Rohirrim, child of kings, slender but as a steel-blade, fair but terrible" (LotR 823).

In this context, the sword's place within the order of time and space must be of interest, as its origins seem to define its purpose and destination as well. Merry's Númenórean sword from the Barrow-Downs exemplifies this principle most clearly. Fraught with a history of defeat in the war against Angmar, it strikes back against the Lord of the Nazgûl and establishes symmetry across an immense expanse of time, thereby fulfilling its own fate.[60] A vast cycle of injury and revenge transcends the historical moment and raises questions about the sword's position in time. As heirlooms, certain blades – such as Narsil – become the carriers of a continuous history and the memories attached to it. Other swords, such as the barrow-blades or Sting and Glamdring, lie dormant for extensive periods, to reawaken in the hands of a new (and sometimes unlikely) keeper. Their great age (often stressed in Tolkien's descriptions) clearly contributes to their power and defines their capacity of connecting temporally discrepant spheres. Swords such as Merry's blade or Sting cut across time and space: they play their part within a conflict of mythical proportions that exceeds individual recollection by far and links the fall of Númenor or Gondolin to the Ring-war at the end of the Third Age. The memory encapsulated in the sword itself induces the collapse of a spatial and temporal abyss.

As agents of history, fate and memory, swords like Gurthang or Sting oscillate between inanimate artefact and animate being. Tolkien's works provide no conceptual background for their specific nature, but when Melian first identifies 'malice' in Anglachel, she also observes: "The dark heart of the smith still dwells in it" (S 243; CH 97). The implication here (and elsewhere) is that swords absorb certain qualities of their makers and possess the ability to retain them – which amounts to an independent recollection, accumulated over time, constituting the 'soul' of the sword. If Théoden's vigour and courage are rekindled by the touch of the hilt, it is the sword's own memory of heroic excellence that achieves this effect.

However, Gurthang's 'cold voice' as well as the light emitted by Sting or Glamdring point to a more articulate and active capacity: the ability to respond to a specific challenge. Gurthang speaks when all of Túrin's social and familial ties have been irrevocably severed. Sting or Glamdring flicker in recognition

---

60 The description suggests that the sword itself rather than Merry's will is the driving force behind the attack: "Merry's sword had stabbed him from behind, shearing through the black mantle, and passing up beneath the hauberk had pierced the sinew behind his mighty knee." Correspondingly, the sword's disintegration – "it writhed and withered and was consumed" – is couched in terms of heroic death: "So passed the sword of the Barrow-downs, work of Westernesse. But glad would he have been to know its fate who wrought it slowly long ago in the North-kingdom when the Dúnedain were young, and chief among their foes was the dread realm of Angmar and its sorcerer king. No other blade, not though mightier hands had wielded it, would have dealt that foe a wound so bitter, cleaving the undead flesh, breaking the spell that knit his unseen sinews to his will." (LotR 824)

of their hereditary enemies. But while the Black Sword kills indiscriminately, the blades from Gondolin distinguish between friend and foe and set their light against an encroaching darkness. Their commonality lies in the ability to respond and reflect, which provides an important clue to the nature of the radiance emanating from the ancient elvish swords: they reflect an invisible light that belongs to a different location in time or space, and in this they resemble the Phial with its 'magical' ability to shine with the light of Eärendil even within suffocating, subterranean darkness.

This reflective ability encompasses memory and sometimes extends beyond it. Only once does Andúril, too, shine with a light of its own – in the formidable presence of Gandalf the White:

> There he stood, grown suddenly tall, towering above them. His hood and his grey rags were flung away. His white garments shone... The sword of Aragorn, stiff in his motionless hand, blazed with a sudden fire. (LotR 483)

The light that shines through Gandalf is mirrored by the sword's 'sudden fire'. As before, when Aragorn declared himself in Rohan, a transhistorical light – now emanating from the wizard – reveals his and Gandalf's identity within a mythical reality, highlighting the different nature of their respective power:

> The others gazed at them in silence as they stood there facing one another. The grey figure of the Man, Aragorn son of Arathorn, was tall, and stern as stone, his hand upon the hilt of his sword; he looked as if some king out of the mists of the sea had stepped upon the shores of lesser men. Before him stooped the old figure, white; shining now as if with some light kindled within, bent, laden with years, but holding a power beyond the strength of kings. (LotR 489)

Certainly, swords flare, blaze and flash throughout medieval literature as well as Tolkien's descriptions of heroic battle. The difference between 'ordinary' blades and 'animate' swords appears to reside in the capacity to remember light[61] or – in the specific case of Andúril – to recognize a supernatural or spiritual (rather than a natural) source of light.[62] In Tolkien's description of

---

61 This may be true of Narsil as well: unlike Andúril it apparently not only reflected but retained the light of the sun and moon.
62 Tolkien's figuration of the 'shining sword' therefore moves beyond mere 'creation from philology', as Whetter and McDonald argue: "It seems likely that these kennings and descriptions of gleaming, flashing swords, particularly those from *Beowulf*, have been

this unique event, time and perception are transformed, so that Aragorn appears as one of the mythical Sea-Kings from a distant era. Once again, we see the convergence of distinct historical moments in the flash not of a moment but of a sword's blade.

As instruments of division between life and death, swords belong to an existential sphere of intensified experience and sharpened vision. Tolkien has taken this quality to a point where a mythical order of time may emerge, and a new order of meaning is established. During these moments of rupture and recognition, the sword truly operates as a hinge between light and darkness and creates an opening for perceptions that transcend the limited mortal awareness and the history of Men.

Bibliography

Bloch, Marc. *The Royal Touch: Sacred Monarchy and Scrofula in England and France*. Routledge & Kegan Paul: London, 1973

Bloch, Marc and Jacques LeGoff. *Die wundertätigen Könige*. Übersetzt von Claudia Märtl. München: C. H. Beck, 1998

La Chanson de Roland. Oxford text and English translation. Ed. Gerard J. Brault. University Park: Pennsylvania State UP, 1984

The Complete Sagas of Icelanders: Including 49 Tales. Ed. Vidar Hreinsson. 5 Vols. Reykjavik: Eiriksson, 1997

Flieger, Verlyn. "Frodo and Aragorn: The Concept of the Hero." *Understanding 'The Lord of the Rings'. The Best of Tolkien Criticism*. Eds. Neil D. Isaacs and Rose A. Zimbardo. Boston, New York: Houghton Mifflin Company, 2004, 122-145

Frazer, James. *The Golden Bough. A Study in Magic and Religion*. 1922. London: Macmillan Press, 1983

Garth, John. *Tolkien and the Great War. The Threshold of Middle-earth*. Boston, New York: Houghton Mifflin, 2003

Girard, René. *Violence and the Sacred*. Translated by Patrick Gregory. Baltimore: The Johns Hopkins University Press, 1977

Haug, Walter. "Die Grausamkeit der Heldensage. Neue gattungstheoretische Überlegungen zur heroischen Dichtung." *Studien zum Altgermanischen. Festschrift für H. Beck*. Ed. Heiko Uecker. Berlin, New York: Walter de Gruyter, 1994, 303-326

Heinzle, Joachim. "Zur Funktionsanalyse heroischer Überlieferung: das Beispiel der Nibelungensage." *New Methods in the Research of Epic – Neue Methoden der Epenforschung*. Ed. Hildegard L.C. Tristram. Tübingen: Gunter Narr, 1999, 201-221

---

adapted into mystical Middle-earth swords that physically glow when enemies are near or that shine in battle. Indeed, we might go farther and say, in this instance, that we have a possible source in *Beowulf*, or even a series of sources. We certainly seem to have what Shippey describes as 'creation from philology' (*Road* 57): that is to say, the manner in which Tolkien worked not from ideas of plot but from words and names (92)." (Whetter/McDonald 21)

The Kalevala. An Epic Poem after Oral Tradition by Elias Lönnrot. Translated from the Finnish with an Introduction and Notes by Keith Bosley. Oxford, New York: Oxford UP, 1989

Klinger, Judith. "Hidden Paths of Time. March 13th and the Riddles of Shelob's Lair." *Tolkien and Modernity*. Eds. Thomas Honegger and Frank Weinreich. 2 Vols. Zurich: Walking Tree Publishers, 2006, Vol. 2: 143-210

Kraemer, Klaus. "Charismatischer Habitus. Zur sozialen Konstruktion symbolischer Macht." Berliner Journal für Soziologie 12 (2002): 173-187

Livingston, Michael. "The Shell-shocked Hobbit: The First World War and Tolkien's Trauma of the Ring." *Mythlore* 25 (2006): 77-92

Rateliff, John D., Ed. *The History of 'The Hobbit'*. J.R.R. Tolkien. Part 1: Mr. Baggins. London: HarperCollins, 2007

von See, Klaus. "Was ist Heldendichtung?" *Edda, Saga, Skaldendichtung. Aufsätze zur skandinavischen Literatur des Mittelalters*. Heidelberg: Winter, 1981, 154-193

Shippey, Tom. *J.R.R. Tolkien. Author of the Century*. New York, Boston: Houghton Mifflin, 2002

Tolkien, J. R. R. *The Hobbit*. 1937. London: Unwin Hyman Limited, 1990

---. *The Lord of the Rings*. 1954/1955. London: HarperCollins, 1995

---. "The Homecoming of Beorhtnoth Beorhthelm's Son." *Tree and Leaf. Including the Poem 'Mythopoeia'*. 1964. London: HarperCollins, 2001, 119-150

---. *The Silmarillion*. Ed. Christopher Tolkien. 1977. London: George Allen & Unwin, 1979

---. *The Letters of J.R.R. Tolkien*. A Selection edited by Humphrey Carpenter with the assistance of Christopher Tolkien. 1981. London: Houghton Mifflin, 1995

---. "Beowulf: The Monsters and the Critics." *The Monsters and the Critics and Other Essays*. Ed. Christopher Tolkien. 1983. London: HarperCollins, 1997, 5-48

---. "On Fairy-Stories." *The Monsters and the Critics and Other Essays*. Ed. Christopher Tolkien. 1983. London: Harper Collins, 1997, 109-161

---. *The Book of Lost Tales (Part Two)*. (*The History of Middle-earth* 2). Ed. Christopher Tolkien. 1984. London: HarperCollins, 2002

---. *The Lays of Beleriand*. (*The History of Middle-earth* 3). Ed. Christopher Tolkien. 1985. London: HarperCollins, 2002

---. *The Shaping of Middle-earth*. (*The History of Middle-earth* 4). Ed. Christopher Tolkien. 1986. London: HarperCollins, 2002

---. *The War of the Ring*. (*The History of Middle-earth* 8). Ed. Christopher Tolkien. 1990. London: HarperCollins, 1997

---. *The War of the Jewels*. (*The History of Middle-earth* 11). Ed. Christopher Tolkien. 1994. London: HarperCollins, 2002

---. *The Children of Húrin. Narn I Chîn Húrin*. Edited by Christopher Tolkien. London: HarperCollins, 2007

Volsunga saga. The Saga of the Volsungs. Ed. R.G. Finch. London: Nelson, 1965

Weber, Max. *The Theory of Social and Economic Organization*. New York: The Free Press, 1974

---. *Essays in Sociology*. Eds. H.H. Gerth and C. Wright Mills. London: Routledge, 1991

Whetter, K.S. and R. Andrew McDonald. "'In the Hilt is Fame': Resonances of Medieval Swords and Sword-Lore in J.R.R. Tolkien's The Hobbit and The Lord of the Rings." *Mythlore* 25 (2006): 5-28

Language and Violence:
The Orcs, the Ents, and Tom Bombadil

Martin G.E. Sternberg (Bonn)

Tolkien once called *The Lord of the Rings* an "essay in linguistic aesthetics" (L 220), and so we may ask what this extended "essay" of his has to tell us about the relation between language and violence. The point of departure for this paper is rather simple. Language enables us to speak, to form thoughts (at least of certain kinds) and express them. But this freedom is not limitless, as everyone will soon discover when translating a text and groping for words in one language to express concepts which so easily fall to hand in another. Language subjects us to its rules, its definitions and therefore limitations, the transgression of which carries the penalty of becoming incomprehensible to other members of one's language group. Language thus not only allows the expression of certain thoughts, it also hinders or even prevents the expression of others (Fix 20ff). Insofar as thinking depends on language, language can restrict and shape thoughts, and insofar as acting depends on thinking, language can enable, restrict and shape actions, including violent ones.

Language and – or as – Violence

The viability of the question of language and violence, and whether language itself can be qualified as violence, is of course affected by the concept of violence applied. For followers of Johan Galtung's idea that violence is the difference between the possible and the actually reached degree of self-realization (Galtung 9), the answer is an unqualified yes: through its inherent constrictions, language is violence, and violence is part of any kind of symbolic representation in varying degrees.

To those who criticize this concept of violence as an overextension that blurs all distinctions and request that violence must be centred on the body and always means the physical violation of somebody or something (von Trotha 13f, 26f, Popitz 48), the answer is that there may still be a relation between language *and* violence: The preconditions set by language may hinder or facilitate violent action in general or against certain objects. The limitations language and language practices impose on speakers may be the crystallizations of preceding violent conflicts, and overstepping these limits may result in incurring violent sanctions. Opting for a physical concept of violence thus does not invalidate the approach of this paper, but means attending to the interaction between language and physical violence more closely.

I will not deal, however, with the question how Tolkien's invented languages merely *display* the more or less violent attitudes of their speakers, as this has already been done by Helmut W. Pesch and others. Nor will I deal with the magical use of language in conflict. Rather I will try to combine some theories on the relation between language, power and violence to address four questions: How far is language in *The Lord of the Rings* not only an expression but an effective means of violence? Can language violate and even subjugate its speaker? How may it violate the things and beings of which it speaks? Finally, how far does language hinder or enable acts of violence?

In this endeavour, I will rely on four different approaches to these questions. The first approach is Michel Foucault's discourse theory for which power resides in regulating discourse, among other things in determining *who* may say what in which circumstances (Foucault, *Ordnung* 10f). At certain law courts, for example, the plaintiff cannot speak, but only his lawyer who had to pass specific training, examinations and accreditations required by the relevant society. The words in which these requirements are formulated are however in themselves neutral. In different combinations, they could mean all sorts of things. Narrowing down discourse theory to the approach of this paper, the question is whether the chances to partake in discourse might already be regulated or at least prejudiced by the phonetics and structure of the relevant language itself.

Another way in which language exerts constrictions on its speakers is by limiting *what* can be expressed in it. The most famous example of this kind of power is "Newspeak" in George Orwell's *1984*. Here, a totalitarian regime tries to impose a severely modified and impoverished form of English to control and restrict what can be said and consequently thought, so that deviations from the dominant ideology will no longer be feasible because they could neither be communicated nor even conceived (Orwell 417f).

The target of this mode of domination through language is the realm of meanings and notions, and in order to judge Tolkien's invented languages properly, we would need an overview of their complete vocabulary, which we lack. Orwell's approach however can be transformed into the field of Tolkien's linguistic aesthetics. Tolkien wrote that the sound, the music of words can have the same effect as music listened to while reading, which may, when aesthetically fitting, deepen and illuminate the passage read (MC 218).

In his book *Inside Language*, Ross Smith has developed this into the idea that the sound of language reflects the speaker's emotional response to the environment, to the things spoken of (Smith 71-75). If this is the case, it should also work the other way round: The sound of words can establish, even prescribe the mood in which the thing meant is spoken and thought of. Language may thus condition what Martin Heidegger called *Grundstimmung*, the "basic mood". We are always in some kind of mood, be it frightened, joyful or bored, and this mood colours our encounters with things and persons (Heidegger 134-137). Such a mood may be more or less prone to aggression and violence, in the way a person's driving style may be affected by whether it is listening to Hard Rock or a Bach cantata.

The power and violence of language can however not only affect the speaker, but also the things and persons spoken of. Language determines how far their individuality and otherness can express itself in the domain of discourse. A frequently discussed example is gender-biased language wherein the dominance of male expressions somehow represses the feminine presence in society. The potential of language for distorting its object may however be much more fundamental. For Theodor W. Adorno, any application of generalizing abstract terms to an individual entity was inherently and invariably violent because it made the difference of the individual from the general concept disappear (Adorno 153f). This is an act of violence that only names, with their strictly individual applicability, could avoid (61f).

Again, this question of how far a language lends itself to expressing the otherness of things and beings can be married to Tolkien's emphasis on linguistic aesthetics: The phonetic fabric of a language and the language practices of the relevant language group may be more or less suited as a soundbox in which the speaker's emotional response to the environment can resonate and in the process be either dulled or enhanced.

The Black Speech as an Instrument of Rule

he first place to look for a connection between language and violence is obviously the Black Speech of Sauron's making, used by the orcs and others of his servants. When Pippin hears the orcs speak, he describes the sound as hideous and abominable, full of hate and anger (LotR II 53f). The ugly and aggressive sound of the Black Speech does more than just express the nature of their speaker, for the orcs are after all the first to hear it. In them, the Black Speech rouses or at least augments and sustains a suitably aggressive mood: it helps the orcs to stay orcs.

Subjective as such aesthetic judgements are, there is much more to the sound of the Black Speech than mere subjectivism. Its phonetic makeup as analysed by

Helmut W. Pesch consists mostly of plosives. Fricatives appear only as hissing sounds, nasals are limited to the bilabial *m*, and among vocals, those vocals dominate which are formed with the back of the tongue, *a* and *u* (Pesch 150, see also Meile 220). The combined effect of all this is that when speaking the Black Speech as in *ash nazg durbatuluk*, the speaker's tongue moves continually backward to the trachea until blocking his breath, thus effectively strangulating the speaker (Pesch 154). The Black Speech is thus a violent speech even by the standards of those who require violence to affect the body.

The Black Speech grammar continues this theme of repression. The expressions in the inscription on the One Ring for "rule them all" –*durbatuluk*–, "find them" –*gimpatul*– and "bring them all" –*thrakatuluk*– demonstrate that the objects of these verbs "them" or "them all"– are as -*atul* and -*atuluk* mere annexes to the relevant verb. The preposition "in" is likewise represented by the annexed -*ishi*. The basic principle of the Black Speech is thus to make all objects and modifications appendices to the basic verb. From the viewpoint of perceptive and cognitive psychology, this is the simplest form of language because it does not require any intermediate storage of partial linguistic structures in short-term memory. In reducing any objects and personal elements to appendices of processes, the Black Speech shows forth the drive for domination and the inhumanity of Sauron its creator (Pesch 150-156).

These linguistic characteristics make the Black Speech much more than a mere *expression* of Sauron's nature. They make it an *effective instrument* of Sauron's rule. If power manifests itself in the ability to speak, the gagging quality of the Black Speech buttresses Sauron's domination. In hindering speech, the Black Speech hinders Sauron's servants in contradicting him, in questioning their orders, in coordinating acts of resistance or actions without orders. The Black Speech is a language in which it is easier to listen than to speak, easier to obey than to oppose. Being a language not meant to be spoken is thus no perversion of language, but its perfection as a tool of power and means of violence.

The centring of the Black Speech around verbs supports this further because it favours thinking in terms of doing something – especially *to* something. According to Elias Canetti, rulers often aim to arrest their soldiers in a standstill, damming up their energies and keeping them in expectation of orders, to release their energies into the execution of their commander's bidding once the order arrives (Canetti 345ff). The Black Speech does just this: it encourages the orcs or any of Sauron's subjects to think in terms of actions and processes and hinders them in speech acts of their own that may lead to executing deeds of their own.

The low demands the Black Speech makes on resources of memory enhances this further. In bypassing memory as far as possible, it reduces the risk that mental content of one's own may slip into the hearing or repeating of orders given. George Orwell stressed this point explicitly for Newspeak. Here, not grammar but the ease of pronunciation, arrived at by careful phonetic construction, was meant to ensure that speakers could perpetuate the dominant discourse without much effort, allowing for a flowing forth of language "as nearly as possible independent of consciousness" (Orwell 425)[1]. Bypassing memory favours also its withering and thus obstructs the development of individual mental content which could be at odds with Sauron's will. The Black Speech refers its speaker always to a superior master.

This is further borne out by the different impressions the Black Speech makes when spoken by speakers who differ in power. When Gandalf recites the inscription on the ring, "the change in the wizard's voice was astounding. Suddenly it became menacing, powerful, harsh as stone" (LotR I 333). When spoken by subaltern orcs, it is just "hideous" and "abominable", it sounds "full of hate and anger", and fades off into cursing, muttering and ultimately silence (LotR II 53). The Black Speech sounds menacing and powerful only when spoken by somebody who already has great power. Like the ring, it gives power to the already powerful, especially if the speaker is, like Sauron and the ringwraiths, not restricted by the limits of a human anatomy.

So impressive the Black Speech is as an instrument of rule in theory, so abysmally does it fail in practice, and it fails precisely because of the physical violence it inflicts on its speakers. We do not know the different dialects of the Black Speech which developed among the orcs, but we may fairly suppose that a language which puts such pressure on its speakers will spawn dialects which carry a lighter phonetic burden. The splintering of the Black Speech into mutually incomprehensible dialects means that Sauron's servants have to resort to the Common Speech on many occasions, giving Sauron's opponents the opportunity to understand them when it is crucial. Here Tolkien's maxim "oft evil will shall evil mar" proves true again.

Entish Linguistic Pacifism

et us now turn from linguistic aggressiveness to what could be called linguistic pacifism. Regarding the violence language may inflict on or provoke to the things and beings spoken about, there could possibly be no more peaceful and caring language than Entish. In the Entish language, Adorno's mutilation

---

1   Meile comes to a similar conclusion based on the way in which Sauron, in creating the Black Speech, seems to have distorted features of Quenya regarding expressions of possession (Meile 221f), but these distortions could only *be effective* if Quenya were the natural language, the „programming language" for every thinking mind in Middle-earth. Attributing this effect to the grammar of the Black Speech is not dependent on such a supposition.

of individuality by the application of generalizing terms is reduced as far as possible. When Treebeard, Merry, and Pippin are about to leave the rocky shelf on which they met, Treebeard asks the Hobbits how they call such a place, and they answer with abstract terms: hill, shelf, step. For Treebeard, these are hasty words for a thing standing there since that part of the world was shaped, and his own word for it is suitably different: "a-lalla-lalla-rumba-kamanda-lind-or-burume. Excuse me: that is part of my name for it" (LotR II 80).

In the Entish language, names tell the story of the things they belong to, and thus keep, like Treebeard's true name, growing all the time (LotR II 80). By doing so, Entish gives as much room as possible to the individuality of the thing spoken of, and because it tells its story that, after all, is still ongoing, it does not even arrest the thing referred to in its development nor freeze it in a static definition. It is open to future developments. It is telling that Treebeard seems to use name and word synonymously, for a name is the kind of word that is most at peace with its meaning (Adorno 61f).

Already at the level of grammar and vocabulary, Entish is thus an order of knowledge that conserves the development of the thing denoted and the interactions it had with other things in the course of time. Entish makes it impossible to speak about something without representing its history, and thus forces elements of that history back into present consciousness which might have been overlooked in more "hasty" languages – a stark contrast to the Black Speech. Where speech precedes and informs action, such language is bound to hinder any uncaring and rash decisions that might easily violate the Other.

This helps to explain Treebeard's claim that Ents are similar to Elves in that they are less interested in themselves and better at getting inside other things, and more similar to men as they are more changeable and "quicker at taking the colour of the outside" (LotR II 84). The latter part of this claim seems at odds with the placid lives the Ents lead, but it fits in well with their language: in contrast to the Elvish languages which, for all their musicality and capacity for poetic expression, are nevertheless closed and rather stable systems of words and meanings, Entish, due to its narrative character, is constantly adapting itself to the present and the present surroundings.

The Ents' cognitive openness to the individuality and otherness of things and beings around them is reflected in the linguistic aesthetics of Entish and the use to which the Ents put it: Words like *a-lalla-lalla-rumba-kamanda-lind-or-burume* show its musicality and its aptness for stringing together unending songs. On the way to his ent-house, Treebeard "all the while as he walked, he talked to himself in a long running stream of musical sounds" (LotR II 82). This musical soliloquy in spite of the presence of Merry and Pippin as possible partners for communication demonstrates that here, speaking Entish does not serve as a means of communicating with others nor for saving knowledge. It is rather the expression of the impression the environment makes on Treebeard. It may not only express the state of his perceiving mind, but even be coeval with it.

Yavanna said "would that the trees might speak on behalf of all things that have roots, and punish those that wrong them" (S 34). Gayatry Spivak has pointed to the important difference between speaking *about* somebody und speaking *for* somebody, between rhetorical and political representation, that is too often sleighted by those who think to speak of the suppressed subaltern, but who regularly construct him or her after their own measure to stabilize their own subjectivity (Spivak 278ff), so that ultimately, "the subaltern cannot speak" (308), but is always the mute object of dominant discourse. It is fitting that the Ents, who shall both speak and act for subaltern plant-life, have a language that goes a very long way to open up to the Other.

Talking Ents into War

This openness and at least strong reduction in violence of the Entish language has one drawback, however: Like the Black Speech, it hinders speaking, not by strangling its speaker's breath, but by drawing it out of him to exhaustion: "It is a lovely language, but it takes a long time to say anything in it, because we do not say anything in it, unless it is worth taking a long time to say, and to listen to" (LotR II 80). Peaceful and deliberate as Entish is, it is for the very same reason also slow and cumbersome. This has drawbacks once its speakers enter situations in which quick decisions have to be taken: situations of violence.

Wolfgang Sofsky said that violence is always experienced in different modes of time by both the acting and the suffering party. Fights and attacks are connected to time passing very quickly, even blurring into the timeless present of battle (Sofsky 103-114). In this perspective, the Ents' slowness predisposes them for being overcome, for becoming victims. The Ents are so obsessed with listening to the Other, with savouring and unfolding the otherness of things that they are unable to defend the Other they most cling to, the trees whose shepherds they are, from the aggression of those with faster, more aggressive modes of language and thought.

Gandalf compares the coming of Merry and Pippin into Fangorn to small stones falling in the mountains that start an avalanche, yet on close examination, we may seriously wonder what makes them have this effect. It is not the news they bring (though Gandalfs says so), for Treebeard already knows about the destruction the orcs wreak in his woods. He at least suspected that the orcs were Saruman's servants even before hearing the news Merry and Pippin brought, for he already linked the orcs wandering freely in Fangorn to the secrets he told Saruman. Indeed, he says that he was thinking lately what to do about Saruman. The Hobbits' tale may make him see that Saruman is plotting to become a power, and that he is in league with Sauron. But Sauron's war is a storm that an Ent can only "weather or crack" (LotR II 89ff). When the Ents finally march on Isengard, Treebeard calls it not a hasty decision, but one that has long grown in their hearts. So something more than news must have triggered the Ents into action.

My suggestion is that the trigger Merry and Pippin bring into Fangorn consists less in the news they bring than in the language in which they convey them and in which they make Treebeard reflect upon them. With the Common Speech they use, the Hobbits bring a less caring and more superficial, but also faster and more aggressive mode of speech and thus of thought with them that liberates first Treebeard and then the other Ents from the passivity in which their language keeps them. It starts with the fact that Treebeard has no name for them, and has to adapt his vocabulary to fit them in. The Hobbits astonish him with their readiness to give their true names right at the beginning of a conversation with a total stranger. For Treebeard, this is an act of dangerous exhibitionism because, after all, true names tell in his language the story of the things they belong to, and contain knowledge that may be dangerous in the hands of an enemy. The Hobbits thus shatter Treebeard's belief in the power of names, and the care and time that has to be attributed to them. The leaving of the hill they met on illustrates this beautifully and contains the whole further development in a nutshell:

> 'Let us leave this – did you say what you call it?'
> 'Hill?' suggested Pippin. 'Shelf? Step?' suggested Merry.
> Treebeard repeated these words thoughtfully. 'Hill. Yes, that was it. But it is a hasty word for a thing that has stood here since this part of the world was shaped. Never mind. Let us leave it, and go.'
> (LotR II 81)

This scene contains the whole dynamics between speaking, thinking and acting which will ultimately lead the Ents to Isengard: Treebeard wants to do something together with the Hobbits – leaving the hill – and is looking for a word in the Common Speech that escapes him. The Hobbits make suggestions out of which he makes a choice which to him, in typically Entish fashion, seems unsuited for something with such a long history. But now, he pushes his scruples aside: *Never mind. Let us leave it, and go.* Treebeard's chief concern is no longer the exact naming of the object concerned or contemplating its individuality, but the immediately following action of leaving it.

At Treebeard's house, the Hobbits not only tell him certain things. Much more important, they force *him* to recount and reflect the Ents' current situation in the hasty, superficial, and action-prone Common Speech. Time and again, Treebeard stresses the fact that his telling is completely inadequate to its subject: "I cannot tell it properly, only in short", "it was never an Entish song, mark you: it would have been a very long song in Entish" (LotR II 93, 95). With this translation of the Entish situation into the hasty Common Speech, Treebeard's knowledge, despite greatly losing in detail, becomes activated, becomes more readily disposable, speakable, thinkable. In the process, Treebeard becomes hasty and positively heated, needing to cool down under the waterfall of his house. The Hobbits have the greatest effect on Treebeard not by speaking to him but by making him speak through listening to him. The psychoanalyst Jaques Lacan once said that the chief function of an analyst is not to tell something to his or her patient, but to open through his listening a space wherein they can speak. Merry and Pippin perform just such a role as analysts, and it is a nice coincidence that when speaking to them, Treebeard lies on his bed like on an analyst's couch.

After that, the Entmoot decides to march on Isengard rather quickly, at least by Entish standards. Both Treebeard and the Hobbits are duly surprised. We may suppose that Treebeard has somehow infected the moot with his accelerated way of speaking and thinking. The example of Quickbeam shows that there are slower and quicker usages even within Entish. Treebeard's reason for the time an Entmoot usually takes supports this view: "However, deciding what to do takes Ents not so long as going over all the facts and events that they have to make up their minds about" (LotR II 103). The changes the Hobbits effect to Entish speech and thought may speed up especially this process and prevent the toils of deliberation from quenching the impulse for action. The violent speech the Hobbits bring into Fangorn allows Fangorn to rise up in violence against Saruman, to be efficiently violent at all.

This relation between language, its regard for the Other, and violence even works within the separation of Ents and Entwives. In a detailed and thoughtful analysis of the Elvish song in which Treebeard relates this story, Corey Olsen concludes that the Ents' obsession with their woods and the Entwives' with their gardens leads to their mutual estrangement. Requiring the other party "to say my land is best" means a disregard of what the others hold dear. Olsen also detects in the song a contrast between passivity dominating the Ents' parts of the song and activity in that of the Entwives. She sees the Ents leading a contemplative, the Entwives an active life, which she sees as perfectly complementary perspectives without any competition between them. She is sensitive to the fact that the Entwives' love of order and plenty has Sarumanian overtones and may lead to tyranny, yet nevertheless thinks that concessions on both sides, but especially from the Ents, might have avoided their break-up. Instead, Ents and Entwives lose touch with each other and sight of their ultimate aim, which the song states as a life in the West (Olsen 44-47, 50).

Whether this is the avoidable moral failure Olsen deems it to be (see also Chance 180f) is another matter. The Entwives not only love different things than the Ents. Again, the key is language: Regarding the plants they gave their minds to, the Entwives "did not desire to speak with these things, but they wished them to hear and obey what was said to them," bearing "fruit and leaf to their liking" (LotR II 93f). Their breeding activities entail a complete shift from the Ents' "listening" speech to commanding speech, turning their plants into mute subalterns, and constructing them into cultivated plants *by telling them what to be*. The language of the active and the contemplative life are here mutually exclusive, and the mutual exclusivity of the claim "to say my land is best" simply stems from the fact that woods and gardens cannot exist on the same spot. The purpose for which Yavanna created the Ents was the protection of all things growing (S 34f), yet at the heart of agricultural technology are not the blade of axe and ploughshare, but the seeds of crops for which woods are cleared and the soil is ripped open. These plants the Entwives breed and pass on to men (LotR II 94), thus literally laying the seeds for the destruction of the woods of old. Again, a shift in language precedes violence.[2]

When finally comparing the Black Speech with Entish under the aspect of language and violence, we can state that there is indeed a conditional relationship between language and violence. Language may ease or hinder violent dispositions and actions toward other beings. Beyond that, there is a puzzling similarity between both languages. Superficially, they seem to be the exact opposites: Where the Black Speech stifles its own flow with the breath of its speaker, Entish is made to flow on indefinitely. Where the Black Speech blocks and atrophies memory, Entish is in itself a memory of the things denoted by it. Where the Black Speech subjugates every thing to verbs and thus process, in Entish, the things rule the endlessly unfolding story of their names.

---

2   This rift between the language of Ents and Entwives supports Davies' view that there is a constant conflict between civilisation and nature in Middle-earth, and that Tolkien was aware of it (Davies 61-65).

Deep down however, both languages are made not for speaking but listening, subjugating their speakers to the Other: in the case of the Black Speech, it is the one Other Sauron, in the case of Entish, it is the many encountering Others of the Entish environment. There is of course the difference that the Ents want to listen and delight in the things they encounter. It is their chief desire. Ultimately however it seems to have destructive consequences on their consciousness as sentient, individual beings: their tendency to drowse off into treeishness. If speaking of the other means being aesthetically affected by it and recounting its whole history in a language that flows on and on, then it is easy to slip into a kind of trance. The stream of words representing the Other as accurately as possible washes away the differences that hedge the self, and drowns it. For all their differences, the orc raging in the black mass of Sauron's army and the Ent standing on his mountain meadow immovably have one thing in common: they have ceased to be individual beings with a distinct consciousness of their own.

Language and Power in the Old Wood

Some may deem these views on the connection of language and violence a little far-fetched and resulting from philosophies applied from outside to *The Lord of the Rings*, yet they are supported by a character we meet quite early on and with whom the relation between language, power and violence is explicitly reflected upon: Tom Bombadil.

As with the Ents, the Hobbits' first encounter is centred on language: Tom's unceasing flow of vocal utterances that the Hobbits hear long before seeing him, "singing carelessly and happily, but it was singing nonsense". This judgement of "nonsense" is immediately qualified by "or so it seemed" (LotR I 165). The reason for this is given later: "Tom sang most of the time, but it was chiefly nonsense, or perhaps a strange language unknown to the Hobbits, an ancient language whose words were mainly those of wonder an delight" (LotR I 200). Tom's language is non-sense because it is his highly sensual answer to his surroundings.

Out of this sensual nonsense he changes into meaningful speech, but he does so before even noticing the Hobbits. The change occurs when he approaches Old Man Willow, commanding him not to hinder his way, and promptly the wind and the whispering of leaves cease (LotR I 165). The change from nonsensical-sensual to meaningful speech is thus directly linked with a threat of violence of which Tom is indeed capable, as the ensuing liberation of Merry and Pippin shows.

Tom's identity is the starting point for Frodo's dialogue with Goldberry, which turns into a reflection on language, classification, power and rule:

Every now and again they caught, among many a *derry dol* and *merry dol* and a *ring a ding a dillo* the repeated words:

> Old Tom Bombadil is a merry fellow
> Bright blue his jacket is and his boots are yellow.
> 'Fair Lady!' said Frodo again after a while. 'Tell me, if my asking does not seem foolish, who is Tom Bombadil?'
> 'He is', said Goldberry staying her swift movements and smiling.
> Frodo looked at her questioningly. 'He is, as you have seen him,' she said in answer to his look. 'He is the master of wood, water and hill.' (LotR I 171f)

Frodo asks for a definition of Tom Bombadil in general, abstract terms – which is refused him. In Tom's and Goldberry's realm, the question who and what something is in the fabric of abstract generalizations (and thus, in Adorno's view, mutilations) that make up language is foolish indeed because it is not essential. Essential is only that something is, and it is as what it appears, as what it is seen: Tom's description of himself as a merry fellow in a blue jacket and yellow boots, which made Frodo ask, sticks to his external appearance. Because everything belongs to itself in the Old Wood, there is no need to fit it into the strictures of discourse and its order of power.

It is telling that Frodo's and Goldberry's different approaches to language reveal themselves in their misunderstanding concerning the meaning of the word *master*. When Goldberry calls Tom thus, Frodo reaches for the abstract meaning of this word, which refers to rule and ownership. Goldberry however speaks of a master *as Frodo had seen him*, and Frodo *saw* Tom exactly as the kind of master Goldberry describes: somebody who cannot be caught, who might liberate others, but who does not own wood, water and hill. In contrast to Frodo, Goldberry centres on the individual, the present, and the visual.

In the same way as with the Ents, this way of speaking and thinking leads to a certain powerlessness against an outside world of violence and domination. On the council of Elrond, Gandalf speaks against giving Tom the ring for safekeeping: Tom would most likely throw it away one day, "for such things have no hold on his mind (LotR II 347f). This seems astonishing for someone who has, even more than the Ents, an enormous fund of historical knowledge, maybe even a prophetic gift. Questions of domination and power have however no hold in his language and thus no hold in his mind, making Tom unsuitable as the ring's keeper.

The Conflict inside Language

Summing up, it can be stated that there is indeed a relation between language and violence in Tolkien's *The Lord of the Rings*. It exists already at the level of language itself, of phonetics and grammar, even before the range of expressible meanings is considered, still less the meaning of specific texts. Language can facilitate or hinder physical violence, and if concepts of violence are applied that do not require violence to be physical, then the constrictive capacity of language violates both the speaker and the thing spoken in ways described by Foucault, Orwell, and Adorno, so far that the Black Speech can qualify even as physical violence in its gagging effect on the speaker.

Beyond that, there is another and possibly more important peculiarity of Tolkien's approach to violence in and through language: It rests less on binary oppositions of the forbidden and the allowed, truth and error, madness and sanity. It rests on the allocation and consumption of resources: breath, physical strength, and time, gagging orcs, exhausting Ents, with silence as the ultimate result in both cases. This linguistic violence is thus a matter not only of quality but of quantity, it is an economic affair. It is significant that the conflict with Saruman is an economical one as well: The Ents, so consumed by their language of the other, are about to be consumed with their trees as fuel. Because the use of language always feeds off the resources of the speaker, there is, inside language, a permanent conflict between the Own and the Other. The more linguistic and cognitive resources for the Other, the less for the Own, even if the Own consists chiefly in a relation to a specific Other. There is no prospect for permanent peace because an equilibrium reached in specific conditions may prove dysfunctional in others.

This means just stating an interdependence, not a judgement. It is obvious that Tolkien approves of the "linguistic pacifism" in Fangorn and the Old Wood, and he saw the delight in the otherness of things as at the heart of Faery (SWM 101). Yet the costs entailed with this are stated as strongly. It is also noteworthy that this pacifism has its place in realms protected by the fear outsiders have of them. Tom sings in a dreaded wood at whose edge the trees, no longer mute subalterns, whisper at night, passing on not utterances of delight, but news and plots (LotR I 153f).

The violent aspect of language thus never subsides. In consequence, what *The Lord of the Rings* has to tell us as an essay in linguistic aesthetics about violence may be more differentiated, ambivalent and "grey" compared to what it tells from an ethical or metaphysical point of view. It is also more ambivalent than some current thinking about the relation of language and violence: It shares with it many presuppositions and points of critique, but also shows the consequence of fulfilling the claim to lay aside, for the sake of the Other, the domination and violence that rests inside language.

Perhaps all this is not too surprising. Michel Foucault remarked that language, when free from the rules and strictures that form discourse, is just noise wherein no meanings exist and the subject dissolves (Foucault, *Dits* 672, 695). The Ents, Tom, and Goldberry demonstrate that this is already true at the level below discourse, in language itself. If one tries to open up language completely, to refrain from repression as far as possible, to desist from definitions which are always exclusions, one risks to dissolve into noise and disappear if not like Foucault's famous face in the sand on the shore, then like a loose leaf drifting through the woods.

Bibliography

Adorno, Theodor W. *Negative Dialektik*. Frankfurt am Main: Suhrkamp Verlag, ³1982

Canetti, Elias. *Masse und Macht*. Frankfurt am Main: Fischer Taschenbuch Verlag, 1980

Chance, Jane. "Tolkien and the Other: Race and Gender in Middle-Earth." *Tolkien's Modern Middle Ages*. Eds. Jane Chance and Alfred K. Siewers. New York: Palgrave Macmillan, 2009, 171-186

Davis, James, G. "Showing Saruman as Faber: Tolkien and Peter Jackson." *Tolkien Studies 5* (2008): 55-71

Fix, Ulla. »Die Macht der Sprache über den Einzelnen und die Gewalt des Einzelnen über die Sprache«. *Gewalt der Sprache, Sprache der Gewalt*. Eds. Angelika Hoffmann-Corbineau and Pascal Nicklas. Hildesheim/Zürich/New York, 2000, 19-35

Foucault, Michel. *Die Ordnung des Diskurses*. Frankfurt am Main: Fischer Taschenbuch Verlag, 1991

---. *Dits et Ecrits*. Schriften. Ed. Daniel Defert et al., Vol. I. Frankfurt: Suhrkamp, 2001

Galtung, Johan. *Strukturelle Gewalt*. Beiträge zur Friedens- und Konfliktforschung. Reinbeck bei Hamburg: Rowolt Taschenbuch Verlag, 1975

Heidegger, Martin. *Sein und Zeit*. Tübingen: Max Niemeyer Verlag, 2006

Meile, M. G. "Sauron's Newspeak: Black Speech, Quenya, and the nature of mind." *Semiotics around the World: Synthesis in Diversity*. Proceedings of the Fifth Congress of the International Association for Semiotic Studies. Eds. Gerald F. Carr and Irmengard Rauch. Berlin: Mouton de Gruyter, 1997, 219-222

Olsen, Corey. "The Myth of the Ent and the Entwife." *Tolkien Studies 5* (2008): 39-53

Orwell, George. *Nineteen-Eighty-Four*. Oxford: Clarendon Press, 1984

Pesch, Helmut W. »J.R.R. Tolkiens linguistische Ästhetik«. *J.R.R: Tolkien – der Mythenschöpfer*. Ed. Helmut W. Pesch. Meitingen: Corian Verlag Heinrich Wimmer, 1984, 143-160

Popitz, Heinrich. *Phänomene der Macht*. Tübingen: Mohr, 1992

Smith, Ross. *Inside Language. Linguistic and Aesthetic Theory in Tolkien*. Zurich/Berne: Walking Tree Publishers, 2007

Sofsky, Wolfgang. »Gewaltzeit«. *Soziologie der Gewalt*. Ed. Trutz von Trotha. Sonderhefte der Kölner Zeitschrift für Soziologie und Sozialpsychologie Vol. 37. Opladen/Wiesbaden: Westdeutscher Verlag, 1997, 102-121

Spivak, Gayatri Chakravorty. "Can the Subaltern Speak?". *Marxism and the Interpretation of Culture*. Eds. Cary Nelson and Lawrence Grossberg. Basingstoke/London: Macmillan Education, 1988, 271-313

Tolkien, John Ronald Reuel. *Smith of Wootton Mayor*. Extended Edition. Ed. Verlyn Flieger. London: HarperCollins, 2005

---. *The Letters of J.R.R.Tolkien*. Ed. Humphrey Carpenter. London: Allen & Unwin, 1981

---. *The Lord of the Rings*. 4. Aufl. London: Unwin Hyman, 1988

---. *The Monsters and the Critics and Other Essays*. Ed. Christopher Tolkien. London: HarperCollins, 1997

---. *The Silmarillion*. Ed. Christopher Tolkien. New York: Houghton Mifflin, 2004

von Trotha, Trutz. »Zur Soziologie der Gewalt«. *Soziologie der Gewalt*. Ed. Trutz von Trotha. Sonderhefte der Kölner Zeitschrift für Soziologie und Sozialpsychologie Vol. 37. Opladen/Wiesbaden: Westdeutscher Verlag, 1997, 9-56

The Problem of Closure: War and Narrative in *The Lord of the Rings*
Margaret Hiley (Peterborough)

Modern War, Modern Literature

The 20th century can with some justification be called the century of war; its "combined will and technology... made it the bloodiest in the history of the world" (Norris 505). In the first half of the 20th century Europe was ravaged and millions of lives destroyed twice over in the two World Wars, while the second half was dominated by the Cold War, with its ever-present threat of total nuclear annihilation and numerous related proxy conflicts. "War", writes the American author Alfred Kazin, can be seen "as the continued experience of twentieth-century man" (81). Thus it is not surprising that war forms a major topic of the literature of the twentieth century, and the works of J.R.R. Tolkien form no exception.

Tolkien himself fought in the Great War of 1914-1918. Generally, this conflict is seen as the turning-point that finally shattered what was left of the Victorian world-view and way of life. The events of this war fundamentally questioned the 19th century myth of progress, and, in Henry James's words, "plung[ed] civilisation into [an] abyss of blood and darkness" (384). It is apt to quote a prominent author here, as the unprecedented *literary* response to the Great War has earned it the name of the "literary war" (cf. Fussell 155). The War Poets, such as Sassoon, Owen, and Blunden, wrote from the trenches themselves, but the First World War also played a major role in the writing of their contemporaries not actively engaged in military combat. For example, although few of literary Modernism's greatest literary figureheads actually saw active combat, representative works such as Ezra Pound's *Hugh Selwyn Mauberley*, T.S. Eliot's *The Waste Land* or Virginia Woolf's *Mrs. Dalloway* all deal with the horror of the War and the (futile) attempt to come to terms with it afterwards:

> Died some, pro patria,
> non "dulce" non "et decor"...
> walked eye-deep in hell
> believing old men's lies, then unbelieving
> came home, home to a lie,
> home to many deceits,
> home to old lies and new infamy[.] (Pound 100)

Yet the omnipresence of war in the texts of the early 20th century reflects not only the conditions under which they were produced, but also the nature of war itself as "uncontrollable and uncontainable" (Norris 506). As the examples of the World Wars show, war expands; it encroaches upon and takes over geographical locations and cultural spheres unconnected to the initial conflict, and it becomes impossible to find ways to close it off and contain it. It is no coincidence that much of the early 20th century literature (including fantastic texts) that thematises war is also centrally concerned with form and closure, and ways of controlling and containing literary matter. Margot Norris claims that this concern with closure is, among other things, a reflection of war's "problematic of closure" (506).

When investigating the ways in which war appears in texts as both theme and structuring device, it can be seen that texts from the early 20th century in particular frequently resort to war as a way of resolving their central problems of unifying plot, narrative, and form – for war offers the possibility of finally resolving all these problems of unity and closure through the apocalypse (cf. Emig 315). Even texts where the narrative does not focus explicitly on war use war as a way of achieving closure; for example, Virginia Woolf's *Mrs. Dalloway* creates a climax and unifying moment at the end of the novel with the suicide of the shell-shocked Septimus Smith, and Thomas Mann's epic *Zauberberg* sends its protagonist Hans Castorp of to the killing-fields of the First World War.

However, war cannot be appropriated and closed so easily, and this kind of literature's appropriation of war as an aesthetic tool means it is ultimately dependent on it for its existence:

> Krieg… schafft Geschlossenheit durch Apokalypse, Form durch Zerstörung und Kunstwerke aus Fragmenten. Man kann dies als Triumph der Moderne über den Krieg lesen. Man kann es auch als Bankrotterklärung der Moderne vor dem Krieg verstehen, einer Moderne, die sich selbst beständig in den Krieg investieren muss, um bestehen zu können. (Emig 316)[1]

Fantasy and War

n his seminal work *The Great War and Modern Memory*, Paul Fussell claims that "the drift of modern history domesticates the fantastic and normalizes the unspeakable. And the catastrophe that begins it is the First World War" (Fussell 74). This statement cites the centrality of the War in changing perceptions of reality in the modern age, and confirms the War as a significant factor

---

1   War… creates closure through the apocalypse, form through destruction and art from fragments. One can read this as modernism's triumph over war. But one can also read it as modernism's declaration of bankruptcy in the face of war, a modernism that itself must constantly invest in war in order to exist at all. (my translation)

in modern literature's turning away from the conventions of realism towards ironic, subjective and fragmented modes of writing. However, it also introduces another term: that of the fantastic.

The First World War was so far removed from the previous lives and experiences of those fighting that it appeared unreal. One strategy adopted by authors writing about the war was to utilise its unreality and reconstruct the war as a fantastic and supernatural experience. Coherent reality of the kind artfully constructed in a Victorian novel breaks down in the face of war; one way of making sense of the resulting fragments is to ascribe supernatural, magical properties to them. David Jones's war "epic", *In Parenthesis*, combines many graphic and naturalistic passages with others that are clearly mythic and fantastic in nature. What then of war and fantasy texts that inhabit a fully-fledged secondary world?

G.K. Chesterton, writing before the First World War, states that "fairyland [is] at once a world of wonder and of war" (Chesterton 258). This implies that war is a constitutive factor of fantastic worlds. In her study of Tolkien, *A Question of Time*, Verlyn Flieger draws some convincing parallels between these worlds and war:

> In the way that extremes can sometimes meet, War and Faërie have a certain resemblance to one another. Both are set beyond the reach of ordinary human experience. Both are equally indifferent to the needs of ordinary humanity. Both can change those who return... Perhaps worst of all, both War and Faërie can change out of all recognition the wanderer's perception of the world to which he returns, so that never again can it be what it once was. (224)

This would seem to imply that there is some key connection between war and fantasy.

The fact that war features so prominently in the fantasy of the Inklings and that of other writers of their time has been remarked on by several critics. For example, Tom Shippey in *Tolkien: Author of the Century* comments on the problem of evil that is thematised by "authors of the mid-twentieth century" (119) and concludes that this is due to "the distinctively twentieth-century experience of industrial war and impersonal, industrialised massacre; and it is probably no coincidence that most of the authors... were combat veterans of one war or other" (120).

Shippey mentions Tolkien, Lewis, T.H. White, Vonnegut, and Orwell, a group he elsewhere calls "post-war [World War II] writers" (cf. Shippey, "Tolkien as a Post-War Writer"); however, war is also central in earlier fantasy such as E.R. Eddison's *The Worm Ouroboros*, published four years after the First World War, or Lord Dunsany's *Don Rodriguez: Chronicles of Shadow Valley*, published in the same year 1922. Don Rodriguez, travelling through a fantastic version of "the later years of the Golden Years of Spain" (11), comes to a castle where he looks through a magic window, and there sees the history of the world pass in war after war, from antiquity up to modern mechanical warfare:

> Rodriguez saw man make a new ally, an ally who was only cruel and strong and had no purpose but killing, who had no pretences or pose, no mask and no manner, but was only the slave of Death and had no care but for his business. He saw it grow bigger and stronger. Heart it had none, but he saw its cold steel core scheming methodical plans and dreaming always destruction. Before it faded men and their fields and their houses... in all the wars beyond that twinkling window he saw the machine spare nothing... Rodriguez lifted his eyes and glanced from city to city, to Albert, Bapaume, and Arras, his gaze moved over a plain with its harvest of desolation lying forlorn and ungathered, lit by the flashing clouds and the moon and peering rockets. He turned from the window and wept. (59–60)

The centrality of war – especially of total, apocalyptic war – in fantasy can thus be linked historically to the experience of modern warfare. Indeed, it can be claimed that it is war that generates fantasy in the first place, as the fragmentation of reality caused by war necessitates the retreat into the coherent reality of a secondary world.

Rainer Emig postulates in *Krieg als Metapher im 20. Jahrhundert* that the apparent disappearance in war of signs, meaning and language is not really a disappearance, but a transformation (cf. Emig, *Krieg* 47, 324); in this context, one might suggest that fantasy represents one of war's greatest transformations – that of primary reality, through its fragmentation and disappearance, into a secondary one.

If the experience of war is central in the shattering of a consistent primary reality, if war cannot be contained and given meaning through realism, that reality can be transformed into that of a secondary world – a secondary world in which wars feature but can (supposedly) be controlled. In this secondary world, war can – supposedly at least – be contained and used for the sub-creator's purposes. The return in much fantasy to older, heroic forms of battle – face-to-face combat, duelling, weapons such as arrows, swords and protective gear such as body armour and shields – represents an escape from the horrors of modern warfare to a form of conflict to which meaning and value could still be applied. The fact, that most fantasy also deals with an overtly black-and-white view of war, with one side definitely evil and the other more or less good, also shows the longing for a clear-cut separation between friend and foe. However, in ways similar to contemporary modern works, war in fantasy also figures as a means of structure, as central to historical cycles, and – in its apocalyptic shape – as making all things new, erasing the past and enabling a fresh start. But this, once again, means that fantasy needs war – to paraphrase Emig, it must continually invest in war in order to exist.

If Tolkien's *Lord of the Rings* can be classed as war literature (as stated above), then the question arises whether this text uses similar strategies of appropriating and containing war. And if it does, subsequently it must be asked whether *The Lord of the Rings* likewise ends up in ultimate dependence on war.

J.R.R. Tolkien and War

Tolkien is an excellent example of how the Great War became a catalyst for literary expression. Tolkien fought on the Somme, in what he called the "animal horror" (L 72) of the trenches. These experiences certainly influenced the invention of his fantastic secondary world. He first began inventing the "nonsense fairy language" (L 8) that was to become Quenya, or High Elvish, as early as 1912, but it was during his time in the army that his serious work on it took place:

> Lots of the early part of [the mythology] (and the languages) – discarded or absorbed – were done in grimy canteens, at lectures in cold fogs, in huts full of blasphemy and smut, or by candle light in bell tents, even some down in dugouts under shell fire. (L 78)[2]

That this creative work was triggered by the war and the desire "to rationalize it, and prevent it just festering" (L 78) is admitted by Tolkien in the same letter. Yet the War cannot be addressed realistically: it is the fantastic mode that Tolkien needs to express himself: "A real taste for fairy-stories was wakened by philology on the threshold of manhood, and quickened to full life by war" (FS 135). Another interesting fact that may be linked to the War is that Tolkien, who was an excellent artist as well as a writer, gave up sketches and paintings from real scenes and of real people almost completely after his return from France:

---

2 Tolkien actually denied this in a 1967 interview: "That's all spoof. You might scribble something on the back of an envelope and shove it in your back pocket, but that's all. You couldn't write" (cit. Croft 15).

> ...in fact since 1918, almost all of Tolkien's art was related to the fantasy writings that increasingly occupied his thoughts. Only rarely in later years did he draw from nature. He seems largely to have lost interest in doing so, preferring his invented landscapes.
> (Hammond and Scull 31)

Some of Tolkien's fantasy is unmistakeably the product of his service in the trenches; for example, he states that "The Dead Marshes and the Morannon owe something to Northern France after the Battle of the Somme" (L 303). John Garth claims that "the Great War played an essential role in shaping Middle-earth" (Garth xv) and Brian Rosebury sees *The Lord of the Rings* "in certain respects as the last work of First World War literature, published almost forty years after the war ended" (Rosebury 126).

Thus a strong case can be made for seeing Tolkien's fantastic works as a way in which the horrors of his own war experience could be contained and given some kind of meaning ("to rationalize it", as he says himself). But is this attempt at containment ultimately successful? The present paper (rather than tracing Tolkien's war experiences in his work, as has been done frequently before) will examine *The Lord of the Rings* and see how its structure and form evince the fragmentation and discontinuity associated with war, demonstrating the nature of war as "uncontrollable and uncontainable".

War in Middle-earth

Middle-earth's history is recounted in *The Silmarillion*. We are told of Middle-earth's creation at the dawn of Time in the *Ainulindalë*, which tells of the Valar ("the Powers of the World", S 21) and the Fall of the wicked Vala Melkor, who desires to dominate the created world (in the course of the narration Middle-earth's cosmology is set firmly in place). *The Silmarillion* then goes on to give an account of the events of the First Age of Middle-earth: the creation of the Great Jewels, the Silmarils, by the Elf Fëanor, their rape by Melkor, and the ceaseless war made on Melkor by the Elves in order to regain the Silmarils with all its tragic consequences, finally culminating in the apocalyptic War of Wrath in which the Valar cast Melkor out into the Void. The Second Age follows, in which the island of Men, Númenor, is established and destroyed through their own folly; the Númenoreans return to Middle-earth and there face Sauron, Melkor's old ally, who was instrumental in the downfall of their isle, in a great battle that ends the Second Age. *The Lord of the Rings* then deals with the Third Age of Middle-earth and its ending in the War of the Ring, in which Sauron is finally destroyed.

This summary of Middle-earth's history, though extremely brief, should make it clear that Tolkien is here working with a cyclical model of history, and throughout each age we can see history repeating itself. Each of the ages of his world begins with the establishment of great kingdoms or realms: in the First Age, the various elven kingdoms in Beleriand, in the Second Age, Númenor, in the Third, Arnor and Gondor. The beginning of the Fourth Age as recounted in *The Lord of the Rings* likewise sees the re-establishment of Númenorean rule in Gondor after the interim government of the Stewards.

Each Age ends with a cataclysmic war, in which even the shape of the world is changed: Beleriand sinks beneath the sea, Númenor is swallowed by a gigantic wave, and the western shores of Middle-earth are changed time and time again. Each age re-enacts the central struggle of good against evil, a struggle that can never be won, for "the lies that Melkor, the mighty and accursed, Morgoth Bauglir, the Power of Terror and of Hate, sowed in the hearts of Elves and Men are a seed that does not die and cannot be destroyed; and ever and anon it sprouts anew, and will bear dark fruit even unto the latest days" (S 307).

The never ending nature of this struggle ensures that the cycle will be repeated over and over again. To think that it will ever be broken is a fallacy, as Elrond states when he recalls of the Battle of the Last Alliance at the end of the Second Age and the War of Wrath at the end of the First:

> I remember well the splendour of their banners[.] It recalled to me the glory of the Elder Days and the hosts of Beleriand, so many great princes and captains were assembled. And yet not so many, nor so fair, as when Thangorodrim was broken, and the Elves deemed that evil was ended for ever, and it was not so.
> (LotR I 237)

Thus we can see that Tolkien's mythology of Middle-earth structures Middle-earth's history entirely around great wars and battles. In *The Silmarillion*, the five great battles of Elves and Men against Morgoth culminate in the War of Wrath that ends the First Age. The Second Age is marked by the fall of Númenor in an attempted war against the Valar, and ends in the first war against Sauron, the Last Alliance. The Third Age ends with the War of the Ring. War is central to these historical cycles of conflict and is used by Tolkien to structure Middle-earth's history and mythology; it creates a pattern that can be repeated over and over again, giving the history of the secondary world logic and continuity. Yet this means that at the same time, Middle-earth needs war to function as a coherent secondary world and thus becomes dependent on it – Middle-earth without war is (literally) unimaginable.

War appears uncontainable not just on the "macro" level of Middle-earth's broad history; it constantly breaks through "micro" level of plot, repeating itself;

thus in Book One of *The Fellowship of the Ring*, the hobbits are taken prisoner by the Barrow-wights, the evil spirits of warriors long dead. These wights trap the hobbits underground with the intention of transforming them into long-barrow sleepers themselves. The hobbits in their enchanted sleep re-enact past battles: "The men of Carn Dûm came upon us at night, and we were worsted. Ah! The spear in my heart" (LotR I 140).

Another example of this can be seen at Weathertop, where the hobbits and Aragorn are attacked by the Nazgûl led by the Witch-King of Angmar (who is, incidentally, also the leader of the men of Carn Dûm). In this episode, they are forced to re-enact the assault on Amon Sûl by the Witch-King of Angmar that laid waste to it in the first place.

Even more striking is the episode in Moria. In Moria's Chamber of Records the Fellowship discover a book that, although partly slashed and stained and thus rendered illegible, tells them the fate of the Dwarves that lived there:

> 'It is grim reading,' [Gandalf] said. 'I fear their end was cruel. Listen! *We cannot get out. We cannot get out. They have taken the Bridge and second hall. Frár and Lóni and Náli fell there.* Then there are four lines smeared so that I can only read *went 5 days ago*. The last lines run *the pool is up to the wall at Westgate. The Watcher in the Water took Óin. We cannot get out. The end comes*, and *then drums, drums in the deep*. I wonder what that means. The last thing is written is in a trailing scrawl of elf-letters: *they are coming*. There is nothing more.'
>
> (LotR I 314)

It may seem strange that a Dwarf should have made a record of his colony and kept it, very practically for the Fellowship, up till the moment he died (though maybe not so strange if one gives credit to Tolkien's statement that he wrote parts of his mythology "down in dugouts under shell fire" L 78). However, it is important for the novel not just because it fills in information; it sets the scene for a repetition of that very tragedy:

> Gandalf had hardly spoken these words, when there came a great noise: a rolling *Boom* that seemed to come from the depths far below, and to tremble in the stone at their feet. They sprang towards the door in alarm. *Doom, doom* it rolled again, as if huge hands were turning the very caverns of Moria into a vast drum... 'They are coming!' cried Legolas. 'We cannot get out,' said Gimli. 'Trapped!' cried Gandalf. 'Why did I delay? Here we are, caught, just as they were before.'
>
> (LotR 315)

It is not just by chance that Legolas and Gimli repeat the sentences they have just heard Gandalf read out. Thus we can see that in Middle-earth war and violence appear to repeat themselves perpetually.

War is, besides the main structuring element, also the driving dynamic force behind the plots of *The Silmarillion* myths and *The Lord of the Rings*. It is not enough to simply invent a fantastic secondary world and then describe it – the lack of enthusiasm that many readers (even hardcore Tolkien fans) show towards the *Ainulindalë* and the *Valaquenta* sections of *The Silmarillion* demonstrates this. A story needs to be told about this world, it cannot remain static – and storytelling implies change and dynamics.

The dynamics that Tolkien resorts to are, as we have seen, those of conflict. Without conflict Middle-earth would be static, so that conflict must be introduced from the start. Here we can perceive the incontainability of war noted above: it cannot be restricted, and if used to structure a world and create a plot it ultimately determines the material of that world. None of the tales of Middle-earth remain unaffected by war – the love stories of Beren and Lúthien and Aragorn and Arwen are tales of love under the threat of complete annihilation, and even figures as peripheral as Tom Bombadil are drawn into the master-plot of the War of the Ring. Indeed, the Ring itself, the ultimate weapon and both the cause and the means of war, becomes the focal point of the narrative.

The Ring is not just the centre of control over the characters' fates, but controls the narrative itself. As Valerie Rohy argues: "the true meaning of the ring… is its command of meaning. In narrative terms, the ring's value lies not in its ability to *rule over*, but in its ability to *rule off* the spaces of the novel, portioning the text by its own measure [; it is] the crucial nexus without which there can be no coherent story of Middle-earth" (Rohy 931). No coherent story of Middle-earth without the Ring; no coherent story of Middle-earth without war.

Here an interesting paradox becomes apparent: fantasy texts such as Tolkien's fear (war's) fragmentation and the modern acceleration of reality, retreating into a secondary world in order to preserve coherence; but they obviously also fear stagnation, and thus have to resort to the dynamics unleashed by war.

The attitude demonstrated towards war by some of the main characters is deeply ironic. For example, Faramir is often quoted by Tolkien critics as an example of how the author himself disapproved of war, and did not want to glamourise it: "War must be, while we defend our lives against a destroyer that would devour all; but I do not love the bright sword for its sharpness, nor the arrow for its swiftness, nor the warrior for his glory. I love only that which they defend: the city of the Men of Númenor" (LotR II 656).

The irony behind this is that of course the realm of Gondor established itself through war and violence, and not just war against Sauron; the men of Númenor colonise the Western shores of Middle-earth: "Great harbours and strong towers they made, and there many of them took up their abode; but they appeared now rather as lords and masters and gatherers of tribute than helpers and teachers" (S 320). In this way, Gondor can be seen as a civilization that constitutes itself through the very thing that destroys it – war. This paradoxical structure is once again representative of a text which both condemns war and is dependent on it for its structures.

Fragmentation: the Form of *The Lord of the Rings*

We have seen now how Tolkien's narrative uses war as a means of structure. Even though the text depends heavily on war to create meaning and coherence, one might nevertheless conclude that the war does after all remain enclosed safely within the narrative – between the near-circle running from Bilbo's party to Sam's return to Bag End.

But that is of course not all there is to the text. Surrounding the main bulk of the narrative is a mass of other texts: a prologue and several appendices. These texts are artfully arranged in imitation of a critical edition. This suggests that, in fact, the central narrative is incomplete and perhaps not fully to be understood without the enlightening other texts clustered around it – as the editor states: "their principal purpose is to illustrate the War of the Ring and its origins, and to fill up some of the gaps in the main story" (LotR III 1009). However, these other texts themselves are incomplete; they are fragments that have supposedly survived from the early Fourth Age of Middle-earth. The whole body of text that makes up *The Lord of the Rings* is thus actually a collection of fragments.

That this fragmentation can be seen as a result of the narrative's investment in war is borne out by Alyson Booth, who states that "the dislocations of war often figure centrally in [the] form [of texts], even when the war itself seems peripheral to [their] content" (Booth 4). Tolkien's text, that portrays history as a never-ending succession of wars that destroy culture rather than preserving it, presents us with what is left after the wars are over: a collection of debris, of fragments; it presents us with its own incompleteness.

The log-book discovered by the fellowship in Moria can thus be seen as a symbol of the narrative itself: it is "the remains of a book" rather than a whole book: "It had been slashed and stabbed and partly burned, and it was so stained with black and other dark marks like old blood that little of it could be read" (LotR 313). The record of Balin's folk, their narrative, has been subjected to the same violence that the characters have; the same could be said to go for *The Lord of the Rings* as a whole – it is "the remains of a book", the remains of the Red Book; it is what has survived the violence described within its pages. As such, it is clear that the text itself pays dearly for its dependence on and investment in war and violence; ultimately, it must capitulate before the nature of war as "uncontrollable and uncontainable".

Conclusions

There is some scholarship dedicated to Tolkien and war. Much of this criticism links his writings to war biographically, tracing Tolkien's experience of the two World Wars and seeking to find parallels to that experience in his work. While the importance of these war experiences is undeniable and the traces of it are plainly to be found, the fact remains that the wars in Tolkien's works are *not* either of the World Wars; thus comparing them to those wars, while inevitable, must form a one-sided approach. It is surprising that most criticism, while frequently citing Tolkien's injunction that his *Lord of the Rings* should not be read primarily as a comment on the World Wars (and World War II in particular), proceeds to do precisely that, asking how aspects of the Wars reappear in altered form in his works.[3]

Of course Tolkien is not the only writer of fantasy to use war to structure his or her secondary world and achieve narrative coherence. Indeed, the vast majority of modern fantasy makes use of war as both theme and device. From C.S. Lewis's space romances, that cast our world as "a kind of Ypres Salient in the universe" (Lewis 184) and his tales of Narnia that end in the Last Battle, to contemporary novels such as Christopher Paolini's *Eragon* tetralogy,[4] war seems ubiquitous in fantastic secondary worlds. Given the connections between the fantasy genre and war cited above, one might ask whether there is any fantasy without war. Does fantasy, as a genre, *have* to invest in war in order to exist at all? And does it, as the same time, seek to evade responsibility for this investment by displacing its wars into a secondary world? There seem to be only few fantasy texts that do not focus on war in some form or other; Ursula Le Guin's *Earthsea* novels are perhaps the most notable example, but even in these war features from the opening pages of *A Wizard of Earthsea* onwards, even if the main characters are not warriors.

At the very least the connection between the fantasy genre and war might merit further exploration, for Tolkien, as one of the fathers of modern fantasy, was perhaps one of the first to adopt the narrative strategies made available by war, but he certainly was not the last.

---

3   A recent example of this approach is Janet Brennan Croft's *War and the Works of J.R.R. Tolkien*. Croft carefully and convincingly traces World War I and World War II themes in Tolkien's work, examines examples of military leadership in it and measures the texts against Tolkien's own views on war. However, she entirely neglects to ask what textual function war itself plays in Tolkien's novels and his mythology as a whole when the works are taken for themselves, without relation to their concrete historical background. That war ultimately is used as a way of ordering history and achieving textual closure is not perceived.

4   Three volumes of the *Inheritance* quartet have been published so far (*Eragon*, 2003; *Eldest*, 2005; *Brisingr*, 2008); there is as yet no publication date set for the final volume.

Bibliography

Booth, Allyson. *Postcards from the Trenches*. Oxford: OUP, 1996

Chesterton, G.K. "Fairy Tales". *All Things Considered*. London: Everyman, n.d. 253-258

Croft, Janet Brennan. *War and the Works of J.R.R. Tolkien*. Westport, CT: Praeger, 2004

Dunsany, Lord. *Don Rodriguez: Chronicles of the Shadow Valley*. Holicong, PA: Wildside, 2002

Emig, Rainer. *Krieg als Metapher im 20. Jahrhundert*. Darmstadt: Wissenschaftliche Buchgesellschaft, 2001

Flieger, Verlyn. *A Question of Time: J.R.R. Tolkien's Road to Faërie*. Kent, OH: Kent State UP, 1997

Fussell, Paul. *The Great War and Modern Memory*. London: OUP, 1975

Garth, John. *Tolkien and the Great War*. Boston: Houghton Mifflin, 2003

Hammond, Wayne G. and Christina Scull. *J.R.R. Tolkien: Artist and Illustrator*. London: HarperCollins, 1995

Kazin, Alfred. *Bright Book of Life. American Novelists and Storytellers from Hemingway to Mailer*. London: Secker and Warburg, 1974

Lewis, C.S. *Out of the Silent Planet*. London: Pan, 1952

Norris, Margot. "Modernisms and Modern Wars". *Modern Fiction Studies* 44:3 (Fall 1998): 505-509

Rohy, Valerie. "On Fairy Stories". *Modern Fiction Studies* 50:4 (Winter 2004): 927-948

Rosebury, Brian. *Tolkien: A Cultural Phenomenon*. Basingstoke: Palgrave, 2003

Shippey, Tom. "Tolkien as a Post-War Writer". *Scholarship and Fantasy: The Tolkien Phenomenon*. Ed. Keither J. Battarbee. Finland: U of Turku P, 1993, 217-236

---. *J.R.R. Tolkien: Author of the Century*. London: HarperCollins, 2000

Tolkien, J.R.R. *The Silmarillion*. London: Allen & Unwin, 1979

---. "On Fairy-Stories". *The Monsters and the Critics and Other Essays*. London: HarperCollins, 1990, 109-161

---. *The Lord of the Rings*. London: HarperCollins, 1997

The Legends of the *Trojan War* in J.R.R. Tolkien

Guglielmo Spirito (Assisi)

> In 1990, the Colombian Ministry of Culture set up a system of itinerant libraries to take books to the inhabitants of distant rural regions. For this purpose, carrier book bags with capacious pockets were transported on donkey's backs up into the jungle and the sierra. Here the books were left for several weeks in the hands of a teacher or village elder who became, de facto, the librarian in charge. Most of the books were technical works, agricultural handbooks and the like, but a few literary works were also included. According to one librarian, the books were always safely accounted for. 'I know of a single instance in which a book was not returned', she said. 'We had taken, along with the usual practical titles, a Spanish translation of the *Iliad*. When the time came to exchange the book, the villagers refused to give it back. We decided to make them a present of it, but asked them why they wished to keep that particular title. They explained that Homer's story reflected their own: it told of a war-torn country in which mad gods mix with men and women who never know exactly what the fighting is about, or when they will be happy, or why they will be killed.' (Manguel 6)

Only someone who has suffered through war, injustice, misfortune, someone who has learned how far 'the domination of force' extends 'and knows how *not* to respect it, is capable', according to Simone Weil, 'of love and justice' (Manguel 222; Weil). 'When waterdrops have worn the stones of Troy / And blind oblivion swallowed cities up'– wrote Shakespeare – (*Troilus and Cressida* (III, 2, 197).

Indeed, the city of Troy was lost, its location forgotten, faded into misty golden legends, alive only in memory trough literature and tales. In 1873, using the *Iliad* as his travel guide, Schliemann unearthed at Hisarlik the fabled city of Troy. From the 17th century on, readers had imagined that it was possible to find 'Priam's six-gated city', as Shakespeare called it. Once again it was easier to believe, with the words of Doris Lessing, that 'Myth does not mean something untrue, but a concentration of truth' (Manguel 208). Troy in the *Iliad* is both a city and an emblem for the story of a war whose beginning and end are not chronicled in the poem. It seems to be an everlasting conflict, providing a useful mirror for all future anguished centuries.

1. Status Quaestionis: 'classic' against 'northern'?

aymond Queneau, in his Preface to Flaubert's *Bouvard et Pécuchet*, states that 'every great work of literature is either the *Iliad* or the *Odyssey*', a statement which goes far beyond Thomas Howard's on C.S. Lewis' *Till We have faces*: 'There is really no such thing as making up a whole new story in any event: we are told that there are only ten or a dozen possible plots in the whole world. Every narrative presents some variation on these few, basic patterns' (Howard 207f). Perhaps it even goes beyond Jorge Luis Borges' bold assertion in *Los cuatro siclos*, where he says that

> Four are the stories. One, the oldest, is that of a strong city whom valaint men surround and defend. The defenders know that the city will be given up to iron and fire and that their battle is useless... Centuries have being adding elements of magic... Other, linked with the first, is that of a return...The third is that of a quest... We can see in it a variation of the former... The last story is that of the sacrifice of a god... Four are the stories. All the time that remains to us we shall keep telling them, transformed. (Borges 1128)

Homer (the overwhelming presence we call 'Homer') is a shadowy figure whose first biographers (or inventors) believed had been born not long after the Sack of Troy. But we don't know anything about Homer, although it is otherwise with Homer's books. Two of our old metaphors tell us that all life is a battle and that all life is a journey; whether the *Iliad* and the *Odyssey* drew on this knowledge or whether this knowledge was drawn from the *Iliad* and the *Odyssey* is, in the final count, unimportant, since a book and its readers are both mirrors that reflect one another endlessly.

Whatever their nebulous origin, most scholars now assume that the poems ascribed to Homer began as scattered compositions of various kinds that eventually coalesced and became perfectly interwoven to form the two stories we now know – one describing the tragedy of a single place, Troy, which is fought over by many men; the other telling the homecoming adventures of a single man, who makes his way back from Troy through many dangerous places. Troy came to stand for all cities and Ulysses for every man (cf. Manguel 2; Nagy, *Questions*).

If this is true, Tolkien's work should be no exception, as his 'classical' education would suggest. 'I cannot agree with you', says Hippias to Socrates in one of Plato's *Dialogues* – and some tolkienist scholars with him. Socrates answers: 'Nor can I agree with myself, Hippias, and yet that seems to be the conclusion which, as far as we can see at present, must follow from our argument'. There speaks a man not afraid of allowing his thoughts absolute freedom to explore.

'The west must stop *hectoring* China over human rights, the Olympics chief has warned' – was written in the *Financial Times* on April 27 2008. 'Hectoring' seems to be slang for 'a blustering turbulent fellow', in allusion to the provocative character of *Hector,* the Trojan hero. Well, I hope that no one shall need to label 'hectoring' what we are about to discuss.

2. 'Homer' (& 'Classics') in Tolkien: what we already know

> It is commonly said that Tolkien based most of his *Legendarium* on Northern literature, favouring above all Anglo-Saxon, Old Norse, Germanic and Finish sources. While it cannot be any serious scholar's purpose to contest the general truth of this assessment, the undeniably pervasive influence of Northern literature should not be allowed to drive out, on principle and without careful case-by-case examination, each and every possible competing source from other mythologies (Stevens 120-1). There is a great deal of Greek mythology assimilated and transformed within the *Legendarium*, albeit unacknowledged.
>
> (Libran-Moreno, *Lives* 15)

We are already in 'Trojan matter' here. Tolkien's reticence for source-hunting (cf. L 418) seems natural enough, for he was not so much – borrowing a term from G.W. Dasent – interested in the 'bones' as he was in the 'soup' (cf. Libran-Moreno, *Lives* 50; Flieger 123). Even Verlyn Flieger mentions the 'bitter ending typical of the *Iliad*', while speaking of the defeat and disillusionment which come on Frodo (125; see also Chance 8 and Slack 115). 'Homer and Virgil (together with some other authors) as sources and analogues to Tolkien have already bee studied at some lengh', says Gergely Nagy (*Myths* 81), and he named David Greenman, Mac Fenwick, John W. Houghton, James Obertino, Donald Morse. 'Traditions are an integral part of the present, and old stories lie behind our new ones' (86.96). We should add David Paul Pace, Kenneth Reckford, Robert Morse, Martin Simonson, Alex Lewis and Elizabeth Currie, Christina Scull and Wayne Hammond.

I thought it not necessary to report or repeat here most of their documentation and conclusions.

3. Other 'Homers': 'post-homerica' and 'non-homeric' Epics. The 'Trojan Genre'

he author of the *Iliad* seems to have had two distinct aims that were not strictly compatible. One was to construct an epic around a gripping personal drama, and that was a stroke of pure genius. The other was to incorporate as much traditional material as possible in order to create a wider panorama of the *Trojan War*, even at the cost of some loss of overall cohesion. That, however, is the justification for the title *Iliad*, from Ilion the old name of Troy, rather than *Achilleid*. The legends of the *Trojan War* were actually preserved by a wider tradition than the Homeric epics themselves. Some are lost, for of the six Cyclic epics dealing with the *Trojan War* (*Kypria, Aithiopis, Little Iliad, Sack of Ilion, Returns, Telegony*) only a few quotations survive (Quintus xii-xiii; Burgess). Virgil's *Aeneid* gave the Romans a national Epic and a place in the mythical past of the *Trojan War*, making of Rome a daughter of Troy (cf. Erskine).

Long before, and after, 'Homer' became the inspiration for Alexandrians and Romans until the 5th century AD. Saint Augustine's *De Civitate Dei*, for example, begins with a long analysis of the various ways in which the ancient authors described and commented on the fall of Troy. But soon, after the beginning of the long barbaric wars that devastated the Italian peninsula, books became objects and relics rather than vessels for stories, and even the tale of the archetypal siege vanished into the obscure past. Homer became a monument in the West, known by hearsay to exist somewhere and respected from afar. In the Eastern half of the Empire, however, Homer continued to be read and was part of the social imagination.

A number of Byzantine writers based their stories on Dictys of Crete's *A journal of the Trojan War (Ephemeris belli troiani)* and Dares the Phrigian's *The History of the Fall of Troy (De excidio Troiae historia)*, who were thought to give first-hand accounts on the war in which they had taken part. Far for being authentic records of the events, both accounts were probably composed in the first century AD. Both stories were translated into Latin and, in this new version, Dares' account, since it narrated the events from the point of view of Aeneas' people – the Trojans –, now became more popular than his Greek colleague's. Dares' text was quoted as the primary source by all those who retold the history of Troy, overtaking the popularity of the *Iliad*. Towards 1165, a clerk from Normandy, Benoit de Sainte-Maure, based his account of the *Trojan War, Le Roman de Troie*, on the chronicle of Dares. And here starts the medieval version of the history (cf. Benoit; Manguel 76f). It was followed by the *Iliad*, a Latin epic written between 1183 and 1190 by an English clerk, Joseph of Exeter (cf. Mora).

4. Singing of Troy and 'Trojanness'

Saint Gregory of Nazianzus in his *Christus Patiens* inspired by Euripides used Hecuba's voice to express Mary's sorrow. While adopting dozens of Homeric and Classical *exempla*, nevertheless in his *Poems* he says that he will *not* sing of Troy (cf. Gregorio 144). Unlike him, here I *do* choose to sing of Troy, although I recognize some risks in doing it.

To some degree the very familiarity of the texts gets in our way. We *think* we know 'Homer' and the 'homeric tradition' and its classical boundaries, and of course, we believe we know Tolkien even better. We may have to set these texts at some distance before we can recover them in a wider way, after discovering how narrow our view easily becomes. This is an area which has led to some miscomprehension as if 'northern' and 'southern' – or 'Vikings' and 'Greeks' –, were somehow mutually exclusive. Even very serious and deep scholars – such as Verlyn Flieger and Tom Shippey – seem to have been vulnerable to feel such temptation. Burns notes that

> By 1892, when Tolkien was born, English popular thought had for some time been turning from the classical world. Southern tastes and southern considerations, particularly from mid-century onward, had been increasingly replaced by Northern ideals. Britain's Nordic ancestry was taken up like a banner and pointed to as indicative of all that the nation should hold in highest esteem... The English, who had previously played down their Northern ties, now chose to deny their Southern past, to see the South as un-English, as decadent, feeble, and lacking in vigour or will... Neither position is just, of course. Culturally, linguistically, racially, England's heritage is mixed; but Northern Romanticism, and that human knack of ignoring what doesn't appeal, now allowed the English to see themselves basically as Norsemen only slightly diluted in race, as Vikings only slightly tempered by time.
> (Scull/Hammond, *Guide* 650)

Nevertheless, the Gallipoli campaign, with its battlefield opposite the road – and the site of Troy –, produced a good number of 'war poets' that got inspiration from good old Homer. For instance, Charles Sorley's poem (Lewis/Currie 84):

> *Of clash of arms. Of council's brawl,*
> *Of beauty that must early fall,*
> *Of battle hate and battle joy*
> *By the old windy walls of Troy...*

> In the words of one commentator, 'As the long, prosperous years of the Pax Britannica succeeded one another, the truth about war was forgotten, and in 1914 young officers went into the battle with the *Iliad* in their backpacks and the names of Achilles and Patroclus engraved upon their hearts.' But the names on Tolkien's heart now were Beowulf and Beorhtnoth...Homer's *Iliad* is in part a catalogue of violent deaths, but it is set in a warm world where seas are sunlit, heroes become demigods, and the rule of the Olympians is unending. The Germanic world was chillier and greyer. It carried a burden of pessimism, and final annihilation awaited *Middangeard* (Middle-earth) and its gods. (Garth 42f)

John Garth's point is of course valid, if we assume that the 'Iliad' that Tolkien knew was only the 'homeric one'; once the medieval Trojan legends enter the picture the situation may became quite different.

At this point, being *politically incorrect*, I may need to disappoint both 'parties' – the 'northern' and the 'southern'. While I recognize easily the incompleteness of overstressing the 'northernness', I shall not overstress the 'Greekness' either, not only because of the evidence of a misbalanced weight in favour of the first, but because I sustain – if anything –, more the *'Trojanness'* than the 'Greekness' of some of these sources. And even more: I dare suspect that this 'Trojanness' *include and contains threads of both 'northernness' and 'southernness', waved in a elaborate and colourful pattern of 'Trojan' pigments*. Perhaps this risk of conflict belongs itself to the logic of the *Iliad*: there is not complete manhood without war, although war is terrible, as Hector forcefully said, with a sensibility closer to Faramir's than to Boromir's (cf. Redfield xii). Indeed, the *Iliad* 'is the greatest war story ever told, but it's not fundamentally about war...but rather about how great men confront tragedy, learn moderation and become wise' (Thomas 84). Perhaps the 'Troy genre' should become a sort of (honest) *Trojan Horse* to overcome the defensiveness of those involved in the debate?

5. The Transmission of the Tale: 'from Saxon Stories and Tudor Myths to the First-War Poets'[1]

The medieval fascination with Troy, and particularly the cult of 'Trojanness' in late-fourteenth- and early-fifteenth-century England is one of these Stories and Myths. Until Schliemann exposed its ruined foundations, Troy was

---

1 Wood 41.

a phenomenon of the imagination, a kind of aperture through which fantasies of the past might be glimpsed darkly. The symbolic appropriation of Troy is at once a means of creating a past, present, and future in accord with specific ideals and also a means of mobilizing that imagined historicity in gestures of self-invention and self-definition. As is true for Schliemann, medieval claimants to Trojanness invent not just Troy but also themselves in the process of imagining the ancient city. Not only Schliemann, but also Sigmund Freud. He elaborates on this metaphor in the course of describing a recent analytic success: 'I still scarcely dare to believe it properly. It is as if Schliemann had dug up Troy, considered legendary, once again' (Federico X).

Scores of European states and their rulers claimed Trojan origins, following the popular medieval belief that after the fall of Troy, its handful of survivors were dispersed to the several corners of Europe to found individual new Trojan settlements. The appropriation of the Trojan past was always a sort of imperial gesture for the European present. Cities and rulers were linked to Troy through mythic genealogies that often claimed Aeneas as their common forefather. The medieval 'Trojan matter', through different streams, is widespread in France, Spain, and Italy (cf. D'Agostino). In England, Geoffrey of Monmouth made popular the idea that London had ancestral ties to Troy. In Geoffrey's *Historia Regum Britanniae*, Diana appears to Brutus, a great-grandson of Aeneas, and explains that the *translatio imperii* from the ancient world to the modern one will be achieved through him and his heirs:

> Brute, past the realms of Gaul, beneath the sunset lieth an island, girt about by ocean…Seek it! For there is thine abode for ever. There by thy sons again shall Troy be builded; there of thy blood shall Kings be born, hereafter Sovran in every land the wide world over… When he came to the river Thames, he walked along the banks till he found the very spot best fitted to his pure pose. He therefore founded his city there and called it New Troy…
>
> (Federico XIV)

After Geoffrey, it was also widely repeated – though not universally accepted – that King Arthur was descended from Brutus, and through him, from Aeneas (cf. Brandsma). The fantasised quality of Troy as an empire permits equally fantastic visions of new Trojan greatness and specifically encourages the creation of the idea of England as a nation. The writers of this period, in turning collectively to Trojan stories, help create the canon of the medieval matter of Troy and, more broadly, English literary history in the later Middle Ages. But Geoffrey's vision is balanced by the 'other' book of Troy – that is Guido delle Colonne's *Historia destructionis Troiae*, which does not have such a strong 'Virgilian perspective'. Copying and adapting Benoit de Saint-Maure's 1160 *Le*

Roman de Troie from French verse into Latin prose, while claiming faithfully to follow Dares and Dictys, Guido's 1287 *Historia* must be seen as one of the initiators of the propagandistic tradition of Trojan interpretation. Guido's three Middle English translations are part of a tradition which includes John Lydgate's *Troy Book, The Laud Troy Book* and the alliterative *Destruction of Troy*.

We may say that 'insofar as the process of remembering or renarrating is a process of becoming... representations of the matter of Troy were vital to authorial, regnal, and national identity formation in late-medieval England.' (Federico XIX). As Michel Foucault writes, placeless places of this kind – like Troy – are like a mirror, insofar as the play between the real and the not real, as exists in a mirror (or in a narrative), describes identity formation:

> Starting from this gaze that is, as it were, directed toward me, from the round of this virtual space that is on the other side of the glass, I come back toward myself; I begin again to direct my eyes toward myself and to reconstitute myself there where I am.
> (Federico XX)

Chaucer's *House of Fame* and the anonymous *Sir Gawain and the Green Knight*, each embeds an ancient myth within a frame that explores how narratives of the past – imagined to have a past in Troy – are transmitted into the present scene in new Troy. And – for the *Gawain* poet – destined to self-destruct in the future.

Troilus and Criseyde revisits the matter of Troy as it was explored in *House of Fame*. The physical setting is situated almost entirely within the walls of war-time Troy. The text retells what had to happen; but it also imagines the city before its fall and considers what may have happened in a different future. It is concerned especially with how the past interacts with the future: old Troy is pretendedly present in the poem; it is not yet fallen. Likewise, the new Troy of the 1380s is not yet gone. This moment – the reign of Richard II – is a moment of national self-definition, and Troy – new and old –, serve as a crucial symbol (cf. Federico 66).

The perpetually lost quality of Troy in the late medieval period is essential to its structuring power. Troy's absence, or lack, in other words, is precisely its strength. Paradoxically the writers, while claiming Trojan precedents, contribute to Troy's disappearance in the process of producing its significance. These authors relate the structures, characters, and themes already familiar in the Trojan narrative, creating themselves through replication rather than remembering Troy itself. Aeneas creates Chaucer in his image: he is the 'father of English poetry' just as Aeneas is the father of Western Europe. Both, in their own way, were like actors in a drama or epic which is always progressive, always heading for the world it only appears to have left behind. A claim to a particular past, such as Troy, involves, alongside the attempt to arrest the present, a journey through the past, creating and recreating itself, hardly a 'claim' since it is always in process, of necessity incomplete. Troy and new Troy leave behind themselves texts as witnesses to a creation of an empire of English letters: *Troilus and Criseyde* inspired the Scottish poet Robert Henryson to produce a sequel, *The Testament of Cresseid*. In 1474 William Caxton included the story in his *Recuyell of the Historyes of Troye*. Finally William Shakespeare, who famously had 'small Latin, and less Greek', made use of these various versions as sources for his *Troilus and Cressida* (cf. Manguel 79).[2]

Keats, or at least so he said, had come to Homer through Chapman's 1598 translation of the *Iliad* in opulent fourteen-syllable lines. 'The Classics!' Blake raged. 'It is the Classics, & not Goths nor Monks, that Desolate Europe with Wars' (Manguel 138ff). How far Homer's poems – or the Trojan legends – travelled is a matter of conjecture but, for instance, scholars have recognized in an Icelandic saga composed about 1300, *The Story of Egill One-hand and Asmundr the Berserks' Killer*, the influence of the *Odyssey*, in particular the story of the encounter between Ulysses and the Cyclops, which latter, in English folklore, became 'Jack and the Beanstalk' (cf. Manguel 87). Dante and his contemporaries, in the southern part of Europe, accepted the time-honoured glorification of Homer as an undisputed fact, and read him, if at all, in Latin translations such as the popular anonymous paraphrase of the *Iliad* known as the *Ilias latina*, probably written in the first century AD (cf. D'Agostino 21-27.121-128).

Petrarch kept, with devotional care, a Greek manuscript of Homer which he didn't know how to read. To the friend who sent it to him from Constantinople, he wrote: 'Your Homer lies mute by my side, while I am deaf by his, and often I have kissed him saying: 'Great man, how I wish I could hear your words!'. At Petrarch's suggestion, and with the help of Boccaccio, a Calabrian monk of Greek origin, their friend, translated the *Odyssey* and the *Iliad* into Latin, both very badly (Manguel 94). Aeneas Silvius Piccolomini, who became Pope Pius II, having a good knowledge of Greek, found an exquisite reason for studying the ancient authors: 'The commerce of language', he wrote, 'is the intermediary of love' (Manguel 108).

Greek was almost lost in the South and survived in the North: from the 17th century onwards, Homer was being rigorously studied in English, German and Scandinavian universities, while in Italy, Spain, Portugal, and France he was neglected for the sake of Virgil. However it is true what Battista Guarino wrote, that 'the *Aeneid* is like a mirror of Homer's works, and there is almost nothing in Virgil that does not have an analogue in Homer' (Manguel 108ff; cf. Erskine).

---

2 Simonson gives a good synthesis of the western Trojan tradition (43f). Instead, for a 'Ioreth's lengh answer' we have two omnicomprehensive studies (Behr; Latacz, *Homer*).

6. Tolkien's 'Trojan' explicit Texts

For Tolkien, translation not only made a work of the past available to modern readers who could not read the older language, it was also a means by which the translator could study the text and get closer to the thought of its author. His translation of *Sir Gawain and the Green Knight* was published by his son Christopher in 1975, but at least from the 20's he was familiar with it. His translation was rebroadcasted by the BBC in 1953 (Scull/Hammond, *Guide* 771; *Chronology* 141.420).

The noblest knight of the highest order of Chivalry refuses adultery, places hatred of sin in the last resort above all other motives, and escapes from a temptation that attacks him in the guise of courtesy through grace obtained by prayer. That is what the author of *Sir Gawain and the Green Knight* was mainly thinking about, and with that thought he shaped the poem as we have it.

It was a matter of contemporary concern, for the English. *Sir Gawain* presents in its own way, more explicitly moral and religious, one facet of this movement of thought out of which also grew Chaucer's greatest poem, *Troilus and Criseyde*. Those who read *Sir Gawain* are likely to read the last stanzas of Chaucer's work with a renewed interest.

> But if Chaucer's poem is much altered in tone and import from its immediate source in Boccaccio's *Filostrato*, it is utterly removed from the sentiments or ideas in the Homeric Greek poems on the fall of Troy, and still further removed (we may guess) from those of the ancient Aegean world. Research into these things has very little to do with Chaucer. The same is certainly true of *Sir Gawain and the Green Knight*, for which no immediate source has been discovered. For that reason, since I am speaking of this poem and this author, and not of ancient rituals, nor of pagan divinities of the Sun, nor of Fertility, nor of the Dark and the Underworld, in the almost wholly lost antiquity of the North and of the Western Isles – as remote from Sir Gawain of Camelot as the gods of the Aegean are from Troilus and Pandarus in Chaucer – for that reason I have not said anything about the story, or stories, that the author used… Chaucer was a great poet, and by the power of his poetry he tends to dominate the view of his time taken by readers of literature. But he was not the only mood or temper of mind in those days. There were others, such as this author, who while he may have lacked Chaucer's subtlety and flexibility, had, what shall we say? – A nobility to which Chaucer scarcely reached.
> (GPO 6f)

Troy is mentioned at the beginning of the translated text:

> When the siege and the assault had ceased at
> Troy, and the fortress fell in flame to firebrands
> and ashes, the traitor who the contrivance of
> treason there fashioned was tried for his treachery, the
> most true upon earth - it was Aeneas the noble and his
> renowned kindred who then laid under them lands, and
> lords became of well-nigh all the wealth in the Western Isles.
> (GPO 17)

Beside Tolkien's formation in 'classics' (cf. L 172), his performance at Exeter (Scull/Hammond, *Chronology* 22, 28-39) and his mentioning of a 'Homeric' patriarchal state for men from Númenor and heroic horsemen from Rohan (cf. L 154.159), he himself recognizes that his work is founded on an earlier matter which includes, as it were, Homer – and Virgil:

> There are, I suppose, always defects in any large-scale work of art;
> and especially in those of literary form that are founded on an
> earlier matter which is put to new uses – like Homer, or Beowulf,
> or Virgil, or Greek and Shakespearean tragedy! (L 201)

To Stanley Unwin he wrote 'I have received one postcard… containing just the words: *sic hobbitur ad astra*' (L 23) which is an allusion to *Aeneid* IX. 641 (cf. L 435). He also mentions to Christopher the unpublished C.S. Lewis' 'new translation in rhymed alexandrines of the Aeneid' (L 93.440). He explicitly mentioned Troy: 'The Mouths of Anduin and the ancient city of Pelargir are at about the latitude of ancient Troy' (L 376). And adds: 'I was recently engaged in the books of Mary Renault; especially the two about Theseus, *The King Must Die*, and *The Bull from the Sea*.' Here, in *The Bull from the Sea*, by the way, Troy is mentioned briefly:

> So we went on, and rounded Mount Athos safely, and sighted
> Thasos where they mine the gold of Troy. A Trojan fllet was there,
> loading, and must have had a king's ransom aboard. But one does
> not bite the gryphon's tail, where the head can reach so quickly.
> (79)[3]

---

3   Towards the bitter end, young Achilles appears, and old Theseus, guest as Skyros, says: 'As we sat in the window, Lykomedes showed him to me, climbing up the long stairs of the rock. Up he came, out of the evening shadow into the last kiss of the sun, as springy and brisk as noonday, his arm around a dark-haired friend. The god who sent him that blazing pride should not have added love to be burned upon it. His mother will lose her pains, for he carries his doom within him. He did not see me; and yet his eyes spoke to mine…' (236)

In *The Book of Lost Tales* (II 196.203): 'Nor Bablon, nor Ninwi, nor the towers of Trui...' Christopher notes that 'the original text of *Tuor A* had *Babylon, Niniveh, Troy*'.

In *On Fairy-Stories* is mentioned Iphigeneia, daughter of Agamemnon, and the legend of her sacrifice at Aulis (FS 49.80) as a significant example for literary critics of making useful – and intelligent – questions to receive useful answers. *Agamemnon*, by Aeschylus, among other Greek plays was used by Tolkien as back as 1913, together with Chaucer's *Troilus and Criseyde* (cf. Scull/Hammond, *Chronology* 37.40; Garth 63).

In *The Lord of the Rings*, we have 'the beacons of Gondor alight, calling for aid' (731); for Hammond and Scull the reference to the *Iliad* is spontaneous (*Companion* 509). 'And so the companies came' (LotR 753) – Tolkien wrote on a working synopsis for *The Lord of the Rings*: 'Homeric catalogue. Forlong the Fat. The folk of Lebennin' (WR 229), thus comparing the arrival of the reinforcements at Minas Tirith to the catalogue of ships and the list of Trojan leaders in Homer's *Iliad*. Todd Jensen adds that when Aeneas has to fight to ensure the preservation of the Trojan kingdom that he has founded in Italy, there is a similar catalogue of the leaders in the stories of both sides. (Cf. *Companion* 524)

In one of the early versions of his famous paper *Beowulf: the Monsters and the Critics*, Tolkien makes this remark:

> This is not a military judgment – we are not asserting that, if the Trojans had employed a Northern king and his warriors, they would have driven Agamemnon and Achilles and all the Achaeans into the sea more decisively than the Greek hexameter routs the alliterative line (though this is highly probable). (Drout 119)

I would like to add a detail, small perhaps and rather personal, but eloquent in my view. Priscilla Tolkien sent me a card from Oxford on 23-07-2006: 'The card shows a favourite view of my father's with his room in Merton College looking out over Christchurch Meadows. He called it the Walls of TROY!'

7. Trojan medieval Narrative: an unexpected Guest?

David Bratman, commenting Libran-Moreno assertions, puts her among those 'sober writers which attempt humbler classical or post-classical parallels', and says that 'she declares that Tolkien was more familiar with classical literature than the common stereotype would have it, but she does not get hot and bothered about this' (288). Not so sober seems to be for the critic *The*

Forsaken Real of Tolkien: Tolkien and the Medieval Tradition by Alex Lewis and Elizabeth Curie, although Bratman recognized that they 'make some interesting comparisons of the *Silmarillion*, in particular, with the little known medieval legends of Troy which are their subject' (288); Minas Tirith, for them, as Gondolin, 'is Troy'. While I agree with critical remarks on their book, nevertheless I am deeply gratefull to Alex Lewis, for his intuitions worked as a *sting* on me, urging me to rediscover the medieval Trojan legendarium: and was indeed a merry meeting.

I think it is proper to recall here some points about the medieval legends on the *Trojan War*, as they 'offered a distinctive version of the longest lived story in Europe' (Lewis/Currie 21):

- They were very popular and widespread.
- They existed alongside and intertwined with most of medieval storytelling to an astonishing degree, and became a symbolic element of the *imaginarium* in the configuration of England as a nation (and of English letters).
- They shaped the perception of the 'true tradition' of Troy – opposite to the old 'Greek' one –, in which the Trojans are the heroes and the Greeks the villains.
- We may be certain that Tolkien knew these legends rather well.

In the pro-Trojan medieval narrative, as in Tolkien's tales of Gondolin and Gondor, it is the besieged people inside Troy who are the heroes, and the besiegers outside Troy who are the villains. Indeed, the common saying 'beware of Greeks bearing gifts' translates Virgil's *Aeneid*: 'Timeo Danaos et dona ferentes' (II, 49), and was taken as a pejorative statement about Greeks in general based on the sentiments of that pro-Trojan stance (Lewis/Currie 6). Also William Morris worked with the Trojan material in a way which was much influenced by the medieval versions of the story (Cf. Lewis/Currie 22).

Probably, the most important instance of Trojan legends being linked with seemingly unrelated material appears in Snorri Sturluson's *Edda*. What is not usually noticed is that Snorri makes skilful use of the Trojan legends. He presents the Norse 'gods' as descendants or refugees from Troy, who were able to rule over the primitive North by reason of their superior skills; in time, the real story was forgotten; history became myth and men became gods. This material appears in Snorri's *Prologue*, in *Gylfaginning* and in *Skaldskaparmal*. He makes a more daring equation between principal characters in the tale of Troy and the Aesir of Scandinavian myth. In this account Ragnarök becomes the *Trojan War*, Hector is Thor, Neoptolemus son of Achilles is the Fenris-wolf because of his behaviour, etc. (Lewis/Currie 12).

If all this is true, then how may we not recall (for the sake of 'Trojanness') Tolkien's old and consistent fascination for Icelandic, *Edda* and *Saga*? (Scull/Hammond, *Guide* 273.468.650f; *Chronology* 40.141)

8. Towards a new Possibility – Hints of more *Trojan Material* in Tolkien's Works

- The alliterative Guido delle Colonne's *Historia Destructionis Troiae*, Lydgate's *Troy Book* and the *Laud Troy Book* describe a golden-silvery tree that the Greeks' ambassadors see at Troy (XII, 57; Lewis/Currie 48.76-77), which resembles the depiction of the trees in Gondolin: 'On either side of the doors of the palace were two trees, one that bore blossom of gold and the other of Silver, nor did they ever fade…' (LT 2 160). In *Unfinished Tales* and *The Silmarillion,* as is known, we have them too.
- The epithet 'silver-footed' – or Celebrindal –, belongs to Idril, Turgon's daughter, of Gondolin. But before that to Thetis, Achilles' mother (cf. *Iliad*, XVIII, 52-55).
- '…in a flash leapt into midstream from the arching bank / but he, the river, surged upon the man/ with all his currents in a roaring flood…' (*Iliad*, XXI, 237-240) – It recalls the flood at Bruinen's Ford?
- 'Forty black ships had crossed the sea with these / who now drew up their companies on the flank' (*Iliad*, II, 530). – May we recall the black ships of the Corsars, that Aragorn used for the rescue of Minas Tirith?
- 'We shall be themes of song for men of the future' (*Iliad* VII, 430-432). – As in Helm's Deep and The stairs of Cirith Ungol?
- Guido delle Colonne's *Historia Destructionis Troiae* (III, 13-14) mentions a ring of invisibility (given by Medea to Jason). It is also present in Lydgate's *Troy Book* (I, 2987-3200). He who carried the ring 'would immediately become invisible, with the result that while he was carrying it in his hand, the means of seeing him would appear to no-one' (Lydgate 69; Lewis/Currie 199). – Remembering Bilbo's Ring, it should appear rather obvious to speak of a surprising coincidence?
- The water-loving willow, in Homer's *Odyssey*, has a deadly secret for it stands at the gate of Hades, and is bringer of death. This was richly elaborated in later patristic tradition (Rahner 289-297). – May we think on the Old Man Willow?
- Ulysses said '…the dead came surging round me, / hordes of them, thousands raising unearthly cries, / and blanching terror gripped me… (*Odyssey* XI, 723-726). A similar throng of souls confronts Virgil's Aeneas in the Underworld. The ghosts 'crowd the shore in front of him, forced to

- wait one hundred years before they are allowed to cross over (*Aeneid*, VI, 306-314). – Does not The Paths of the Dead come to mind?
- Faramir, we know, was Tolkien's favourite, as that the Trojan Hector was the character Homer loved most (Zoja 138). In Faramir it may seem that Hector is still alive, after all. In Chaucer, Hector makes Criseyde part of the community – 'ye yourself in joie / Dwelleth with us, while yow good list, in Troie' (I, 118-119; Federico 78). – They remind us of Faramir's words to Éowyn? Both – Faramir and Hector –, live through intolerable pressure, but they keep their dignity and nobility, despite everything. Both fight a war they have not chosen, but they fight it to defend the relationships in which they believe and in which they are grounded: their city, their family, their people. And for that they face fate – and doom – sacrificing themselves. Both are capable of feeling the sorrow of others, one with Frodo and Éowyn; the other with Helen. Hector – as Faramir – is hero *à la mesure de l'homme* (Romilly 38). Indeed, in both shines a *mélange* of heroism and sufferance, courage and tenderness. In fact, Hector – not Achilles – is presented consistently in the Trojan medieval legends as *the* perfect model of chivalrous hero – as Faramir was –, with a pre-eminent place among the Nine Worthies, and he is portrayed in manuscripts, sculptures, vitraux and tappestries in all western Europe, including England (cf. Engels).
- Achilles was warned by his olympian horse, who spoke briefly before dying, as the valinorian brave dog Huan did (*Iliad* XVIII, 59-60; 88-93; 329-332).
- Ulysses, in Sophocles' *Ajax*, spoke with pity when he see his humiliated adversary, not unlike Frodo – and later Sam – seeing the poor wretched Gollum (Romilly 245.280; it is a well documented feeling in Greek texts).
- Last but not least, we should not forget two famous Trojans: *Ganimede* and *Tithonus* (cf. Woodford 38-45; Lefkowitz 36-41; Davidson 169-200). Their fate speaks about the risks, fears and bitterness that come as doom upon mortals involved in love with immortals. It has an inspiring similarity with the same theme in *Athrabeth Finrod ah andreth* (MR 303-366, cf. Spirito).

9. Conclusion

At the end of our little *odyssey* through texts, we can't boast – as Schliemann did – of a fabulous discovery of a fabled long lost City, or that we discovered *Priam's golden Treasure* (in fact, Troy's Gold is lost again, except a very tiny part, kept now at Moscow's Pushkin Museum). Perhaps some little dust of that gold had nevertheless remained in our fingers, after searching Trojan footprints in J.R.R. Tolkien's work. It seems to me that some glittering allows us to think so; at least, I hope it is so.

By being able to draw some hints of the link with the *Trojan War* legends, Tolkien can be seen as fitting into the great literary tradition of Europe also under this prospective. The line stretches from Homer, the Classics ('southern') and Dares and Dyctis, through the medieval ('northern') recasting of the Trojan story – 'from Saxon Stories and Tudor Myths' – until the Professor.

Shortly before his death in 1832, Goethe finished the last section of his autobiography, *Dichtung und Wahrheit*. In it, he hails his century as one fortunate enough to have witnessed the rebirth of Homer (cf. Manguel 167). 'Even Goethe shrank from tackling this material (of the *Trojan War*) and reinterpreting it – but not Tolkien' (Lewis/Currie 254). Fyodor Dostoyevsky goes much further:

> ...Homer (a legendary man, he was perhaps like Christ, an incarnation of God sent to us) can be compared only to Christ and not to Goethe. Try to understand him, brother, try to grasp the meaning of the Iliad (admit it – you haven't really read it, have you?). Don't you realize that in the *Iliad* Homer gave to the whole ancient world a scheme for spiritual and earthly life with the same force as Christ gave it to the modern world? ...   (38)

A Greek author who called himself, after the philosopher, 'Heraclitus', composed in the first century AD a series of commentaries on Homer. The first of these reads:

> From the very earliest infancy young children are nursed in their learning by Homer, and swaddled in his verses. We water our souls with them as though they were nourishing milk. He stands beside each of us as we start out and gradually grown into men, he blossoms as we do, and until old age we never grow tired of him, for as soon as we set him aside we thirst for him again; it may be said that the same limit is set to both Homer and life.
> (Manguel 236f)

We dare to say, the same thing – or more – on Tolkien's account …

Bibliography

Benoit de Saint-Maure. *Le Roman de Troie*. Paris: Le livre de poche, 1998

Behr, Hans-Joachim. *TROIA – Traum und Wirklichkeit*. Stuttgart: Theiss, 2001

Brandsma, Frank. "Arthur". *A Dictionary of Medieval Heroes*. Eds. Willem Gerritsen & Anthony van Melle. Woodbridge: The Boydell Press, 1998, 32-44

Borges, Jorge Luis. *Obras Completas*. Buenos Aires: Emecé Editores, 1974

Bratman, David. "The Year's Work in Tolkien Studies 2005". *Tolkien Studies* 5 (2008): 271-297

Burgess, Jonathan. *The Traditions of the Trojan War in Homer & the Epic Cycle*. Baltimore/London: The Johns Hopkins University Press, 2004

Carpenter, Humphrey (Ed.). *The Letters of J.R.R Tolkien*. Boston: Houghton Mifflin, 2000

Chance, Jane. "Introduction: A 'Mythology for England?'". *Tolkien and the Invention of Myth. A Reader*. Lexington: The University Press of Kentucky, 2004, 1-16

Chaucer, Geoffrey. *Troilus and Criseyde*. London: Dent, 1974

D'Agostino, Alfonso. *Le gocce d'acqua non hanno consumato I sassi di Troia. Materia Troiana e letterature medievali*. Milano: CUEM, 2006

Davidson, James. *The Greeks & Greek Love*. London: Wiidenfeld & Nicolson, 2007

Dostoyevsky, Fyodor. *Selected Letters of Fyodor Dostoyevsky*. Eds. Joseph Frank & David Goldstein. New Brunswick/London: Rutgers University Press, 1987

Drout, Michael D.C. (Ed.). *Beowulf and the Critics by J.R.R. Tolkien*. Temple: Arizona Center for Medieval and Renaissance Studies, 2002

Engels, I.J. "Hector". *A Dictionary of Medieval Heroes*. Eds. Willem Gerritsen & Anthony van Melle. Woodbridge: The Boydell Press, 1998, 139-145

Erskine, Andrew. *Troy between Greece and Rome. Local Tradition and Imperial Power*. Oxford: Oxford University Press, 2003

Federico, Sylvia. *New Troy. Fantasies of Empire in the Late Middle Ages*. Minneapolis-London: University of Minnesota Press, 2003

Flieger, Verlyn. "Frodo and Aragorn: The Concept of the Hero". *Understanding* The Lord of the Rings. *The Best of Tolkien Criticism*. Boston: Houghton Mifflin Company, 2004, 122-145

Garth, John. *Tolkien and the Great War. The Threshold of Middle-earth*. London: HarperCollins, 2003

Gregorio Nazianzeno. *Poesie/2*. Roma: Città Nuova, 1999

---. *La Passion du Christ. Tragédie*. Paris: Les Editions du Cerf, 1969

Greenman, David. "Aenedic and Odyssean Patterns of Escape and Return in Tolkien's 'The Fall of Gondolin' and *The Return of the King*". *Mythlore* 18,2 (1992): 4-9

Guido de Columnis. *Historia Destrictionis Troiae*. Cambridge: The Medieval Academy of America, 1936

Hammond, Wayne and Christina Scull. *The Lord of the Rings. A Reader's Companion*. London: HarperCollins, 2005

Houghton, John. "Commedia as Fairy-Story: Eucatastrophe in the Loss of Virgil". *Mythlore* 17,2 (1990): 29-32

Howard, Thomas. *C.S. Lewis – Man of Letters. A Reading of his Fiction*. San Francisco: Ignatius Press, 1987

Latacz, Joachim (Ed.). *Homer. Der Mythos von Troia in Dichtung und Kunst*. München: Hirmer, 2008

Lefkowitz, Mary. *Greek Gods, Human Lives. What can we learn from the myths*. New Haven/London: Yale University Press, 2003

Lewis, Alex and Elizabeth Currie. *The Forsaken Realm of Tolkien. J.R.R. Tolkien and the Medieval Tradition*. Medea Publishing, 2005

Libran-Moreno, Miryam. "Greek and Latin Amatory Motifs in Éowyn's Portrayal". *Tolkien Studies* 4 (2007): 73-97

---. "Parallel Lives: The Sons of Denethor and the Sons of Telamon". *Tolkien Studies* 2 (2005): 15-52

Lydgate, John. *Troy Book: Selections*. Kalamazoo: Western Michigan University, 1998

Fenwick, Mac, "Breastplates of Silk: Homeric Women in *The Lord of the Rings*". *Mythlore* 21,3 (1996): 17-23

Manguel, Alberto. *Homer's* The Iliad *and* The Odyssey. *A Biography*. London: Atlantic Books, 2008

Mora, Francine. *L'Iliade. Epopée du XIIe siécle sur la Guerre de Troie*. Turnhout: Brepols, 2003

Morse, Robert. *Evocation of Virgil in Tolkien's Art.Geritol for the Classics*. Chicago: Bolchary-Carducci Publishers, 1986

Nagy, Gergely. "Saving the Myths.The Re-creation of Mythology in Plato and Tolkien". *Tolkien and the Invention of Myth. A Reader*. Lexington: The University Press of Kentucky, 2004, 81-100

Nagy, Gregory. *Homeric Questions*. Austin: University of Texas Press, 1996

Obertino, James. "Moria and Hades: Underworld Journeys in Tolkien and Virgil". *Comparative Literature Studies* 30 (1993): 153-169

Pace, David Paul. "The Influence of Vergil's *Aeneid* in *The Lord of the Rings*". *Mythlore* 6,2 (1979): 37-38

Quintus of Smyrna. *The Trojan Epic. Posthomerica*. Baltimore/London: The Johns Hopkins University Press, 2007

Rahner, Hugo. *Greeks Myths and Christian Mystery*. New York: Biblo and Tannen, 1971

Reckford, Kenneth. "Some Trees in Virgil and Tolkien". *Perspectives of Roman Poetry: A Classical Symposyum*. Austin: University of Texas Press, 1974, 56-91

---. "There and Back Again - Odysseus and Bilbo Baggins". *Mythlore* 14,3 (1988): 5-9

Redfield, James. *Nature and Culture in the* Iliad. *The Tragedy of Hector*. Durham/London: Duke University Press, 1994

Renault, Mary. *The Bull from the Sea*. London: Arrow Books, 2004

Romilly, Jacqueline de. *Hector*. Paris: Editions de Fallois, 1997

Scull, Christina and Wayne Hammond. *The J.R.R. Tolkien Companion and Guide. Chronology and Reader's Guide*. London: HarperCollins, 2006

Shakespeare, William. *Troilus and Cressida*. Ware: Wordsworth Classics, 1993

Shippey, Tom. "Tolkien and the Appeal of the Pagan. *Edda* and *Kalevala*". *Tolkien and the Invention of Myth. A Reader*. Lexington: The University Press of Kentucky, 2004, 145-162

Simonson, Martin. "An Introduction to the Dynamics of the Intertraditional Dialogue in *The Lord of the Rings*: Aragorn's Heroic Evolution". *Tolkien and Modernity 2*. Eds. Thomas Honegger & Frank Weinreich. Zurich/Jena: Walking Tree Publishers, 2006, 75-113

---. *The Lord of the Rings and the Western Narrative Tradition*. Zurich/Jena: Walking Tree Publishers, 2008

Slack, Anna. "Slow-Kindled Courage. A Study of Heroes in the Works of J.R.R. Tolkien". *Tolkien and Modernity 2*. Eds. Thomas Honegger & Frank Weinreich. Zurich/Jena: Walking Tree Publishers, 2006, 115-141

Spirito, Guglielmo. "Wolves, Ravens, and Eagles. A mythic presence in The Hobbit". *Hither Shore* 5 (2008): 47-66

Thomas, Carol and Craig Conant. *The Trojan War*. Norman: University of Oklahoma Press, 2007

Tolkien, John Ronald Reuel. *Morgoth's Ring. HoMe X*. London: HarperCollins, 1994

---. *Sir Gawain & the Green Knight. Pearl. Sir Orfeo*. London: HarperCollins, 1995

---. *The Book of Lost Tales. II. HoMe II*. London: HarperCollins, 2002

---. *The Lord of the Rings*. London: HarperCollins, 1995

---. *The War of the Ring. HoMe VIII*. London: HarperCollins, 1990

---. *Tolkien On Fairy-stories. Expanded Edition, with Commentary and notes*. Eds. Verlyn Flieger & Douglas Anderson. London: HarperCollins, 2008

Weil, Simone and Rachel Bespaltoff. *War and the Iliad*. New York: New York Review Books, 2005

Wood, Michael. *In search of the Trojan War*. London: BBC Books, 2005

Woodford, Susan. *The Trojan War in Ancient Art*. Ithaca: Cornell University Press, 1993

Zoja, Luigi. *Il gesto di Ettore. Preistoria, storia, attualità e scomparsa del padre*. Torino: Bollati Boringhieri, 2008

›contraria contrariis curantur‹ –
Krankheitsheilung als Kampf in Tolkiens
The Lord of the Rings
Petra Zimmermann, Braunschweig

Are they doctors?‹ he asked Ron quietly. ›Doctors?‹ said Ron, looking startled. ›Those Muggle nutters that cut people up? Nah, they're healers.‹ (J.K. Rowling, Harry Potter and the Order of the Phoenix)

Wie in der Zauberwelt von *Harry Potter* obliegt auch in Tolkiens *The Lord of the Rings* das Heilen von Krankheiten nicht akademisch ausgebildeten Ärzten im Sinne unserer realen Welt, sondern ›Heilern‹, deren Können weit über erlernbares Wissen hinausgeht.[1] Neben dem Halbelben Elrond ist es vor allem der rechtmäßige Erbe des Königsthrons, Aragorn, der als Heiler in Erscheinung tritt und sich dabei therapeutischer Methoden bedient, die sich zwischen rationaler Medizin und Magie bewegen.[2]

Es mag seltsam anmuten, dass ausgerechnet derjenige, der als oberster Kriegsherr und Träger des Schwertes Andúril Gewalt ausübt, gleichzeitig als Heiler Gesundheit wiederherstellt: »it is a thing passing strange to me that the healing hand should also wield the sword«, wie es der Vorsteher der Häuser der Heilung in Minas Tirith ausdrückt (LotR III 285). Zerstörung und Rettung von Leben liegen in ein- und denselben Händen. Abgesehen davon, dass die Gewaltausübung mithilfe des Schwertes durch die Idee eines gerechten Krieges legitimiert erscheint[3], sind Kriegsführung und Krankheitsheilung auch durch ein gemeinsames Moment miteinander verknüpft:

---

1 Zumindest in Gondor gibt es gleichwohl eine ›akademische‹ Medizintradition und Heilkundige, die sich in dieser Tradition bewegen, ohne als echte ›Heiler‹ zu überzeugen. Über die medizinische Überlieferung in Gondor heißt es: »For though all lore was in these latter days fallen from its fullness of old, the leechcraft of Gondor was still wise, and skilled in the healing of wound and hurt, and all such sickness as east of the Sea mortal men were subject to« (LotR III 160). Der Vorsteher der Häuser der Heilung zählt sich zwar selbst zu den Heilern (»But for long years we healers have only sought to patch the rents made by the men of swords«, LotR III 286), jedoch werden wir als Leser nie Zeuge seiner Heilkunst. Darüber hinaus existiert ein Kräutermeister, der allerdings eher mit seinem theoretischen Wissen brilliert, als tatsächliche heilerische Fähigkeiten erkennen lässt (vgl. LotR III 167).
2 In einem Brief Tolkiens heißt es: »Aragorn's ›healing‹ might be regarded as ›magical‹, or at least a blend of magic with pharmacy and ›hypnotic‹ processes« (L 200). Es sei darauf hingewiesen, dass in früheren Zeiten Medizin und Magie nie zu trennen waren, sondern immer Hand in Hand gingen (vgl. Silva 96 und Pollington 26).
3 Vgl. Birks in diesem Band.

den Kampf.[4] Wie der auf dem Schlachtfeld ausgetragene Ringkrieg ist in Tolkiens Roman der therapeutische Prozess ein Kampf zwischen Gegensätzen. Dabei kommt bei allen angewandten Therapieverfahren, ob physikalischen, phytotherapeutischen oder magischen, ein grundlegendes, aus der Antike stammendes Prinzip zum Tragen: ›contraria contrariis curantur‹ – eine Krankheit wird durch den Gegensatz dessen, was die Krankheit kennzeichnet, kuriert.

Im Folgenden wird zunächst untersucht, welche Rolle Krankheiten allgemein in Tolkiens Mittelerde spielen und wodurch sie hervorgerufen werden. Im Anschluss werden die verschiedenen Heilmethoden dargestellt und auf das oben genannte Prinzip der Gegensätzlichkeit zurückgeführt. Den Heilungsversuchen sind Grenzen gesetzt, was abschließend erörtert wird.

1. Krankheit als Ausnahmeerscheinung

Krankheit gehört bei den Lebewesen Mittelerdes, anders als in unserer realen Welt, nicht zu den Alltagserfahrungen. So scheint beispielsweise bei den Hobbits im Auenland Krankheit nicht vorgesehen zu sein. Weder ist von kranken Hobbits die Rede noch in logischer Konsequenz von Personen und Institutionen, die die Bekämpfung von Krankheiten zum Ziel haben (Ärzte, Krankenhäuser). Wie die in Anhang C von *The Lord of the Rings* abgedruckten Stammbäume illustrieren, erreichen Hobbits in der Regel ein hohes Alter von ca. 100 Jahren und sterben dann, wenn sie die natürliche Lebensspanne ausgeschöpft haben. Ein vorzeitiger Tod wie z.B. bei Frodo Baggins' Eltern oder bei Lotho Sackville-Baggins ist durch äußere Einwirkungen (Unfall bzw. Mord) bedingt.

Wie ist dieses Phänomen der Abwesenheit von Krankheit zu erklären? Bei der Beantwortung dieser Frage erscheint ein Blick auf das antike medizinische Denken hilfreich. In der Antike wurde Krankheit als »Entgleisung aus der Harmonie der natürlichen Gleichgewichte« (Schipperges 33) angesehen, die idealerweise sowohl auf der mikrokosmischen Ebene des menschlichen Körpers als auch auf

---

4   Diese gedankliche Verbindung zwischen medizinischem und militärischem Bereich war im Sprachgebrauch der frühmittelalterlichen Medizin keineswegs unüblich. So heißt es etwa im altenglischen, sich zwischen Magie und Medizin bewegenden *Lacnunga*: »God, through impenetrable defence, shield me with your might from every quarter, release all my body's limbs sound, shielding each of them with a light shield so that the dark devils shall not hurl arrows into my sides...« (Pollington 207 ff). Laut Pollington wies die ›Ausbildung‹ eines Heilers sogar gewisse Parallelen zu der eines Kriegers auf: »The symbolic cultural parallel is plain: the shaman will fight for his people against the forces of disease and misfortune, just as the warrior will fight against human foes« (Pollington 60).

der makrokosmischen Ebene der Natur existieren. Wo eine Harmonie innerhalb von Mikro- und Makrokosmos und im Verhältnis der beiden zueinander besteht, hat Krankheit keine Chance. Nach dem griechischen Arzt Galen ist »alle Natur... eingebettet in die Wohlgeordnetheit aller Dinge, den ›kosmos‹, ist geleitet von Mitte und Maß (mesotes) und alles in allem im Konsens eines ›ethos‹, eines allgemein verbindlichen Bezugssystems« (Schipperges 38).

Die Wohlgeordnetheit, das Eingebundensein in den Kosmos und in ein ethisches Beziehungsgefüge spielt bei den Hobbits eine wichtige Rolle. Im Auenland, das Christopher Garbowski als »the almost archetypical small homeland« (Garbowski 167) bezeichnet, leben sie im Einklang mit sich selbst und ihrer Umwelt. Dieser harmonische Zustand beruht auf einer engen Verbundenheit mit der Erde. Merry Brandybuck macht diese Verbundenheit mit der Erde ganz deutlich, indem er sagt: »It is best to love first what you are fitted to love, I suppose: you must start somewhere and have some roots, and the soil of the Shire is deep« (LotR III 174).[5]

Wo solch eine Verbundenheit existiert, können Krankheiten nicht entstehen. Erst wenn die ursprüngliche Harmonie durch innere oder äußere Ursachen ins Durcheinander gerät, sind Krankheiten die Folge.

Im Laufe der Romanhandlung werden nun mehrere Romanfiguren, Hobbits wie auch Vertreter anderer Ethnien, mit Krankheit konfrontiert. Vordergründig betrachtet handelt es sich immer um die Folgen von äußerer Gewalteinwirkung:
• Frodo erleidet Verletzungen durch Messer, Stachel und Zähne.
• Éowyn und Merry tragen aus dem Kampf mit dem Anführer der Ringgeister Armverletzungen davon.
• Faramir wird durch einen Pfeil schwer verletzt.

Bei näherer Betrachtung zeigt sich jedoch, dass die Krankheitszustände viel komplexer sind und sich nicht monokausal nur auf äußere Verletzungen zurückführen lassen.

2. Die komplexe Ätiologie von Krankheiten

Dass aus Faramirs Pfeilverletzung ein lebensbedrohlicher Zustand erwachsen konnte, gibt Rätsel auf, denn »the wound was not deep or vital« und wurde zudem fachgerecht versorgt (LotR III 166). Aragorn zählt eine Reihe möglicher Krankheitsursachen auf, unter denen die Wunde nur eine untergeordnete

---

5   Bezeichnenderweise heißt es für das erste Friedensjahr nach Ende des Ringkrieges und der Wiederherstellung der Ordnung im Auenland: »And no one was ill...« (LotR III 369).

Rolle spielt: »Weariness, grief for his fathers's mood, a wound, and over all the Black Breath« (LotR III 166). Andere Faktoren, nämlich die innere, emotionale Verfasstheit des Patienten sowie vor allem die von außen induzierte Krankheit des Schwarzen Atems wirken ineinander und sind im Zusammenspiel für die Schwere der Erkrankung verantwortlich.

Dass dabei eine innere Disharmonie erst die Voraussetzung dafür schafft, dass eine äußere Krankheitsursache wie der Schwarze Atem ihre Wirkung entfalten kann, zeigt sich im Vergleich zwischen Merry und Éowyn, die beide vom Schwarzen Atem befallen sind, aber ihre Krankheit auf recht unterschiedliche Weise bewältigen. Während es von Merry heißt »But these evils can be amended, so strong and gay a spirit is in him« (LotR III 172), seine innere Disposition also den Einfluss des Schwarzen Atems zügelt, ist Éowyns Zustand aufgrund einer vorbestehenden inneren Disharmonie um vieles ernster.

Wir betrachten zunächst ›Melancholie‹ als innere Krankheitsursache, im Anschluss daran den ›Schwarzen Atem‹ als äußere Ursache.

2.1 Innere Krankheitsursache: Melancholie

Wie Aragorn und Gandalf feststellen, ist der Beginn von Éowyns Krankheit weit vor ihrer Verletzung durch den Ringgeist anzusetzen. Die ihr verhasste Rolle als Frau, die ihr Selbstentfaltung und eine ihrer Tapferkeit entsprechende Betätigung versagt, sowie die unerfüllte Liebe zu Aragorn haben sie in eine tiefe Depression gestürzt, die nicht heilbar ist. Traurigkeit und Erstarrung sind Kennzeichen ihres Zustandes, dessen Heilung weder möglich noch aus ihrer Sicht wünschenswert erscheint. Das Bild, mit dem Aragorn sie beschreibt – eine weiße Lilie, deren Lebenssaft vom Frost vereist ist –, lässt ihre Todesgestimmtheit erahnen, die sie selbst offen ausspricht:

> And it is not always good to be healed in body. Nor is it always evil to die in battle, even in bitter pain. Were I permitted, in this dark hour I would chose the latter. (LotR III 286)

Ihr Zustand ließe sich nach der antiken Vier-Säfte-Lehre als Melancholie, Schwarzgalligkeit, klassifizieren. Jedem der vier Säfte (Blut, gelbe Galle, schwarze Galle, Schleim) sind in diesem System zwei Qualitäten zugeordnet – der Schwarzgalligkeit die Qualitäten ›kalt‹ und ›trocken‹ (vgl. Ackerknecht 39). Beide spiegeln sich im obigen Bild wider: der Frost ist ›kalt‹, der vereiste, nicht mehr fließende Lebenssaft ›trocken‹. Nach der antiken Entsprechungslehre ist die Schwarzgalligkeit auch mit dem Element ›Erde‹ verbunden. Bezeichnenderweise wendet sich Éowyn, als sie schließlich durch Faramirs Liebe doch von ihrer Melancholie befreit wird, auch von dieser ›Erd-Störung‹, vom Unfruchtbaren und Trockenen ab: »I will be a healer, and love all things that *grow* and are *not barren*« (LotR III 294, Herv. P.Z.).[6]

Wodurch ist ihre Schwarzgalligkeit entstanden? Denken wir noch einmal an die Definition von Krankheit als »Entgleisung aus der Harmonie der natürlichen Gleichgewichte« zurück. Der Disharmonie in Éowyns Säftehaushalt entspricht ihre ›Entgleisung‹ aus dem sozialen Werteschema: Als Frau geboren, jedoch mit dem Mut und dem Kampfgeist eines Mannes ausgestattet, steht sie im Konflikt mit der patriarchalischen Gesellschaftsordnung. Für sie scheint kein Platz in der Gesellschaft zu sein: »…her part seemed to her more ignoble than that of the staff he [King Théoden] leaned on« (LotR III 169). Mit ihrem Wunsch, ihre Liebe zu dem zukünftigen König Aragorn möge von ihm erwidert werden, verlässt sie zudem das oben zitierte Prinzip von »Mitte und Maß«.

Ihre Heilung ist erst vollständig, als sie ihre ›natürliche‹ Position im sozialen Wertegefüge anerkennt: »I will be a shield-maiden no longer…« und: »No longer do I desire to be a queen…« (LotR III 294), wie sie Faramir gegenüber erklärt.

2.2 Äußere Krankheitsursache: der Schwarze Atem

Éowyn, Merry und Faramir und viele andere mit ihnen sind seit Ausbruch des Ringkrieges von einer seltsamen Krankheit befallen: dem Schwarzen Atem oder Schwarzen Schatten, der von den Ringgeistern hervorgerufen wird (vgl. LotR III 161). Gegen diese Krankheit scheint es keine Rettung zu geben: Wer an ihr leidet, versinkt in immer tieferen Traum, Kälte und Dunkelheit und stirbt schließlich. Auch Frodos dramatischer Zustand nach seiner Stichverletzung auf der Wetterspitze ist auf den Schwarzen Atem zurückzuführen: Frodo gleitet allmählich in eine andere Welt über – die Welt der Ringgeister.

Die Art und Weise, wie diese Krankheit die Lebewesen Mittelerdes befällt, ist rational nicht erklärbar. In Frodos Fall ist noch ein direkter Übertragungsweg nachgewiesen, nämlich mittels des Messers, durch das Frodo verletzt wurde und dessen Spitze in der Wunde stecken blieb. Bei Merry und Éowyn ist der Kontakt mit dem ›Krankheitsauslöser‹ schon weniger direkt: die Krankheit scheint sich von dem Arm, der die Waffe gegen den Anführer der Ringgeister

---

6   Bei Merry hingegen liegt keine ›Erd-Störung‹ vor (s.o.), was seine Heilung beschleunigt.

führte, weiter zu verbreiten. Bei Faramir dagegen reicht bereits die physische Nähe eines der Ringgeister aus, um ihn so zu schwächen, dass er durch die später hinzukommende Pfeilverletzung an den Rand des Todes gerät. Allein die Präsenz der Ringgeister und deren Schrei, der alle Lebewesen mit »cold blades of horror and despair« (LotR II 265) erfüllt, können die Krankheit auslösen.

Tolkien greift hier auf den in der mittelalterlichen Volksmedizin verbreiteten Gedanken zurück, dass Krankheiten von Dämonen ausgesandt werden. Hierbei könnte die altenglische Sammlung medizinischer Texte *Lacnunga* ihm wichtige Anregungen vermittelt haben.[7] E. Pettit bemerkte erstmals gewisse Parallelen zwischen zwei darin enthaltenen Zaubersprüchen und Tolkiens Roman: Zum einen werden im »Nine Herbs Charm« neun Heilmittel gegen neun Gifte angerufen, wobei uns die Zahl Neun an die Gegenüberstellung der neun Gefährten in der Ringgemeinschaft mit den neun Ringgeistern denken lässt. Zum anderen enthält der Zauberspruch »Against a Sudden Stitch« (»Wið færstice«) die Vorstellung, dass Krankheiten von Göttern, Elfen oder Hexen mittels eines Speer- oder Pfeilschusses verursacht werden.

Hier lassen sich Parallelen zu dem Angriff der Schwarzen Reiter auf der Wetterspitze ziehen: Berittene Angreifer werden mithilfe eines kleines Speeres abgewehrt; die in der Wunde verbliebene Messerspitze wird eingeschmolzen (vgl. Leibiger).

Aber die beiden Zaubersprüche lassen sich noch weiter gehend auf die Krankheit des Schwarzen Atems beziehen: Bei den neun Giften handelt sich nämlich um »infections or illnesses from *onflygnum*, flying infections thought to enter their victim through the mouth and ears« (Leibiger) – fliegende Krankheitsbringer, wie die auf fliegenden Kreaturen reitenden Ringgeister. Darüber hinaus entspricht der »sudden stitch« der Wirkung, die der Schrei der Ringgeister ausübt (»cold blades«). Beim Schwarzen Atem handelt es sich also um eine dämonische Krankheit, die quasi durch die Luft und wie ein imaginäres Messer in den Körper ihrer Opfer eindringt.[8]

---

7   Dass Tolkien dieses Werk kannte, zeigt sich daran, dass er einen Namen daraus entlehnte: Quickbeam, der hastige Ent mit einer Vorliebe für Ebereschen, ist im *Lacnunga* ein Heilmittel gegen Entzündungen: »Against inflammation: take quickbeam bark« (Pollington 211). Diesen Baum gibt es in der Realität nicht, möglicherweise handelt es sich aber um die Eberesche (vgl. Pollington 151).
8   In altenglischen Medizintexten, darunter auch im »Nine Herbs Charm«, ist darüber hinaus der Gedanke verbreitet, dass Krankheiten von giftigen Schlangen verursacht werden: »There is hardly a symptom... that is not at one time or another ascribed to ›worm‹ [OE ›wyrm‹ = Schlange] in the literature. There is a constant association of ideas of the poison of the serpent and the supposed venom of the ›worm‹...« (Mullis). In The Lord of the Rings vertritt Gríma »Wormtongue« die Position der Gift versprühenden Schlange: »Think you that Wormtongue had poison only for Théoden's ears?«, wie Gandalf Éomer am Krankenbett seiner Schwester Éowyn fragt und damit ihre oben als Melancholie be-

3. Heilung durch das Prinzip der Gegensätzlichkeit (›contraria contrariis curantur‹)

Alle Versuche, der Krankheit des Schwarzen Atems Herr zu werden, sind durch ein aus der Antike bekanntes Therapieprinzip gekennzeichnet, nämlich den hippokratischen Leitsatz ›contraria contrariis curantur‹: »Beschwerden werden durch das ihnen Entgegengesetzte behoben, jede Krankheit nach ihrer Eigenart«.[9] Dieses Prinzip findet sich auf mehreren therapeutischen Ebenen.

3.1 Wärme gegen Kälte

Die Krankheit des Schwarzen Atems ist durch ein extremes Kältegefühl gekennzeichnet, das sich bei fortschreitendem Krankheitsverlauf immer weiter im Körper ausbreitet (»... a deadly chill was spreading from his shoulder to his arm and side«, LotR I 264). Dieses Kältegefühl verschlimmert sich bei klimatischen Bedingungen, die durch Kälte und Feuchtigkeit geprägt sind. Z.B. heißt es im Fall von Frodos Stichverletzung: »The cold and wet had made his wound more painful than ever...« (LotR I 270). Demgegenüber verbessert sich sein Befinden bei Sonnenschein: »Even Frodo felt better in the morning light...« (LotR I 273). Dieses in der Natur bereits angelegte Wirkprinzip wird auch in der Therapie genutzt, indem Aragorn die Anweisung gibt, Frodo neben das Feuer zu legen und ihn warm zu halten (vgl. LotR I 264). Als weitere Maßnahme wird die Wunde mit heißem Wasser gewaschen (vgl. LotR I 264). Hier finden wir also auf einer physikalischen Ebene das Prinzip, die Krankheit durch den Gegensatz dessen, was sie charakterisiert, zu behandeln.[10]

3.2 Duft gegen Schwarzen Atem: Athelas

Bei der Therapie des Schwarzen Atems spielt die Arzneimitteltherapie eine wichtige Rolle. Das einzige Heilkraut, das in *The Lord of the Rings* vorkommt, ist Athelas. Es handelt sich um eine Pflanze, die an schattigen Orten wächst und ursprünglich aus Númenor stammt. Ihre wirksamen Bestandteile sind die

---

schriebene Krankheit auch auf die Einflüsterungen dieser ›Schlange‹ zurückführt (LotR III 169). Zu ›worm‹ als Krankheitsursache vgl. auch Pollington 462.
9 Der Leitsatz findet sich in Hippokrates' Schrift *De locis in homine*. Hier zitiert nach *Leitfaden der Homöopathie*, Hg. Jan Geißler u. Thomas Quak, München: Elsevier 2005, S. 9.
10 Auch Éowyns Heilung hat zumindest auf metaphorischer Ebene mit der Auflösung von Kälte durch Wärme zu tun, denn der für ihren melancholischen Zustand bezeichnende bittere Frost weicht »the first faint presage of Spring« (LotR III 288). Eine Träne ist ein äußeres Zeichen für das Tauen ihres inneren ›Eises‹. Später heißt es »And suddenly her winter passed, and the sun shone on her« (LotR III 294).

langen Blätter, die zerdrückt und in heißes Wasser gegeben einen scharfen, süßen Duft entwickeln. Zur therapeutischen Anwendung wird die betroffene Körperpartie mit dem Sud gewaschen oder der Kranke atmet den Duft ein. In der offiziellen Heilkunde wird Athelas wenig Bedeutung beigemessen. In der Volksmedizin setzt man sie allerdings als Aufguss gegen Kopfschmerzen ein.

Über dieses Kraut existiert ein alter Reim, dem der Kräutermeister in Minas Tirith eine Bedeutung abspricht, der aber tatsächlich entscheidende Hinweise darauf enthält, wogegen Athelas wirkt und wie es diese Wirkung entfalten kann:

> When the black breath blows and death's shadow grows
> and all lights pass, come athelas! come athelas!
> Life to the dying in the king's hand lying! (LotR III 167)

Athelas ist *das* Mittel der Wahl gegen den Schwarzen Atem; allerdings entwickelt es diese Wirkung nur in den Händen des ›Richtigen‹, nämlich des Königs, weshalb es auch »kingsfoil« (Königskraut) genannt wird. Darüber hinaus wirkt es bei Verletzungen schmerzlindernd und Kälte austreibend.

Auf Athelas wird bereits in früheren Werken Tolkiens angespielt, so im *Silmarillion (Of Beren and Lúthien)*, wo Lúthien Berens Pfeilwunde mit einem »herb out of the forest« versorgt und ihn »by her arts and by her love« heilt (S 213). Im *Lay of Leithian* wird dieselbe Episode folgendermaßen erzählt:

> Huan came and bore a leaf,
> of all the herbs of healing chief,
> that evergreen in woodland glade
> there grew with broad and hoary blade. (RS 197)

Laut Christopher Tolkien schrieb sein Vater »athelas« an den Rand dieser Passage (vgl. RS 197). Interessanterweise verwendet Tolkien ein Wort zur Beschreibung der Pflanzenblätter – »blade« –, das außer »Blatt« auch »Messer, Klinge« bedeuten kann. Wie in der antiken, im 16. Jahrhundert durch Paracelsus ausgearbeiteten Signaturenlehre[11] verweist das Aussehen der Pflanze hier auf ihren Anwendungsbereich, nämlich Verletzungen durch Klingen bzw. der Messerstichen (»cold blades«, s.o.) ähnlichen Wirkung des Schwarzen Atems.[12]

Haben wir es hier mit dem Prinzip der Ähnlichkeit zu tun (das Aussehen entspricht dem Anwendungsbereich), so verweist die Wirkung von Athelas

---

11 »Hinter vielen Vorstellungen steht der uralte Glaube an die ›Signatur‹ der Pflanzenwelt, derzufolge die Heilkräuter dem aufmerksamen Beobachter durch ihre Form selbst zeigen, wofür oder wogegen sie angewendet werden sollen...« (Telesko 20).
12 Auch in dem oben erwähnten Zauberspruch »Against a sudden stitch« spielt die Signaturenlehre eine Rolle: die drei in dem Zauberspruch aufgeführten Heilkräuter sind ebenso wie die Blätter von Athelas wie Speere geformt (vgl. Pollington 476).

wiederum auf das Prinzip der Gegensätzlichkeit: der Duft, den Ioreth als
»wholesome« (gesund, heilsam) beschreibt, wird dem krankheitsbringenden
Schwarzen Atem gegenübergestellt. Um Dämonisches austreiben zu können,
muss die Heilpflanze aber selbst über übernatürliche Kräfte verfügen. Dies zeigt
sich vor allem in zwei Bereichen, nämlich einerseits in einer Beziehung zwischen
Heilkraut und Patient, andererseits einer Beziehung zwischen Heilkraut und
Heiler. Beide Beziehungen sind nicht auf rationale Weise zu erklären, wodurch die
medizinische Therapie mit einer magischen Komponente vermischt wird.[13]

Beziehung zwischen Heilkraut und Patient
Athelas erzeugt auf geheimnisvolle Weise bei jedem einzelnen Erkrankten genau
den heilenden Duft, den er bzw. sie für die individuelle Heilung benötigt.

Bei Merry (und auch bei der nicht erkrankten Ioreth) sind es offensichtlich
Assoziationen mit der jeweiligen Heimat: Merry erwacht durch den Duft von
»orchards, and of heather in the sunshine full of bees« (LotR III 172), wobei
die Obstgärten an das Auenland denken lassen. Ioreth fühlt sich an die Rosen
in Imloth Melui erinnert, wo sie ihre Kindheit verbrachte (vgl. LotR III 168).
Für Faramir ist es die Erinnerung an »dewy mornings of unshadowed sun in
some land of which the fair world in Spring is itself but a fleeting memory«
(LotR III 168). Vielleicht ist mit dem geheimnisvollen Land das untergegangene
Númenor gemeint, das Faramir in seinen Träumen gegenwärtig ist. Im Falle
von Éowyn erzeugt Athelas »an air wholly fresh and clean and young«, eine
Luft, die von schneebedeckten Bergen oder von silbrigen Gestaden, die in weiter
Ferne vom Meeresschaum weggewaschen werden, zu stammen scheint (LotR
III 171). Auch dies könnte mit der Heimat der Erkrankten in Verbindung ge-
bracht werden, denn Rohan wird im Süden vom Gebirge Ered Nimrais (weißes
Gebirge) begrenzt, und das Meer, in den der durch Rohan fließende Fluss Isen
mündet, liegt weit entfernt im Westen.

Dass diese Assoziationen nicht auf subjektiven Täuschungen der Erkrankten
beruhen, sondern von den Umstehenden ebenfalls wahrgenommen werden
(ohne dass sie im Einzelnen wissen können, was der Duft zu bedeuten hat),
wird ganz deutlich gemacht: »the fragrance that came to each« (LotR III 168)
heißt es, oder »it seemed to those who stood by« (LotR III 171).

Beziehung zwischen Heilkraut und Heiler
Athelas entfaltet seine Wirkung erst in den Händen des ›Richtigen‹, nämlich
des Königs. Diese Beziehung zwischen Heilkraut und Heiler zeigt sich bereits
in ihrer gemeinsamen Herkunft, denn Athelas war ursprünglich in Númenor

---

13 Unter »magischer Heilkunde« versteht man laut Jütte »alle Heilmethoden..., die sich
auf geheimnisvolle Naturkräfte im Kosmos berufen und diese übernatürlichen Kräfte
mithilfe bestimmter Techniken und ›Medien‹ auf den kranken menschlichen Körper zu
lenken und damit einen Heilprozeß in Gang zu setzen suchen« (Jütte 67).

beheimatet, so wie auch Aragorns Vorfahren. Auf diesen Zusammenhang spielt Tolkien an, wenn angesichts von Aragorns Heilungserfolgen die Frage gestellt wird, ob diese vielleicht auf »some forgotten power of Westernesse [= Númenor]« (LotR III 171) zurückzuführen seien.

Darüber hinaus besteht auch eine Analogie bezüglich des äußeren Erscheinungsbildes: Die Pflanze wächst im Dickicht, ist schwer aufzufinden, den meisten ohnehin unbekannt und sieht unscheinbar aus. Eben diese Merkmale gelten auch für Aragorn, der jahrzehntelang ›undercover‹ als Ranger durch die Wälder streifte und von dem niemand vermutet hätte, dass er der Anwärter auf den Königsthron sei. Bezeichnend ist hier Frodos Ausruf: »I thought he was only a Ranger« (LotR I 290). Bilbos Gedicht über Aragorn »All that is gold does not glitter« gibt diesen Widerspruch zwischen wahrem Kern und äußerer Erscheinung sehr schön wieder. Das Königskraut ist damit auch ein Abbild des Königs selbst.

Die Tatsache, dass sich die Heilkraft einer Pflanze nur in den richtigen Händen entfaltet, lässt eine spezielle Auffassung über das Wesen von Pflanzen erkennen, wie sie beispielsweise bei den Kelten verbreitet war. Danach verfügen Pflanzen neben den chemisch nachweisbaren Inhaltsstoffen auch über ein feinstoffliches Potential: »Die Druiden hatten bei ihren schamanischen Reisen in die Geisterwelt erkannt, dass eine Pflanze neben ihren Inhaltsstoffen einen Energiekörper besitzt, der Kräfte ausstrahlt...« (Krämer 104). Dieser Energiekörper stelle dem erkrankten Menschen »Informationen zur Verfügung, die er als Anstoß zur Selbstheilung benötigt« (Krämer 105). Da jede Krankheit und jeder Kranke sich von anderen unterscheidet, sind auch unterschiedliche energetische Informationen gefordert, um den Selbstheilungsprozess in Gang zu setzen. Dies erklärt, warum Athelas auf den einzelnen Patienten zugeschnittene Heildüfte entwickelt.

Die energetische Sichtweise impliziert auch, dass es jemanden geben muss, der diese Kräfte freizusetzen vermag: Es existiert eine spirituelle Beziehung zwischen Heiler und Heilpflanze, welche therapeutisch genutzt wird, um Heilung zu bewirken. Wie im keltischen Schamanentum verwendet Aragorn dabei eine »Heilpflanze, die zu ihm selbst passt...« (Krämer 63).

3.3 Heilende Hände gegen destruktive Kräfte: Aragorn als spiritueller Heiler

Nach der physikalischen Wärme- und der arzneipflanzlichen, aber bereits magisch gefärbten Dufttherapie haben wir es noch mit einer dritten Ebene des ›Contraria‹-Prinzips zu tun, die ganz im spirituellen Bereich angesiedelt ist. Aragorns Hände, in denen er als Kriegsherr sein Schwert hält und Gewalt ausübt, sind andererseits auch Instrumente, mit denen er Heilung erwirkt. Auf diese Doppelfunktion wird im Text immer wieder hingewiesen: »wielder of the Sword Reforged, victorious in battle, whose hands bring healing« (LotR III 297) oder »strength and healing were in his hands« (LotR III 298). Nicht nur auf dem Schlachtfeld, sondern auch am Krankenbett ist Aragorns Handlungsweise durch einen Kampf geprägt, in diesem Fall durch einen Kampf mit dem Krankheitsdämon in Form des Schwarzen Atems: »And those that watched felt that some great struggle was going on« (LotR III 167). Dieser Kampf gegen den Krankheitsdämon wird unter Zuhilfenahme bestimmter Rituale geführt.

Rituale spielen in vielen ›vorwissenschaftlichen‹ Medizinpraktiken eine wichtige Rolle, so z.B. im Keltentum. Hier hatten Rituale »das Ziel, dass der Druide seinen Geist auf den Geist der Pflanze einstimmte« (Krämer 105). Rituale können wir auch bei Aragorn beobachten, der Gesang, Worte, Berührungen und Behauchen einsetzt, bevor er die Athelas-Therapie beginnt. Damit wird die Energie, die in der Heilpflanze steckt, in die richtigen Bahnen gelenkt.

Gesang, Worte, Rufen
Nach Jahn wirken »alle ›Medizinen‹, ›Talismane‹, ›Zauberkörner‹, ja selbst Gifte... nicht ohne das Wort« (zit. n. Rätsch 14). Auch Aragorn setzt das Wort ein, um auf den Patienten einzuwirken, aber auch, um die Waffe, mit der eine Wunde herbeigeführt wurde, zu neutralisieren. Bevor er sich Frodo zuwendet, singt er über dem Griff des Dolches »a slow song in a strange tongue« (LotR I 265). Unverständlich sind auch die Worte, die er dann zu Frodo spricht. Wir können nur vermuten, dass es sich um Beschwörungsformeln handelt, eine Form des ›Besprechens‹, wodurch der Krankheitsdämon aus dem Patienten herausgetrieben werden soll. Dass die Worte unverständlich sind, erhöht dabei noch ihre magische Wirksamkeit (vgl. Cameron 134).

Faramir, Éowyn und Merry ruft Aragorn bei ihren Namen, um sie aus ihrem komatösen Zustand zu erwecken. Dabei ist im Falle von Faramirs Heilung ein interessantes Phänomen zu beobachten: Aragorns Stimme wird immer leiser, als ob er sich von den anderen entferne und nun in einem dunklen Tal wandere, »calling for one that was lost« (LotR III 167). Aragorn scheint sich in eine andere Welt zu begeben, in die, wo der Kranke weilt. Hier klingt die ebenfalls im Keltentum verbreitete Vorstellung an, dass der Heiler die Fähigkeit besitze, in die ›Anderswelt‹ zu reisen.[14] Faramir, Merry und Éowyn, alle schon an der Schwelle des Todes, werden von Aragorn zurückgerufen. Dieses Zurückrufen scheint der wichtigste Teil der Therapie zu sein, denn Aragorn betont, dass nun (noch bevor er das Heilkraut anwendet) das Schlimmste vorüber sei.

Berührungen
Auch Berührungen, d.h. Körperkontakt zwischen dem Heiler und Patienten, spielen im therapeutischen Prozess eine wichtige Rolle. Dabei scheint die Berüh-

---

14 Die Fähigkeit, Verbindung zur Anderswelt aufzunehmen, zeigt sich bei Aragorn auch daran, dass er als der Erbe Isildurs in der Lage ist, auf den Pfaden der Toten das Geisterheer herbeizurufen und es zu führen (vgl. LotR III, »The Passing of the Grey Company«).

rung zum einen diagnostische Erkenntnisse zu liefern, denn Aragorn ist durch das Anfassen von Faramirs Hand und Stirn in der Lage, Aussagen über dessen Zustand zu treffen. Umgekehrt fühlt er durch Berührung von Éowyns Hand, wie das Leben in ihren Körper zurückströmt. In der Hauptsache jedoch dient der Körperkontakt dazu, heilende Energien auf den Patienten zu übertragen. Dies kann in Form von Berührungen mit der Hand (bei Faramir und Merry) oder durch einen Kuss (bei Éowyn) geschehen. Deutlich sieht man, wie dieses Ritual die Energie des Heilers verzehrt: »For Aragorn's face grew grey with weariness...« (LotR III 167).

Anhauchen
Aragorn überträgt nicht nur Energien auf die Patienten, sondern auch auf die Heilpflanze. Da Athelas am besten frisch wirkt, das herbeigebrachte Kraut jedoch bereits zwei Wochen alt ist, scheint es notwendig zu sein, die Pflanze zu ›beleben‹: »Then taking two leaves, he laid them on his hands and breathed on them...« (LotR III 168).

In den Ritualen, die der Heilpflanzentherapie vorausgehen bzw. die diese unterstützen, zeigt sich eine enge Verflechtung von Medizin und Magie, die sogar etymologisch nachweisbar ist: Sie ist bereits in dem von Tolkien verwendeten Wort ›leech‹ angelegt.[15] Dessen germanische Protoform *lækjaz* bedeutet ›enchanter‹ und bildet gleichzeitig die Wurzel des Altirischen *liaigh*, ›Arzt‹ (vgl. Pollington 41). Damit ist der Heiler schon von der Begrifflichkeit her Magier und Arzt in einer Person, eine Verflechtung, die sich deutlich bei Aragorns therapeutischem Vorgehen zeigt.

Noch eine weitere Personalunion spielt bei Aragorn eine wichtige Rolle, nämlich diejenige zwischen König und Heiler. Nicht durch äußere Symbole der Macht wird er als König identifiziert, denn die Königsinsignien (das Königsbanner und den Stern von Elendil) legt er vor den Toren Minas Tiriths ab. Vielmehr ist es seine Heilkraft, durch die der alte Spruch »The hands of the king are the hands of a healer« seine Bestätigung findet. Es ist ausgerechnet Faramir, der ›Rivale‹ Aragorns in Bezug auf die Herrschaft über Gondor, der nach seiner Heilung die Identifizierung Aragorn = König vornimmt: »My lord, you called me. I come. What does the king command?« (LotR III 168).

Die Verbindung zwischen Königtum und heilender Macht ist tief in der mittelalterlichen Tradition verwurzelt.[16] Hier existierte die Vorstellung, dass

---

15 Prinz Imrahil fragt z.B.: »Are there no leeches among you?« (LotR III 142).
16 »His [Aragorn's] power over sickness, resembling that of medieval kings to cure the ›king's evil‹, is taken by all as a divine gift, which can belong only to a sovereign« (Kocher 154 f). Flieger verankert das Konzept des heilenden Königs in einer noch früheren Epoche, indem sie es auf das frühkeltische Prinzip von »sacral kingship« zurückführt (Flieger 133).

die Krankheit Skrofulose, auch King's Evil genannt, durch »royal touch«, also Berührung vonseiten eines Königs, geheilt werden könne. Erst König George I (1660–1727) machte dieser Praxis in England ein Ende, während sie in Frankreich noch bis zum Jahr 1825 ausgeübt wurde (vgl. *Wikipedia*, Scrofula, und Day 108). Auch im altenglischen *Lacnunga* wird ein weiser König erwähnt, der Heilkraft besaß (vgl. Pollington 241).

Tolkien greift hier auf diese Traditionslinie zurück, um einerseits die Legitimität von Aragorns Herrscheranspruch zu untermauern, andererseits aber auch Aragorns ›magische Fähigkeiten‹ in einem bestimmten Licht erscheinen zu lassen: Wie Tolkien in einem Brief beschreibt, handelt es sich nicht um eine Form von Magie, die man sich aneignen kann, sondern um eine inhärente Kraft, die sich aus Aragorns besonderer Abstammung speist.[17] Wohl auch deshalb hat Tolkien die oben erwähnte Formulierung »some forgotten *power* of Westernesse« (Herv. P.Z.) gewählt statt »art or wizardry«, wie es noch im Entwurf heißt (WR 396). Mit dieser Leben rettenden Heilkraft stellt Aragorn den Gegenpart zu den Leben vernichtenden Kräften Saurons dar (vgl. Kranz 21).

4. Grenzen der Heilung

Ob mit rationalen oder magischen Therapiestrategien – nicht alle Krankheiten können geheilt werden. So stellt Aragorn Éowyns vollständige Genesung in Frage, »unless other healing comes which I cannot bring« (LotR III 170). Die Heilung kommt tatsächlich, nämlich in Gestalt von Faramir, der Éowyns Melancholie durch seine Liebe zu ihr aufbricht. Auch bei Beren waren es nicht die Heilpflanze Athelas und Lúthiens Heilkunst allein, die Genesung brachten: Auch hier ist die Liebe als Therapeutikum (»by her arts and by her love«, S 213) von mindestens gleich hohem Rang.

Dieser Weg steht Frodo nicht offen. Seine singulären Leiden haben ihn außerhalb von »Mitte und Maß« gestellt und ihn damit zu einem gesellschaftlichen Außenseiter gemacht: »Frodo dropped quietly out of all the doings of the Shire, and Sam was pained to notice how little honour he had in his own country« (LotR III 371). Seine Verletzungen sind nicht mit anderen teilbar[18] und zumindest in Mittelerde unheilbar: »Alas! there are some wounds that cannot be wholly cured« (LotR III 325), wie Gandalf bemerkt.

---

17 »Anyway, a difference in the use of ›magic‹ in this story is that it is not to be come by ›lore‹ or spells; but is in an inherent power not possessed or attainable by Men as such... A. is not a pure ›Man‹, but at long remove one of the ›children of Lúthien‹« (L 200).
18 Frodo versucht, seine wiederkehrenden Beschwerden vor den anderen zu verbergen: »All that day [Jahrestag seiner Stichverletzung] he was silent« (LotR III 325). »Frodo was ill again in March, but with a great effort he concealed it...« (LotR III 372).

Auf Frodos Frage »Where shall I find rest?«(LotR III 325) hat Arwen bereits eine Antwort gegeben: »If your hurts grieve you still and the memory of your burden is heavy, then you may pass into the West, until all your wounds and weariness are healed« (LotR III 306).

»The West«, Aman[19], wohin das Schiff Frodo am Ende bringt, ist als eine Art Paradies zu verstehen, das außerhalb Mittelerdes liegt. Man verlässt die physische Welt, indem der Weg dorthin nicht mehr der Krümmung der Erdoberfläche folgt, sondern der »straight road« Richtung Westen (vgl. L 411).

Für Frodo als einem Sterblichen bedeutet der Eintritt in die Unsterblichenlande nicht die Verleihung der Unsterblichkeit, sondern einen zeitlich befristeten Aufenthalt zur Heilung seiner körperlichen und seelischen Verletzungen: »this is strictly only a temporary reward: a healing and redress of suffering« (L 198). Am Ende stehen doch der Tod und das Eingehen in Welten, von denen auch die Elben keine Kenntnis haben (vgl. L 411). Mehrmals verwendet Tolkien für diesen Heilungsprozess den Ausdruck »purgatory« (Fegefeuer), worunter er ein Fegefeuer des Friedens und der Heilung (vgl. L 411) versteht.

Vollständige Heilung ist damit nicht Sache der Medizin, sondern erhält eine transzendente Dimension: Sie ist erst möglich, wenn man den Weltenkreis verlassen hat. So finden wir zum Schluss noch einmal das Prinzip der Heilung durch Gegensätzlichkeit (›contraria contrariis curantur‹): der Welt der Ringgeister, aus der die Krankheit des Schwarzen Atems stammt und in die die Kranken, kann ihnen nicht geholfen werden, eingehen, wird eine Welt der Heilung gegenübergestellt: »a far green country under a swift sunrise« (LotR III 378).

Bibliographie

Ackerknecht, Erwin H. *Geschichte der Medizin*. 7., überarb. u. erg. Aufl. v. Axel Hinrich Murken. Stuttgart: Enke, 1992

Cameron, Malcolm Laurence. *Anglo-Saxon Medicine*. Cambridge: Cambridge University Press, 1993

Carpenter, Humphrey, Ed. with assistance of C. Tolkien. *The Letters of J.R.R. Tolkien*. London: HarperCollins, 1995

Day, David. *Tolkiens Welt. Die mythologischen Quellen des Herrn der Ringe*. Stuttgart: Klett-Cotta, 2003

Garbowski, Christopher. *Recovery and Transcendence for the Contemporary Mythmaker: The Spiritual Dimension in the Works of J.R.R. Tolkien*. Zurich/Berne: Walking Tree Publishers, [2]2004

---

19 Aman: »the undying lands of Valinor and Eressëa« (L 410); an anderer Stelle setzt Tolkien das Ziel der Fahrt Richtung Westen nur mit Eressëa gleich (vgl. L 198).

Jütte, Robert. *Geschichte der Alternativen Medizin. Von der Volksmedizin zu den unkonventionellen Therapien von heute*. München: C.H. Beck, 1996

Kocher, Paul. *Master of Middle-earth. The Fiction of J.R.R. Tolkien*. New York: Ballantine Books, 1977

Krämer, Claus. *Keltische Heilkunst*. Freiburg i.Br.: Bauer, 2002

Kranz, Gisbert. »Der heilende Aragorn«. *Inklings-Jahrbuch* 2 (1984): 11-24

Leibiger, Carol A. "Charms". *J.R.R. Tolkien Encyclopedia. Scholarship and Critical Assessment*: www.routledge-ny.com/ref/tolkien/charms.html (11.8.2009)

Mullis, Paul: "The Ravens Warband. How to get better the Anglosaxon Way (or Not As the Case May Be": www.millennia.fs2.com/medicine.htm (27.7.2009)

Pettit, Edward. "J.R.R. Tolkien's Use of an Old English Charm". *Mallorn* 40.11 (2002): 39-44

Pollington, Stephen. *Leechcraft. Early English Charms, Plant Lore, and Healing*. Hockwold-cum-Wilton: Anglo-Saxon Books, 2000

Rätsch, Christian. *Lexikon der Zauberpflanzen aus ethnologischer Sicht*. Graz: Akad. Druck- u. Verl. Anst., 1988

Schipperges, Heinrich. *Krankheit und Kranksein im Spiegel der Geschichte*. Berlin u.a.: Springer, 1999

„Scrofula". Artikel in der englischsprachigen Version von Wikipedia: en.wikipedia.org/wiki/Scrofula (11.8.2009)

Silva, Raymond. *Magie in der Medizin – gestern und heute: von ungewöhnlichen Heilweisen und Heilerfolgen*. Genf: Ariston Verlag, 1988

Telesko, Werner. *Die Weisheit der Natur. Heilkraft und Symbolik der Pflanzen und Tiere im Mittelalter*. München u.a.: Prestel, 2001

Tolkien, Christopher (Ed.). *The History of Middle-earth VI. The Return of the Shadow*. London: HarperCollins, 2002

---. *The History of Middle-earth VIII. The War of the Ring*. London: HarperCollins, 1990

Tolkien, John Ronald Reuel. *The Lord of the Rings*. Vol. I-III. London: Unwin Paperbacks, ³1979

---. *The Silmarillion*. Ed. Christopher Tolkien, London: Allen & Unwin, 1979

Zusammenfassungen der englischen Beiträge

Perspektiven auf den Gerechten Krieg in Tolkiens *Legendarium*
Annie Birks

Wie in der *Ainulindalë* gezeigt wird, ist Krieg in Mittelerde keine Wahlmöglichkeit: Schon eingangs werden zugleich die Samen von Harmonie und Missklang gesät und zwischen dem Alpha und dem Omega werden sich Rassen und Individuen entweder auf die ›Große Musik‹ einstellen oder dem Missklang widmen. Ihre Wege werfen ein Schlaglicht auf die Perspektiven ihres Schöpfers – oder, vom Leser aus gesehen, ihres Subschöpfers.

Wegen der zentralen Lage von Kriegsführung in der Geschichte Mittelerdes widmet sich dieser Beitrag den Motivationen der an Konflikten beteiligten Rassen und Personen unter der Fragestellung, ob sie mit scheinbar berechtigten Intentionen geführt werden oder nicht, ob sie defensiv, präventiv oder aggressiv sind. Von wissenschaftlichen Positionen aus gesehen (z.B. aus der Sicht des Augustinus) und aufgrund der kurz- und langfristigen Ergebnisse der Feindseligkeiten in der Geschichte Mittelerdes soll versucht werden, die Perspektiven auf das Konzept des ›Gerechten Krieges‹ in Tolkiens Sekundärwelt zu identifizieren.

Dagor dagorath und Ragnarök: Tolkien und die Apokalypse
Michaël Devaux

Die Lektüre der *Edda* war für Tolkien entscheidend – für seine universitäre Karriere wie für seine literarische. Man findet dort die „Götterdämmerung", die Ragnarök. Tolkien hat diese Episode anlässlich der Redaktion des *Silmarillion* (schon im *Buch der Verschollenen Geschichten*) wieder aufgenommen, Christopher Tolkien aber im *Silmarillion* von 1977 wegfallen lassen. In diesem Beitrag wird die Beziehung zwischen narrativer Struktur, den Ereignissen (z.B. der Rolle des Mondes und der Sonne) sowie den unterschiedlichen Personen in der *Edda* und bei Tolkien (Tulkas, Manwë, Fionwë, Túrin, Eärendil und Melkor) untersucht. Außerdem werden die mehr oder weniger wichtigen Veränderungen besprochen, die diese Episode in den verschiedenen Versionen des *Silmarillion* erfahren hat (LT 2 282-283; SM 40, 165; MR 399; LR 333; WJ 247; UT 511). Die Christianisierung des *Legendarium* bedenkend, wird versucht, auszumachen, wo sich diese Entwicklung für diese Legende ausmachen lässt, indem die zweite Prophezeiung Mandos' mit der Schlacht von Armageddon in der Johannes-Offenbarung verglichen wird.

Der Autor schlägt (mit P. Louis Bouyer, einem Freund Tolkiens vom Oratorium) eine eschatologische Interpretation der Dagor dagorath, der Schlacht der Schlachten, vor. Er folgert, die *Edda* diene letztlich als paradoxes Modell ohne Ähnlichkeiten (vgl. L 149), während die gemeinsamen Elemente mit der Apokalypse zunehmen. Die Frage der Interpretation ist die bedeutendste. An den vierfachen Schriftsinn erinnernd, konzentriert er sich auf die Tatsache, dass Tolkien keine Allegorie der Apokalypse geschrieben hat, sondern eine Parabel (im von Robert Murray SJ definierten Sinn) – die Entsprechungen bestehen nicht Begriff für Begriff. Die Logik Mittelerdes erlegt ihr Neuschreiben der Apokalypse und der *Edda* nicht auf, ohne die Freiheit des Lesers zu respektieren.

Einen sauberen Boden zu bestellen – Eine Tolkien'sche Sicht des Krieges
Anna E. Slack

Dieser Beitrag untersucht Facetten der Tolkien'schen Sicht des Krieges in seinem berühmtesten Werk *The Lord of the Rings*, indem die Ursachen, Motive und Ziele des Krieges und seine Führung im Kontext der literarischen und spirituellen Untermauerungen seins Werkes analysiert werden. Er beginnt mit einem Überblick über den überwältigend makrokosmischen Aussichtspunkt, der vom Fantasy-Genre im Generellen und der heroischen Fantasy im Speziellen eingenommen wird, und zeigt, wie dieser oft dazu führt, Konflikte als archetypischen »Krieg im Himmel« wiederzugeben. Indem dieses Konzept besonders auf *The Lord of the Rings* angewandt wird, untersucht der Beitrag, wie Konflikt dort gezeichnet wird, und argumentiert, dass Tolkien eher ein – durch individuelle Charaktere und die literarischen Traditionen, für die sie symbolisch stehen, fokalisiertes – Spektrum von Antworten auf Gewalt und Konflikt denn eine dogmatische Sicht bietet. Die Analyse dieses Spektrums führt schließlich zu Tolkiens in diesem Beitrag *ius in delectu* genanntem Konzept – nicht nur im Krieg gerecht zu sein, sondern, wichtiger noch, in der Wahl. Im Kern untersucht der Beitrag, wie dieser Gedanke der heroischen moralischen Wahl als entscheidend für Kriegs- und Friedenszeiten – und als das eigentliche Ziel von beiden – angesehen wird.

Das Vermächtnis von Schwertern: Belebte Waffen und die Ambivalenz heroischer Gewalt

Judith Klinger

Schwerter sind in Tolkiens Texten nicht allein Werkzeuge der Gewalt, sondern auch Träger dynastischer Identität und kollektiver Erinnerung – und zudem von ganz eigener Lebendigkeit erfüllt. Ihre Ursprünge, Namen und mythischen Qualitäten verweben sich untrennbar mit Identität, Schicksal und Geschichte ihrer jeweiligen Träger. Tolkien greift darin auf weit verbreitete mittelalterliche Traditionen zurück.

In der Vormoderne ist das Schwert keineswegs unbelebtes Instrument oder bloßes Symbol der Macht, es spielt vielmehr eine aktive Rolle als Mittler von Herrschaft und Privilegien, Vorbestimmtheit und Eigen-Macht. Am Schnittpunkt zwischen strahlendem Ruhm und bedrohlicher Vernichtung führt das Schwert zugleich die Ambivalenz heroischer Gewalt vor Augen: Ob gewaltsam kulturelle Ordnung geschaffen wird oder der heroische Exzess seine Strahlkraft jenseits sozialer Normen entfaltet, steht buchstäblich auf Messers Schneide. Solche Ambivalenzen sind auch in Tolkiens Texten über Mittelerde sichtbar. Neben den verhängnisvollen Konsequenzen katastrophaler Kriege steht der Glanz heroischer Schwertgewalt, der sich weder mit pazifistischen Tendenzen noch mit moderner Gewaltkritik verrechnen lässt.

Am Beispiel von Aragorn, Túrin sowie Frodo und Sam wird gezeigt, wie sich Geschichte und Gebrauch der Schwerter jeweils mit Fragen von Gewaltlegitimation, Eigenwillen und Schicksalhaftigkeit sowie Integration und Ausgrenzung verbinden.

Aragorns charismatischer Herrschaft ist mit dem ›Schwert, das zerbrochen war‹ die Erinnerung an Verlust und Niedergang eingeschrieben. Letztlich begründet diese Dialektik von Verlust und Rückeroberung die integrative Wirkung königlicher Schwertgewalt.

Dagegen steht Túrins Allianz mit dem ›schwarzen Schwert‹ im Zeichen schicksalhafter Desintegration, wobei ihm die Fremdartigkeit Anglachels zugleich heroischen Status jenseits sozialer Gemeinschaft zuweist.

Im Fall der Hobbits begleitet das elbische Schwert eine Grenzüberschreitung, die aus der eigenen Kultur hinausführt und eine Anverwandlung an das Fremde vorzeichnet. Stings geheimnisvolles Leuchten weist zudem darauf hin, dass sich die Wirkmächtigkeit belebter Schwerter insgesamt nicht auf heroische Gewalttaten beschränkt: Ihre besondere Magie situiert sie am Schnittpunkt von Zeit, Geschichte und Mythos und bewahrt die Erinnerung an ein überzeitliches Licht.

Sprache und Gewalt:
die Orks, die Ents und Tom Bombadil
Martin G.E. Sternberg

Tolkien hat den *Herrn der Ringe* einmal einen »Essay in linguistischer Ästhetik« genannt, und so soll die Frage gestellt werden, ob sich aus diesem Essay auch ein Zusammenhang zwischen Tolkiens erfundenen Sprachen und Gewalt ermitteln lässt. Auf der Grundlage von theoretischen Ansätzen von Michel Foucault, Theodor W. Adorno, George Orwell und Ross Smith wird untersucht, wie weit Tolkiens erfundene Sprachen bereits durch ihre Beschaffenheit vorherbestimmen, *wer* sprechen kann, was gesagt werden kann, wie sehr die Eigenheit des Anderen in ihnen Ausdruck finden kann und wie die von ihnen hervorgerufenen Stimmungen das Verhalten ihrer Sprecher beeinflussen.

Eine Analyse der Schwarzen Sprache zeigt, dass diese aufgrund ihrer Phonetik sogar körperliche Gewalt ausübt, weil sie den Sprecher am Atmen und damit Sprechen hindert. Mit der Möglichkeit zum Sprechen behindert sie auch das Widersprechen und zeigt sich als Herrschaftsmittel, indem es leichter ist zu gehorchen als sich zu widersetzen. Ihre Grammatik lässt alles nur als das Objekt von Prozessen erscheinen und begünstigt so eine Haltung, die alles nur als Verfügungsmaterial für Handlungen ansieht. Weiter hält ihre ästhetische Wirkung die Orks in einer aggressiven Grundstimmung.

Das Entische dagegen ist eine Sprache, die sich der Individualität des Benannten so weit wie möglich öffnet. Ihre Worte erzählen die Geschichte der Dinge, zu denen sie gehören. Sie spiegeln sie so in ihren Details und fixieren sie nicht einmal in einem bestimmten Zustand, sondern bleiben als Geschichten offen für ihre zukünftigen Entwicklungen. Wie Treebeard zeigt, eignet sich ihre Musikalität für das Formen endloser Lieder, die zum Resonanzkörper der ästhetisch-emotionalen Begegnung mit der Umwelt des Sprechers werden. Sie hat aber auch nachteilige Auswirkungen auf den Sprecher: Sie ist zeitaufwendig, fördert endlose Überlegungen ohne Entscheidung und eine Schwerfälligkeit, die die Ents anfällig macht für Aggressionen schneller sprechender und darum schneller denkender Wesen. Es wird gezeigt, dass der eigentliche Beitrag Merrys und Pippins zum Aufgerütteltwerden der Ents in einer aggressiveren Sprache und Art des Sprechens liegen, die sie nach Fangorn bringen. Erst hierdurch werden die Ents wieder gewaltfähig.

Ein ähnliches Bild bietet Tom Bombadil. Auch hier geht eine nonsenshafte Sprache, deren Hauptfunktion der Ausdruck von Wunder und Erstaunen über das Begegnende ist und die von schematisierenden Festlegungen absieht, Hand in Hand mit einer Unfähigkeit, in den Kategorien von Macht und Gewalt zu denken, die Tom als Hüter des Rings ungeeignet macht.

Tolkiens imaginäre Sprachen zeigen so einerseits ein waches Bewusstsein für die Fähigkeit von Sprache, die Individualität des Anderen zu verletzen, aber sie zeigen auch die Kosten eines linguistischen Pazifismus. Diese Kosten sind überwiegend quantitativer Art: der Verbrauch von Atem, Kraft, Zeit und Erinnerungsvermögen, die die Ents so sehr belasten, dass das Entische letztlich wie die Schwarze Sprache zu einer Fessel ihrer Sprecher wird.

Von der Schwierigkeit, den Abschluss zu finden: Krieg und Erzählstrukturen in Tolkiens *Der Herr der Ringe*
Margaret Hiley

Der amerikanische Schriftsteller Alfred Kazin schrieb 1973, dass der Krieg die dominante und durchgehende Erfahrung des Menschen im 20. Jahrhundert sei: »War is the continued experience of twentieth-century man« (*Bright Book of Life*). Diese durchgehende Erfahrung ist vielleicht der Grund, weshalb viele namhafte Schriftsteller des 20. Jahrhunderts Krieg in ihren Werken darstellen und thematisieren. J.R.R. Tolkien bildet dazu keine Ausnahme.

Dieser Artikel möchte untersuchen, wie die ständige Präsenz des Krieges in Tolkiens Werken nicht einfach die Zeit ihrer Entstehung reflektiert, sondern auch das unkontrollierbare und uneindämmbare Wesen des Krieges aufweist (cf. Margot Norris: »[war is] uncontrollable and uncontainable«). Der Krieg spielt eine zentrale Rolle in den Konfliktzyklen, die die Geschichte Mittelerdes strukturieren, und bildet die treibende Dynamik in der Handlung des *Silmarillion* und des *Herrn der Ringe*. Die saubere Unterteilung historischer Epochen durch eine Abfolge von Kriegen – der Krieg des Zorns, das Letzte Bündnis, der Ringkrieg – kann als Versuch gesehen werden, den Krieg durch eine fiktionale Erzählung einzugrenzen. Aber dadurch, dass Tolkiens Werke den Krieg als Strukturmittel verwenden, machen sie sich gleichzeitig davon abhängig: Mittelerde braucht den Krieg, um als kohärente Sekundärwelt zu funktionieren – eine Welt ohne den Krieg ist unvorstellbar.

Die Fragmentierung und Desorientierung, die durch den Krieg ausgelöst werden, erscheinen auch in der gebrochenen und diskontinuierlichen Form vieler moderner Texte und sind auch in Tolkiens Meisterwerk zu erkennen. Während der Rückzug in eine fantastische Welt als Versuch gewertet werden kann, eine narrative Kohärenz zu bewahren, die in realistischer Fiktion nicht mehr möglich ist, resultiert die Abhängigkeit der Erzählung vom Krieg dennoch in einer brüchigen, unvollständigen Form. Die Menge an »historischen« Dokumenten, die den Hauptteil des Buches umgibt, impliziert, dass die Erzählung ohne sie nicht zu verstehen ist; aber sie selbst sind unvollständig, durch den Krieg zerstört. Letztlich zeigt *Der Herr der Ringe* als fragmentierter und gebrochener Text das Wesen des Krieges als unkontrollierbar und uneindämmbar auf.

Der Krieg scheint in der modernen Fantasy allgegenwärtig. G.K. Chesterton beschreibt die Märchenwelt als eine Welt von Wundern und gleichzeitig von Kriegen (»fairyland is at once a world of wonder and of war«), und Verlyn Flieger behauptet in *A Question of Time*, dass Faërie und Krieg eine gewisse Ähnlichkeit besitzen (»War and Faërie have a certain resemblance to one another«). Die Überlegung liegt nahe, ob Fantasy als Genre in den Krieg investieren muss, um überhaupt zu bestehen; gleichzeitig versucht es, die Verantwortung dafür zu vermeiden, indem es seine Kriege in eine Sekundärwelt verschiebt. Tolkien als ein Gründervater der modernen Fantasy ist einer der Ersten, die diese Strategie wählen, aber er ist bestimmt nicht der Letzte.

Die Legenden des Trojanischen Krieges bei J.R.R. Tolkien
Guglielmo Spirito OFM

Gleichwohl nicht bestritten werden kann, dass Tolkien den Großteil seines *Legendariums* auf nordische Literatur gegründet und dabei vor allem angelsächsischen, altnordischen, germanischen und finnischen Quellen den Vorrang gegeben hat, sollte dieser überall vorhandene Einfluss nicht dazu verleiten, unsere Aufmerksamkeit von anderem inspirierenden Material abzulenken, das in gewisser Weise von nicht geringerer Bedeutung ist.

Eines davon sind die Legenden des Trojanischen Krieges, die in der westlichen – und englischen – Kultur nicht nur in ihrer homerischen ›klassischen‹ Form verwurzelt sind, sondern auch – und besonders – durch ihre mittelalterliche Rezeption und Transformation. Material und Einflüsse aus den Zyklen des Trojanischen Krieges (von vor Homer bis zu Chaucer und über ihn hinaus) können an zahlreichen Stellen in Tolkiens Werk ausgemacht werden. In diesem Beitrag werden einige Hinweise auf diese gewöhnlich uneingestandene Präsenz gegeben.

Summaries of the German Essays

Is there Power without Violence?
Thomas Fornet-Ponse

The relationship between governmental power and violence with its question of legitimating governmental power over individuals, the necessity of monopoly of force, etc. is one of the most important topics of political philosophy. This paper addresses this issue in Tolkien's work by examining the 'constitutions' of the Shire, Gondor, and Rohan; the relationship between 'state' and individual in these countries; the Istari as cases of great personal power; Eru, Ainur and the Children of Ilúvatar as exampled of an ontologically grounded power structure; and finally Tal-Elmar as an instance for colonialisation.

The analysis shows that in Tolkien's work there is an implicit connexion of power and violence since he did not describe a Utopian political system that has no need of a monopoly of force. Furthermore, in Gondor and Rohan, the law established by the monarchs is valid not only for the subjects, but for all persons in their country, even if only temporarily. An important element which is present in all analysed texts is the temptation to rule over other persons instead of helping them – which is also the root of war. While the Valar and especially Aragorn do not succumb to this temptation, there are numerous counterexamples like Melkor, Sauron, Saruman, Denethor, etc.

According to Tolkien, wise people use their power for the benevolence of others; they counsel and help without wishing to exert their power beyond certain limits.

Violence and the Depiction of Violence in Tolkien's Output in Comparison to Contemporary Theories of Violence and Aggression
Friedhelm Schneidewind

There are frequent discussions on whether and how much Tolkien's portrayal of war and violence was influenced by his personal experiences or by political and social events. It is equally interesting to analyse to what extent common ideas of man's behaviour in his time influenced his work. Here we have to consider two basic theories of aggression and aggressiveness prevalent then and now: The idea that aggressiveness/aggression is based on instinct(s) and the assumption that aggressiveness is a reactive behaviour, e.g. a reaction to intrinsic and extrinsic reasons or stimuli. After presenting the most important theories and models, the essay shows that Tolkien's work clearly reflects one of the prevailing main tendencies. Wherever we look at Tolkien's texts, we will always find a modern depiction of aggression and aggressiveness as a reaction towards personal and/or familial, or social situations or threats. In *The Lord of the Rings* and other of Tolkien's writings, we find not only "... an almost modern and very humane understanding of ethics..." (Frank Weinreich), but also a modern understanding of aggression and aggressiveness.

The Minstrels' War: Song and Power in J.R.R. Tolkien's Middle-earth
Julian Tim Morton Eilmann

In the tale "Of Beren and Lúthien", which is of central importance for the narrative of the *Silmarillion*, Tolkien depicts a fight between Felagund and Sauron. Astonishingly, the antagonists do not fight with the help of arms, but with poetry and song. *The Lord of the Rings* also includes scenes in which characters do battle with magical songs, e.g. the strife between Tom Bombadil and Old Man Willow or the barrow-wight. Tolkien introduces the reader to the term "songs of power" for tunes that are used in this way as instruments of conflict. Starting from this observation, this essay analyses the relation between song and power in greater detail, thus illuminating the problem of art and magic which is crucial for Tolkien's poetology.

With a precise interpretation of the usage of "songs of power" in the middle-earth mythology and a comparison with Tolkien's poetological concept of "sub-creation" as presented in *On Fairy-Stories*, this article makes clear that the term "songs of power" indicates an aesthetic as well as ethic question: On the one hand, the word "song" is positively associated in Tolkien's texts with art, (Elvish) enchantment, aesthetics, and poetry. The term "power", on the other hand, refers to the semantic field of negative words like domination, bewitchment and greed. Tolkien's differentiation of magic and art culminates in the notion that Elvish enchantment "is artistic in desire and purpose" and only used "for specific beneficent purposes", while the magician is characterized by his egocentric lust and the intention to "terrify and subjugate" other beings. Considering the fact that "songs of power" have the potential of controlling other free wills, a middle-earth singer is faced with the ethical question whether the utilisation of his enchanting power in form of magical songs is appropriate for conflict situations.

In this context, the essay points to similarities between the character of Lúthien Tinúviel and the sirens of Greek and Roman mythology. As the *Silmarillion* indicates, Lúthien shares with the sirens uttermost physical beauty and mastery in "songs of power", an aspect that is present in the whole tale. Her and other protagonists' songs are used as sleep spells; however, in this case the moral disposition of the singer is crucial as well.

Altogether, the problem of an adequate use of "songs of power" refers to the heart of Tolkien's poetology, which deals with the importance of the creative potential for the human being. Tolkien emphasises the fundamental artistic desire and power of the individual in all his poetological and fictional texts and ultimately declares it a human right. Considering this Tolkien's poetic work can be understood not only as a defence of poetic imagination, but an apologia of art itself.

Courtly Acteurs and Heroic Violence in Tolkien's *Farmer Giles of Ham*
Patrick Brückner

Farmer Giles of Ham – undoubtedly – is a comic text. Its specific relevance, however, is rooted in the way this comic effect is generated, i.e., in the manner Tolkien's text juxtaposes and commingles divergent concepts of courtly and heroic violence. Consequently, one must refrain from reducing *Farmer Giles of Ham* to its comic passages alone. Its very violence – or rather the dialectic process it describes – represents a Tolkienian construction of heroic history, which is bound irrevocably to heroic prowess.

"contraria contrariis curantur": Healing Diseases as a Battle in Tolkien's *The Lord of the Rings*
Petra Zimmermann

This article focuses on the nature of disease and healing in Tolkien's Middle-earth. Using the example of the Hobbits, it can be shown that being ill is not part of their everyday experience, but that illnesses only gain major importance during the War of the Ring. Diseases are elicited by disharmonies of inner or outer origin, a weakness of the inner harmony allowing an outer disharmony to invade a person's body. The Black Breath, a deadly sickness spread by the Ringwraiths, is an example of a disease with an outer origin. In this context, Tolkien refers to demonological concepts from the Middle Ages, in which diseases are believed to be caused by flying venom.

Tolkien assigns the curing of diseases mainly to the future king, Aragorn, thus referring to the connection between 'healing' and 'kingship' that are deeply rooted in the medieval world of ideas. Aragorn's healing method is based on the Hippocratic guideline of fighting against an illness by applying its contrary (*contraria contrariis curantur*). This concept of fight forms the link between Aragorn's healing capacities and his skills as a captain of war: the healing hands are simultaneously instruments wielding a sword.

The principle of contrariness in healing diseases can be found on several levels:

1) The physical level: sensations of coldness, which are a symptom of the Black Breath, are relieved by the application of heat.

2) The partly phytotherapeutical, partly magical level: the fragrant herb Athelas is used as a remedy against the foul influence of the Black Breath.

3) The energetic-spiritual level: Aragorn's healing hands fight against destructive forces of the enemy, using magical rituals during the healing process.

4) The metaphysical level: Aragorn's healing skills fail in view of Frodo's exceptional sufferings. Only by being granted the opportunity to leave Middle-earth and to find a temporary refuge in Aman Frodo can hope for a complete cure of his wounding. In his case, healing can neither be achieved by medical nor by magical means, but gains a transcendental dimension.

Rezensionen/Reviews

Adam Lam, Nataliya Oryshchuk (eds.): How We Became Middle-earth. A Collection of Essays on *The Lord of the Rings*

(Cormarë Series 13), Zurich/Jena: Walking Tree Publishers, 2007, 432 pp., Softcover

Harriet Margolis, Sean Cubitt, Barry King, Thierry Jutel (eds.): Studying the Event Film *The Lord of the Rings*

Manchester, New York: Manchester University Press, 2008, 358 pp., Hardcover

Knapp sechs Jahre nach dem letzten Teil des weltweiten New-Line-Blockbusters *The Lord of the Rings* (2001-2003) sind die akademischen Nachbeben noch immer mit schöner Regelmäßigkeit zu beobachten. Abgesehen von unzähligen Aufsätzen in wissenschaftlichen Online- und Print-Zeitschriften sind allein im deutsch- und englischsprachigen Raum bisher vier umfassende, monografisch angelegte Studien zum Gesamtphänomen des New-Line-Franchise erschienen. Hinzu kommen etwa ein halbes Dutzend Sammelbände, die sich mit der Analyse der Filme, ihrer Produktion, der cross-medialen Vermarktung bzw. Verwertung, ihrer globalen Rezeption und – vor allem – ihrem Status als Verfilmungen eines der populärsten Romanwerke des 20. Jahrhunderts befassen.

Als von den Filmen selbst prominent ins Bild gerückter Drehort und real existierender geografischer Brennpunkt der mit der Welt J.R.R. Tolkiens und Peter Jacksons verbundenen Fantasien der Fangemeinde rückt neuerdings Neuseeland zunehmend ins Zentrum der Beschäftigung mit den kulturellen Folgen des Medienphänomens. Der Sammelband *How We Became Middle-earth*, herausgegeben von den beiden an der Universität von Canterbury (Christchurch, Neuseeland) lehrenden Kulturwissenschaftlern Adam Lam und Nataliya Oryshchuk, nimmt seine Perspektive auf die von den Filmen gezeitigten Veränderungen in der Wahrnehmung Neuseelands ganz bewusst im Schnittpunkt zwischen wissenschaftlicher Reflexion und persönlicher Erfahrung der einzelnen Autoren ein. So stehen »harte« Forschungsdaten wie die Umfrageergebnisse über das Neuseelandbild beim internationalen Trilogie-Filmpublikum, gewonnen im Rahmen des International *The Lord of the Rings* Audience Research Project (2003-2004) von Martin Barker und Ernest Mathijs, oder die Diskursanalyse der Fan-Nutzung von Internet-Ressourcen (Robin Anne Reid) neben subjektiven Berichten über eigene Besuche der Drehorte (Lynette R. Porter, Lisa Wong), entsprechenden Fotoessays (Bill J. Jerome) oder einer kritischen Würdigung der Computerspiele aus dem persönlichen Spielerlebnis eines Vaters und seines 13-jährigen Sohnes heraus (Kenneth und Simon Henshall). Diese Durchmischung der Reflexionsebenen kann zwischen den einzelnen Beiträgen, zuweilen auch innerhalb eines Beitrags, zu abrupten Wechseln in der Form der Argumentation führen, sie ist von den Herausgebern jedoch durchaus beabsichtigt. Dies wird bereits im ersten Teil des Buches signalisiert, in dem sich die Beiträger nicht nur mit ihren akademischen oder außerakademischen Tätigkeiten vorstellen, sondern auch Einblick in ihre individuellen Lektürebiografien gewähren und sich in der Mehrzahl als Fans von Tolkiens Trilogie wie auch der Verfilmungen von Peter Jackson zu erkennen geben.

Beeindruckend in der Gesamtschau ist einerseits die Breite der Gegenstände, die in *How We Became Middle-earth* in den Blick genommen werden (sie reichen vom literarischen Werk Tolkiens über die Kino- und DVD-Fassungen der Filme bis hin zu Websites, Computerspielen, touristischen Theme Tours und den alle Aktivitäten und Medienprodukte verbindenden Fanpraktiken), und andererseits die Vielfalt der theoretischen Kontexte und methodischen Herangehensweisen, die neben literatur- und kommunikationswissenschaftlichen, postkolonialistischen, feministischen, ideologie- und ökologiekritischen Ansätzen auch kulturgeografisch, camusianisch-existentialistisch und zenbuddhistisch inspirierte Lektüren umfasst. Der aus diesem bunten Kaleidoskop entstehende Eindruck ist zwar notwendig ein gemischter. Er sollte jedoch nicht über zwei Grundlinien hinwegtäuschen, die dem Band am Ende doch eine konzeptionelle Konstanz verleihen und ihm seinen Stellenwert in der Flut der Literatur sichern: Er besteht zunächst in dem allen Beiträgen gemeinsamen Vorgehen, Tolkiens Schriften und Jacksons Verfilmung in Bezug auf Neuseeland als imaginäres Mittelerde der Fans auf einer gemeinsamen diskursiven Ebene anzusetzen ohne vorgeschaltete Bewertungen oder disziplinär begründete Kategorisierungen. Vor allem aber besticht der Sammelband *How We Became Middle-earth* in seinem bisher einzigartigen Versuch, eine Kontinuität zwischen Fandiskurs und wissenschaftlicher Diskussion herzustellen, die den einen in die andere übergehen lässt und in der sich beide wechselseitig erhellen.

Nichts, so möchte man meinen, könnte einem anderen, soeben erst erschienenen Sammelband zum Thema ferner liegen: Bereits seit geraumer Zeit angekündigt, stellt *Studying the Event Film* die jüngste Etappe in der rapide wachsenden film- und medienwissenschaftlichen Auseinandersetzung mit dem

Gegenstand dar. Es ist das erklärte Ziel dieses Sammelbandes, eine studentische und allgemeine Leserschaft am Beispiel von Jacksons *The Lord of the Rings* mit den übergreifenden Eigenschaften des »Event Film«-Phänomens vertraut zu machen (S. 1). Diese Zielsetzung wird von der auch hier eingenommenen, dezidiert neuseeländischen Perspektive leider in hohem Maße konterkariert, die die Zusammensetzung der Beiträger und die inhaltliche Ausrichtung der einzelnen Kapitel deutlich prägt. Obwohl die Organisation des Bandes sichtlich bemüht ist, alle Dimensionen der Medien und Kontinente überschreitenden Produktions-, Vermarktungs- und Rezeptionsgeschichte von New Lines *The Lord of the Rings* abzudecken, findet sich deren gemeinsamer Bezugspunkt doch immer wieder in den konkreten Auswirkungen der Dreharbeiten, Darstellungsstrategien und Rezeptionsformen dieses speziellen »Event Films« auf das kulturelle Selbstverständnis Neuseelands (und insbesondere der Rolle, die dessen Film- und Steuerpolitik in diesem Zusammenhang gespielt haben). Ungeachtet der wertvollen Erkenntnisse, die – wie nicht zuletzt *How We Became Middle-earth* unter Beweis stellt – eine solche »lokale« Perspektive im Einzelfall bietet, scheinen viele der Beobachtungen, Hypothesen und Ergebnisse sich damit nur sehr vermittelt auf eine grundsätzliche Ebene zu heben und auf andere »Event Filme« übertragbar.

Lässt man das akademische Marketing-Manöver einmal außer Acht, den Sammelband als systematisch angelegte, lediglich exemplarisch vorgehende Einführung in das Medienformat des »Event Films« zu positionieren, so ist sein Fokus auf den Produktionsstandort Neuseeland und die dort zu beobachtenden kulturellen Auswirkungen von Peter Jacksons Mammutprojekt durchaus als Stärke und entscheidendes Differenzkriterium gegenüber ähnlich angelegten Untersuchungen wie etwa Kristin Thompsons *The Frodo Franchise: The Lord of the Rings and Modern Hollywood* (2007) zu betrachten. Im Vergleich zur Vielzahl anderer aktueller Studien zum Thema wird der Gebrauchswert des Buches allerdings dadurch zusätzlich eingeschränkt, dass die Arbeit an den einzelnen Beiträgen in der Mehrzahl schon im Frühjahr 2005 abgeschlossen wurde (vgl. S. 20). Auf seitdem entstandene Untersuchungen bzw. Medienprodukte kann also nur punktuell – vor allem im Einleitungskapitel oder einigen der jeder Buchsektion vorangestellten »Dossiers« der Herausgeber – eingegangen werden.

So bleibt am Ende der Eindruck, dass viele der für sich genommen verdienstvollen Analysen und Überlegungen – etwa zur Bedeutung der Computerspiele (Brett Nicholls) und DVD-Versionen (Craig Hight), zum Sound Design (Jo Smith) und zu Howard Shores filmmusikalischem Opernstil (Judith Bernanke), zum paradoxen Realitätseffekt digital generierter visueller Effekte (Sean Cubitt) oder zur Rolle von »Kreativindustrien« im transnationalen Produktionsprozess (Danny Butt) – an anderer Stelle nicht unbedingt geistvoller, jedoch schon umfassender und auch methodisch fundierter angestellt worden sind. Eine der Ausnahmen, die nicht spezifisch auf Neuseeland bezogen sind, bildet in dieser Hinsicht Sean Cubitts und Barry Kings so umsichtige wie kenntnisreiche, dabei äußerst kritischer Diskussion der prekären Stellung des Schauspiels, verstanden im herkömmlichen Sinne einer emotional homogen ausgestalteten, individuell differenzierten Rolleninterpretation. Auf überzeugende Weise wird dargelegt, welch durchgreifenden Transformationsprozess die schauspielerische Figurendarstellung unter den besonderen Bedingungen des ›modularen‹ und in hohem Maße reale und digitale Figuren, Aktionen und Milieus synthetisierenden Herstellungsprozesses von *The Lord of the Rings* durchläuft (S. 111-125).

Mit Blick auf die literarische Vorlage des Blockbusters fällt auf, dass Fragen des vielfältigen Medienwechsels von Tolkiens Roman hin zu den Kino- und Extended-DVD-Fassungen sowie den Adaptionen für Computerspiele und Merchandising-Produkte weitgehend außen vor bleiben. Auch darin unterscheidet sich der Sammelband – jedoch nicht unbedingt zu seinem Vorteil – von bisher, in *How We Became Middle-earth* ebenso wie in Kristin Thompsons Standardwerk *The Frodo Franchise*, stark dominierenden Erklärungsansätzen an die Zugkraft der Verfilmung. *Michael Wedel*

Stratford Caldecott, Thomas Honegger (eds.): Tolkien's *The Lord of the Rings*. Sources of Inspiration.

Zurich/Jena: Walking Tree Publishers, 2008, 237 pp., Paperback

This book bears testimony to a conference which took place at Exeter College, Oxford, in 2006, and which still is the only conference ever held about Tolkien studies at his former college. The outstanding setting led to this conference volume offering articles roughly divided into three major topics: biographical, mythos and modernity, mythos and logos.

John Garth enlarges on his seminal biography *Tolkien and the Great War* with more material from Tolkien's time at Exeter College, concentrating on his student life and the impact of the War on Exeter. He further illustrates creative links of his aspirations as poet and writer with fellow students. Peter Gulliver, Edmund Weiner and Jeremy Marshall are editors for the *Oxford English Dictionary* and follow up on their interesting publication *The Ring of Words* with more examples from the OED archives on how Tolkien worked and how language sparked in him flurries of creative output – not to forget the importance of the correct plural of 'dwarf', i.e. 'dwarves.' Verlyn Flieger rounds off the 'biographical' section with an article on the connection of two of Tolkien's closest friends, Rob Gilson and Geoffrey Smith, who died during World War I with one of his main literary characters, Frodo Baggins. She convincingly likens Frodo's losses to Tolkien's own situation after losing two of his best friends in battle.

Patrick Curry begins the second section (mythos and modernity) by a comparison of the concept of 'enchantment' in *The Lord of the Rings* with Verlyn Flieger's findings in *A Question of time*, Jan Zwicky's dichotomy of the 'lyrical' and 'technological' and Robert Hepburn's idea of 'wonder.' Following Tolkien's elucidation of enchantment in *On Fairy Stories* he makes a good point in saying that neither pure enchantment nor technological exploitation would work for human existence, only a well-balanced equilibrium. Any need for enchantment is given a bitter sweet taste in the realisation that there is a need for it but one may never depend on it. Marek Oziewicz likens Tolkien's own life, career and concept of myth with Italian philologist Giovanni Battista Vico's writings, stating that their recent success lies in their affirmation of the "value of myth and poetic understanding in the construction of human individuals and societies." Peter M. Candler Jr., touches in *Frodo and Zarathustra: Beyond Nihilism in Tolkien and Nietzsche* on different concepts as seen by these two authors who were both philologists but does not quite succeed in providing a coherent argument. Starting off the third section (mythos and logos) Leon Pereira OP posits that Tolkien's own mindset as a Roman-Catholic Christian, his *Weltanschauung*, is at the heart of his writing and that understanding his work is only possible from a theistic point of view. Unfortunately, the Dominican friar does not produce a fully convincing argument. Alison Milbank raises an interesting point in finding close links between Tolkien's own concept of fantasy as exemplified in *On Fairy Stories* and what he called 'Chestertonian fantasy.' Both Chesterton and Tolkien had been influenced by resurgent Thomism in their time and the question as to how creativity also had a religious dimension. Guglielmo Spirito OFM Conv. addresses the image of light in Tolkien's work from the viewpoint of its healing power as it has been described in Roman-Christian theology drawing on an impressive number of diverse resources. The last article is by Stratford Caldecott, organizer of the conference, who tackles the ever fascinating question of 'Tolkien's project', a mythology for his England, by following different lines of tradition such as the Atlantis story, Britain's celtic heritage, and the influence of romanticism on this very English author while always keeping in mind Tolkien's avid Catholicism.

Meeting Priscilla Tolkien, Walter Hooper and Robert Murray SJ in the Rector's very own home during this conference at Exeter College was exceptional and one can only hope that this collection of generally well-conceived articles may provide an inkling of this one-time experience.

Marcel R. Bülles

Jonathan B. Himes, Joe R. Christopher, Salwa Khoddam (eds.): Truths Breathed Through Silver. The Inklings' Moral and Mythopoeic Legacy.

Newcastle: Cambridge Scholars Publishing, 2008, xviii + 160 pp., Hardcover

In diesem Band sind zehn Vorträge und Reden versammelt, die im Laufe einer Dekade (1998-2007) auf den Tagungen der C.S. Lewis & Inklings Society gehalten worden sind. Wie der Titel schon andeutet, liegt der Schwerpunkt auf moralischen und mythopoetischen Fragestellungen bei Lewis, Tolkien und MacDonald, wobei die meisten Beiträge einen deutlich theologischen Akzent tragen (auch wenn sie nicht von Fachtheologen verfasst worden sind). Gleichwohl die Bezugnahme auf die Inklings im Titel insofern etwas irreführend wird, weil MacDonald nicht dazugehörte und Charles Williams und andere bestenfalls am Rand erwähnt werden, bieten die Artikel doch interessante Einsichten und Perspektiven; zudem werden inhaltliche Gemeinsamkeiten sehr deutlich.

Eröffnet wird der Band nach einer Einführung von Jonathan Himes von einem Beitrag von Joe R. Christopher über die drei von C.S. Lewis erläuterten Wege zu Gott – über logische Kategorien bzw. die Vernunft (weil diese jenseits der Natur liege, müsse sie zu einer Heteronatur bzw. Übernatur gehören), über moralische Werte (d.h. naturrechtlich) sowie über die Vision des Transzendenten bzw. die Sehnsucht.

Anschließend untersucht Rolland Hein anhand der drei Autoren, wie Mythen auf Transzendentes verweisen können, indem sie die zentralen Themen des Lebens adressieren und sich somit auch die Weltsicht einer Person verändert. Zudem kommt der Vorstellungskraft eine besondere Rolle zu.
Salwa Khoddam setzt sich in ihrem Beitrag mit *The Magician's Nephew* von C.S. Lewis unter der Fragestellung auseinander, wie sich die Ruinenstadt Charn und der neugeschaffene Garten zu klassischen, biblischen und säkularen Motiven verhält und wie beide als Orte eingesetzt werden, in denen die Reise und Kämpfe der christlichen Seele stattfinden.

Der nächste Beitrag Jonathan Himes' widmet sich mit *The Dark Tower* einem unvollendeten Werk C.S. Lewis' (dessen Verfasserschaft allerdings nicht völlig gesichert ist), das er als (eher misslungene) Allegorie der Lust deutet – was wohl auch ein Grund gewesen sein mag, es nicht zu veröffentlichen; eine ähnliche Thematik habe Lewis in *That Hideous Strength* sehr gelungen verarbeitet.

Es folgt ein Aufsatz von David Oberhelman über eine kurze Geschichte von Bibliotheken in Mittelerde, die mit ihrem Ausgangspunkt in der Oralkultur der Valar über die diversen Verschriftungen und die Rückkehr der elbischen Zivilisation zur Oralkultur im dritten Zeitalter (mit Erinnerungen an die Schriftkultur) zum Aufstieg der Hobbits als den größten Buchproduzenten ähnlich komplex verlaufen sei wie die realweltliche.

Ebenfalls mit Tolkien setzt sich Jason Fisher auseinander, der anhand verschiedener Beispiele das Motiv des »glücklichen Falls« (der *felix culpa*) in Tolkiens *Legendarium* untersucht: Melkors Einführung von Hitze und Kälte, die zu Wolken und Schnee führte; Fëanors ›Fall‹, der großartige Tage im ersten Zeitalter ermöglichte; der Fall der Númenorer, der letztlich die Überwindung Saurons fördert, etc.

Wieder mit Lewis – den *Screwtape Letters* – beschäftigt sich Tom Shippey, der fragt, was Screwtape mit ihrem »philologischen Arm« meine und wie dieser wirke. Korrekt dürfe nicht von Philologen, sondern müsse von Verbiziden gesprochen werden: Denn sie bemühten sich darum, Worten ihre ursprüngliche Bedeutung zu entziehen und sie zu leeren Formeln zu machen – wie Shippey anhand von *life, bourgeois, healthy* etc. erläutert und dabei auch eine Parallele zu George Orwell zieht, der Ähnliches behandele.

Für viele Leser sicherlich überraschend, bespricht David L. Neuhouser in seinem Beitrag, welche Rolle die Mathematik im geistlichen Werdegang MacDonalds spielte – z.B. mit ihrer Schönheit, ihrer Schärfung des Verstandes, der Vorstellungskraft, den Paradoxen, die es ermöglichen, mit religiösen Paradoxen umzugehen, sowie der Parallele zwischen dem Befolgen bekannter mathematischer Gesetze und dem Gehorsam gegenüber Gott.

Im vorletzten Artikel untersucht Kerry Dearborn, wie Lewis, Tolkien und MacDonald in *Out of the Silent Planet, The Fellowship of the Ring, Princess and Curdie* und *The Great Divorce* beschreiben, wie Fremden oder Reisenden mit Offenheit und Liebe begegnet werden kann und wie eine solche Gastfreundschaft auf diese wirkt – als Beispiel kann z.B. die Transformation Gimlis in der Begegnung mit Galadriel genannt werden.

Abgeschlossen wird der Band durch eine »Dinner's Speech« von Thomas Howard, in der er mit autobiographischem Einschlag die drei Autoren als spirituelle Mentoren vorstellt.

Thomas Fornet-Ponse

Jeremy Mark Robinson: J.R.R. Tolkien. The Books, The Films, The Whole Cultural Phenomenon. Including a Scene-by-Scene Analysis of the 2001-2003 *Lord of the Rings* Films.

Maidstone: Crescent Moon Publishers, 2008, 801 pp., Paperback

Angesichts des Vorhabens, in einem umfangreichen Buch »the whole cultural phenomenon J.R.R. Tolkien« kritisch-analytisch zu behandeln, mag ein Leser geneigt sein, über kleinere Ungenauigkeiten in der Lektüre oder thesenartige Behauptungen hinwegzusehen – träten sie nicht in der Häufigkeit auf wie im ersten Teil dieses Buches. Gerade für eine kritische Analyse ist es zudem sehr nachteilig, wenn immer wieder Behauptungen und eigenwillige Deutungen (z.B. Fëanor als fähiger Heerführer, 114) nicht weiter belegt werden. Da eine ausführliche Besprechung sämtlicher Behauptungen angesichts des Pensums wohl kaum möglich war – gleichwohl Robinson an manchen Stellen abschweift und z.B. von Sauron als Werwolf zur Verbindung von Dracula oder Werwölfen zur Menstruation gelangt (151f) –, hätte sich der Autor wohl besser mit einem geringeren Vorhaben begnügt. Denn so hinterlässt er den Leser oft mit Informationen, mit denen wenig anzufangen ist.

Zudem ist die gewählte Sprache großenteils stark umgangssprachlich geprägt und fallen flapsige Bemerkungen wie über die Begegnung der Gefährten mit Galadriel nicht immer positiv auf: »She doesn't invite any of them back to her rooms in the mallorn trees, for instance, for a little brandy, chocolates and backgammon« (116). Noch stärker fällt dieser an Diskussionen in Internetforen erinnernde (und wohl teilweise auch von dort stammende) Stil im der Verfilmung von 2001-2003 gewidmeten Teil auf.

Aufgebaut ist das Buch in drei Sektionen, wobei die erste neben ›klassischen‹ Themen der Tolkienfoschung wie Quellen, Sprache, Religion, einzelnen Figuren auch die ›Tolkien Industry‹ Popmusik, die Beziehung zu *Harry Potter* und *Star Wars* sowie Illustrationen bespricht. Allerdings wird hier eine klare Struktur vermisst, zumal sich der Autor zuweilen von seinen Assoziationen leiten lässt. So endet das Kapitel zu Sprache, Stil und Humor mit folgendem Absatz: »So to typeset *The Lord of the Rings* extra keys were required for accents. It took a careful attention to detail with its many unusual names and references. Then there were the maps.« (57)

Der zweite Teil befasst sich mit *The Lord of the Rings*. Hier wird die Entstehungs- und Publikationsgeschichte sehr ausführlich dargestellt. Der Autor kommt aber auch auf narrative Strategien sowie Ideen und Techniken Tolkiens zu sprechen, wobei auch hier Schwächen in der Deutung auffallen – z.b. deutet er Gandalfs Hinweise auf eine im Hintergrund wirkende höhere Macht als schicksalhafte Bestimmung, die die narrative Spannung aufhebe (307).

Im dritten Teil bietet der Autor sehr viel Informationen über die diversen Verfilmungen und Adaptionen und listet z.b. sämtliche Abweichungen (d.h. Auslassungen, Veränderungen und Hinzufügungen) der Verfilmung von 2001-2003 zum Buch auf, bevor er sich der Analyse der einzelnen Szenen zuwendet. In dieser bemüht er sich deutlich darum, die Filme primär als Filme und nicht als Literaturillustrationen zu untersuchen, womit dies der interessanteste und am ehesten gewinnbringende Teil des Buches sein dürfte, auch wenn Robinson andere Kritiker und ihre Positionen nur sehr selten nennt. So kann er einige Abweichungen zwar als wenig getreu zu Tolkiens Werk, aber als in einem typischen Hollywood-Film funktionierend ansehen – Beispiel: der auf lange redelastige Szenen folgende Wargüberfall in *The Two Towers*. Viele der Abweichungen hält er indes für nicht nötig und darüber hinaus schwach umgesetzt (in *The Return of the King* z.B. die Trennung von Frodo und Sam), weshalb er auch die Filme deutlich kritisiert.

Angesichts der großen methodischen und inhaltlichen Mängel besonders im ersten Teil ist dieses Buch sowohl wenig für Einsteiger als auch in weiten Teilen kaum gewinnbringend für Kenner der Materie. Ausgenommen davon ist am ehesten die Informationsfülle im Bezug auf die Filme und ihre Analyse, wobei auch dies dem Anspruch einer kritischen Analyse nicht völlig gerecht werden und insofern eher als erste Annäherung oder zur Informationsbeschaffung dienen kann.

Thomas Panti

Krisztina Sebők: Roots of Middle-earth Seeds of Fantasy: Mythical and Literary Heritage in *The Lord of the Rings*, and J.R.R. Tolkien's Classic as Fantasy
Saarbrücken: VDM Verlag Dr. Müller, 2008, 66 pp., Softcover

Krisztina Sebők sets out to discover Tolkien's literary roots and attempts to demonstrate why his work can be categorized as fantasy literature. Due to the relative shortness of this volume and the vastness of the subjects suggested by the title it comes as no surprise that she has to narrow the scope of her study by focusing on the character level of *The Lord of the Rings* in the

first part and relying on oversimplification in the second part – a decision that might have been necessary for practical reasons but that does not prove advantageous to the book.
It is needless to say that Sebők is not the first critic to take an interest in the literature that inspired Tolkien in his sub-creation. There are numerous highly original and enlightening investigations into that matter, e.g. the well-known *Road to Middle-earth* or *J.R.R. Tolkien: Author of the Century* by Tom Shippey and Sebők seems to acknowledge their scholarly value; but in her argumentation she relies so heavily on those works that one is inclined to wonder if one's time would not be better invested in consulting those books instead.

In the first part of this book Sebők assures us of the impact that Old Norse mythology, legends and fairy tales – she limits her investigation to the *Elder Edda*, Arthurian legends and Grimm's *Children's and Household Tales* and more or less disregards Tolkien's scholarly contributions to that field of study – had on Tolkien's oeuvre by basically juxtaposing various characteristics of the dwarves, elves, hobbits and Istari that populate Middle-earth with those of similar creatures to be found in the more ancient literature.

In doing so, she unfortunately barely scratches the surface of the literary pieces in question and due to the lack of an elaborate analysis of the characters, connected motifs and their importance for the work as a whole, she can hardly contribute an original thought to the discussion of Tolkien's literary sources.

Sebők begins the second part by naming several characteristics of fantasy literature but without quite giving a coherent and satisfying definition thereof and follows Shippey in his assertion that fantasy is a literary mode rather than a genre. Once that is established, she spots the aforementioned features of fantasy fiction in *The Lord of the Rings* and comes to the unsurprising conclusion that it can indeed be assigned to that mode.

This volume might be informative for interested readers who have only just begun to discover Tolkien's literary work and its far-reaching roots but it can hardly be recommended to those who are looking for an extensive scholarly analysis of the subject. Despite some minor mistakes in grammar and vocabulary – I was surprised to learn that, besides having written Tolkien's biography, Carpenter also wrote his bibliography – it is a quick and easy read, which will hopefully induce those who pick it up to delve deeper into the discussed subject.

Doreen Triebel

Eduardo Segura: Mitopoeia y Mitología. Reflexiones Bajo la Luz Refractada.
Vitoria: Portal Editions, 2008, xxxiv + 333 pp., Paperback

Mit dieser Aufsatzsammlung beginnt der neu gegründete spanische Verlag Portal Editiones sein Verlagsprogramm, das u.a. der Auseinandersetzung mit den Inklings und verwandten Autoren, aber auch der Publikation von Originaltexten dieser Art gewidmet ist. Die insgesamt 14 Beiträge dokumentieren die wissenschaftliche Auseinandersetzung Eduardo Seguras mit J.R.R. Tolkien der letzten Jahre. Die meisten sind schon an anderen Orten publiziert worden, nun aber gesammelt (und leichter) zugänglich.

Sein Anliegen ist es, die These zu erläutern, Tolkien sei ein Mythopoet (im Sinne seines Gedichts *Mythopoeia*) gewesen, und dem Leser dabei zu helfen, die ästhetischen, philosophischen und literarischen Schlüssel zu verstehen, die die außerordentliche Anziehungskraft der Tolkien'schen Zweitschöpfung begründen. Dieser eher einführende Charakter der ursprünglichen Aufsätze und Vorträge entstammt auch den Entstehungsbedingungen, da die meisten für ein breiteres Publikum verfasst wurden. Dementsprechend diskutiert Segura weniger verschiedene Positionen der Sekundärliteratur zu den behandelten Oberthemen, sondern stellt Tolkiens Überlegungen (vor allem in *Mythopoeia* und *On Fairy-Stories*) in den Vordergrund; beim theoretischen Hintergrund verweist er zudem des Öfteren auf G.K. Chesterton, C.S. Lewis und O. Barfield.

Gerahmt von einer Einführung und einem Nachwort teilen sich die Beiträge der Sammlung in folgende Themenbereiche auf, jeder mit einer speziell für diesen Band verfassten Einleitung:

Zunächst widmet sich Segura dem Charakter von Erzählungen und besonders von Märchen, wobei er zunächst den Leser bzw. Adressaten der Werke Tolkiens in den Blick nimmt (inklusive der hierfür bedeutenden Frage der Verbindung zwischen Realität und möglichen Welten) und anschließend die Positionen Tolkiens und Chestertons zu Märchen skizziert.

Im zweiten Teil behandeln vier Artikel die von Segura in Anlehnung an Tolkien ›Mythopoeia‹ genannte Kunst, Geschichten zu erzählen. Darunter fallen Überlegungen zur schöpferischen Vorstellungskraft, Tolkiens Umgang mit Worten bzw. sein Charakter als Philologe (!), eine ausführliche Reflexion über Wörter und die Verbindung von Leben und Erzählungen anhand des Gedichts *Mythopoeia* sowie über die Verbindung von Wahrheit, Mythos und Welt.

Der nächste Teil setzt sich mit der zweitschöpferischen Praxis Tolkiens auseinander, d.h. mit einzelnen Werken. Sehr ausführlich (allerdings nicht ganz so wie in seiner in *Hither Shore* 3 besprochenen Dissertation) bespricht er die Entwicklung der Erzählerstimme Tolkiens vom *Hobbit* bis zum *Lord of the Rings*; dann die Bedeutung der Freundschaft jenseits aller Hoffnung im *Lord of the Rings*; ferner führt er in die *Unfinished Tales* ein; schließlich nähert er sich angesichts der Fragen der Ästhetik und der Gabe in *Leaf by Niggle* der Poetik (nicht Poesie!) Tolkiens an.

Der letzte Teil ist mit vier Beiträgen der cinematographischen Umsetzung bzw. Adaption des Tolkien'schen Werkes durch Peter Jackson gewidmet: Segura zeigt sehr deutlich die Möglichkeiten und Unmöglichkeiten eines solchen Unterfangens (besonders in der Postmoderne) auf und bemüht hierfür das Konzept der Transposition. Auf diese Weise kann er Kritik an den Filmen relativieren, ohne deswegen seine Kritik z.B. an den Figurenzeichnungen zu verschweigen.

Der Epilog ist insofern bemerkenswert, als Segura hier erläutert, inwiefern diese Aufsatzsammlung eine Etappe seines intellektuellen Werdegangs abschließt und welchen Themen er sich in Zukunft zuwenden will: zum einen einer tieferen Auseinandersetzung mit der Philosophie der Kunst auf der Basis der Poetik Tolkiens und zum anderen der Untersuchung einiger bislang in der Literaturgeschichte und komparativen Literaturwissenschaft kaum beachteter Aspekte des Lebens und Werkes einiger Autoren der Inklings.

Segura bietet mit dieser Aufsatzsammlung eine gut lesbare und sehr hilfreiche Einführung in Tolkiens Werk und in seinen Charakter als Mythopoet. Gleichwohl er damit kein völliges Neuland betritt (dies aber im Blick auf den einführenden Charakter der Beiträge auch gar nicht beansprucht), zeugen seine Ausführungen von einem hohen Verständnis des besonderen Charakters des Schaffens Tolkiens und können daher auch jenen Lesern empfohlen werden, die sich schon länger mit ebendiesen Fragen beschäftigt haben.

Thomas Fornet-Ponse

Gregory Bassham, Eric Bronson: *Der Herr der Ringe* und die Philosophie. Klüger werden mit dem beliebtesten Buch der Welt.
Stuttgart: Klett-Cotta, 2009, 288 Seiten, Hardcover

Bei dem amerikanischen Verlag Open Court, Chicago, erscheint eine Reihe namens *Popular Culture and Philosophy*, die zeitgenössische Erscheinungen – meist Bücher, Filme oder Fernsehsendungen und deren Autorinnen/Autoren, aber auch schon einmal durchaus das Baseballspiel als solches – in einen philosophischen Kontext stellt und mit den Methoden der Philosophie untersucht, interpretiert und Bezüge zu philosophischen Lehren herstellt.

Das ist beispielsweise für die Fernsehserie *Buffy – the Vampire Slayer* und die *Matrix*-Filmtrilogie gut gelungen. Dieser Erfolg liegt an den Autoren, die für diese immer als Sammelbände angelegten Bücher gewonnen werden konnten, aber auch daran, dass das jeweilige Thema erst neu erschlossen wurde.

Der Herr der Ringe bietet sich natürlich im Besonderen dafür an, ihn in Verbindung mit Philosophie zu setzen. Allerdings ist die Ringerzählung im Gegensatz zu *Matrix* und *Buffy* eine von der Sekundärliteratur außerordentlich gut ausgeleuchtete Materie, bei der man also sehr gespannt sein darf, was da philosophisch Neues herauszuholen ist. Und es stecken sicher noch viele Themen in Mittelerde, die man genauer betrachten kann, so dass der Rezensent den Sammelband mit Spannung erwartete. *Der Herr der Ringe und die Philosophie* beleuchtet allerdings nichts Neues, so dass dieses Buch sicherlich keine Pflichtlektüre für den Tolkienkenner darstellt.

Die Anthologie umfasst abzüglich Vorwort 13 Artikel von elf Autoren und zwei Autorinnen. Es lohnt nicht, jeden Beitrag einzeln zu behandeln, weshalb ich nur aufzähle, dass Eric Katz über Moral in Mittelerde im Vergleich zur platonischen Philosophie schreibt; sich Theodore Schick mit Technik und Technologie befasst; Alison Milbank den Ring als Objekt der Begierde beschreibt und ihn auf diese Weise mit Moralität verbindet; Gregory Bassham untersucht, wie Tolkien Glück und Lebenssinn darstellt; Eric Bronson die Elben denkwürdigerweise als Existenzialisten vorstellt; Douglas K. Blunt die Hobbits als nicht-nietzscheanische Personen entdeckt; Scott A. Davison eine für den Anspruch äußerst knappe Darstellung von Gut und Böse bei Tolkien gibt; Aeon J. Skoble erstaunlicherweise über Sünde und Tugend redet, ohne Tolkiens viele nichtfiktionale Äußerungen dazu auch nur zu erwähnen; Bill Davis sich ganz interessant über Tod und Unsterblichkeit bei Tolkien auslässt; Joe Kraus, sekundärliteraturfrei, über Tolkiens Schwierigkeiten mit der Moderne spricht; Andrew Light dem Thema Umwelt ein paar Seiten widmet; Thomas Hibbs ein wenig über Willensfreiheit spekuliert und J. Lenore Wright sich dem Motiv des Reisens als Reise durch das Leben widmet. Dass drei Beiträge aus dem englischen Original fehlen, schmerzt nicht (es wundert nur, dass deren Beiträger im Vorwort, S. 10, noch mitgezählt werden, was nicht für die Sorgfalt spricht, mit der das Buch zusammengestellt wurde). Statt der fehlenden Beiträge gibt es noch acht Seiten mit Zitaten bekannter Philosophen, die in der Originalanthologie nicht stehen und deren Sinn sich dem Leser auch nicht erschließt, denn mit Mittelerde haben sie nichts zu tun.

Pauschalieren soll man ja möglichst nicht, aber in diesem Fall geht es, denn die Artikel sind von gleichartigem Niveau. Die Beiträge sind von Profis verfasst und so gut geschrieben, dass man ihnen auch ohne philosophische Vorbildung gut folgen kann. Das liegt aber sicherlich auch daran, dass sie sich auf einführendem Niveau bewegen, das man auch in der Mittelstufe als Lektüre verwenden könnte. Dies jedoch in pädagogischer Hinsicht nur sehr bedingt, da die Sichtweisen durchweg arg verkürzt sind und ihren Themen über weite

Strecken nicht gerecht werden. Der Platonbeitrag etwa referiert das Gleichnis vom Ring des Gyges und schließt daraus, dass auch der Eine Ring besser nicht verwendet werden sollte, weil er korrumpiert. Das stimmt natürlich, lässt aber so viele Möglichkeiten aus, dass es schmerzt.

Wenn man schon Platon und Tolkien hinsichtlich ihrer ethischen Ansichten vergleicht, so wäre es ungleich wichtiger gewesen, auf die in Tolkiens christlicher Überzeugung wurzelnde Individualität von Moral einzugehen und diese der Kollektivmoral bei Platon kontrastierend gegenüberzustellen. Eine Kollektivmoral, die natürlich in der Ideenlehre wurzelt, die ihrerseits aber – man muss gar nicht nur von Moral bei Platon reden! – einen faszinierenden Einfluss auf Tolkien gehabt hat. So hätte man einen Zirkel erhalten, der die Gesamtheit Mittelerdes dem einflussreichsten Philosophen der menschlichen Geschichte gegenübergestellt hätte. Stattdessen nur Gyges. Schade.

Ähnliches gilt für die anderen Beiträge, deren Themen von anderen Autorinnen und Autoren seit Jahren durchweg ertragreicher behandelt werden. Wenn denn überhaupt Mittelerde im Fokus stand – Theodor Schicks Technikbeitrag etwa ist spannende Science-Fiction-Thematisierung, aber der Tolkienpart wirkt seltsam angeklatscht, als sei Mittelerde nun wirklich nicht des Autors eigentliches Interesse. Diese Kritik gilt auch, wenn man dem Umstand Rechnung trägt, dass es sich um eine Anthologie handelt, die naturgemäß große Themen auf viel zu engem Raum zu behandeln hat. Die Anthologien von *Walking Tree Publishers* etwa beweisen durchweg, dass so etwas auch auf hohem Niveau geht.

Wer einen ersten Blick hinter die Kulissen des HdR werfen will, um eine Ahnung zu bekommen, welcher Reichtum sich dort verbirgt, bekommt einen gewissen Eindruck davon. Doch bei dem einführenden Niveau der Beiträge in *Der Herr der Ringe und die Philosophie* stellt sich die Frage, ob, wenn man denn in intensivere Betrachtungen Mittelerdes einsteigen will, es nicht lohnendere Einstiege gibt. Und die gibt es. Etwa die ebenfalls bei Klett-Cotta erschienenen Bücher von Tom Shippey *Autor des Jahrhunderts* und *Der Weg nach Mittelerde*, die fast alle der Themen des Sammelbandes auch behandeln, aber mit deutlich mehr Tiefe, unter Einbezug vieler weiterer Aspekte und verfasst von jemandem, der Tolkiens Werk ausgewiesenermaßen bestens kennt.

Was bezüglich der Werkkenntnis seitens der Autoren des Sammelbandes auffällt, ist, dass diese zwar Philosophieprofis mit universitärem Hintergrund sind, sie aber im Bereich der Tolkienforschung sich bisher kaum publizierend hervorgetan haben. Da hätte die/der eine oder andere durch Tolkienpublikationen ausgewiesene Fachfrau/Fachmann die bessere Wahl dargestellt. Der Eindruck mangelnder Tolkienexpertise entspringt aber nicht nur geringer Bekanntheit in der Tolkienforschung, sondern vor allem dem Umstand, dass die zitierte Literatur von barer Unkenntnis der Forschungslage zeugt.

So wird einmal Shippey zitiert, und es gibt ein Zitat aus *Tolkien's Art* von Jane Chance. Keine Verlyn Flieger, kein Patrick Curry, kein Matthew Dickerson (deren wichtigste Bücher waren 2003, als das englische Original erschien, alle schon erhältlich). Und Tolkien selbst kommt auch kaum zu Wort, denn außerhalb von Nennungen der Ringerzählung, des *Silmarillion* und des *Hobbit* gibt es zusammen eine Handvoll Zitate aus den *Lost Tales*, der *History* und den *Briefen* sowie ein(!) Zitat aus *On Fairy-Stories*, dem philosophischen(!) Werk Tolkiens par excellence. Diese Missachtung der Quellen wie der Forschungsliteratur ist bei einer ernstzunehmenden Anthologie nicht zumutbar.

Ein Wort noch zur Umsetzung des Bandes: Diese ist auf gewohnt hohem Klett-Cotta-Niveau, was die Ausstattung, vor allem aber die gute Übersetzung angeht – es ist nicht nötig, die Artikel im amerikanischen Original zu lesen. Was Klett-Cotta sich da allerdings an Untertitel geleistet hat, ist schon ein bisschen peinlich, gehört es doch von der Diktion her (»Klüger werden mit ...«) eher auf die Beraterseiten einschlägiger Jugendmagazine. Aber vielleicht war das auch beabsichtigt, denn das Niveau ist, wie gesagt, ähnlich jener Periodika.

Für den deutschen Untertitel sind die Herausgeber jedoch nicht verantwortlich, die das Buch im Original mit »One Book to Rule Them all« untertitelten. Wenn aber auch der Untersuchungsgegenstand *Der Herr der Ringe* pfiffig mit »ein Buch, die anderen zu beherrschen« beschrieben wäre, so gilt dies in keiner Weise für den vorliegenden Sammelband, der keine bleibenden Spuren in der Tolkienforschung hinterlassen wird und zu dem es – auch für den interessierten Laien und auch in deutscher Sprache – reichliche Alternativen gibt.

Frank Weinreich

Fabian Geier: J.R.R. Tolkien
Reinbek bei Hamburg: Rowohlt, 2009, 157 Seiten, broschiert

Der letzte Beweis, dass ein Mensch eine unhintergehbare Person der Zeitgeschichte wurde, ist immer dann gegeben, wenn einer der großen Verlage sein Leben der Aufnahme in die hauseigene Biographienreihe für wert befindet. Wie etwa in die Reihe *rowohlts monographien,* die nun auch den Professor bedenkt. Das ist eine weitere schöne Ehre für Tolkien. Wichtiger ist jedoch, dass die Biographie in gute Hände gelegt wird, und das hat der Verlag getan, als er das 150-Seiten-Werk Dr. Fabian Geier überantwortete, der der Aufgabe voll gerecht wurde.

In diesem Zusammenhang sei vorab daran erinnert, was die Aufgabe dieser vergleichsweise dünnen Bände in den entsprechenden Reihen von Junius, Beck oder eben Rowohlt ist: Sie sollen die Porträtierten zuallererst einem noch nicht informierten Publikum auf 100 bis 200 Seiten vorstellen. Unter diesen Umständen sind keine neuen Forschungsergebnisse zu erwarten – ebenso wenig darf man kontroverse oder hochinnovative Standpunkte erwarten oder dass auch nur Raum bestünde, besonders in der Tiefe zu schürfen. Das hat alles seine Berechtigung und ist dem Anlass vollkommen angemessen, doch der Autor der entsprechenden Lebensläufe hat dadurch eben auch nur geringe Möglichkeiten, dem Werk seinen Stempel aufzudrücken.

Und doch gelingt Geier innerhalb dieses engen Rahmens ein informatives und eigenständiges Porträt, das auch der Tolkienkenner mit Gewinn liest. Die Darstellung ist klar und weitestgehend fehlerfrei, die Gewichtung, wo sie denn außerhalb der notwendig zu referierenden Lebensdaten und -umstände gesetzt werden kann, ist klug gewählt und die hinzugezogene Sekundärliteratur deckt die Aufgabe unter Berücksichtigung auch der neueren Erkenntnisse ab. Anzufügen ist, dass das Ergebnis zudem sehr gut geschrieben ist und sich einfach angenehm liest.

Geier geht chronologisch vor und verbindet wie üblich – und sicherlich auch vorgegeben – die biographischen Ereignisse mit der Bedeutung, die sie für das Werk haben könnten. Dabei bewegt Geier sich in plausiblen Bahnen und man hätte sich vielleicht ein wenig mehr Innovation und die eine oder andere neue Idee gewünscht, was in Anbetracht der oben beschriebenen engen Grenzen aber nicht möglich war. Aber seiner Aufgabe einer informativen und neutralen Darstellung wird Geier damit gerecht.

Er stützt sich im Wesentlichen auf die unausweichliche Biographie Carpenters, auf die Briefe sowie auf Aussagen Christopher Tolkiens und bezieht sich für neuere Ergebnisse, vor allem auf Hammond und Scull. Das verbindet er gekonnt und kann so alles unterbringen, was für eine angemessene Vorstellung von Tolkien und seinem Werk nötig ist. Die Literaturliste umfasst auch sonst die meisten wichtigen Werke, und wenn einige fehlen, so ist dies vermutlich nicht Geier anzulasten als vielmehr den Umständen, dass sie erstens nicht nötig waren für das zu Sagende und dass es zweitens keinen Platz gab, ihre Schwerpunkte zu verfolgen.

Interpretationen und Wertungen finden sich nur gering dosiert, wie zu erwarten war; aber wo Geier sie anbringt, sind sie überzeugend. Für den Tolkienkenner bedeutet dies natürlich, dass er wenige Anhaltspunkte für neue Ideen und auch wenige Punkte findet, an denen er sich reiben und entwickeln könnte. Doch auch wer sich bei Tolkien auskennt, findet manch anregende Formulierung, die weiterzuspinnen sich lohnt. Etwa wenn Geier mit wenigen Worten erklärt, warum das Werk inhaltlich abgeschlossen ist: »Der große Bogen ist mit dem Ringkrieg und dem Fortgang der Elben beendet, und ein Zustand ist erreicht, in dem Tolkiens Universum in ein historisches Zeitalter eintritt. Hier lässt sich keine neue Welt mehr aufbauen, sondern man kann nur noch

Geschichten erzählen« (S. 128). Oder wenn er konstatiert, »sicher hat Tolkien die Fantasy nicht erfunden – aber es sagt viel über seine Wirkung aus, dass es heute nicht wenige gibt, die genau das glauben« (S. 137).

Dass und warum das so ist, erklärt Geier, und deshalb ist sein Buch ein Gewinn. Wenn Tolkien also als zeitgeschichtliche Persönlichkeit nun auch von Rowohlt geehrt und anempfohlen wird, so hat der Verlag den Richtigen gefunden, um das angemessen umzusetzen.

Frank Weinreich

Mark T. Hooker: The Hobbitonian Anthology of Articles about J.R.R. Tolkien and his *Legendarium*.
Llyfrawr: CreateSpace, 2009, 268 pp., Paperback

This book is another of Mark T. Hooker's delightful collections of articles on various aspects of Tolkien's works. A few of these are (revised) reprints from older publications, but most of the contents consist of new stuff. As you might expect by now, most are about Hooker's main areas of interest, i.e., name studies and comparative Tolkien translation.

The section on "Names" takes up around one third of the book. With the exception of a few rather short pieces, Hooker usually delves deeply into possibly etymologies or literary sources/analogues for the names in question (among which are Bilbo, Boffin, Farmer Maggot, and Puddifoot), never being afraid of stepping off the beaten path and even introducing the occasional whimsical train of thought. He is fully aware that his analyses in places may run counter to Tolkien's intentions as stated by the man himself, but that never stops Hooker from engaging in his own line of enquiry.

In these "Names" articles, the author displays a thorough knowledge of linguistics, etymology, and history, and is also very well versed with even obscure sources of literature. For instance, Hooker manages to trace the name Bilbo back to a French literary hero by the name of Bilboquet, and that of Tom Bombadil to the sound of the bell in the Tom Tower of Christ Church, Oxford.

Furthermore, Hooker also manages to transfer Tolkien's concepts into other cultural identities, combining this with his intimate knowledge of many Tolkien translations to give us comments about the ways certain names and concepts have been translated, and often improvements aimed at translations that want to localise Tolkien's names.

His article on The Ivy Bush (short but to the point) is an excellent example of this approach: First, there is an explanation of why exactly someone might want to call an inn thusly and then, we get a suggestion at how to arrive at a parallel way of naming that specifically fits German culture. This is excellent work.

The second section is simply called "Many Things." Its aim is to take a closer look at certain linguistic peculiarities of Tolkien's works (like the term "nine days wonder" or the Hundredweight Feast), explain them in their English cultural relevance, and then look at ways of translating them.

Of special interest here is an article on how people are addressing one another in *The Hobbit*, and how this has been handled in various translations, based on the differentiation of the familiar vs. the deferential forms of address in the languages in question. The ensuing study is a must read for any student of comparative Tolkien translation.

Section Three gives a short survey of all Hobbit translations Hooker is familiar with (we're talking Belorussian, Bulgarian, Czech and Slovak, Dutch, German, Polish, Russian, Serbian, and Ukrainian here!), listing things that stand out, obvious mistakes, innovative solutions, and the like. While not of equal use to anyone, this is a valuable repository of sage translatorial advice and comment.

Section Four is somewhat more specialised, dealing with the Russian translations of *Leaf by Niggle*.

All in all, this book is a highly interesting and worthwhile read for anyone interested in speculating about how and why Tolkien used language the way he did, and it is invaluable for someone interested in Tolkien translation. Even if you already know much about these subjects, you are bound to learn quite a few new things and/or find that new vistas for research have opened up for you.

Rainer Nagel

Douglas Charles Kane:
Arda Reconstructed. The Creation of the Published *Silmarillion*.
Bethlehem: Lehigh University Press, 2009, 280 pp., Hardcover

Mit diesem Buch hat sich Douglas Charles Kane einer wichtigen (und großen Fleiß erfordernden) Aufgabe angenommen, nämlich die Entstehung des von Christopher Tolkien und Guy Kay herausgegebenen *The Silmarillion* zu untersuchen. Auch wenn seine Datenbasis nur die *History of Middle-earth* ist und er darüber hinaus keine Archivstudien verfolgt hat (womit es fraglich bleibt, ob er alle relevanten Quellen berücksichtigt hat), sind seine Ergebnisse doch sehr interessant und für weitere Studien ein guter Ausgangspunkt. Sehr deutlich stellt er heraus, welche Passagen von *The Silmarillion* auf welche Texte und Entwicklungsstufen des *Silmarillion*-Komplexes zurückgehen sowie wo und in welchem Umfang Christopher Tolkien als Herausgeber in den Textbestand eingegriffen, d.h. diesen verändert, erweitert oder verkürzt hat.

Schon in seiner Einleitung nennt Kane mehrere Ergebnisse und kritisiert einige Abweichungen Christopher Tolkiens als von den Vorlagen zu stark abweichend, da die erwünschte Konsistenz auch im vorliegenden Text nicht völlig erreicht werden konnte. Sicherlich diskutiert werden kann über die dabei deutlich werdenden Präferenzen Kanes, denn ein stärkerer Einbezug jener Texte mit stark philosophischem Charakter (gerade in *Morgoth's Ring*) hätte möglicherweise nicht eine so breite Leserschaft erreicht.

Die detaillierte Analyse folgt in drei Teilen dem Aufbau des *Silmarillion* (*Ainulindalë* und *Valaquenta*; *Quenta Silmarillion* sowie *Akallabêth*, *Of the Rings of Power and The Third Age* nebst Anhängen), wobei er bezüglich des Kapitels ›Of Maeglin‹ auf die nicht zu ergänzenden Aussagen Christopher Tolkiens in *War of the Jewels* verweist. Zu jedem besprochenen Kapitel gibt der Verfasser zunächst die Hauptquellen an (auch tabellarisch dargestellt), nennt die wichtigsten Abweichungen und äußert zuweilen Vermutungen über deren Motivation. Sehr deutlich wird dabei, an welchen Stellen Christopher Tolkien eingreifen musste, um verschiedene Quellen zu einer durchgehenden Narrative zu verbinden, wobei auch die scheinbar ohne Not – und für viele sicherlich in überraschendem Umfang – gemachten Abweichungen, z.B. Verschiebungen von Teilen der *Ainulindalë* in ein anderes Kapitel, klar benannt werden.

Während diese Arbeit von großer Hilfe als Materialsammlung für weitere Untersuchungen sein könnte, verbleibt seine verschiedentlich geäußerte Kritik an den Entscheidungen Christopher Tolkiens zuweilen recht thetisch sowie sehr subjektiv und hätte von einer gründlicheren Ausarbeitung profitiert.

Sehr schön wäre es zudem gewesen, wenn Kane die von ihm herausgearbeiteten durchgängigen Veränderungen detaillierter dargestellt hätte: So sei die Rolle von mindestens acht weiblichen Charakteren durch editorische Entscheidungen geringer geworden; seien philosophische Überlegungen im Vergleich zu den Quellen unterrepräsentiert, seien einerseits wichtige Teile der Geschichte komprimiert worden und andererseits sei die Geschichte über den Untergang Doriaths größtenteils neu geschaffen worden sowie der narrative Kontext aufgegeben worden, wonach *The Silmarillion* als Kompilation verschiedener menschlicher und elbischer Quellen erschienen wäre. Schließlich sei das Nettoergebnis der zahlreichen kleineren sprachlichen Veränderungen »a work with language that is significantly different than that used by the author« (262). Auch dies wäre weiterzuverfolgen.

Thomas Panti

Alex Lewis, Elizabeth Currie: The Epic Realm of Tolkien. Beren and Lúthien.

Moreton-in-the Marsh, Gloucestershire: ADC Books, 2009, 232 pp., Softcover

Here we go again – as in their previous books (especially *The Forsaken Realm of Tolkien*), the authors explore Tolkien's indebtedness to various (medieval) sources, with special focus on the tale of Beren and Lúthien (other tales will be the subject of two more books announced). Before we discuss the content, maybe a few comments on the presentation and layout of the text.

The cover-illustration is once more a nice ornament by Ruth Lacon (aka Elizabeth Currie), in the style which has become the hallmark of the series. The layout of the text is in line with that of the two other books by the same authors. These two volumes had been self-published by Lewis and Currie, which means the books had not gone through the usual copy-editing processes. Viewed from a professional point of view, the layout is in dire need of improvement. Thus, we find bold print and underlining for titles and subtitles, which is a no-no in professional printing. Indentation of the paragraphs is erratic, as is the marking of book titles by means of italics (or not). Longer quotes are not set off, nor are they marked by a different font-size. The indication of sources immediately after the quotes is correct but would profit from using an internationally accepted format such as that of the MLA.

On the other side, the layout as it is mirrors to some extent the content of the book itself. It, too, would have profited from some critical copy-editing and proofreading. To put it bluntly: Lewis and Currie attempt to argue that the tale of *Culhwch and Olwen* and the tale of *Perceval* (in its various versions) as well as some other Arthurian legends provided Tolkien with the underlying blueprint for his tale of Beren and Lúthien (in its different forms).

The authors argue on the level of general parallels of plot, but also by means of parallels between names – thus constructing a case for Tolkien's indebtedness to the Celtic/Arthurian tradition. The method is the same as in *The Forsaken Realm of Tolkien*, where they were arguing for the story of Troy to provide the blueprint for Tolkien's tale of *The Fall of Gondolin*; and the mistakes and weaknesses are also the same.

Firstly, many of the common plot elements identified are also to be found in many other folk-tales – a brief look into Antti Aarne and Stith Thompson's list of structural elements of folk-tales will prove, if you are inclined to believe so, Tolkien's indebtedness to Inuit, Papuan, Chinese, Japanese etc. folk-tales, all of which share the same motifs. Malory's *magnum opus* is a veritable treasure-cove for almost anything you need. Tolkien, of course, knew the medieval texts analysed by the authors – but he also knew a lot of other stories and tales and the ingredients of his 'cauldron of stories' do not come from one or two sources only, but rather from the 'decomposed' elements found in the fertile humus of his imagination, which had been fed by a plethora of texts. It is, on this level, rather pointless to go looking for 'sources'.

Secondly, the etymological relationship between the names in Tolkien and in some of the sources may be due rather to their common 'Celtic' background than to Tolkien's specific use of a tale. Thirdly, the authors rely too much on translations, summaries and encyclopaedia entries, often without consulting the primary texts.

Lastly, they are not up-to-date concerning scholarship even in the area of their expertise. Discussing Beren and Lúthien's disguise as vampire-bat and werewolf, they correctly point to the Middle English romance *William of Palerne* – yet fail to refer to or even mention (sorry for blowing my own trumpet) my article on exactly this point. The fact that this article was published in the one and only international academic journal on Tolkien studies, *Tolkien Studies* 1 (2004), and not in some obscure anthology, makes it even worse. I may hasten to add that I have not taken this oversight personally, but it is symptomatic for the way the authors treat secondary literature.

To sum up: the study is a rather misguided and to my mind pointless exercise in reading the story of Beren and Lúthien as a creative 're-writing' of *Culhwch and Olwen* (plus some elements from *Perceval* and other Celtic/Arthurian tales).

And whereas it is likely that Tolkien's attempts at 'framing' his tales take up ideas found in Geoffrey of Monmouth, the authors ask for some suspension of critical disbelief when they argue that the Ælfwine-figure has a lot in common with Coleridge's mariner in *The Rime of the Ancient Mariner*.

The Forsaken Realm of Tolkien may have given us some new ideas about Tolkien's possible (and as yet neglected) sources. *The Epic Realm of Tolkien* fails to do so this time – and I think the authors would do better to leave it at that rather than publish two more books on the topic. *Thomas Honegger*

John S. Ryan:
Tolkien's View: Windows into his World.
Zurich/Jena: Walking Tree Publishers, 2009,
xv + 286 pp., Softcover

Professor John Ryan is one of an elite, and sadly vanishing, coterie of scholars who actually knew Tolkien, and this close personal association gives him an invaluable vantage point from which to approach Tolkien's work (x). Likewise, Ryan's education and career followed in the blueprint of Tolkien's own, from his "'colonial' nurture" to a "strictly classical education" followed by "a discipline move back to the west of Europe, to the older Germanic languages, and Old English and Old Norse in particular" (loc.cit.). While a student at Merton College, Ryan both studied under Tolkien and interacted with him in "many unplanned and more social meetings…, many walks and pacings together with him around the College Garden" (loc.cit.). In short, he acquired a much better sense of the man, *intra muros*, than many of the scholars of the past four decades have been able to do. He had first-hand exposure to "the Tolkien mental climate" (xiii).

In addition to having known Tolkien personally, Ryan has been one of the most prolific scholars of his work. At the same time, he is one of the least read, mainly because most of his published work is long out of print. That unfortunate situation is largely remedied by a new collection from Walking Tree, published in two volumes (the second to appear in 2010). The present review concerns the first volume only.

While readers' tastes will certainly vary, the material collected here should appeal to a broad range of interests. The essays in the present collection fall into three broad categories. The majority may be categorized as Quellenforschung, or the study of Tolkien's sources. In some cases, Ryan attempts to identify the source(s) of individual words or phrases, as in "Before Puck – the Púkel-men and the *puca*"; while in others, Ryan highlights more general wellsprings of source material. Even better, Ryan points to works often overlooked – e.g., Elizabeth Wright's *Rustic Speech and Folk-Lore* (1913) or William Craigie's *Scandinavian Folk-Lore: Illustrations of the Traditional Beliefs of the Northern Peoples* (1896) – as the "richly veined source[s]" (45) Tolkien mined for his *Legendarium*. He might have added F.J. Child and Thomas Keightley, *inter alia*, but perhaps these folklorists will make an appearance in the volume to come.

Other essays in the collection explore more general critical approaches to Tolkien's fiction. This group contains several important papers, of which the most important may well be the one with the most typographically challenging title: "By 'Significant' Compounding "We Pass Insensibly into the World of the Epic"". This is an insightful look at the prose style of *The Hobbit* in the light of Tolkien's comments in *On Translating Beowulf*, originally written a year or two after *The Hobbit*. Tolkien's prelude to *The Lord of the Rings* is often treated as an immature children's story by comparison to its sequel, but Ryan demonstrates that this such cavalier treatment may be misguided. He collates a wealth of illustrative cases — kennings, epithets, examples of "[t]he compounding habit" (128-129) — in what is even today a pretty novel comparison, one usually reserved for Tolkien's more 'serious' works (e.g., Michael Drout's essay on "Tolkien's Prose Style and its Literary and Rhetorical Effects"). As part of his conclusion, Ryan notes that "concordances would be needed to quantify the relative contextual frequency of compounds in *The Hobbit* as against the … prose style of *The Lord of the Rings*" (127), seeming to call for an extension or addition to Professor Blackwelder's *Tolkien Thesaurus* (published the year before).

Now, of course, Blackwelder's concordance to *The Lord of the Rings* is long out of print, and a concordance to *The Hobbit* is still an unfulfilled desideratum.

The remainder of the essays are of a more biographical nature, collecting facts and dates of Tolkien's education and professional life. One of these, "The Oxford Undergraduate Studies in Early English and Related Languages of J.R.R. Tolkien (1913-1915)", is a very interesting look at Tolkien's undergraduate studies and examinations; while another, "J.R.R. Tolkien: Lexicography and other Early Linguistic Preferences", is perhaps the only extended exploration that has ever been made of Tolkien's three substantial essays for *The Year's Work in English Studies*. These essays will inevitably be treated as raw material for subsequent scholarship, rather than as conclusive on their own. In some cases they have been superseded by the research of others (e.g., Peter Gilliver, *et al.*, Wayne Hammond and Christina Scull).

But even so, they remain valuable for Ryan's intimate knowledge of Oxford, and specifically Merton College (where Tolkien taught from 1945-1959). This institutional knowledge survives in both Ryan's own memory and an impressive collection of university documents, both ably deployed in many of these essays. Ryan turns up and turns over many wonderful resources overlooked by (or unavailable to) scholars today – e.g., contemporary syllabi, examination papers, and other ephemera of Oxford. For one example, from *The Oxford University Gazette*, 9 December 1932: "[t]he chief event of the year was the complete reorganization of the philological section of the Library carried out by Professor Tolkien, Mr C.L. Wrenn and the Assistant Librarian Mr J.L.N. O'Loughlin" (quoted 94). As a side note, Scull and Hammond add that this complete reorganization was completed by January 28 (162-163). Was 1932 really so uneventful that its "chief event" occurred in the first month of the year?

Tolkien's View is well organized and attractively presented, with decorative illustrations by Anke Eißmann and a beautiful cover photograph of Merton Meadows, as viewed from Tolkien former rooms. The book contains a complete bibliography and an index, quite valuable in a collection with such varied and densely packed contents. I have found a few errors – e.g., *IWES* for *YWES* (78), an extraneous footnote (92), and the lecture *On Fairy-Stories* was delivered in 1939, not 1938 (103, *et passim*) – but apart from such occasional slips, the quality of the book is very high. Ryan's style often dips into the inkhorn; I personally find this parts of his charm, but some readers may be put off. Other essays sometimes read more like dense and hasty outlines – in his own words: "treatment [that] is selective and impressionistic" (51).

It is a collection best read in its historical context, as many of Ryan's findings are dated and have been improved on by subsequent scholars; however, Ryan was one of the first (and still one of the few) scholars to dig into the most arcane corners of Tolkien's professional life for evidence of the thinking behind his fiction. Frequently, Ryan calls for further research which has regrettably never come to pass. Today's scholars might well take note of both these points; there is still much to learn from Professor Ryan's example.

Jason Fisher

Works consulted:

Blackwelder, Richard E. *A Tolkien Thesaurus*. Garland Reference Library of The Humanities, Vol. 1326. New York: Garland Publishing, 1990

Drout, Michael D.C. "Tolkien's Prose Style and its Literary and Rhetorical Effects." *Tolkien Studies* 1 (2004): 137-162

Gilliver, Peter, Jeremy Marshall, and E.S.C. Weiner. *The Ring of Words: Tolkien and the Oxford English Dictionary*. Oxford: Oxford University Press, 2006

Scull, Christina and Wayne G. Hammond. *The J.R.R. Tolkien Companion and Guide: Chronology*. Boston: Houghton Mifflin, 2006

Thomas Scholz: Weit entfernte Wunder. Zur Konstruktion von Raum und Zeit in der englischen Fantasyliteratur am Beispiel von J.R.R. Tolkiens *The Hobbit*.

(ALPH 4) Frankfurt am Main: Peter Lang, 2009, 145 pp., Paperback

The size of this slim volume (145 pages) must not be taken as an indicator of its critical value. The first 40 pages or so are dedicated to a discussion of the genre of 'fantasy' and constitute the traditional 'Forschungsüberblick', a typically German academic exercise that aims to demonstrate the author's familiarity with all the existing literature on his topic. Luckily, Scholz does not aim at comprehensiveness and discusses 'only' a selection of important publications that are of relevance for his 'project'.

This 'project', then, is an analysis of *The Hobbit* in view of the three aspects assumed to be typical for the genre of fantasy. The first is the use of atavistic timeframes and Scholz aims at analysing the structure of temporal regression in Tolkien's book. Second comes the question in how far the creation of inner consistency is dependent on secondary history. Third and last, the possibility of a Bakhtinian chronotope for 'fantasy' is explored. These three areas of investigation take up the remainder of the study.

Scholz opens the main section with a discussion of the phenomenon of the dual regress as found in *The Hobbit*. On the one hand, we have a 'time level' in the Shire that is to be equated with rural England in the 18th or 19th centuries. The world outside the Shire, on the other hand, is more indebted to the European Middle Ages – which usually provide the 'time frames' for works of fantasy and could thus be called 'the norm'. Therefore, the use of an 18th/19th-century timeframe asks for an explanation, which Scholz finds in its function as a transitional location, especially for the 'early' readers of *The Hobbit*, who could not yet be expected to be familiar with the later prevalent use of the Middle Ages in fantasy. Similarly, the function of instances of 'linguistic regress' in figures such as the trolls or Gollum are investigated, as well as the general topos of 'degeneration from a Golden Age'.[1]

---

1 Although Scholz's study uses some of the most important secondary sources for his book, he develops his ideas rather independently from the mainstream of Tolkien studies and the specialist is often able to see parallels to existing studies. On the topos of the 'decay from a Golden Age', e.g., see Dirk Vanderbeke's paper 'Language, Lore and Learning in

The use of secondary history, i.e. references to a fictional past of the protagonists or their people, as a means to create inner consistency is the focus of the following (rather short) chapter. Again, it is noticeable that the occurrence of secondary history is uneven and differs greatly from one culture to another. The 'secondary history' of the dwarves, for example, is much more pronounced than that of the hobbits. Scholz is content to point out future areas of research, which is why he calls this chapter 'a promising building site'.

Last comes the question whether it is possible to establish a typical and distinct 'fantasy chronotope' (in the Bakhtinian sense of the word). The author focuses first on the 'adventure time chronotope', which seems to occur in the 'adventures' of Thorin & Co. However, most of the 'adventures' in *The Hobbit* are part of a meaningful sequence of events and thus differ from the Bakhtinian 'adventure time chronotope' which is characterised by randomness of events. Furthermore, Tolkien complements this modified 'adventure time chronotope' by the 'everyday time chronotope' with clear recurrent structures and events (e.g. mealtimes, postal deliveries, etc.). The framing of the central 'adventure time chronotope' by means of the 'everyday time chronotope' at the beginning and end points towards the ritualistic structure of the book with, according to van Gennep, 'separation' – 'liminal period' – 'aggregation' (i.e. return). However, as Scholz correctly points out, the story also presents several chronotypes interacting with each other within the 'liminal period' section. Thus we have the 'adventure time chronotype' of Thorin & Co. intruding upon the 'everyday time chronotype' of those people they 'visit' (Bilbo, trolls, Beorn etc.).

All in all, even though none of Bakhtin's chronotopes really fits the literary structure of *The Hobbit*, and thus of fantasy, it is possible to deduce from the analysis that the 'everyday time chronotope' is applied to signal the reader 'fantasy normality' (however much this may deviate from 'real world normality'), whereas the 'adventure time chronotope' is used to introduce the 'fantasy fantastic'.

As mentioned in the opening paragraph, Scholz's study is relatively short but it contains more stimulating ideas and suggestions for research than many of the thicker books in print. It is a pity that its content is only available in German and it is to be hoped that some of his ideas will find their way into the mainstream of Tolkien studies where they would interact with and complement profitably the approach by Martin Simonson's study of the intertraditional dialogue in *The Lord of the Rings*.[2]

Thomas Honegger

The Lord of the Rings', in Thomas Honegger (ed.), *Reconsidering Tolkien*, Zurich/Berne: Walking Tree Publishers, 2005, 129-151.

[2] Scholz, at the time of writing his book, seemed to have been unaware of Simonson's 2008 book and reached his conclusions independently of Simonson's (often similar or complementary) thoughts on *The Lord of the Rings*.

Pia Skogeman:
Where the Shadows Lie: A Jungian Interpretation of Tolkien's *The Lord of the Rings*.
New York: Chiron Publications, 2009, 232 pp., Paperback

Studies approaching Tolkien's work from a psychoanalytical point of view are rare and few between. There has been, to my knowledge, as yet only one monograph published in English, namely Timothy O'Neill's illuminating and informed *The Individuated Hobbit. Jung, Tolkien and the Archetypes of Middle-earth* (1979), which discusses Tolkien's mythology in a Jungian framework. It is, unfortunately, no longer in print. Pia Skogeman's Jungian interpretation of *The Lord of the Rings* could thus fill a gap.

The book was originally published in Danish in 2004, and has now been translated into English. It is written in an almost jargon-free, easily understandable English – almost too 'easy' for my taste, yet maybe perfect for the main (American) target readership. Although Skogeman introduces and explains the main critical terms (archetype, archetypal image), she does not place her approach into the larger framework of Jungian studies (unlike O'Neill, who gives an excellent introduction) – a lack she is obviously aware of, since she points the reader towards a helpful website (www.nyaap.org) where he can find the basics of Jungian psychoanalysis conveniently summarized. This, however, does not really make up for the overall lack of an explicit theoretical framework for her study.

The book then more or less retells the story of the central characters and provides 'psychological notes' and explanations. We thus learn that the four hobbits (Frodo, Sam, Merry, and Pippin) represent the four psychological functions (thinking, feeling, sensation, and intuition respectively), that Tom Bombadil is a trickster figure and Goldberry a typical anima figure (a point already made by O'Neill), and that Boromir is the shadow to Aragorn the hero figure etc.

The interpretations proposed by Skogeman are, within a Jungian framework, understandable and easy to follow, but the 'net profit' from reading the 200-odd pages is very slim indeed. Too much of the text consists of a simple re-telling of the story and the actual critical analysis often takes up only a fraction of the space and does not penetrate deeply.

Furthermore, there are no references to secondary sources within the text (a short bibliography at the end lists the most important studies used) and only a meagre handful of studies on Tolkien have been used. This lack of Tolkien-expertise is also reflected in the fact that some of the Danish names have not been 'backtranslated' (we find, e.g. page 36: 'Torben' for English Ted Sandyman, and page 114: 'Dysterharge' for English Dunharrow) and is a deplorable step backwards – O'Neill back in 1979 not only knew and covered all the available works by Tolkien, but was also conversant with the (back then rather limited) secondary literature.

All in all, Skogeman's book may provide a very basic introduction to a possible application of some of Jung's ideas and concepts onto *The Lord of the Rings* for general readers who have neither Jung nor Tolkien at their fingertips. Tolkien scholars, on the other side, won't profit from this book and we can go on waiting for a study that unites competence in Jungian analysis with Tolkien scholarship – or hope for a revised edition (or even simply a reprint) of O'Neill's *The Individuated Hobbit*.

Thomas Honegger

J.R.R. Tolkien: The Legend of Sigurd and Gudrún. Edited by Christopher Tolkien.
London: HarperCollins, 2009, 377 pp., Hardcover

Any addition to the posthumous Tolkien canon is welcome because it gives an insight into the working of a unique philological mind. It is particularly valuable when it reveals his interaction with a series of texts from a compilation which has exercised the European imagination for over 250 years. The legend told in Tolkien's two long-awaited Eddaic poems should be even more familiar to German readers than to English ones, since it was developed into a German national myth in the 19th century, although the characters may be more familiar under the names Siegfried and Kriemhild from the *Nibelungenlied*. The old story has been re-worked by numerous authors, from Friedrich de la Motte Fouqué (the romantic drama *Der Held des Nordens*, 1808-1810), via Hebbel and Wagner to Jürgen Lodemann (post-modern novel, *Siegfried und Krimhild*, 2002).

However, the essential difference between these re-writings and Tolkien's is that he has not used the traditional material to create a new work of his own, rooted in his own time and connecting to contemporary ideas; Christopher Tolkien explicitly distances his father's work from Wagner's on these grounds (10), although this may be no more than a variation on "Both rings were round, and there the resemblance ends". Indeed, the problem with these two poems is knowing how to place them in the Tolkien canon, since they are neither wholly new adaptations, nor are they translations of the original poems in the strict sense, as is for example his "Sir Gawain".

In fact what Tolkien was attempting was an imaginative recreation: the Music played aright, to use an analogy from his own mythology. There is no indication that a complete verse narrative of the whole cycle ever existed in Old Norse; at any rate it would be difficult for a modern reader to make sense of the miscellaneous collection of short lays in the *Codex Regius*, compiled by an anonymous 13th century antiquarian, if the story were not told more clearly in other sources. Several of the poems are magnificent as dramatic vignettes, but they simply do not add up to a cohesive whole, even in the translation of a poet of international stature like Auden. Tolkien resolved the difficulties of continuity by re-working the elements of the story into two longish narrative poems in the original Norse verse form, one extending to the death of Sigurd and the other telling the subsequent fate of the Burgundian kings.

As might be expected, Tolkien adds his own interpretation by tightening up the motivation of the characters and adding a small but significant addition to the teleology: in a re-casting of the Völuspá ('Upphaf') it is prophesied that only a hero who has passed through death can defeat the World Serpent and make possible a new age. This draws a clear parallel to his drafts from the same period about Túrin, who was to return to defeat Morgoth in the last battle. That there was almost from the beginning a Sigurd element in Túrin merged in with the Kullervo element is proved by an entry in the Quenya Lexicon which makes Turambar a (possibly mistaken) calque on Sigurd, but it is revealing to find the same motif echoed on the other side of the equation.

We know from experience that Tolkien's verse is perfectly capable of standing on its own, but it is difficult to imagine this edition of the poems without the very detailed supporting materials supplied by Christopher Tolkien. In addition to notes on the individual poems, there is an introduction to the *Elder Edda* and an appendix on the historical origins of the different strands of the legends, which is useful whether one is reading Tolkien's poems or the actual *Edda*. What is absolutely indispensable is a concise explanation of the verse form, taken in part from Tolkien's own account in *On Translating Beowulf*. The Old Norse *fornyrðislag* is a very concise form, the appreciation of which is greatly helped if the reader is conscious of the constantly varying rhythms running through it. In this, non-native speakers may even have a slight advantage, since they will be paying closer attention to how the words fit together, while the native speaker might be tempted to rely on a subconscious sense of (modern) prosody and so gloss over the detail. For a German reader it might be analogous to reading Goethe's *Römische Elegien* with a conscious awareness of how the alternation of the Classical hexameter and pentameter is superimposed on the natural rhythms of the German language.

This close attention to the form is important, since Tolkien clearly set great store by improving his alliterative technique, which he regarded as a way of increasing his empathy with old Germanic poetry. One unexpected bonus of the present volume is a fragment of a rendering of the Old Norse *Atlakviða* into the much more expansive Old English alliterative verse. It seems as if Tolkien was trying to do no less than explore for himself the differences in the expressive nature of these two once flourishing literary languages.

However, it should not be thought that the poems in this book are a dry exercise in literary archaeology, even though they seem to have been written for his own instruction without any thought of publication. Certainly they require a degree of effort on the part of the reader, but nevertheless they can be read as a tightly written, gripping narrative in its own right, following the tale through from its mythical beginnings up to the personal tragedy of Gudrún. They may even encourage some to come to the Old Norse verses with an enhanced receptiveness and understanding, which was perhaps what moved Tolkien to compose them in the first place.
Allan Turner

Tolkien Studies. An Annual Scholarly Review. Volume VI. 2009
Morgantown: West Virginia University Press, 364 pp., Hardcover

Yearbooks have a comforting effect – at least if they are published with such regularity and in such high quality as *Tolkien Studies*. Once a year a nicely produced, beautifully made volume arrives in your mail, in my case perfectly timed for the term break. Although *Tolkien Studies* has also been available in electronic form for some time (to be accessed via Project Muse), I prefer the appealingly designed volumes with their red half-leather covers for my private reading. The sixth volume of *Tolkien Studies*, running to 364 pages, comprises nine full papers, three items in the 'Notes and Documents' section, the substantial book-review part, the very useful 'The Year's (2006) Work in Tolkien studies', and the bibliography of Tolkien-related works for 2007.

The scholar honoured this time for his contribution in Tolkien studies is John D. Rateliff, of most recent fame for his two-volume edition-cum-study of the history of *The Hobbit*. His paper gives convincing reasons for studying the earlier drafts and versions of Tolkien's works. Rateliff correctly points out that many scholars have elucidated why Tolkien wrote his stories, but not how. The aim of his paper is therefore to look at the possible reasons for the (overwhelmingly positive) effect on readers, which, as Rateliff argues, cannot be solely attributed to the plot and action elements of the story. Style and form are of almost equal if not greater importance, and he illustrates the way Tolkien's craft contributes to the enjoyment of the story by means of three case studies.

Rather surprisingly, his analysis calls for a re-assessment of Tolkien's composition technique. His main point is that Tolkien would not correct minor contradictions or mistakes if they serve a narrative function. Thus, next to the well-established figure of 'Tolkien the sub-creator', who pays close attention to the details of his world, we have to put Tolkien the storyteller, who is sometimes willing to sacrifice total coherence in favour of a good read.

The series of peer-reviewed essays opens with a paper by Jakobsson, who discusses the encounter between Bilbo and Smaug as a kind of translation of the encounter between Sigurd and Fafnir from the *Völsunga Saga*. While I agree with Jakobsson's general argument, I have several smaller bones to pick with him. First, he does not consider Anne C. Petty's highly relevant analysis of Smaug (see chapter 2 of her book *Dragons of Fantasy*) for his discussion of the dragon. Secondly, the logic of interpreting Bilbo's passing through the small passage to the Great Hall where Smaug lies sleeping on the treasure as representing the process of birth seems flawed. The process of birth is usually from womb (Great Hall) through the birth canal (small passage) into the outside world (outside world) – and not the other way round. Thirdly, the argument that Smaug's ability to speak puts him into a category different from that of the traditional dragon seems to me not convincing. True, dragons that are able to talk have, ever since Kenneth Grahame's *The Reluctant Dragon* (1899), suffered from the danger of anthropomorphism. Yet I see the ability to speak as a consequence rather than the cause of such a development and Smaug remains, to my mind, the *draco* par excellence (see my recent paper 'A good dragon is hard to find').

The third essay, by Jill Fitzgerald, is a welcome and long overdue re-publication of Tolkien's Middle English poem *The Clerkes Complainte*, hitherto only available in *Arda* 4 (1984) (my own attempts to have it re-published as part of Tom Shippey's volume of essays *Roots and Branches* were not successful). Fitzgerald prefaces her transcription of the poem (based on the facsimile published in *Arda* 6) by a discussion of Tolkien's scholarly engagement with Chaucer's work and places it within the larger framework of the university political controversy between Lit. and Lang. Why this paper-cum-edition was included in the essay section and not in 'Notes and Documents', is not quite clear – it is certainly a borderline case. Yet whatever its categorical affiliations – it does exactly what

I asked for in my review of TS 5 (HS 5) in connection with the re-publication of *The Reeve's Tale* in TS, namely to provide an overview of the academic and scholarly background as well as the context to the piece under discussion.

No TS volume without some source studies. This time it is Stefan Ekman who fills the breach with a fine paper on landscape echoes from the Middle English *Pearl* in Arda. He takes Tolkien's poem *The Nameless Land* (composed in the same metre as *Pearl*) as the starting point for his analysis and shows how landscape-motifs and elements from *Pearl* appear in this poem and, as a consequence of the poem moving more and more into the universe of Arda, also in the texts of the *Legendarium*.

Ford and Reid provide a comparative though not contrastive analysis of Aragorn's journey towards kingship as depicted in the book and in Jackson's movies. The authors' attempt to avoid simple contrasting (this is in the book, but not in the movie) is to be applauded and must be seen as a step forward when compared with many of the previous studies dealing with the same topic.

However, it might have proven reader-friendlier to put the theoretical considerations at the beginning of the essay, and not towards the end. Also, the authors should have done their (research) homework; they seem to have consulted neither Connie Veugen's nor Martin Simonson's nor Arvidsson's contributions on this very topic. These flaws do not invalidate their results, but we have arrived at a stage in Tolkien studies where it is no longer possible to work in splendid isolation without running the risk of simply repeating what others have found out on this topic before. Therefore, 'even' a Tolkien scholar should consult the MLA bibliography before starting on his or her project. There the authors would have found both Veugen's and Simonson's papers with a basic search 'Tolkien' and then 'search within results: Aragorn' – or, alternatively, an email to the ever-so watchful and knowledgeable compilers of the *Tolkien Studies* bibliographies would probably also have been of help.

The following contribution, by Cynthia M. Cohen, belongs to the growing area of Eco Criticism (see e.g. Dickerson and Evans, or Campbell). She starts by giving a comprehensive overview of all the passages in *The Lord of the Rings* where trees are of relevance, discusses possible sources for the concept of talking and walking trees and makes a valiant attempt towards a coherent categorisation. Of special significance is the question of the ontological status of Ents and Huorns.

Taking into account the original drafts, where Treebeard was a giant rather than a tree-herd, her careful and knowledgeable analysis is able to make a single aspect of Tolkien's creation (trees and tree-like beings) meaningful for a more general appreciation of his creative impulse.

Josh Long then gives us an inspired and meaningful discussion of Tolkien's *Smith of Wootton Major* within a Bloomian framework. He selects two of the four ways in which the anxiety of influence manifests itself – namely *clinamen* and *tessera*, corrective swerve and antithetical completion respectively. Tolkien, when asked to write a preface to MacDonald's *The Golden Key* in 1964, re-read the work and found it at odds with his own ideas about faery and faery-stories. His own faery tale *Smith of Wootton Major* can thus be seen as his creative attempt to remedy all those things he disliked in MacDonald's story and, in the course of this, to redeem the word 'fairy'. Long's application of Bloom's critical concepts to *Smith* makes good sense and is an important contribution to our understanding of Tolkien's motivation in writing this story.

Verlyn Flieger takes a new look at the not-so-new problem of Fate, Predetermination and Free Will. Her basic argument is that we must take seriously Tolkien's sometimes conscious vagueness and contradictions in matters of who has Free Will (Men) and who is bound by the workings of Fate (Elves). She comes to the conclusion that Tolkien is not simply copying any of the existing systems, but that he uses his authorial freedom to create a new situation by having Men and Elves follow different paths. Flieger is certainly correct in highlighting some of the problematic and seemingly contradictory elements in Tolkien's underlying fabric of fate, yet I am not quite sure whether these points add up to a sufficiently strong case for construing a new and experimental view of the old problem. The idea is an intriguing one, but I feel that Tolkien's ideas and concepts are still to be accommodated within Catholic orthodoxy.

The three articles in the 'Notes and Documents' sections contain two that are primarily concerned with Tolkien's development of the Elvish languages. The first, and shorter, of the two presents Tolkien's ideas on the Elvish word for fate (and thus provides an appropriate coda to Flieger's preceding paper). The second provides a discussion and list of the basic vocabulary of Quenya. The third article, however, is a learned and informed analysis of the Old English poem *The Wanderer* and its importance for Tolkien as a scholar as well as an author and man.

The extensive review section (some seventy pages), the useful short-summaries of David Bratman's *Year's Work* (2006), and the bibliography of works related to Tolkien (in English) for 2007 rounds off this nicely edited and produced volume.

Thomas Honegger

Works consulted:

Arvidsson, Håken, *Aragorn: Tales of the Heir of Isildur*, Lund: Department of English, Lund University, Sweden, 2004: middle-earth-journeys.com/forums/viewtopic.php?t=134&postdays=0&postorder=asc&start=15 (Part of this thesis was published in *Mallorn* 44: 47-59)

Campbell, Liam, *The Ecological Augury in the Works of J.R.R. Tolkien*, Zurich/Jena: Walking Tree Publishers, 2010 (forthcoming)

Dickerson, Matthew and Jonathan Evans, *Ents, Elves, and Eriador: The environmental vision of J.R.R. Tolkien*, Lexington, KT: The University Press of Kentucky, 2006

Honegger, Thomas, 'A good dragon is hard to find or, from *draconitas* to *draco*', in Fanfan Chen and Thomas Honegger (eds.), *Good Dragons are Rare*, Frankfurt etc.: Peter Lang, 2009, 27-59

Petty, Anne C., *Dragons of Fantasy*, Crawfordville, FL: Kitsune Books, 2nd edition, 2008

Simonson, Martin, 'An Introduction to the Dynamics of the Intertraditional Dialogue in *The Lord of the Rings*: Aragorn's Heroic Evolution', in Thomas Honegger and Frank Weinreich (eds.), *Tolkien and Modernity 2*, Zurich/Berne: Walking Tree Publishers, 2006, 75-113

Veugen, Connie, 'A Man, lean, dark, tall: Aragorn Seen Through Different Media', in Thomas Honegger (ed.), *Reconsidering Tolkien*, Zurich/Berne: Walking Tree Publishers, 2005, 171-209

Unsere Autoren und Autorinnen

Annie Birks lehrt Englische Sprache und Literatur an der Katholischen Universität des Westens in Angers (Frankreich). Sie erwarb kürzlich ihr Doktorat an der Sorbonne über »Honorierung in den Werken J.R.R. Tolkiens«. Im Fokus ihrer gegenwärtigen Forschungsinteressen liegen im Wesentlichen die theologischen Perspektiven der Schriften Tolkiens.
annie.birks@neuf.fr

Patrick Brückner studierte an der Universität Potsdam Germanistische Mediävistik und Soziologie mit dem Schwerpunkt Soziologie der Geschlechterverhältnisse sowie Volkswirtschaftslehre. Er arbeitet über Genderfragen in den Werken Tolkiens und hat gemeinsam mit Judith Klinger an der Universität Potsdam mehrere Seminare zu »Tolkien und das Mittelalter« gehalten. Seine Veröffentlichungen beinhalten Beiträge zu *Hither Shore*, den *Arbeiten zur Literarischen Phantastik* sowie *Tolkien and Modernity 2* (Walking Tree Publishers).
patricbrueckner@aol.com

Marcel Bülles, Gründungsvorsitzender der Deutschen Tolkien Gesellschaft, studierte Anglo-Amerikanische Geschichte und Anglistik in Köln und Aberdeen und arbeitet derzeit freiberuflich als Übersetzer und Journalist rund um Mittelerde. Sein Promotionsvorhaben behandelt »The emergence of a cult. The Lord of the Rings in the United States«.
marcel.buelles@tolkiengesellschaft.de

Michaël Devaux hat an der Sorbonne in Paris in Philosophie über Leibniz promoviert und viele Publikationen über Leibniz und Descartes vorzuweisen. Er lehrt Philosophie der Erziehung an der Universität Caen. Über die theologischen Dimensionen des Werks Tolkiens hat er zahlreiche Aufsätze veröffentlicht und ist zudem Präsident der Französischen Tolkiengesellschaft »La Compagnie de la Comté« sowie Chefredakteur des La Feuille de la Compagnie.
michael.devaux@gmail.com

Julian Tim Morton Eilmann studierte in Aachen und Nottingham Geschichte, Germanistik und Kunstgeschichte und ist gegenwärtig Referendar für das Gymnasiallehramt. Neben seinen akademischen Arbeiten ist er seit drei Jahren bei einer Film- und TV-Produktion als Autor von Reportagen und historischen Dokumentationen tätig und darüber hinaus Inhaber einer Kunstgalerie und Kurator einer Künstlerstiftung. Schwerpunkte seiner Tolkien-Forschungen sind Tolkiens Lieder und Gedichte sowie die Filmadaption von Peter Jackson.
julianeilmann@web.de

Jason Fisher ist ein unabhängiger amerikanischer Gelehrter mit dem Schwerpunkt J.R.R. Tolkien und germanische Philologie (inkl. Altenglisch und Altnordisch). Er hat zahlreiche Aufsätze und Rezensionen in verschiedenen Büchern und Zeitschriften über Tolkien und die Inklings publiziert sowie zahlreiche Vorträge darüber gehalten. visualweazel@yahoo.com

Thomas Fornet-Ponse studierte Katholische Theologie, Philosophie und Alte Geschichte in Bonn und Jerusalem, war 2006/07 Studienleiter beim Theologischen Studienjahr in Jerusalem und promoviert gegenwärtig in Katholischer Theologie. Er veröffentlichte zahlreiche Aufsätze zu Tolkien, Pratchett und Lewis. Er war bis 2009 Beisitzer im Vorstand der Deutschen Tolkien Gesellschaft und ist inhaltlicher Koordinator des Tolkien Seminars sowie von *Hither Shore*.
hither-shore@tolkiengesellschaft.de

Margaret Hiley erwarb ihren Doktor in Glasgow mit einer Arbeit über die Inklings und ihre kontroverse Beziehung zur literarischen Moderne (wird bei Walking Tree Publishers 2010 erscheinen). Sie hat über verschiedene Aspekte der Fantasy und Science Fiction vorgetragen und publiziert, an den Universitäten Glasgow und Regensburg unterricht und arbeitet gegenwärtig als Lektorin für Englisch am University Centre Peterborough, wo sie zudem die Studiengänge in Arts und Sciences koordiniert. margaret.hiley@peterborough.ac.uk

Thomas Honegger, Prof. Dr. phil, hat in Zürich promoviert und zahlreiche Bände zu Tolkien, mittelalterlicher Sprache und Literatur herausgegeben und verschiedene Beiträge zu Chaucer, Shakespeare und zu mittelalterlichen Romanzen publiziert. Seit 2002 lehrt er als Professor für Mediävistik an der Friedrich-Schiller-Universität Jena.
www2.uni-jena.de/fsu/anglistik/homepage/Honegger3.htm

Judith Klinger, Dr. Phil., hat nach einem Studium der Germanistik und Anglistik an der Universität Hamburg und dem Studium Dokumentarfilm und Fernsehpublizistik an der Hochschule für Fernsehen und Film, München, über Identitätskonzeptionen im Prosa-Lancelot promoviert. Nach einer Lehrtätigkeit an der Universität Bayreuth ist sie seit 1995 am Lehrstuhl für Germanistische Mediävistik der Universität Potsdam beschäftigt und verfolgt ihr Habilitationsprojekt im Bereich der Gender Studies. jklinger@rz.uni-potsdam.de

Rainer Nagel, Dr. phil., arbeitet am Lehr- und Forschungsbereich für Englische Sprachwissenschaft an der Johannes-Gutenberg-Universität Mainz mit den Forschungs¬schwerpunkten Sprachgeschichte, Übersetzungswissenschaft, Wortbildung und Fachsprachenforschung. Ferner ist er als Autor und Redakteur bei diversen Rollenspielen sowie als Übersetzer und Lektor bei verschiedenen Verlagen tätig.

Friedhelm Schneidewind studierte Biologie und einige Semester Informatik. Aktuell ist er tätig als freier Dozent u. a. für Öffentlichkeitsarbeit und Mediengestaltung sowie als Leiter einer Mittelaltermusiktruppe, als Autor, Journalist, Herausgeber und Verleger. Bekannt ist er darüber hinaus als Autor, u. a. mehrerer Lexika aus dem Fantasy-Bereich und mehrerer Bücher zu Tolkien.
www.friedhelm-schneidewind.de

Anna Slack erhielt ihren MA in Cambridge im März 2009. Zwischen 2006 und 2008 arbeitete sie als Lehrerin für Englisch als Fremdsprache an einer privaten Sprachschule in Palermo (Sizilien). Gegenwärtig unterrichtet sie Englische Sprache und Literatur an der St. Gabriel's School, ist die englische Chefredakteurin von PortalEditions, wofür sie einen Aufsatzband zu C.S. Lewis herausgibt und die Autorin verschiedener Artikel zu Tolkien.
AnnaSlack@cantab.net

Guglielmo Spirito OFM Conv., Prof. Dr. theol., geboren in Buenos Aires, studierte vor seinem Eintritt in den Franziskanerorden Philosophie und Ägyptologie, erwarb in Rom sein theologisches Lizenziat am Camillianum und sein Doktorat (mit der Spezialisierung in Spiritualität) am Antonianum. Seit 1994 ist er Professor für Patristik, Franziskanische Spiritualität und Literatur (vor allem Tolkien) am Theologischen Institut Assisi und an der Päpstlichen Fakultät des Heiligen Bonaventura in Rom. Er lehrte auch in Kroatien, Rumänien, Russland, Mexiko, England, Kanada, Armenien und Ägypten. Über Tolkien hat er verschiedene Essays, Aufsätze und Bücher publiziert; er ist Mitglied der Italienischen Tolkiengesellschaft. fraguspi@gmail.com

Martin G.E. Sternberg hat von 1990 bis 1996 Alte Geschichte, Mittlere Geschichte, Kunstgeschichte sowie Rechtswissenschaft studiert. Er arbeitet als Referent bei einer Bundesbehörde. Ein Schwerpunkt seines Geschichts- und Philosophiestudiums lag in der Spätantike und im frühen Christentum.
lasgalen@web.de

Doreen Triebel studierte Englische und Amerikanische Literatur und Sprache, Psychologie und Deutsch als Fremdsprache an der Universität Jena, der University of Nottingham und der Illinois State University. Gegenwärtig verfolgt sie ein Dissertationsprojekt in Englischer Literatur und lehrt an der Universität Jena. Doreen-T@gmx.de

Allan Turner, Ph.D., studierte Deutsche Philosophie, Mediävistik and Allgemeine Linguistik. Seine Dissertation in Übersetzungswissenschaften untersucht die inhärenten Probleme bei der Übersetzung philologischer Elemente in *The Lord of the Rings*. Sein Interessensschwerpunkt liegt gegenwärtig im Stil der

Werke Tolkiens. Er unterrichtet Englische Sprachpraxis und British Cultural Studies an der Universität Jena.
allangturner@aol.com

Michael Wedel, Dr. phil., Professor für Mediengeschichte im digitalen Zeitalter an der Hochschule für Film und Fernsehen »Konrad Wolf« in Potsdam-Babelsberg. Veröffentlichungen u.a.: *Die »Herr der Ringe«-Trilogie. Attraktion und Faszination eines populärkulturellen Phänomens* (zus. mit L. Mikos, S. Eichner, E. Prommer, Konstanz: UVK 2007).

Frank Weinreich, Dr. phil., arbeitet als freier Autor und Lektor in Bochum. Er studierte Kommunikationswissenschaften, Philosophie und Politikwissenschaften an der Ruhr Universität Bochum und erlangte mit einer Arbeit über Ethik den Doktorgrad der Philosophie an der Hochschule Vechta. Er hat zahlreiche Veröffentlichungen über Fantasy, Mythologie und besonders das Werk Tolkiens vorgelegt.
fw@polyoinos.de

Petra Zimmermann, Dr. phil, absolvierte ihr Studium der Musikwissenschaft, Germanistik und Geschichte an der Universität Köln, der TU Berlin und der FU Berlin sowie ein Zusatzstudium »Deutsch als Fremdsprache« an der Humboldt-Universität Berlin. Sie promovierte im Fachgebiet Musikwissenschaft. Nach Stationen als DAAD-Lektorin an Universitäten in Polen und der VR China und als Lehrbeauftragte an der TU Braunschweig ist sie seit 2005 Redakteurin und Übersetzerin für den Medizinverlag Urban & Fischer/Elsevier sowie seit 2007 Lehrkraft für besondere Aufgaben am Internationalen Zentrum der TU Clausthal
petra.zimmermann@gmx.net

Our Authors

Annie Birks teaches English language and literature at the Université Catholique de l'Ouest, in Angers, France. She has recently received a doctorate from the Sorbonne on "Retribution in the Works of J.R.R. Tolkien." Her current research interests focus essentially on the theological perspectives of Tolkien's writings.
annie.birks@neuf.fr

Patrick Brückner is a student of German Medieval Literature, Women's Studies and Sociology at the University of Potsdam. He is working on aspects of gender in the works of J.R.R. Tolkien and held joint seminars with Judith Klinger on "Tolkien and the Middle Ages" at the University of Potsdam. His publications include contributions to *Hither Shore*, to *Arbeiten zur Literarischen Phantastik*, and *Tolkien and Modernity 2* (Walking Tree Publishers).
patricbrueckner@aol.com

Marcel Bülles is the founding chairman of the German Tolkien Society. He studied Anglo-American History as well as English Studies in Cologne and Aberdeen. He is currently working as a free-lance translator and journalist with a focus on Middle-earth. His emerging PhD thesis: "The emergence of a cult. The Lord of the Rings in the United States."
marcel.buelles@tolkiengesellschaft.de

Michaël Devaux holds a Ph.D. from the Sorbonne in Paris, has worked extensively on Leibniz, Descartes and is currently teaching philosophy of education at Caen University. He has published numerous articles on the theological dimension of Tolkien's works and is president of the French Tolkien Society La Compagnie de la Comté and editor-in-chief of *La Feuille de la Compagnie*.
michael.devaux@gmail.com

Julian Tim Morton Eilmann studied History, German Philology, and History of Arts at Aachen and Nottingham and is currently working as student teacher. Furthermore, since three years he is working as a journalist and author of films and TV productions, and as a developer of historical TV documentation. In addition, he is fulfilling the functions of gallery owner and conservator for an artists' foundation. His works on Tolkien focus on Tolkien's songs and poems and the adaptation by Peter Jackson.
julianeilmann@aol.com

Jason Fisher is an independent American scholar specialising primarily in J.R.R. Tolkien and Germanic Philology (including Old English and Old Norse). He has published numerous articles and book reviews in several books and journals and as presented papers on J.R.R. Tolkien and the Inklings in a variety of academic settings and conferences. visualweazel@yahoo.com

Thomas Fornet-Ponse studied Catholic Theology, Philosophy, and Ancient History at Bonn and Jerusalem. He worked as an inspector of Studies at 'Theologisches Studienjahr Jerusalem'. He was a committee member of the German Tolkien Society and has been charged with conceptually coordinating the Tolkien Seminars as well as *Hither Shore*.
hither-shore@tolkiengesellschaft.de

Margaret Hiley holds a Ph.D. from the University of Glasgow dealing with the Inklings and their controversial relationship to literary modernism (to be published by Walking Tree Publishers 2010). She has published and lectured on various aspects of fantasy and science fiction. She has taught at the Universities of Glasgow and Regensburg and now is Lecturer in English at the University Centre Peterborough, where she also coordinates the degrees in the Arts and Sciences.
margaret.hiley@peterborough.ac.uk

Thomas Honegger holds a Ph.D. from the University of Zurich. He edited several volumes on Tolkien, medieval language and literature, and published papers on Chaucer, Shakespeare, and mediaeval romance. He teaches, since 2002, as Professor for Mediaeval Studies at the Friedrich Schiller University Jena (Germany).
www2.uni-jena.de/fsu/anglistik/homepage/Honegger3.htm

Judith Klinger, Dr. phil., studied German Philology and English Philology at the University of Hamburg, then studied documentary filming and TV media studies at the University of TV and film at Munich. Ph.D. thesis on concepts of 'identity' in the prose Lancelot. Taught at Bayreuth University and has been employed at the chair of German Mediaeval Studies at Potsdam University since 1995. She is currently working on a post-doctoral thesis in the field of gender studies. jklinger@rz.uni-potsdam.de

Rainer Nagel, Dr. phil., is currently teaching English and Linguistics at Johannes Gutenberg University, Mainz; his research specialities are the history of English, translation studies, word-formation, and special-language research. He has also written and edited numerous role-playing publications and has worked extensively as a translator.

Friedhelm Schneidewind studied Biology and, for a few terms, Computer science. He is currently working as a teacher and adviser for a variety of topics, mainly including DTP/media presentation/multimedia and public relations. He is an author, journalist, publisher and musician. Furthermore, he is known as author of several books and encyclopaedias.
www.friedhelm-schneidewind.de

Anna Slack was awarded her MA in Cambridge in March, 2009. Between 2006 and 2008 she worked as a teacher of English as a Foreign Language at a private language school in Palermo, Sicily. She currently teaches English Language and Literature at St. Gabriel's School, is the General English Editor of *PortalEditions*, for whom she is editing a volume of essays on C.S. Lewis and the author of various papers on Tolkien.
AnnaSlack@cantab.net

Guglielmo Spirito OFM Conv., Prof. Dr. theol., was born in Buenos Aires and studied Philosophy and Egyptology before joining the Order of Saint Francis in the 1980s. In Rome he obtained the Degree (Licenza) in Pastoral Theology of Health Care at the Camillianum and the Doctorate in Theology with specialism in Spirituality at the Pontifical Ateneum Antonianum. Since 1994 he is professor of Patristic and Franciscan Spirituality and of Theology and Literature (especially J.R.R. Tolkien) at the Theological Institute of Assisi and at the Pontifical Faculty of Saint Bonaventure in Rome. He gave courses in Croacia, Romania, Russia and Mexico, and lectures in England and Canada, Armenia and Egypt. On Tolkien he had published various essays, articles, and books. He is also a member of the Società Tolkieniana Italiana.
fraguspi@gmail.com

Martin G.E. Sternberg studied Ancient History, Mediaeval History, History of Arts, and Law at Münster from 1990 to 1996. He is currently working in a federal authority. During his studies, he specialised in Late Antiquity and Early Christianity.
lasgalen@web.de

Doreen Triebel studied English and American Literature and Linguistics, Psychology and German as a Foreign Language at the Friedrich Schiller University Jena, the University of Nottingham and Illinois State University. She is currently pursuing a Ph.D. in English Literature and teaches at the University of Jena.
Doreen-T@gmx.de

Allan Turner, Ph.D., studied German Philology, Mediaeval Studies, and General Linguistics. His Ph.D. thesis in translation studies examines the problems inherent in translating the philological elements in *The Lord of the Rings*. His main focus of interest is currently on the stylistics of Tolkien's works. He teaches English language skills and British Cultural Studies at the University of Jena.
allangturner@aol.com

Michael Wedel, Dr. phil., is professor for Media History in the Digital Age at the University of Film and Television "Konrad Wolf" in Potsdam-Babelsberg and has edited inter alia *Die "Herr der Ringe"-Trilogie. Attraktion und Faszination eines populärkulturellen Phänomens* (with L. Mikos, S. Eichner, E. Prommer, Konstanz: UVK 2007).

Frank Weinreich, Dr. phil., works as an advisor and independent author in Bochum. He studied media science, philosophy and science of politics at Bochum University and did his PhD on bio-ethics at Vechta.
fw@polyoinos.de

Petra Zimmermann, Dr. phil., studied Science of Music, German Philology, History, and German in Cologne and Berlin and obtained her doctorate in 1995 at TU Berlin. She worked as a lecturer for the German Academic Exchange Service (Deutscher Akademischer Austauschdienst) at universities in Poland and the Peoples' Republic of China, as a lecturer at the language centre of TU Braunschweig, as editor and translator for the publishing house Urban & Fischer/Elsevier and is currently lecturer at the International Centre of TU Clausthal.
petra.zimmermann@gmx.net

Siglenverzeichnis

Die Schriften von J.R.R. Tolkien werden im Text jeweils ohne Angabe des Verfassernamens mit den folgenden Siglen zitiert. Die jeweils benutzte Ausgabe findet sich im Literaturverzeichnis.

AI:	The Lay of Aotrou and Itroun
ATB:	The Adventures of Tom Bombadil and other Verses from the Red Book / Die Abenteuer des Tom Bombadil und andere Gedichte aus dem Roten Buch
AW:	Ancrene Wisse and Hali Meiðhad
B:	Die Briefe von J.R.R. Tolkien
BA:	Bilbos Abschiedslied
BB:	Baum und Blatt
BGH:	Bauer Giles von Ham
BLS:	Bilbo's Last Song
BMC:	Beowulf: The Monster and the Critics
BT:	Blatt von Tüftler
BUK:	Beowulf: Die Ungeheuer und ihre Kritiker
BW:	Die Briefe vom Weihnachtsmann
CH:	The Children of Húrin
CP:	Chaucer as a Philologist
EA:	The End of the Third Age (History of Middle-earth 9). Auszug
EW:	English and Welsh / Englisch und Walisisch
FC:	Letters from Father Christmas
FGH:	Farmer Giles of Ham
FH:	Finn and Hengest
FS:	On Fairy-Stories
GD:	Gute Drachen sind rar
GN:	Guide to the Names in the Lord of the Rings
GPO:	Sir Gawain and the Green Knight, Pearl, and Sir Orfeo
H:	The Hobbit / Der Hobbit / Der kleine Hobbit
HB:	The Homecoming of Beorhtnoth Beorhthelm's Son
HdR:	Der Herr der Ringe
HdR I:	Der Herr der Ringe. Bd. 1. Die Gefährten
HdR II:	Der Herr der Ringe. Bd. 2. Die Zwei Türme
HdR III:	Der Herr der Ringe. Bd. 3. Die Rückkehr des Königs / Die Wiederkehr des Königs
HdR A:	Der Herr der Ringe. Anhänge
HG:	Herr Glück
HH I/II:	The History of the Hobbit
HL:	Ein heimliches Laster
KH:	Die Kinder Húrins
L:	The Letters of J.R.R. Tolkien
LB:	The Lays of Beleriand (History of Middle-earth 3)
LN:	Leaf by Niggle
LotR:	The Lord of the Rings

Siglenverzeichnis

LotR I:	The Fellowship of the Ring. Being the first part of The Lord of the Rings
LotR II:	The Two Towers. Being the second part of The Lord of the Rings
LotR III:	The Return of the King. Being the third part of The Lord of the Rings
LotR A:	The Lord of the Rings. Appendices
LR:	The Lost Road and other Writings (History of Middle-earth 5)
LSG:	The Legend of Sigurd and Gudrún
LT 1:	The Book of Lost Tales 1 (History of Middle-earth 1)
LT 2:	The Book of Lost Tales 2 (History of Middle-earth 2)
MB:	Mr. Bliss
MC:	The Monsters and the Critics and Other Essays
ME:	A Middle English Vocabulary
MR:	Morgoth's Ring (History of Middle-earth 10)
My:	Mythopoeia
NM:	Nachrichten aus Mittelerde
OE:	The Old English Exodus
OK:	Ósanwe-Kenta
P:	Pictures by J.R.R. Tolkien
PM:	The Peoples of Middle-earth (History of Middle-earth 12)
R:	Roverandom
RBG:	The Rivers and Beacon-hills of Gondor
RGEO:	The Road Goes Ever On (with Donald Swann)
RS:	The Return of the Shadow (History of Middle-earth 6)
S:	Silmarillion
SD:	The Sauron Defeated (History of Middle-earth 9)
SG:	Der Schmied von Großholzingen
SGG:	Sir Gawain and the Green Knight / Sir Gawain und der Grüne Ritter (Essay)
SM:	The Shaping of Middle-earth (History of Middle-earth 4)
SP:	Songs for the Philologists
SV:	A Secret Vice
SWM:	Smith of Wootton Major
SWME:	Smith of Wootton Major Essay
TB:	On Translating Beowulf
TI:	The Treason of Isengard (History of Middle-earth 7)
TL:	Tree and Leaf
ÜB:	Zur Übersetzung des Beowulf
ÜM:	Über Märchen
UK:	Die Ungeheuer und ihre Kritiker. Gesammelte Aufsätze
UT:	Unfinished Tales
VA:	Valedictory Address
VG 1:	Das Buch der Verschollenen Geschichten 1
VG 2:	Das Buch der Verschollenen Geschichten 2
WJ:	The War of the Jewels (History of Middle-earth 11)
WR:	The War of the Ring (History of Middle-earth 8)

Index

Adorno, Theodor W.	154, 156f, 163f, 219
Ainulindalë	29, 31f, 34, 38, 40, 51, 102f, 113, 173, 176, 216, 244
Andúril	→ Schwerter
Angmar	142, 145, 147, 175
Aragorn (Elessar)	14, 28f, 39, 43-50, 56, 112, 121, 124f, 131, 134-139, 144, 148f, 175f, 193, 200, 202f, 205, 207, 209-212, 218, 222, 225, 252, 257
Aristoteles/Aristotle	30, 124
Ar-Pharazôn	36f, 53f
Arwen	176, 213
Auenland (Shire)	42-48, 50, 55, 66, 126, 142, 145, 201f, 208, 212, 222, 250
Augustinus/Augustine	29-32, 112, 121, 183, 216
Beleriand	33f, 110, 174
Beren	35, 70, 78f, 107, 176, 207, 212, 223, 245f
Bilbo	142-145, 177, 193, 209, 242, 251, 256
Boromir	18, 31, 44, 49, 66, 136f, 185, 252
Caudimordux	→ Schwerter
Chance, Jane	48, 63, 86, 161, 182, 202, 239
Christianity/christian/christlich	29f, 41, 106, 108f, 117ff, 121, 126, 217, 230, 231, 239
Chrysophylax	→ Drachen
Curry, Patrick	11, 230, 239
Denethor	23, 36, 38f, 44f, 48ff, 56, 70, 123ff, 222
Devaux, Michaël	52, 102, 216, 260, 264
Dickerson, Matthew	11, 25, 51, 239, 257
Drachen: Chrysophylax, Smaug	65, 67f, 86, 88-98, 144, 256
Eärendil	52, 105-108, 114, 148, 216
Edda	104f, 192f, 216f, 235, 253f
Elendil	36, 44, 53, 135f, 144, 211
Elessar	→ Aragorn
Elrond	134, 136f, 163, 174, 200
Éomer	22, 28f, 36, 46ff, 50, 135, 138, 206

Éowyn	46f, 120, 123ff, 146, 194, 202-212
Eru (Ilúvatar)	29, 31ff, 35, 50f, 53, 55, 78, 113, 222
Faramir	31, 36, 44f, 48f, 54, b66f, 138, 176, 185, 194, 202, 204f, 208, 210ff
Fëanor	34, 51f, 173, 232, 233
Flieger, Verlyn	131f, 170, 182, 184, 211, 221, 229f, 239, 258
Foucault, Michel	153, 164f, 187, 219
Frieden (Peace)	23, 30, 49, 62, 73, 75f, 140, 244, 253, 258, 265
Frodo	14, 31, 40, 44, 48, 50, 65f, 71, 121f, 124, 126f, 134ff, 142-1446, 163, 182, 194, 201f, 204, 206, 209f, 212f, 218, 225, 228ff, 234, 252
Gandalf	11, 36, 39f, 45f, 49f, 70, 75, 105, 109, 121, 124, 130, 135, 144, 148, 156, 158, 163, 175f, 203, 205, 212, 234
Garbowski, Christopher	113, 202
Garth, John	131, 173, 185, 191, 229
Gerechter Krieg (Just War)	28-39, 42, 118f, 121, 176, 200, 216
Gimli	14, 135f, 175f, 232
Glamdring	→ Schwerter
Gondor	42-49, 55, 67, 131, 134-138, 174, 176f, 191f, 200, 211, 222
Great War (World War I)	11, 118, 131, 168ff, 172f, 178, 229f
Gríma (Wormtounge)	49, 121, 205
Gurthang	→ Schwerter
Hammond, Wayne	173, 182, 184, 189ff, 193, 241. 248f
Harry Potter	200, 233
Heilung/Heiler	200f, 203f, 206, 208-213
Ilúvatar	→ Eru
Just War	→ Gerechter Krieg
Krieg	39, 42f, 45, 47f, 50f, 53f, 56, 58, 65f, 68, 70, 86, 92, 96, 169, 171, 200ff, 204, 216, 217, 218, 220, 221, 241
Legolas	14, 136, 176
Lewis, C.S.	29, 102, 108, 170, 178, 190, 231f, 236
Lúthien Tinúviel	52, 70, 77-80, 176, 207, 212, 223f, 245f
Magic/Magie	10, 21f, 24, 71-83, 131f, 135, 140, 145, 148, 153, 170f, 181, 200f, 211f, 218
Mandos	34, 78, 104ff, 142, 217
Manwë	51f, 105f, 108, 216
Melkor (Morgoth)	31-34, 37, 38f, 42, 51-54, 56, 70, 79, 81ff, 105-108, 110,113, 139, 141f, 173f, 216, 222, 232, 244, 254
Merry	14, 44, 47ff, 123f, 132, 142, 145, 147, 157-162, 202ff, 208, 210f, 219, 252
Minas Tirith	31, 43, 48, 124, 191ff, 200, 207, 211
Monarchie, Königtum	43-47, 56, 222
Mordor	31, 45, 119, 124, 132, 135, 146
Morgoth	→ Melkor
Narsil	→ Schwerter
Nazgûl	50, 132, 143, 146f, 175
Noldor (auch Quenta Noldorinwa)	35f, 51ff, 103, 105-108,
Númenor, Númenórer, Númenorean	31f, 35, 37, 41, 44, 46f, 52-56, 110, 138, 142, 145, 147f, 173f, 176, 190, 206, 208f, 232

Old Man Willow (Weidenmann)	71f, 76, 79f, 162, 193, 223
Peace	→ Frieden
Pippin	14, 23, 44ff, 48f, 142, 145, 154, 157-160, 162, 219, 252
Remarque, Erich Maria	11, 25
Ritter	67, 86-97
Rohan/Rohirrim	28, 42, 46-49, 56, 67, 119-122, 130, 146, 148, 190, 208, 222
Sam(wise Gamgee)	14, 44, 48, 66, 124-127, 134, 136, 142-146, 177, 194, 212, 218, 234, 252
Saruman	36, 38f, 43f, 47, 49f, 54, 56, 83, 121f, 144ff, 159ff, 164, 222
Sauron	28, 33-39, 42, 49ff, 53-56, 67, 70, 76, 78f, 81, 83, 110, 112f, 117, 135ff, 154ff, 159, 162, 173f, 176, 212, 218, 222f, 232f
Schwerter	65f, 90-97, 131, 134, 136-148, 200, 209, 218
Scull, Christina	173, 182, 184, 189ff, 193, 241, 248f
Shippey, Tom	25, 35, 86, 90, 99, 102, 131, 149, 170, 184, 232, 235, 239, 256
Shire	→ Auenland
Simonson, Martin	182, 188, 251, 257
Smaug	→ Drachen
Stich	→ Schwerter
Sub-creation, ~tor, ~ted, ~tive	38, 73, 76, 82, 102, 111, 125, 127, 171, 216, 223, 235, 256
Tal-Elmar	53ff, 222
Théoden	46-49, 119-124, 130f, 147, 204f
Thomas v. Aquin/Thomas Aqunias	30f, 112, 121
Tom Bombadil	71f, 76, 152, 162f, 176, 219, 223, 242, 252
Tulkas	32, 105f, 216
Túrin	105-108, 134, 139-142, 144, 147, 216, 218, 254
Valar	32, 34, 36, 44f, 47, 49-53, 55f, 106, 139, 173f, 222, 232
Valinor	32, 34f, 51f, 82, 105, 108, 213
War	10ff, 20ff, 24f, 28-34, 36-41, 54, 102, 108, 116-127, 130f, 135, 137ff, 142, 144-147, 158f, 168-174, 176ff, 180, 183ff, 187f, 192, 194f, 220f, 222, 223, 224, 225, 229, 244
Weidenmann	→ Old Man Willow
Weinreich, Frank	11, 12, 20, 25, 42-46, 67, 68, 223
Williams, Charles	102, 231
World War I	→ Great War
Wormtongue	→ Gríma